FOURTH EDITION

GROUPS
Process and Practice

FOURTH EDITION

GROUPS
Process and Practice

Marianne Schneider Corey
Private Practice

Gerald Corey
California State University, Fullerton
Diplomate in Counseling Psychology,
American Board of Professional Psychology

BROOKS/COLE PUBLISHING COMPANY
PACIFIC GROVE, CALIFORNIA

Brooks/Cole Publishing Company
A Division of Wadsworth, Inc.

Printed in the United States of America
10   9   8   7   6   5   4   3   2

Library of Congress Cataloging-in-Publication Data

Corey, Marianne Schneider, [date]
    Groups : process and practice / Marianne Schneider Corey, Gerald
Corey. — 4th ed.
        p.   cm.
    Includes bibliographical references and index.
    ISBN 0-534-16122-7 :
    1. Group psychotherapy.   I. Corey, Gerald.   II. Title.
RC488.C5955   1991
616.89′152—dc20   90-26069
                                                                            CIP

Sponsoring Editor: *Claire Verduin*
Editorial Associate: *Gay C. Bond*
Production Editor: *Fiorella Ljunggren*
Manuscript Editor: *William Waller*
Permissions Editor: *Carline Haga*
Interior and Cover Design: *Terri Wright*
Typesetting: *Bookends Typesetting*
Cover Printing: *Phoenix Color Corporation*
Printing and Binding: *The Maple-Vail Book Manufacturing Group*

To the memory of our fathers,
Heinrich Schneider and Dr. Joseph Corey,
and to the memory of Jerry's nephew,
Jeff Corey

ABOUT THE AUTHORS

MARIANNE SCHNEIDER COREY is a licensed marriage and family therapist in private practice in Idyllwild, California, and is a National Certified Counselor. She received her master's degree in marriage, family, and child counseling from Chapman College. She is a clinical member of the American Association for Marriage and Family Therapy and holds memberships in the California Association of Marriage and Family Therapists, the American Association for Counseling and Development, the National Organization for Human Service Education, the Association for Religious and Value Issues in Counseling, and the Association for Specialists in Group Work.

Marianne has been actively involved in leading groups for different populations, providing training and supervision workshops in group process, and facilitating self-exploration groups for graduate students in counseling. She sees groups as the most effective format in which to work with clients and finds it the most rewarding for her personally. With her husband, Jerry, Marianne has conducted workshops, continuing-education seminars, and personal-growth groups in Germany, Belgium, Mexico, and China as well as regularly in the United States. Each year, she offers her time to California State University at Fullerton for training and supervising student leaders in group-counseling classes and for

co-leading weeklong residential growth groups. In her free time she enjoys travel-
ing, reading, visiting with friends, and hiking.

Marianne has co-authored several articles in group work, as well as the following books (published by Brooks/Cole Publishing Company):

- *Group Techniques*, Second Edition (1992, with Gerald Corey, Patrick Callanan, and J. Michael Russell)
- *I Never Knew I Had a Choice*, Fourth Edition (1990, with Gerald Corey)
- *Becoming a Helper* (1989, with Gerald Corey)
- *Issues and Ethics in the Helping Professions*, Third Edition (1988, with Gerald Corey and Patrick Callanan)

Marianne and Jerry have been married since 1964. They have two adult
daughters, Heidi and Cindy, and have made their home in the mountain community of Idyllwild, California. Marianne grew up in Germany and has kept in
close contact with her family in that country.

GERALD COREY is a professor of human services and counseling at California State University at Fullerton and was the coordinator of the university's
Human Services Program from 1983 to 1991. A licensed psychologist, he received
his doctorate in counseling from the University of Southern California. He is a
Diplomate in Counseling Psychology, American Board of Professional Psychology;
is a National Certified Counselor; and is registered as a National Health Service Provider in Psychology. He is a Fellow of the American Psychological Association (Counseling Psychology) and a Fellow of the Association for Specialists in
Group Work. In 1991, he received the Outstanding Professor of the Year Award
from California State University at Fullerton.

Jerry has a special interest in teaching group-counseling courses and also
teaches classes in theories and techniques of counseling, ethical and professional
issues, and the counseling profession. With his colleagues, he regularly gives
presentations at state and national professional conventions, conducts in-service
training workshops for group workers, offers weeklong residential growth groups,
and conducts training workshops in the United States. He has also done
workshops in Germany, Belgium, Mexico, and China. In his leisure time, Jerry
likes to travel, hike in the mountains, and bicycle.

Recent publications by Jerry, all with Brooks/Cole Publishing Company, are:

- *Group Techniques*, Second Edition (1992, with Marianne Schneider Corey, Patrick Callanan, and J. Michael Russell)
- *Theory and Practice of Counseling and Psychotherapy*, Fourth Edition (and *Manual*) (1991).
- *Case Approach to Counseling and Psychotherapy*, Third Edition (1991)
- *I Never Knew I Had a Choice*, Fourth Edition (1990, with Marianne Schneider Corey)
- *Theory and Practice of Group Counseling*, Third Edition (and *Manual*) (1990)
- *Becoming a Helper* (1989, with Marianne Schneider Corey)
- *Issues and Ethics in the Helping Professions*, Third Edition (1988, with Marianne Schneider Corey and Patrick Callanan)

PREFACE

THIS BOOK OUTLINES the basic issues and key concepts of group process and shows how group leaders can apply these concepts in working with a variety of groups.

In Part One, we deal with the basic issues in group work. The introductory chapter presents views on theory applied to practice, a discussion of group-leadership issues, and an overview of the types of group. In this new edition we give increased coverage in Chapter 2 to the ethical and professional aspects of group leadership.

In Part Two, separate chapters deal with group-process issues for each phase in the evolution of a group. A few of these issues are designing a group and getting one started, working effectively with a co-leader at each stage of a group, member roles and leader functions, problems that can occur at different times in a group, and techniques and procedures for facilitating the group process. There is updated material summarizing the practical applications of research literature at the various stages of a group.

In this edition we have added many more examples illustrating a variety of leader interventions in response to common problems. In many cases we have provided sample member/leader dialogues to demonstrate our own style. Each chapter in this part contains a summary of the characteristics of the particular stage, along with the functions of leaders and members. The chapters conclude with several exercises.

Some other topics that receive expanded coverage in the fourth edition are concrete examples of the group process in action; practical examples of leadership styles; the role of understanding cultural factors in group work; examples of resistance of individuals in groups; strategies for working with the resistance of an entire group; therapeutic factors in a group accounting for personal change; examples of effective and ineffective member behaviors; the role of cohesion, self-disclosure, and feedback; and ways of terminating both open and closed groups. Chapter 8 puts group process and practice in perspective by providing a single example of a member's fears and showing different interventions appropriate for each of the stages of a group. It also highlights trends in group work, guidelines for working effectively with cultural diversity in groups, and ways of combining research and practice. This chapter puts many of the topics covered in Parts One and Two into a nutshell for review purposes. We have also included the *Ethical Guidelines for Group Counselors* of the Association for Specialists in Group Work. The reading list at the end of Part Two, which has been updated and expanded considerably, is offered to help readers round out their knowledge of the topics discussed in the first two parts of the book and pursue a deeper understanding of areas of special interest.

In Part Three, we show how the basic concepts examined in Part Two can be applied to specific therapeutic groups. We offer guidelines for leaders who want to design groups specifically for children, adolescents, adults, and the elderly. We have also updated the discussion of issues in working with these special populations. New to this edition is an expanded coverage of a variety of groups appropriate to many settings. Different practitioners have provided a description of their groups, such as a group for children of divorce, a group with adolescents and parents, a group for children of alcoholics, an aftercare group for adolescents in drug rehabilitation, and an adult group for personal growth. We have also added descriptions of the following special groups: groups for weight control, AIDS support groups, bereavement groups, and groups for people with cancer.

Although we describe a number of techniques, we discourage the reader from using any technique without first developing a sound rationale for doing so in a particular situation. We focus on the unique needs of each age group and how to meet them; we discuss ethical, legal, practical, and professional guidelines; and we offer an expanded and updated list of suggested readings for each type of group. In many ways this is a "how to" book, but it is also a book about the "why" of group leadership.

Groups is intended for graduate and undergraduate students majoring in psychology, sociology, counseling, social work, education, and human services who are taking courses in group counseling or group leadership. It is also a practical manual for practitioners who are involved in leading groups and for counselors who are training to lead various types of group. Others who may find this book useful in their work are social workers, rehabilitation counselors, teachers, pastoral counselors, correctional workers, and marriage and family therapists.

An *Instructor's Manual* for this fourth edition is available. It contains multiple-choice test items, questions for reflection and discussion, additional exercises and activities, reading suggestions for instructors in preparing classes, a survey of current practices in the teaching of group-counseling courses, and examples of course outlines. We also describe our approach to workshops in training and supervising group leaders, which can be incorporated into many group courses.

Acknowledgments

We want to express our appreciation to J. Michael Russell and Patrick Callanan, both of whom continue to be very influential in helping us refine our views of group process and practice. Both of them have been co-leading weeklong residential personal-growth groups with us for 19 summers as well as working with us in the residential training workshops we offer for group leaders. We wish to recognize Mary Moline and Helga Kennedy, who also co-lead these residential workshops with us. These friends and colleagues have an influence on our style of group leadership that is reflected in the pages of this book.

The reviewers for this fourth edition have been instrumental in making important changes from the earlier editions. We appreciate the comments and suggestions of these prerevision reviewers: Joseph D. Dameron, University of North Texas; Earl Folse, Nicholls State University; Rosemarie S. Morganett, Indiana University Southeast; Bernard Nisenholz, California State University, Northridge; William Schiller, Northeastern State University; and Jerrold L. Shapiro, Santa Clara University. Three people reviewed the revised manuscript and offered useful comments: Paul Blisard, College of the Ozarks; Holly Forester-Miller, University of West Virginia College of Graduate Studies; and Diane Meadow, University of Southern California. We appreciate Katie Dutro's work in compiling the indexes and Debbie DeBue's assistance in typing the manuscript.

We thank the following people for granting us permission to describe their groups in Part Three: Lupe and Randy Alle-Corliss, Sandi Burns, Marilyn Chandler, Julianne Christinson, Nancy Ceraso English, Linda Gilbert, Wayne Huey, Paul Jacobson, Deborah Lambert, Steven Lanzet, Karen Kram Laudenslager, Kathleen McNamara, Michael Nakkula, and Phil Piechowski. We hope that their innovative programs inspire those who read this book to think of their own special designs for a group.

The dedicated members of the Brooks/Cole team continue to offer support for all of our projects. We wish to express our appreciation to Fiorella Ljunggren, production services manager, and to Claire Verduin, managing editor and psychology editor, for their interest in the revision process and for their helpful perspectives. We are especially indebted to William Waller, the manuscript editor, whose talent has contributed much to the readability and clarity of our book.

Marianne Schneider Corey
Gerald Corey

CONTENTS

CHAPTER 4
INITIAL STAGE OF A GROUP 105

CHAPTER 5
TRANSITION STAGE OF A GROUP 145

CHAPTER 6
WORKING STAGE OF A GROUP 189

CHAPTER 11
GROUPS FOR ADULTS 351

CHAPTER 12
GROUPS FOR THE ELDERLY 399

GROUPS
Process and Practice

PART ONE

INTRODUCTION:
Basic Issues in Group Work

Through the workshops we offer around the country, we have
become aware of a growing interest in using group approaches with
a wide variety of populations. In these visits to other states, however, we still hear comments like "What are those Californians up to
now?" Those who are not familiar with groups are often suspicious
about the purpose and value of them. Even though the reputation of
groups has suffered from some poor practices in the past, we are
convinced that groups have much to offer. The effort involved in
setting up and leading groups is considerable, yet we think that this
commitment is essential if the group movement is to be viewed with
respect. In Part One we discuss the fundamentals of group work
and provide guidelines for beginning your own work as a group
leader.

CHAPTER 1

Introduction to Group Work

FOCUS QUESTIONS

Introduction

The Theory behind the Practice
     Our theoretical orientation
     Developing your own theory of group practice

An Overview of the Various Types of Groups
     Group therapy ▪ Group counseling
     Personal-growth groups ▪ T-groups, or laboratory-training groups
     Structured groups ▪ Self-help groups

Group Leadership
     Problems and issues facing beginning group leaders
     Personal characteristics of the effective group leader
     Survey of group-leadership skills
     An integrated view of leadership skills

The Co-Leadership Model
     The basis of co-leadership
     Advantages of the co-leadership model
     Disadvantages of the co-leadership model

Exercises
     Attitude questionnaire on group leadership
     Self-assessment of group-leadership skills
     Evaluation of group leaders

3

FOCUS QUESTIONS

1. If you were applying for a job that entailed leading groups, how would you address these questions: "What theoretical orientation guides how you lead groups? How would you set up a group? How do you view your role as a leader?"
2. What are some advantages of practicing within a single theoretical perspective? some disadvantages? What value can you see in developing an eclectic stance by drawing on concepts and techniques from diverse theoretical perspectives? Are there any drawbacks?
3. Beginning group leaders face a number of concerns in setting up and leading groups. What worries do you have about leading your first group? If you have had some experience in group work, what problems did you face when you began?
4. What personal characteristics, skills, and specialized knowledge do you associate with effective group leaders? Which of these attributes do you see as being most crucial in competently leading groups?
5. What are some advantages and disadvantages of co-leadership of a group, both for the group members and for the co-leaders?

Introduction

Our hope is that, from its very beginning, this book will get you excited about the prospect of leading groups and about the value of group work. This chapter discusses our theory of group work, which obviously influences the way we function in groups. It also deals with the personal characteristics desirable in group leaders, describes basic skills needed for effective leadership, and explains our preference for co-leadership. The chapter includes an overview of the various types of groups, and it ends with a look at recent trends in group work.

The Theory behind the Practice

Our Theoretical Orientation

We are sometimes asked to declare what theory we follow. Neither of us subscribes to any single theory in its totality. Rather, we function within an eclectic (or integrative) framework, which we continue to develop as we practice. We respect the contributions that many theorists have made to the field. We freely borrow concepts and techniques from most of the contemporary therapeutic models and adapt them to our own unique personalities. Our conceptual framework takes into account the *thinking*, *feeling*, and *behaving* dimensions of human experience. Thus, our theoretical orientations and leadership styles are primarily a function of the individuals we are and the experiences we see unfolding in the groups we lead.

We value those therapies that emphasize the *thinking* dimension. Though many clients can benefit from an emotional catharsis (the release of pent-up feelings), some kind of cognitive work is also essential if the maximum benefit is to be gained. Therefore, we draw heavily on transactional analysis, behavior therapy, rational-emotive therapy, and other cognitive-behavioral approaches. From transactional analysis we adopt a focus on early parental messages that group members incorporated and early decisions that they made about themselves and others in response to these parental injunctions. We typically challenge members to begin to think about these decisions, some of which may have been necessary for their psychological survival as children but now are clearly out of date. We hope that members will eventually be able to make necessary revisions that can lead them to live more freely. Like cognitive-behavioral and rational-emotive therapists, we stress paying attention to one's "self-talk." How are members' problems actually caused by the assumptions they make about themselves, about others, and about life? How do members create their problems by the thoughts and beliefs they cling to? How can they begin to free themselves by critically evaluating the sentences they repeat to themselves? In other words, many of our group techniques and procedures are designed to tap members' thinking processes, to help them think about events in their life and how they have interpreted these events, and to work on a cognitive level to change certain belief systems. We have even suggested that members experiment with saying aloud new sentences, even if they don't believe what they are saying, just to have the experience of telling others something different about themselves.

In working with group members, we also emphasize the value of helping them identify and express their *feelings*. We find that the following theories guide us in facilitating emotional expression in group sessions: The person-centered approach emphasizes the value of listening with understanding and encouraging people to put into words what they are feeling in the moment. The experiential therapies, such as psychodrama and Gestalt, place value on expressing feelings in action-oriented ways; techniques are available to release buried feelings and to enable members work through emotional barriers.

Thinking and feeling are vital components in the therapeutic process, but we see another dimension as essential if the goal is behavior or personality change: *behaving*, or *doing*. Members can spend countless hours gaining insights and ventilating pent-up feelings, but at some point they need to get involved in an action-oriented program of change. In this way they bring feelings and thoughts together by applying them to real-life situations. We think there is considerable merit in reality therapy's focus on current behavior. Group leaders can ask useful questions such as these: "What are you doing?" "What do you see for yourself now and in the future?" "Does your present behavior have a reasonable chance of getting you what you want now, and will it take you in the direction you want to go?" If the focus of group work is on what people are doing, there is a greater chance that they will also be able to change their thinking and feeling (Glasser, 1985).

In Chapter 7, on ending a group, we focus on strategies and techniques to assist members in consolidating what they've learned in their group experience and applying new behaviors to situations they encounter every day. We focus on "contracts," "homework assignments," action programs, self-monitoring techniques, support systems, and self-directed programs of change. These approaches all stress the role of commitment on the members' part to practice new behaviors, to follow through with a realistic plan for change, and to develop practical methods of carrying out this plan in everyday life.

Underlying our integrated focus on thinking, feeling, and behaving is our philosophical leaning toward the existential approach, which places primary emphasis on the role of choice and responsibility in the therapeutic process. We do not perceive or treat group members as helpless victims of forces that are beyond their control. Although we can appreciate that people are strongly influenced by certain traumatic events, we do not subscribe to the view that people are *hopelessly* "scripted" during early childhood or that they can do nothing now to change any negative conditioning from the first five years of life. Basically, we challenge people to look at the choices they *do* have and to accept the responsibility for choosing for themselves. Most of what we do in our groups is based on the assumption that people can exercise their freedom to change situations. In those cases where it is not possible to change a difficult situation, we work with members on changing their attitudes toward it or the way they react to it. The group context offers people opportunities to learn how to use the freedom they have.

Of necessity, this discussion of our theoretical orientation has been brief. If you want a more elaborate discussion of the various theoretical orientations than is given here, see *Theory and Practice of Group Counseling* (G. Corey, 1990).

Developing Your Own Theory of Group Practice

Attempting to lead groups without having an explicit theoretical rationale is like flying a plane without a flight plan. Though you may eventually get there (and even find the detours exciting), you're equally likely to do nothing but fly aimlessly in circles and run out of patience and gas. If you operate in a theoretical vacuum or cannot draw on theory to support your interventions, your groups probably will not reach a productive stage.

We don't see theory, however, as a rigid, step-by-step prescription for how you should function as a leader. Rather, theory is a general framework that helps you make sense of the many facets of group process, gives direction to what you do and say in a group, and helps you think about the possible results of your interventions. We encourage you to look at all the contemporary theories to determine what concepts and techniques you can incorporate into your leadership style. The theoretical stance you develop is most meaningful if it is closely related to your own values, beliefs, and characteristics.

In co-leading groups, we do not consciously think about what theory we are using with what clients. Yet sometimes we rely more on one type of intervention than another, depending on the needs of the clients. In deciding on techniques to introduce, we take into account an array of factors about the group members. We consider their readiness to confront an issue, their cultural backgrounds, their value systems, and their trust in us as leaders. It is also important to keep in mind the level of cohesion and trust that the members have established among themselves. We are inclined to use more confrontive interventions with relatively well-functioning members, for example, and to draw on supportive approaches when we work with clients who are unable to benefit from confrontation. If members are highly emotional, we challenge them to think about how the decisions they have made affect the way they feel and act. With individuals who have a tendency to intellectualize or rehearse what they say, we employ emotive techniques as a way of helping them overcome some of their blocks to effective functioning. We have a rationale for using the techniques we employ, and our interventions generally flow from some particular theoretical framework. Our concern is to help clients identify and experience whatever they are feeling, identify ways in which their assumptions influence how they feel and behave, and experiment with alternative modes of behaving.

Thus, we hope that you have some underlying purpose for suggesting a particular technique, introducing an exercise, or inviting members to participate in an experiment. By thinking about the different models of therapeutic groups, you may be stimulated to examine questions such as:

- What is the basic nature of human beings?
- How can I incorporate my philosophy of human nature into the way I lead groups?
- Can people be trusted to determine their own direction in a group, or do they need strong intervention to keep them moving productively?
- Should the goals of the group be determined by the members? by the group leader? by both?
- How specific should the goals be?
- Should the group leader be a facilitator? director? expert? consultant? resource person?
- How much responsibility for the group's work lies with the leader? with the members? To what degree should the group be structured by the leader?

- What are your views on selecting a co-leader and working with one? Ideally, how would you divide responsibility with a co-leader?
- Is it best to work with one group member at a time or to encourage maximum interaction among members? How can you introduce techniques that will maximize working on themes and linking the work of several members simultaneously?
- How much personality change is desirable? Should the focus be on attitude change or on behavior change?
- What are the functions of group members?
- In what ways must the structure or the techniques of a group be adapted to the clients' cultural frames of reference?
- What techniques are the best for a particular group? Why?
- What are the criteria for measuring the success of a group?

A theory can help you to clarify many of these questions. Ultimately, the most meaningful perspective is one that reflects your values and personality. A theory is not something divorced from you as a person. At its best it is an integral part of the person you are and an expression of your uniqueness. If you are a student in training, it is unrealistic to expect you to have already integrated a well-defined theoretical model into your practice. This process may take years of extensive reading and practice in leading groups. We encourage you to devote considerable time to thinking about and discussing with others your ideas about group practice.

Developing a personalized theory that guides your practice is obviously an ongoing process, for ideally your model will continually undergo revision. With increased experience you will develop new questions, try new experiments, and put clinical hunches to the test. By talking to fellow group leaders, you can get ideas for modifying your old practices to fit your new knowledge.

You can limit yourself by subscribing totally to the tenets of a single theoretical viewpoint. If you become a devotee of one approach, you may overlook critical aspects of human experience and unduly limit your effectiveness with different clients by attempting to force them to fit your theory. Remember that each theory has something unique to offer and that it is essential to continually refine the personalized theory of group process that guides the interventions you make.

There are some dangers in encouraging an eclectic approach. At its worst, eclecticism can be an excuse for sloppy practice that lacks a systematic rationale. It can be a disorganized process of merely picking bits and pieces from various theories without any integrating framework. In developing a personalized integrative approach, it is important to be alert to the problems that can arise from mixing theories with incompatible philosophical assumptions. As Lazarus (1989) has observed, if eclectic practitioners choose their theories and techniques strictly on the basis of subjective appeal, the result can be chaos. Thus, in working toward the goal of an integrative perspective, it is essential that you be aware of irreconcilable differences among the systems that make a merger impractical, if not impossible.

At its best, however, eclecticism can be a creative synthesis of selected concepts and techniques from a variety of systems. Systematic eclecticism, or a truly integrative approach, implies that as a practitioner you are thoroughly grounded in the various theories, that you are open to the idea that the techniques that flow from these theories can be unified in some ways, and that you are willing to continually test your hypotheses to determine how well your interventions are working. If you have developed an integrative approach, you are able to wisely select a range of techniques to meet the special needs of the members in your groups. Such a perspective is the product of a great deal of clinical practice, and it involves considerable reading, researching, and theorizing. There are clear indications that since the early 1980s counseling and psychotherapy have been characterized by a rapidly developing movement toward integration and eclecticism (G. Corey, 1991b).

Throughout this book we refer to your ability to draw on your life experiences and your personal characteristics as one of your most powerful therapeutic tools. Particularly important is your willingness to examine how your personality and behavior either hinder or facilitate your work as a group leader. Although it is essential to become well grounded in the theories underlying group work, to acquire the skills needed to conduct groups, and to gain supervised experience as a group leader, we do not see these as sufficient to make you an effective leader. You must also be willing to take an honest look at your own life to determine if you are willing to do for yourself what you challenge group members to do.

An Overview of the Various Types of Groups

Throughout the book *therapeutic group* is used as a general term to indicate various types of groups. *Therapeutic* does not refer to the treatment of emotional and behavioral disorders. Rather, the broad purpose of a therapeutic group is to increase people's knowledge of themselves and others, help them clarify the changes they most want to make in their life, and give them some of the tools necessary to make these desired changes. By interacting with others in a trusting and accepting environment, participants are given the opportunity to experiment with novel behavior and to receive honest feedback from others concerning the effects of their behavior. As a result, they learn how they appear to others.

In this book we use the term *therapeutic group* to refer to group counseling, group therapy, group guidance, T-groups, structured groups, task groups, awareness groups, consciousness-raising groups, self-help and leaderless groups, and personal-growth groups, among others. Different groups differ with respect to goals, techniques used, the role of the leader, and the kind of people involved. The following brief descriptions will give you some idea of the diversity of these groups.

Group Therapy

Group therapy originated in response to a shortage during World War II of personnel trained to provide individual therapy. At first, the group therapist assumed a traditional therapeutic role, frequently working with a small number of clients with a common problem. Gradually, leaders began to experiment with different roles and various approaches. Over time, practitioners discovered that the group setting offered unique therapeutic possibilities. Exchanges among the members of a therapy group are viewed as instrumental in bringing about change. This inter-action provides support, caring confrontation, and other qualities not found in individual therapy. Within the group context members are able to practice new social skills and apply some of their new knowledge.

People generally participate in group therapy to try to alleviate specific symptoms or psychological problems, such as depression, sexual difficulties, anxiety, and psychosomatic disorders. Some therapy groups are organized for the purpose of correcting a specific emotional or behavioral disorder that impedes people's functioning. Thus, many individuals in these groups are in need of remedial treatment rather than developmental and preventive work. In group therapy attention is given to unconscious factors and one's past and to the reconstruction of major aspects of the personality. Therapy groups are thus typically of longer duration than most other types.

A variety of methods are employed in the conduct of therapy groups, including techniques designed to induce regression to earlier experiences, methods to work with unconscious dynamics, and procedures aimed at helping members reexperience traumatic situations so that catharsis can occur. The therapist is typically interested in creating a climate that fosters a corrective emotional experience. The process of working through psychological blocks that are rooted in past experiences often involves exploring dreams, interpreting resistance, dealing with transference that emerges, and helping members develop a new perspective on "unfinished business" with significant others.

Group Counseling

The counseling group usually focuses on a particular type of problem, which may be personal, educational, social, or vocational. It is often carried out in institutions such as schools, college counseling centers, and community mental-health clinics and agencies. This type of group differs from a therapy group in that it deals with conscious problems, is not aimed at major personality changes, is generally oriented toward the resolution of specific and short-term issues, and is not concerned with treatment of the more severe psychological and behavioral disorders.

Group counseling has preventive and educational purposes as well as remedial aims. The group involves an interpersonal process and problem-solving strategies that stress conscious thoughts, feelings, and behavior. The focus of the group is often determined by the members, who are basically well-functioning individuals who do not require extensive personality reconstruction and whose problems relate to the developmental tasks of the life span or finding means to cope with stresses of a situational crisis. The group is characterized by a growth orientation, with an emphasis on discovering inner resources of personal strength and constructively dealing with barriers that are preventing optimal development. Members are able to develop interpersonal skills that can equip them to better cope with both current difficulties and future problems. The group provides the support and the challenge necessary for honest self-exploration.

The group counselor's job is to structure the activities of the group, to see that a climate favorable to productive work is maintained, to facilitate members' interactions, to provide information that will help the members see alternatives to their modes of behavior, and to encourage them to translate their insights into concrete action plans. To a large extent group leaders carry out this role by teaching the members to focus on the here and now and to establish personal goals that will provide direction for the group.

Participants in group counseling often have problems of an interpersonal nature, which are ideally explored in a group context. Members are able to see a reenactment of their everyday problems unfold before them in the counseling group. The group becomes a microcosm of society, with a membership that is diverse but that shares common problems. The group process provides a sample of reality, with the struggles that people experience in the group resembling their conflicts in daily life. Through feedback members are encouraged to see themselves as others do. They have a chance to experience themselves as they did in their original family, reliving conflicts they had with parents and siblings. There is also a chance to practice new ways of behaving, for the empathy and support from other members help clients identify what they want to change and how to bring about change. Participants can learn to respect differences in culture and values and can discover that, on a deep level, they are more alike than different. Although their circumstances may differ, their pain and struggles are universal.

Fairly detailed descriptions of counseling groups for clients of various ages are provided in Part Three of this book. In Chapter 9 there is a group program for elementary schoolchildren that is structured along educational and therapeutic lines. A counseling group for adolescents that deals mainly with the normal developmental concerns of this period is found in Chapter 10. There are several examples of group-counseling programs for various adult populations in Chapter 11. In Chapter 12 support groups and counseling groups for the elderly are described, along with guidelines for setting up and facilitating these groups.

Personal-Growth Groups

Personal-growth groups offer an intense experience intended to help relatively healthy people function better on an interpersonal level. Rather than being aimed at curing personality problems, such groups are developmental, in that they explore personal issues that most people struggle with at the various transition periods in life. The rationale for these groups is that the support and challenge they provide help participants make an honest self-assessment and determine specific ways in which to change their patterns of thinking, feeling, and acting. Although participants can benefit from the feedback they receive from others, it is ultimately up to them to decide what changes they want to make. Participants can compare the perceptions they have of themselves with the perceptions others have of them and then decide for themselves what they will do with this information.

Personal-growth groups range from those with an open structure, in which participants shape the direction of the group, to those characterized by a specific focus. But they share the following goals:

- helping people develop more positive attitudes and better interpersonal skills
- using the group process as a way of facilitating personality change
- helping members transfer newly acquired skills and behavior learned in the group to everyday life

Although personal-growth groups are often led by social workers, psychologists, or counselors, they may also be led by paraprofessionals in some settings. Regardless of who leads these groups, we think that training and supervision in group process is essential, even if it is on-the-job training. Although the clients in these groups are typically not highly disturbed, such groups can be counterproductive if they are led by people who lack the knowledge and skills to facilitate interaction. Examples of personal-growth groups for adults are provided in Chapter 11.

T-Groups, or Laboratory-Training Groups

T-groups, also referred to as training groups, laboratory-training groups, or sensitivity-training groups, tend to emphasize the human-relations skills required for successful functioning in a business organization. In such groups the stress is on education through experience in an environment in which experimentation can occur, data can be analyzed, new ideas are encouraged, and decisions can be made or problems solved.

These groups are frequently task oriented, and the focus is on specific organizational problems, such as: How can leadership become a more shared function? By what vehicle can employees creatively express themselves?

The focus of T-groups is on the group process rather than on personal growth. (*Group process* refers to the stages of development of a group and the interactions that characterize each stage.) Members are taught how to observe their own interactions and also how to develop a leadership role so that they can continue the groups on their own.

Structured Groups

Groups structured to focus on a particular theme are being increasingly used by agencies, schools, and college counseling centers. Although the specific topic varies according to the interests of the leader and the population of the group, such groups share the aim of providing members with increased awareness of some life problem and the tools to better cope with it. Generally, the sessions are about two hours each week, for 4 to 15 weeks. Depending on the population, some group sessions may be as short as 30 to 45 minutes, especially with children or clients with a short attention span.

At the beginning of these structured groups it is common to ask the members to complete a questionnaire on how well they are coping with the area of concern. Such groups make use of structured exercises, readings, homework assignments, and contracts. When the group comes to an end, another questionnaire is often used to assess the members' progress.

This list will give you some idea of the scope of topics for structured groups:

- stress management
- assertion training
- eating disorders (bulimia and anorexia)
- women in transition
- dealing with an alcoholic parent
- learning coping skills
- managing relationships and ending relationships
- overcoming perfectionism
- support for incest victims

Part Three of this book provides a variety of examples of short-term structured groups. At this time you might skim the passages dealing with a structured group for repeat dieters, in Chapter 11; a group for women with a history of incest, in Chapter 11; groups for children of divorce, conducted in elementary schools, in Chapter 9; and a high school program for children of alcoholics, in Chapter 10.

Self-Help Groups

Self-help groups serve a critical need for certain populations that is not met by professional mental-health workers. Self-help groups are typically organized around a shared specific problem (such as substance abuse or weight control). Because of this common problem such groups more easily develop into cohesive units. They provide a support system that helps reduce psychological stress and gives the members the incentive to begin changing their lives. The members share their experiences, learn from one another, offer suggestions for new members, and provide encouragement for people who sometimes see no hope for the future.

Examples of self-help groups include Alcoholics Anonymous, Weight Watchers, Mended Hearts, and Recovery, Inc. These groups are led by people who are struggling with the same issues as the members of the group. At times professionals are used as consultants, however.

Group Leadership

Problems and Issues Facing Beginning Group Leaders

Those who are just beginning to lead groups typically feel overwhelmed by the potential problems they face. New leaders ask themselves questions such as:

- Will I be able to get the group started?
- What techniques should I use?
- Should I wait for the group to initiate activity?
- Do I have what it takes to follow through once something has been initiated?
- What if I like some people more than others?
- What if I make mistakes? Can I cause someone serious psychological damage?
- Do I know enough theory? Can I apply whatever I do know in groups?
- Should I share my anxiety with my group?
- What do I do if there is a prolonged silence?
- How much should I participate or involve myself in a personal way in the groups I lead?
- Will I have the knowledge and skills to work effectively with clients who are culturally different from me?
- What if the entire group attacks me?
- How do I know whether the group is helping people change?
- How can I work with so many people at one time?

Whether you are a beginning group leader or a seasoned one, successful groups cannot be guaranteed. Hence, courage is necessary, the courage to function under conditions of uncertainty. You are sure to make mistakes, and if you can admit them, you will learn from them.

It is important that you not be harshly critical of yourself, imposing standards of perfection. In supervising group leaders, we tell trainees that the fear of making mistakes can stifle their creativity and their ability to remain in the present.

One problem that you will probably face as a beginning group leader is negative reactions from members. On the one hand, if you structure a group by using specific techniques, you may be accused by members of constricting their freedom. The members may rebel by refusing to cooperate with the structure. On the other hand, if you do not provide some degree of structure and direction, members may criticize you for allowing them to flounder, and they may wait passively for you to initiate some exercise. You need to learn how to constructively confront those who have these reactions. If you become tight and defensive, the members may, in turn, become increasingly defensive. Such an undercurrent of unresolved hostility will sabotage any further work. How to deal with these situations will be discussed later in this section and at different places in this book.

Beginning group leaders should realize that it will take time to develop leadership skills. Many feel like quitting after leading only a few sessions. Such people usually want to be accomplished leaders without experiencing the self-doubts and fears that may be necessary to their development as leaders. Some feel devastated if they don't receive an abundance of positive feedback. It probably cannot be mentioned too many times that some struggle and uncertainty are almost always a part of learning how to lead well. Nobody expects to perfect any skill (skiing, playing the guitar, making pottery) in a few introductory lessons. Those who finally experience success at these endeavors are the ones who have the endurance to progress in increments. There is probably no better teacher than experience, but unguided experience is often unsatisfactory. Immediate feedback—from a supervisor, from co-leaders, or from other budding leaders in a training group—enables leaders to profit from their experience.

Personal Characteristics of the Effective Group Leader

In our view who the leader is as a person is one of the most significant variables influencing the group's success or failure. In discussing the personality characteristics of the effective group leader with some of our colleagues, we have found that it is difficult to list all of the traits of successful leaders and even more difficult to agree on one particular personality type associated with effective leadership. Following are some personal characteristics that we deem important. As you read about each of these dimensions, reflect on how it applies to you. Consider the degree to which you are at least on the road to acquiring the personal characteristics that you deem important for your success as a group leader.

Courage. One of the most important personal traits of effective group leaders is courage. Courage is demonstrated through your willingness (1) to be vulnerable at times, admitting mistakes and imperfections and taking the same risks that you expect group members to take; (2) to confront others but to stay "with" them as you work out conflicts; (3) to act on your beliefs and hunches; (4) to be emotionally touched by others and to draw on your experiences in order to identify with them; (5) to examine your life; (6) to be direct and honest with members; and (7) to express to the members your fears and expectations about the group process. Just as the members of your groups will have fears, so will you as the leader. By the behavior you model you can teach the members that courage does not mean being without fears; rather, it means acknowledging them and dealing with them.

Willingness to Model. As just mentioned, one of the best ways to teach desired behaviors is by modeling them in the group. Through your behavior and the attitudes conveyed by it, you can create such group norms as openness, seriousness of purpose, acceptance of others, and the desirability of taking risks.

Remember that you teach largely by example—by doing what you expect members to do. Realize that your role differs from that of the group member, but do not hide behind a professional facade. By engaging in honest, appropriate, and timely self-disclosure, you can both participate as a member in the group and fulfill the leadership function of modeling.

Presence. The ability to be emotionally present with group members is extremely important. It involves being touched by others' pain, struggles, and joys. Some members may elicit anger in a group leader, and others may evoke pain, sadness, guilt, or happiness. You become more emotionally involved with others by paying close attention to your own reactions. This does not mean that you will necessarily talk about the situation in your own life that caused you the pain or evoked the anger. It means that you will allow yourself to experience these feelings, even for just a few moments. Fully experiencing emotions gives you the ability to be compassionate and empathic with your clients. At the same time as you're moved by others' experiences, it is important to remain a separate person and to avoid the trap of overidentifying with your clients' situations.

To increase your ability to be present, spend some time alone before leading a group, and block out distractions as much as possible. It is good to prepare yourself by thinking about the people in the group and about ways in which you might increase your involvement with them.

Goodwill and Caring. A sincere interest in the welfare of others is essential in a group leader. It implies that you will not exploit members or use them primarily to enhance your own ego. Your main job in the group is to help members get what they are coming for, not to get in their way. Caring involves respecting, trusting, and valuing people. In some cases it may be exceedingly difficult for you to care for certain group members, but we hope that you will at least want to care. It is vital that you become aware of what kind of people you care for and what kind you find it difficult to care for. You can gain this awareness by openly exploring your reactions to members.

There are various ways of exhibiting a caring attitude. One way is by inviting a client to participate but allowing that person to decide how far to go. Or you can observe discrepancies between a client's words and behavior but confront that person in a way that doesn't intensify fear and resistance. Another way to express caring is by giving warmth, concern, and support when, and only when, you feel it toward a person.

Belief in Group Process. Some counselors really don't believe that groups can bring about significant change in clients, but they continue to lead groups. We think that a deep confidence in the value of group process is positively related to constructive outcomes. You need to believe in what you are doing and trust the therapeutic forces in a group. We continue to find that our enthusiasm and convictions are powerful both in attracting a clientele and in providing an incentive to work. Group leaders who do not genuinely believe in the value of therapeutic work and who do it only for money or power are behaving unethically.

Openness. To be effective, it certainly helps to be open with yourself, open to members of the group, open to new experiences, and open to lifestyles and values that differ from your own. At times, you may want to reveal your own experiences or, at least, the meaning that certain experiences have for you. Openness does not mean that you reveal every aspect of your personal life. Rather, it means that you reveal enough of yourself to give the participants a sense of who you are as a person. It can also enhance group process if you appropriately reveal your reactions to the members and let them know how you are being affected by being with the group.

Your openness tends to foster a corresponding spirit of openness within the group. It allows members to become more open about their feelings and beliefs, and it lends a certain fluidity to the group process. Self-revelation should not be manipulated as a technique; it is best done spontaneously, when it seems appropriate.

Nondefensiveness in Coping with Attacks. Dealing frankly with criticism is related to openness. Group leaders who are easily threatened, who are insecure in their work of leading, who are overly sensitive to negative feedback, and who depend highly on group approval will encounter major problems in trying to carry out a leadership function.

Members may sometimes accuse you of not caring enough, of being selective in your caring, of structuring the sessions too much, of not providing enough direction, of being too harsh, and so forth. Some of the criticism may be fair—you may be insensitive or uncaring at times—and some of it may be an unfair expression of jealousy, testing of authority, power seeking, or projection onto you of feelings for other people. The crucial thing is for you to explore nondefensively with the group the feelings that are behind the criticism.

Personal Power. Personal power does not entail domination of members or manipulation of them toward the leader's end. Rather, it is the dynamic and vital characteristic of leaders who know who they are and what they want. This power involves a sense of confidence in self and a certain charisma. Such leaders' lives are an expression of what they espouse. Instead of merely talking about the importance of being alive, powerful leaders express and radiate an aliveness through their actions.

Power and honesty are closely related. In our view powerful people are the ones who can show themselves. Although they may be frightened by certain qualities within themselves, the fear doesn't keep them from examining these qualities. Powerful people recognize and accept their weaknesses and don't expend energy concealing them from themselves and others. In contrast, powerless people need very much to defend themselves against self-knowledge. They often act as if they are afraid that their vulnerabilities will be discovered.

Clients often badly need to see leaders not only as powerful but also as having all of the qualities that the members are striving for. Such clients may view leaders as perfect. They tend to undercut their own power by giving their leader *all* of the credit for their insights and changes. There is a danger that leaders will become infatuated with clients' perceptions of them as finished products and come to believe this myth. Powerful group leaders can accept credit where it is due and, at the same time, encourage clients to accept their own share of credit for their growth.

Stamina. Group leading can be taxing and draining as well as exciting and energizing. Therefore, you need physical and psychological stamina and the ability to withstand pressure in order to remain vitalized throughout the course of a group. Some novice counselors begin a group feeling excited and anticipating each session—until, that is, the group becomes resistive, clients begin to drop out, or members complain that the group is going nowhere. If you lose most of your stamina at this point, any possibility that the group will be productive may be lost. This means that you need to be aware of your own energy level. Furthermore, it is good to have sources other than your groups for psychological nourishment. If you depend primarily on the success level of your groups for this sustenance, you run a high risk of being undernourished and thus of losing the stamina so vital to your success as a leader. Unrealistically high expectations can also affect your stamina. Those leaders who cling to such expectations of dramatic change are often disappointed in themselves and in what they perceive as "poor performance" on the part of their group. Faced with the discrepancy between their vision of what the group *should* be and what actually occurs, these leaders often lose their enthusiasm and begin to needlessly blame both themselves and the group members for what they see as failure.

Willingness to Seek New Experiences. Your personhood is largely determined by the variety of your life experiences. A narrow range of experiences restricts your capacity to understand the psychological worlds of clients who have different values resulting from different life experiences. Your willingness to put yourself in situations where you can learn about different cultures will be most useful in helping you work effectively with culturally diverse populations. If you genuinely respect the differences among the members of your groups and are open to learning from them, you will win their trust. By contrast, "culturally encapsulated" counselors tend to make rigid and stereotyped generalizations about individuals within a particular cultural group. As a result they tend to impose their world view on the members of their groups. This narrowness demonstrates a lack of respect for the complexity of the human struggles that grow out of various cultural backgrounds.

It is important to learn about human struggles by recognizing and wrestling with your own life issues. If you have lived a fairly sheltered life and have known little pain and strife, how can you empathize with clients who have suffered and have made dramatic life choices? If you have never experienced loneliness, joy, anguish, or uncertainty, what basis do you have for tuning in to the pain that your clients experience? Although it is not possible for you to experience directly everything that you encounter in others, you should at least be willing to identify ways in which you can draw on your own emotions in working with group members. It is unrealistic to expect yourself to have experienced the same problems as all of your clients. But the emotions that all of us experience are much the same. We all experience psychological pain, even though the causes of this pain may be different. One basis for empathizing with clients is being open to the sources of pain in your own life, without being swept up by this pain.

Self-Awareness. A central characteristic of any therapeutic person is an awareness of self, including one's identity, cultural perspective, goals, motivations, needs, limitations, strengths, values, feelings, and problems. If you have a limited understanding of who you are, you will surely not be able to facilitate this kind of awareness in clients. As we've mentioned, being open to new life experiences and divergent lifestyles is one way you can expand your awareness. Involvement in your own personal therapy, both group and individual, is another way for you to become more aware of who you are and whom you might become. Awareness of why you choose to lead groups is crucial, including knowing what needs you are meeting through your work. If you are functioning with dim self-awareness, you could keep yourself blinded for fear of what you might discover. How can you encourage others to risk self-discovery if you are hesitant to come to terms with yourself? You have a potentially rich source of information about yourself if you will reflect on interactions you have had with members of your groups.

Sense of Humor. At times, people take themselves so seriously that they miss an opportunity to put the importance of their problems into perspective. Although therapy is serious business, there are many humorous dimensions of the human condition. The ability to laugh at yourself and to see the humor in your human frailties can be extremely useful in helping members keep a proper perspective and avoid becoming "psychologically heavy." Groups occasionally exhibit a real need for laughter and joking simply to release built-up tension. This release should not be viewed as an escape, for genuine humor can heal. If you can enjoy humor and infuse it effectively into the group process, you will have an invaluable asset.

Inventiveness. The capacity to be spontaneously creative, approaching each group with fresh ideas, is a most important characteristic. Freshness may not be easy to maintain, particularly if you lead groups frequently. You must somehow avoid becoming trapped in ritualized techniques or a programmed presentation of self that has lost all life. If you are able to discover new ways of approaching a group by inventing experiments that emerge from here-and-now interactions, you are unlikely to grow stale. Working with interesting co-leaders is another source of fresh ideas. Getting some distance from groups—for example, by conducting fewer of them, doing other things, or taking a vacation—may also help you gain a fresh perspective.

Inventiveness involves the ability both to detect clues that clients give and to create some way of exploring with them the problems they are hinting at. In this regard it is important for you to have a theoretical perspective to guide your selection of techniques. For instance, we appreciate the psychosocial view of development, so in our groups we invent techniques that help people tap their memories of early childhood experiences. In this way leaders can use the theory or combination of theories they endorse as a source of fresh techniques.

Survey of Group-Leadership Skills

Although the personality characteristics of the group leader are among the most important determinants of group outcomes, we think it is a mistake to assume that being a person of goodwill and approaching your group enthusiastically are all you need to lead effectively. Some personality attributes seem positively related to effective leadership, but these characteristics by themselves are not sufficient. Basic counseling skills specific to group situations must be developed. Like most skills, counseling skills can be taught to some degree, but there is also an element of art involved in using these skills in a sensitive and timely way. Learning how and when to use these skills is a function of supervised experience, practice, feedback, and confidence.

We will now consider some of the skills that you will need to acquire as a competent group leader. As you read, keep in mind that these skills, like your personal qualities, are not sufficient to ensure effective leadership. Unless you are also the kind of person who provides a positive model that your clients can benefit from, your success as a leader will be limited.

Active Listening. It is most important to learn how to pay full attention to others as they communicate, and this process involves more than merely listening to the words. It involves absorbing the content, noting gestures and subtle changes in voice or expression, and sensing underlying messages. Group leaders can improve their listening skills by first recognizing the barriers that interfere with paying attention to others. Some of these roadblocks are not really listening to the other, thinking about what to say next instead of giving full attention to the other, being overly concerned about one's role or about how one will look, and judging and evaluating without putting oneself in the other person's place. Like any other therapeutic skill, active listening exists in degrees. Some leaders are so intent on being in the spotlight that they can't focus on anything outside themselves; other leaders have developed a high degree of perceptivity in discerning others' messages. The skilled group leader is sensitive to the congruence (or lack of it) between what a member is saying in words and what he or she is communicating through body posture, gestures, mannerisms, and voice inflections. For instance, a man may be talking about his warm and loving feelings toward his wife, yet his body may be rigid and his fists clenched. A woman recalling a painful situation may both smile and hold back tears.

Reflecting. Reflecting, a skill that is dependent on active listening, is the ability to convey the essence of what a person has communicated so the person can see it. Many novice group leaders find themselves confining most of their interaction to mere reflection. Somehow it seems safe. And, since members continue to talk, leaders continue to reflect. Carried to its extreme, however, reflection can become a hollow echo, empty of any substance:

Member: I really didn't want to come to the group today. I'm bored, and I don't think we've gotten anyplace for weeks.

Group leader: You didn't want to come to the group because you're bored and the group isn't getting anywhere.

There was plenty of rich material here for the leader to respond to in a personal way, or with some confrontation, or by asking the person and the other members to examine what was going on in the group. Beginning on a reflective level may have value, but staying on that level produces blandness. The leader might have done better to reply "You sound discouraged about the possibility of getting much from this experience." The leader would then have been challenging the member to look at the emotions that lay beneath his words and, in the process, would have been opening up opportunities for meaningful communication.

Clarifying. Clarifying is a skill that can be valuably applied during the initial stages of a group. It involves focusing on key underlying issues and sorting out confusing and conflicting feelings. Thus, a girl might say: "I hate my father, and I wish I didn't have to see him anymore. He hurts me so often. I feel guilty when I feel this way, because I also love him and wish he would appreciate me." The therapist might clarify: "You have feelings of love and hate, and somehow having both of these feelings at once doesn't seem OK." Clarification can help the client sort out her feelings so that she can eventually experience both love and hate without experiencing guilt. However, intervention methods stronger than clarification may have to be used before she can accept this polarity.

Summarizing. When the group process becomes bogged down or fragmented, the skill of summarizing is useful. On the basis of a summary, decisions about where to go next can be made. For example, some members may be arguing that the leader is not providing enough structure and direction, while others are maintaining that the leader is handling the group correctly. If the interaction seems to be turning into a debate, the group leader might interrupt and have each person state briefly how he or she feels about the issue. The leader can then summarize and offer possible alternatives.

At the end of a session the leader might make some summary statements or ask each member to summarize. For instance, a leader might say "Before we close, I'd like each of us to make a statement about his or her experience in the group today and tell where he or she is left." It's a good idea for the leader to make the first summary statement, so that the members will have a model for this behavior. Sometimes, however, the leader may want to close the session with his or her own reactions.

Facilitating. The group leader can facilitate the group process by (1) assisting members to openly express their fears and expectations,

(2) actively working to create a climate of safety and acceptance in which people will trust one another and therefore engage in productive interchanges, (3) providing encouragement and support as members explore highly personal material or as they try new behavior, (4) involving as many members as possible in the group interaction by inviting and sometimes even challenging members to participate, (5) working toward lessening the dependency on the leader, (6) encouraging open expression of conflict and controversy, and (7) helping members overcome barriers to direct communication. The aim of most facilitation skills is to help the group members reach their own goals. Essentially, these skills involve opening up clear communication among the members and helping them increase their responsibility for the direction of their group.

Empathizing. An empathic group leader can sense the subjective world of the client. This skill requires the leader to have the characteristics of caring and openness already mentioned. The leader must also have a wide range of experiences to serve as a basis for identifying with others. Finally, the leader must be able to discern subtle nonverbal messages as well as messages transmitted more directly. It is impossible really to know what another person is experiencing, but a sensitive group leader can make a good guess. It is also important, however, for the group leader to avoid blurring his or her identity by overidentifying with the group members. The core of the skill of empathy lies in being able to openly grasp another's experiencing and at the same time maintain one's separateness.

Interpreting. Group leaders who are highly directive are likely to make use of interpretation, which entails offering possible explanations for certain behaviors or symptoms. If interpretations are accurate and well-timed, they may result in a member's moving beyond an impasse. It is not necessary that the leader always make the interpretation for the client; in Gestalt therapy clients are encouraged to make their own interpretations of their behavior. A group leader can also present an interpretation in the form of a hunch, the truth of which the client can then assess. For instance, an interpretation might be stated as follows: "Harry, I've noticed that, when a person in the group talks about something painful, you usually intervene and become reassuring and in some way try to take that person's pain away. What might that say about you?" It is important that the interpretation be presented as a hypothesis rather than as a fact. Also important is that the person have a chance to consider the validity of this hunch in the group.

Questioning. Questioning is really not much of a skill, and it is overused by many group leaders. Interrogation seldom leads to productive outcomes, and more often than not it distracts the person working. If a member happens to be experiencing intense feelings, questioning is one way of reducing the intensity. Asking "Why do you feel that way?" is rarely helpful. However, appropriately timed "what" and "how" questions do serve to intensify experiencing. Examples are questions such as "What is happening with your body now, as you speak about your isolation?" "In what ways do you experience the fear of rejection in this group?" "What are some of the things you imagine happening to you if you reveal your problems to this group?" "How are you coping with your fear that you can't trust some of the members here?" These questions direct the person to heighten awareness of the moment. Leaders should develop the skill of asking questions like these and avoiding questions that remove people from themselves. Questions that are not helpful include those that search for causes of behavior, probe for information, and the like: "How long have you been seeking your father's approval?" "Why do you feel depressed?" "Why don't you leave home?"

Linking. A group leader who has an interactional bias—that is, who stresses member-to-member rather than leader-to-member communication—makes frequent use of linking. This skill calls on the insightfulness of the leader in finding ways of relating what one person is doing or saying to the concerns of another person. For example, Katherine might be describing her feeling that she won't be loved unless she's perfect. If Pamela has been heard to express a similar feeling, the leader could ask Pamela and Katherine to talk with each other in the group about their fears. By being alert for cues that members have some common concern, the leader can promote member interaction and raise the level of group cohesion.

Confronting. Beginning group leaders are often afraid to confront group members for fear of hurting them, of being wrong, or of inviting retaliation. It doesn't take much skill to attack another or to be merely critical. It does take both caring and skill, however, to confront group members when their behavior is disruptive of the group functioning or when there are discrepancies between their verbal messages and their nonverbal messages. In confronting a member, a leader should (1) challenge specifically the behavior to be examined, avoiding labeling the person, and (2) share how he or she feels about the person's behavior. For example, Danny has been interrupting the group, pelting people with "why" questions and offering interpretations. The leader might intervene: "Danny, I find it difficult to listen to all your questioning and telling people how they are. Most of the time when you enter the group interaction, you interpret others' behavior for them, and I still don't know much about you. I would be interested in getting to know you better."

Supporting. The skill in supportive behavior is knowing when it will be therapeutic and when it will be counterproductive. A common mistake is offering support before a participant has had an opportunity to fully experience a conflict or some painful feelings. Although the intervention may be done with good intentions, it may abort certain feelings that a given member needs to experience. Another mistake is supporting game-playing behavior. For instance, if a woman is playing helpless and trying to convince everyone of how fragile she is, a leader who offers support will, in effect, foster her dependency. What the leader might do instead is confront the member with the fact that she can do for herself what she's pleading for others to do for her. Support is appropriate when people are facing a crisis, when they're venturing into frightening territory, when they attempt constructive changes and yet feel uncertain about these changes, and when they're struggling to rid themselves of old patterns that are limiting. Leaders should remember that too much support can send the message that people are unable to support themselves.

Blocking. Group leaders have the responsibility to block certain activities of group members, such as questioning, probing, gossiping, invading another's privacy, breaking confidences, and so forth. The skill is to learn to block counterproductive behaviors without attacking the personhood of the perpetrator. This requires both sensitivity and directness. Some examples of behavior that need to be blocked are:

- **Bombarding others with questions.** Offenders can be asked to make direct statements out of their questions.
- **Gossiping.** If a member talks *about* another member in the room, the leader can direct the person to speak directly *to* the person being spoken about.
- **Storytelling.** If lengthy storytelling occurs, a leader can intervene and ask the person to say how all this relates to present feelings and events.
- **Breaking confidences.** A member may inadvertently talk about a situation that occurred in another group or mention what so-and-so did in a prior group. This talk should be stopped by the leader in a firm but gentle manner.
- **Invasion of privacy.** If a person pushes another, probing for personal information, this behavior must be blocked by the group leader.

Diagnosing. Diagnostic skills involve more than labeling behavior, identifying symptoms, and figuring out what category a person falls into. They include the ability to appraise certain behavior problems and choose the appropriate intervention. For example, a leader who diagnoses a client as deeply angry must consider the safety and appropriateness of encouraging the client to "let out your pent-up rage." Leaders also need to develop the skill of determining whether a particular group is indicated or contraindicated for a member, and they need to acquire the expertise necessary to make appropriate referrals.

Evaluating. A crucial leadership skill is evaluating the ongoing process and dynamics of a group. After each group session it is valuable for the leader to evaluate what happened, both within individual members and among the members, and to think about what interventions might be used next time with the group. Leaders need to get in the habit of asking themselves questions such as: What changes are resulting from the group? What are the therapeutic and antitherapeutic forces in the group?

The leader must also teach participants how to evaluate, so that they can appraise the movement and direction of their own group. Once the group has evaluated a session or series of sessions, its members can decide what, if any, changes need to be made. For example, during an evaluation at the close of a session the leader and the members are in agreement that the group as a whole has been passive. The leader might say: "I feel the burden of initiating and sense that you're waiting for me to do something to energize you. I'm challenging each of you to examine your behavior and to evaluate to what degree you're personally responsible. Then please think about what, specifically, you're willing to do to change this group."

Terminating. Group leaders must learn when and how to terminate their work with both individuals and groups. They need to develop the ability to tell when a group session should end, when an individual is ready to leave a group, and when a group has completed its work, and they need to learn how to handle each of these types of termination. The skill of terminating a single session or a whole group involves (1) providing the members with suggestions for transferring what they've learned in the group to the environment they must return to, (2) creating a climate that will encourage members to make contracts to do work between sessions or after the group, (3) preparing people for the psychological problems they may face on leaving a group, (4) arranging for a follow-up group, (5) telling members where they can get additional therapy, and (6) being available for individual consultation at the termination of a group. Follow-up and evaluation activities are particularly important if the leader is to learn the impact of the group as a therapeutic agent.

An Integrated View of Leadership Skills

Some counselor-education programs focus mainly on developing counseling skills and assessing competencies, whereas other programs stress the personal qualities, described earlier, that underlie these skills. Ideally, training programs for group leaders give due weight to both of these aspects. In the next chapter, when professional standards for training group counselors are described, we will go into more detail about the specific areas of knowledge and the skills that group workers need.

In concluding this section, we want to acknowledge that you are likely to feel somewhat overwhelmed when you consider all the skills that are necessary for effective group leadership. It may help to remember that, as in other areas of life, you will become frustrated if you attempt to focus on all aspects of this field at once. You can expect to gradually refine your leadership style and gain confidence in using these skills effectively.

Several points about the skills we have discussed need to be emphasized. First, these skills can best be thought of as existing at varying levels, rather than on an all-or-nothing basis. They can be fully mastered and used in a sensitive and appropriate manner, or they can be only minimally developed. Second, these skills can be learned and constantly improved through training and supervised experience. Participating in a group as a member is one good way to determine what a group is about. Leading or co-leading a group under supervision is another excellent way to acquire and refine leadership skills. Third, these skills are not discrete entities; they overlap a great deal. Active listening, reflection, and clarification are interdependent, as are interpreting and diagnosing. Hence, by developing certain skills, a leader automatically improves others. Finally, these skills cannot be divorced from who the counselor is as a person, for the choice of which skills to develop and use is an expression of the leader's personality.

The Co-Leadership Model

The Basis of Co-Leadership

Many who educate and train group leaders have come to favor the co-leadership model of group practice. This model has a number of advantages for all concerned: the group members can gain from the perspectives of two leaders; the co-leaders can confer before and after a group and learn from each other; and supervisors can work closely with the co-leaders during their training and can provide them with feedback. We prefer co-leadership both for facilitating groups and for the training and supervising of group leaders, and we usually work as a team. Although each of us has independent professional involvements (including leading groups alone at times), we very much enjoy co-leading and continue to learn from each other as well as from other colleagues we work with. Nevertheless, we do not want to give the impression that co-leadership is the only acceptable model, because many people facilitate a group alone quite effectively.

In conducting training workshops with university students, we continually hear how they value working with a partner, especially if they are leading a group for the first time. As we discussed earlier, group leaders preparing to meet their first group tend to experience self-doubt, anxiety, and downright trepidation! The task seems far less monumental if they meet their new group with a co-leader whom they trust and respect. In our in-service workshops for group workers we find it useful to observe the trainees as they co-lead so that we can discuss what they are actually doing as they facilitate a group. Then, as we offer feedback to them, we frequently ask them to talk with each other about how they felt as they were co-leading and what they think about the session they have just led. The feedback between these co-leaders can be both supportive and challenging. They can make constructive suggestions about each other's style, and the process of exchanging perceptions can enhance their ability to function effectively as co-leaders.

The choice of a co-leader is important. If the two leaders are incompatible, their group is bound to be negatively affected. For example, power struggles between co-leaders will have the effect of dividing the group. If co-leaders are in continual conflict with each other, they are providing a poor model of interpersonal relating. Such conflict typically leads to unexpressed hostility within the group, which gets in the way of effective work. We are not suggesting that co-leaders will never have conflicts. What is important is that they work out any disputes in a decent and direct manner, for doing so can model ways of coping with interpersonal conflict.

A major factor in selecting a co-leader should be mutual respect. Two or more leaders working together will surely have their differences in leadership style, and they will not always agree or share the same perceptions or interpretations. If there is mutual respect and trust between them, however, they will be able to work cooperatively instead of competitively, and they will be secure enough to be free of the constant need to prove themselves.

It is not coincidence that those with whom we lead are also our closest friends. When several of us work together as a team in leading a workshop or presenting as a panel at a convention, we often receive comments about our style of interacting with one another. For example, people at times remark that our differences in personality and style complement one another. They observe enthusiasm, playfulness, a willingness to openly disagree, an absence of competition, and a liking and respect among us. The point we want to make is that the way we work as a team has a definite impact on the people we work with.

It is not essential that you be best friends with your co-leader. What you need is a good working relationship, which you can achieve by taking time to talk with each other. Although we take delight in our personal and professional relationship, we are also willing to engage in the hard work necessary to be a successful team. This relationship reflects our belief that it is essential that co-leaders get together regularly to discuss any matters that may affect their working as a team. We emphasize discussing how we are feeling in regard to our personal life as well as talking about specific group purposes and making plans for an upcoming group. Further, we tell co-leaders in training to arrange to spend time together both before and after each group session in order to evaluate their leadership and the group's progress, as well as to make plans for future sessions.

Advantages of the Co-Leadership Model

Having acknowledged our clear preference for co-leading groups, we will now present a summary of what seem to us the major advantages of using the co-leadership method:

1. The chance of burnout can be reduced by working with a co-leader. This is especially true if you are working with a draining population, such as severely disturbed individuals who often simply get up and leave, who hallucinate during sessions, and who may be withdrawn or be acting out. In such groups one leader can attend to certain problem members while the other attempts to maintain the work going on in the group.

2. If intense emotions are being expressed by one or more members, one leader can pay attention to those members while the other leader scans the room to note the reactions of other members, who can later be invited to share their feelings. Or, if appropriate, the co-leader can find a way to involve members in the work of someone else. Many possibilities exist for linking members, for facilitating interaction between members, and for orchestrating the flow of a group when co-leaders are sensitively and harmoniously working as a team.

3. If one leader must be absent because of illness or professional reasons, the group can proceed with the other leader. If one of the co-leaders is especially drained on a given day or is temporarily experiencing some emotional pain, the co-leader can assume primary leadership, and the leader having problems can feel less burdened with the responsibility to "be there" for the group members. In such a case it may be appropriate for the co-leader to say to the group that he or she is going through some difficulties personally, without going into great detail. By simply having said this, the leader is likely to feel freer and may be much more present. This admission provides sound modeling for the members, for they can see that group leaders are not beyond dealing with personal problems.

4. If one of the leaders has been strongly affected by a session, he or she can later explore feelings of anger, depression, or the like in some detail with the co-leader. The co-leader can be used as a sounding board, can check for objectivity, and can offer useful feedback. There is no problem of breaking confidentiality in such instances, for the co-leader was also present at the session. However, we do want to emphasize that it is often necessary for leaders to express and deal with such feelings in the session itself, especially if they were aroused in the group setting. For example, if you are aware that you are perpetually annoyed by a given member, you might need to deal with your annoyance as a group matter. In certain cases a group member's concerns might touch your own

"unfinished business," and you might explore your personal issues in the session. This is a time when a competent and trusted co-leader is especially important.

5. An important advantage of co-leading emerges when one of the leaders is affected by another member to the degree that countertransference is present. Countertransference can distort one's objectivity so that it interferes with leading effectively. For example, your co-leader may typically react with hostility or some other intense feeling to one member who is seen as a problem. Perhaps you are better able to make contact with this member, and so you may be the person who primarily works with him or her. You can be of valuable assistance by helping your co-leader talk about, and perhaps even resolve, irrational reactions and attachments toward such a client.

Disadvantages of the Co-Leadership Model

Even with a co-leader you choose, one whom you respect and like, there are likely to be occasional disagreements. This difference of perspective and opinion need not be a disadvantage or a problem. Instead, it can be healthy for both of you, because you can keep yourself professionally alert through constructive challenges and differences. Moreover, if you deal with your differences or conflicts during the session (rather than pretending that they do not exist), you are providing excellent modeling on how to work with conflicts. Most of the disadvantages in co-leading groups have to do with poor selection of a co-leader, random assignment to another leader, or failure of the two leaders to meet regularly:

1. Problems can occur if co-leaders rarely meet with each other. The results are likely to be a lack of synchronization or even a tendency to work at cross-purposes instead of toward a common goal. For example, we've observed difficulties when one group leader thought that all intervention should be positive, supportive, and invitational, whereas the other leader functioned on the assumption that members need to be pushed and directly confronted and that difficult issues should be brought up. The group became fragmented and polarized as a result of the incompatible leadership styles. The main problem was that the leaders did not take the time to discuss their differences.

2. A related issue is competition and rivalry. For example, one leader may have an exaggerated need to have center stage, to be dominant at all times, and to be perceived as the one in control; such a leader might even actively put down the co-leader. Obviously, such a relationship between co-leaders is bound to have a negative effect on the group. In some cases members may develop negative reactions toward groups in general, concluding that all that ever goes on in them is conflict and the struggle for power.

3. If co-leaders do not have a relationship built on trust and respect or if they do not value each other's competence, they may not trust each

other's interventions. Each leader may insist on following his or her own hunches, convinced that the other's are not of value.

4. One leader may side with members against the other leader. For example, assume that Sue confronts a male leader with strong negative reactions and that his co-leader (a woman) joins Sue in expressing her reactions and even invites the members to give feedback to the co-leader. This practice can divide the group, with members taking sides about who is "right." It is especially a problem if one leader has not previously given negative reactions to the other and uses the situation as a chance to "unload" feelings.

5. Co-leaders who are involved in an intimate relationship with each other can get into some problematic situations if they attempt to use time in the session to deal with their own relationship struggles. Although some members may support the co-leaders' "working on their issues" in the group, most clients are likely to resent these co-leaders for abdicating their leadership functions.

We think that it is important that the two leaders have some say in deciding to work as a team. Otherwise, there is a potential for harm for both the group members and the co-leaders. Careful selection of a co-leader and time devoted to meeting together are essential. We encourage those who co-lead groups to spend some time both before *and* after each session discussing their reactions to what is going on in the group as well as their working relationship as co-leaders.

Exercises

There are exercises at the end of each of the chapters in Parts One and Two. These exercises can be done on your own or in class in small groups. The goal is to provide you with an opportunity to experience some of the techniques, issues, group processes, and potential problems that can occur at the various stages of a group's development.

We suggest that you read over all the suggested exercises at the end of each chapter and then focus on those that appeal to you the most or those that seem to have the most potential for clarifying issues for you.

For those of you who are leading a group for the first time, we encourage you to complete these exercises both before you begin leading and then again toward the end of the semester. The comparison will give you a basis for seeing how your attitudes and ideas may evolve with experience.

Attitude Questionnaire on Group Leadership

Following are some statements concerning the role and functions of a group leader. Indicate your position on each statement, using the scale preceding the statements.

1 = strongly agree
2 = slightly agree
3 = slightly disagree
4 = strongly disagree

_____ 1. It is the leader's job to actively work at shaping group norms.
_____ 2. Leaders should teach group members how to observe their own group as it unfolds.
_____ 3. The best way for a leader to function is by becoming a participating member of the group.
_____ 4. It is generally wise for leaders to reveal their private life and personal problems in groups they are leading.
_____ 5. A group leader's primary task is to function as a technical expert.
_____ 6. It is extremely important for good leaders to have a definite theoretical framework that determines how they function in a group.
_____ 7. A group leader's function is to draw people out and make sure that silent members participate.
_____ 8. Group leaders influence group members more through modeling than through the techniques they employ.
_____ 9. It is generally best for the leader to give some responsibility to the members but also to retain some.
_____ 10. A major task of a leader is to keep the group focused on the here and now.
_____ 11. It is unwise to allow members to discuss the past or to discuss events that occurred outside of the group.
_____ 12. It is best to give most of the responsibility for determining the direction of the group to the members.
_____ 13. Leaders should limit their self-disclosures to matters that have to do with what is going on in the group.
_____ 14. If group leaders are basically open and disclose themselves, transference by members will not occur.
_____ 15. A leader who experiences countertransference is not competent to lead groups.
_____ 16. Group leaders should develop a personalized theory of leadership based on ideas drawn from many sources.
_____ 17. To be effective, group leaders must recognize their reasons for wanting to be leaders.
_____ 18. Part of the task of group leaders is to determine specific behavioral goals for the participants.
_____ 19. A leader's theoretical model has little impact on the way people actually interact in a group.
_____ 20. If group leaders have mastered certain skills and techniques, it is not essential for them to operate from a theoretical framework.

_____ 21. Leaders who possess personal power generally dominate the group and intimidate the members through this power.

_____ 22. There is not much place for a sense of humor in conducting groups, because group work is serious business.

_____ 23. Group leaders should not expect the participants to do anything that they, as leaders, are not willing to do.

_____ 24. In groups with co-leaders there is the potential that the members will play one leader against the other like children playing one parent against the other.

_____ 25. For co-leaders to work effectively with each other, it is essential that they share the same style of leadership.

_____ 26. In selecting a co-leader, it is a good idea to consider similarity of values, philosophy of life, and life experiences.

_____ 27. If co-leaders do not respect and trust each other, there is the potential for negative outcomes in the group.

_____ 28. Those who co-lead a group should be roughly equal in skills, experiences, and status.

_____ 29. Co-leaders should never openly disagree with each other during a session, for this may lead to a division within the group.

_____ 30. The group is bound to be affected by the type of modeling that the co-leaders provide.

We suggest that after you have completed this self-inventory, your class break into small groups to discuss the items.

Self-Assessment of Group-Leadership Skills

Review the section on group-leadership skills, and ask yourself to what degree you have mastered the skills described. Rate yourself on the following self-assessment scale for group leaders, and then discuss with a small group of class members why you rated yourself as you did. With your group explore specific things you might do to develop these skills. Rate yourself from 1 to 5 on the following items, using a scale with these extremes:

1 = I am very poor at this.
5 = I am very good at this.

_____ 1. **Active listening.** I am able to hear and understand both direct and subtle messages.

_____ 2. **Reflecting.** I can mirror what another says without being mechanical.

_____ 3. **Clarifying.** I can focus on underlying issues and assist others to get a clearer picture of some of their conflicting feelings.

_____ 4. **Summarizing.** When I function as a group leader, I'm able to identify key elements of a session and to present them as a summary of the proceedings.

_____ 5. **Interpreting.** I can present a hunch to someone concerning the reason for his or her behavior without dogmatically telling what the behavior means.

_____ 6. **Questioning.** I avoid bombarding people with questions about their behavior.

_____ 7. **Linking.** I find ways of relating what one person is doing or saying to the concerns of other members.

_____ 8. **Confronting.** When I confront another, the confrontation usually has the effect of getting that person to look at his or her behavior in a nondefensive manner.

_____ 9. **Supporting.** I'm usually able to tell when supporting another will be productive and when it will be counterproductive.

_____ 10. **Blocking.** I'm able to intervene successfully, without seeming to be attacking, to stop counterproductive behaviors in the group such as gossiping, storytelling, and intellectualizing.

_____ 11. **Diagnosing.** I can generally get a sense of what specific problems members have without feeling the need to label people.

_____ 12. **Evaluating.** I appraise outcomes when I'm leading a group, and I make comments concerning the group's progress.

_____ 13. **Facilitating.** I'm able to help others openly express themselves and work through barriers to communication.

_____ 14. **Empathizing.** I can intuitively sense the subjective world of others in a group, and I have the capacity to understand much of what they are experiencing.

_____ 15. **Terminating.** At the end of group sessions I'm able to create a climate that will foster a willingness in others to continue working after the session.

Evaluation of Group Leaders

The following evaluation form can be used in several ways. Group leaders can use it as a self-evaluation device, supervisors can use it to evaluate group leaders in training, group leaders can evaluate their co-leader with it, and group members can use it to evaluate their leader. These rating scales can be used by leader trainees at several points during a course. The self-evaluation forms can pinpoint progress made and areas needing further work. Rate the leader from 1 to 5 on the following items, using a scale with these extremes:

1 = to an extremely low degree
5 = to an extremely high degree

_____ 1. **Support.** To what degree does the group leader allow members to express their feelings?

_____ 2. **Interpretation.** To what degree is the group leader able to explain the meaning of behavior patterns within the framework of a theoretical system?

_____ 3. **Confrontation.** To what degree is the group leader able to actively and directly confront members when they are engaging in behavior that is inconsistent with what they are saying?

_____ 4. **Modeling.** To what degree is the group leader able to demonstrate behaviors that he or she wishes members to emulate and practice both during and after the session?

_____ 5. **Assignment.** To what degree is the group leader able to direct the members to improve on existing behavior patterns or to develop new behaviors before the next session?

_____ 6. **Referral.** To what degree is the group leader able to make available to members someone who is capable of further assisting them with personal concerns?

_____ 7. **Role direction.** To what degree is the group leader able to direct members to enact specific roles in role-playing situations?

_____ 8. **Empathy.** To what degree does the group leader demonstrate the ability to adopt the internal frame of reference of a member and communicate to the member that he or she is being understood?

_____ 9. **Self-disclosure.** To what degree does the leader demonstrate a willingness and ability to reveal his or her own present feelings and thoughts as it is appropriate to the group-counseling situation?

_____ 10. **Initiation.** To what degree is the group leader able to get interaction going among members or between leader and member?

_____ 11. **Facilitation.** To what degree is the group leader able to help members clarify their own goals and take steps to reach these goals?

_____ 12. **Diagnosis.** To what degree is the group leader able to identify specific areas of struggle and conflict within each member?

_____ 13. **Following through.** To what degree is the group leader able to follow through to reasonable completion work with a member in an area the member has expressed a desire to explore?

_____ 14. **Active listening.** To what degree does the leader actively and fully listen to and hear the subtle messages communicated by group members?

_____ 15. **Knowledge of theory.** To what degree does the leader demonstrate a theoretical understanding of group dynamics, interpersonal dynamics, and behavior in general?

_____ 16. **Application of theory to practice.** To what degree is the leader able to appropriately apply a given theory to an actual group situation?

_____ 17. **Perceptivity and insight.** To what degree is the group leader able to sensitively and accurately extract the core meanings from verbal and nonverbal communications?

_____ 18. **Risk taking.** To what degree is the group leader able to risk making mistakes and to profit from mistakes?

_____ 19. **Expression.** To what degree is the group leader able to express thoughts and feelings directly and clearly to members?

_____ 20. **Originality.** To what degree does the group leader seem to have synthesized a personal approach from a variety of approaches to leadership?

_____ 21. **Group dynamics.** To what degree is the leader able to help a group of people work together effectively?

_____ 22. **Cooperation as a co-leader.** To what degree is the group leader able to work cooperatively with a co-leader?

_____ 23. **Content orientation.** To what degree is the leader able to help members focus on specific themes in a structured group experience?

_____ 24. **Awareness of values.** To what degree is the group leader aware of his or her own value system, aware of the members' value systems, and able to avoid imposing his or her values on the members?

_____ 25. **Flexibility.** To what degree is the group leader able to change approaches—to modify style and technique—to adapt to each unique working situation?

_____ 26. **Awareness of self.** To what degree is the group leader aware of his or her own needs, motivations, and problems, and to what degree does the leader avoid exploiting or manipulating members to satisfy these needs?

_____ 27. **Respect.** To what degree does the group leader communicate an attitude of respect for the dignity and autonomy of members?

_____ 28. **Caring.** To what degree does the group leader communicate an attitude of genuine caring and concern for members?

_____ 29. **Techniques.** To what degree is the leader knowledgeable about techniques and able to use them well and appropriately to help members work through conflicts and concerns?

_____ 30. **Ethical awareness.** To what degree does the group leader demonstrate awareness of and sensitivity to the demands of professional responsibility?

CHAPTER 2

Ethical and Professional Guidelines for Group Leaders

FOCUS QUESTIONS

1. What are some of the things an ethical group leader will be sure to tell prospective members about a group?
2. What is your position on the issue of group leaders' providing individual therapy for members? What are some advantages and disadvantages of this practice?
3. What measures might you take as a leader to ensure confidentiality in your group?
4. What psychological risks do you think are associated with group membership? How can these risks be minimized?
5. What legal issues might you consider in setting up a group? Can you think of some legal safeguards to help you avoid a malpractice suit?
6. What education and training do you think a person needs in order to be a competent leader?
7. What experience and supervision would you like to receive as part of your program in group leadership?
8. What is your position on the issue of private psychotherapy for group leaders? Should group membership be part of a leader's background?
9. What are your thoughts about requiring students to participate in an experiential group-counseling class oriented toward personal growth? What are some of the ethical and practical aspects involved when instructors of group-counseling courses also function in therapeutic ways as a part of teaching the course?
10. Review the ASGW's (1989) *Ethical Guidelines for Group Counselors*, which are reproduced at the end of Chapter 8. What are your thoughts about the value of these guidelines for a group practitioner? Which of the guidelines do you most agree with? Are there any guidelines that you disagree with?

Introduction

For those who are preparing to become group leaders, a thorough grounding in ethical issues is as essential as a solid base of psychological knowledge and skills. Our aim in this chapter is to highlight the ethical issues of central significance to group workers. Both professionals and paraprofessionals must be thoroughly familiar with the ethical standards of their professional specialization. They must also learn to make ethical decisions, a process that can be taught both in group courses and in supervised practicum experiences.

It is our position that students must eventually learn how to apply established ethical codes to a range of dilemmas that they will certainly face as group practitioners. Thus, absolute freedom should certainly not be the rule, nor is "going on intuition" an appropriate path to follow.

One's practice should be guided by established principles that have clear implications for group work. In this chapter we have drawn heavily on the *Ethical Guidelines for Group Counselors* (Association for Specialists in Group Work [ASGW], 1989), as a general framework for exploring a host of ethical issues. The guidelines are reproduced at the end of Chapter 8. In addition to these principles specifically for group work, it is essential that practitioners know and abide by the ethical codes of their respective professions. Professional guidelines that have relevance for group leadership include *Ethical Standards* (American Association for Counseling and Development [AACD], 1988); *Ethical Principles of Psychologists* (American Psychological Association [APA], 1989); *Code of Ethics* (National Association of Social Workers [NASW], 1979); *Standards for the Private Practice of Clinical Social Work* (NASW, 1981); *Code of Ethics for Certified Clinical Mental Health Counselors* (American Mental Health Counselors Association [AMHCA], 1980); *Code of Ethics* (National Board for Certified Counselors [NBCC], 1987); and *AAMFT Code of Ethical Principles for Marriage and Family Therapists* (American Association for Marriage and Family Therapy [AAMFT], 1988).

Although professionals should know the ethical code of their specialization and be aware of the consequences of practicing in ways that are not sanctioned by the appropriate professional organization, such codes alone are not adequate for professional leadership of groups. There will be times when you need to make wise decisions about issues that are not simple and clear. Functioning within the broad guidelines of established ethical codes will be a beginning, but you will have to base your practice on sound, informed, and responsible judgment. To develop such judgment, experience in leading groups is essential, yet it alone is also not enough. You will learn much by consulting with colleagues, by getting continued supervision and training during the early stages of your development as a leader, by doing what is necessary to keep up with recent trends, and by attending relevant conventions and workshops.

Some beginning group leaders burden themselves with the expectation that they should always know the "right" thing to do in every possible situation. In contrast, we expect that you will gradually refine your positions on the issues we raise in this chapter, a process that demands a willingness to remain open and to adopt a self-critical attitude. We do not think that these issues are ever resolved once and for all. They are often complex, and they take on new dimensions as you gain experience as a group leader.

We decided to place this chapter early in the book because the guidelines that we discuss here pertain to all phases of a group's development as well as to each special group population. In the chapters that follow we will return to some of these guidelines, and we will explore ethical and professional issues that especially pertain to a particular period in the group's history or to conducting various types of groups.

Professional Competence and Training

As a group leader you must provide only those services and use only those techniques for which you are qualified by training and experience. It is your responsibility as you market your professional services to accurately represent your competence. Although we encourage you to think of creative ways of reaching diverse populations, we also emphasize the need for adequate training and supervision in leading groups with such members. If you lead groups that are clearly beyond the scope of your preparation, you are not only practicing unethically but are also wide open to a malpractice suit.

Because various professions have differing training and educational standards for group work and because specializations call for various skills, we will not try to specify an "ideal program" that would produce competent group leaders. Rather, we will outline several general areas of professional experience that we consider basic in the development of a capable leader.

The Issue of Leader Competence

Who is qualified to lead groups? What are some criteria by which to determine the level of competence of group leaders? How can leaders recognize their limits?

Concerning the issue of qualification, several factors must be considered. One is the type of group. Different groups require different leader qualifications. Some professionals who are highly qualified to work with college students are not competent to lead children's groups. Professionals who are trained to lead personal-growth groups may lack either the training or the experience necessary to administer group therapy to an outpatient population. Some may be very successful with groups for alcoholics or drug addicts yet be unequipped to lead couples' groups or to work with families. So we can restate the basic question as: Who is qualified to lead *this type* of group with *this type* of population?

There are many ways of becoming a professional group leader. Some of the fields of study that prepare people to lead therapeutic groups are:

- counseling psychology
- clinical psychology
- psychiatry
- educational psychology
- school counseling
- marriage and family counseling
- clinical social work
- pastoral psychology or pastoral counseling
- child and adolescent psychology

- rehabilitation counseling
- community mental-health counseling
- human services

Other disciplines that can help prepare professionals for group work are sociology and philosophy. Course work in personality theory, human growth and development, abnormal psychology, clinical techniques, theories of counseling, and vocational and career development can also be helpful. The main point is that no one discipline has a monopoly when it comes to offering valuable information and training to potential group leaders. Each type of therapeutic group calls for a different type of training and experience.

During the professional education of counselors who hope to work as group leaders, at least one course in the theory and practice of group counseling is essential. Unfortunately, it is not uncommon to find only one such survey course available to students in a master's degree program in psychology or counseling.

Another issue related to competence is that of licenses, degrees, and credentials. In our judgment the training that leads to the attainment of such certification is usually valuable, but degrees alone do not indicate that a person is a qualified leader. A person may hold a Ph.D. in counseling psychology and be licensed to practice psychotherapy yet not be equipped, either by training or by personality, to practice *group* work. At the same time, we can conceive of a paraprofessional, without a degree or a license, who could competently lead or co-lead certain types of therapeutic groups.

Group leaders need to recognize their limitations. Toward this end, they might well ask themselves:

- What kinds of clients am I capable of dealing with?
- What are my areas of expertise?
- What techniques do I handle well?
- How far can I safely go with clients?
- When should I consult another professional about a client?
- When should I refer a client to someone else?

Professional group workers know their limitations and recognize that they can't lead all kinds of groups or work with all kinds of clients. They familiarize themselves with referral resources and don't attempt to work with clients who need special help beyond their level of competence. Furthermore, responsible group workers are keenly aware of the importance of continuing their education. Even licensed and experienced professionals will attend conventions and workshops, take courses, seek consultation and supervision, and get involved in special training programs from time to time.

Truly competent group workers also have reasons for most of the activities they suggest in a group. They are able to explain to their clients the theory behind their group work and how it influences their practice. They can tell the members in clear language the goals of a group, and they can state the relationship between the way they lead the group and these goals. Effective group leaders are able to conceptualize the group process and to relate what they do in a group to this model. They continually refine their techniques in light of their model. In short, they possess the knowledge and skills that are described next.

Professional Standards for Training Group Workers*

The revised and expanded version of the *Professional Standards for the Training of Group Workers* (ASGW, 1990) is awaiting action by the new association's Executive Board. (The former board has approved the document.) Because these standards have not been officially approved at the time of this writing, we will refer to the material as a "working document." One of the provisions of this draft is that all professional counselors should possess basic *knowledge* and *skills* in group work. This set of core competencies provides the foundation on which specialized training in group work is built. The working document emphasizes that training in the core knowledge and skill competencies alone does not prepare counselors to independently conduct any of the specialty groups. To do so, leaders must receive advanced training.

Knowledge. In the area of knowledge competencies the ASGW takes the position that all group counselors should be able to:

- Define the distinguishing characteristics of the four major specializations in group work: task groups, guidance groups, counseling groups, and psychotherapy groups.
- Identify the basic principles of group dynamics.
- Discuss the basic therapeutic ingredients of groups.
- Identify one's own strengths and weaknesses, values, and other personal characteristics that have an impact on members.
- Describe the ethical issues special to group work.
- Discuss the research on group work and understand how it relates to one's academic preparation.
- Describe the characteristics associated with the typical stages in a group's development.
- Describe the facilitative and debilitative roles and behaviors that group members may assume.

*Adapted from a working document, *Professional Standards for the Training of Group Workers,* by permission of the Association for Specialists in Group Work, a division of the American Association for Counseling and Development, 5999 Stevenson Avenue, Alexandria, VA 22304.

- State the advantages and disadvantages of group work and the situations in which it is appropriate or inappropriate as a form of therapeutic intervention.
- Describe the therapeutic factors of group work.
- Identify strategies for recruiting and screening prospective group members.
- Understand the importance of group and member evaluation.

Skills. In the area of skill competencies the ASGW contends that qualified group workers should be able to effectively:

- Encourage participation of the members of a group.
- Observe and identify group-process events.
- Attend to group members' behavior.
- Clarify and summarize members' statements.
- Open and close group sessions.
- Impart information in groups at appropriate times.
- Model appropriate behavior for group members.
- Engage in appropriate self-disclosure in the group.
- Give and receive feedback in the group.
- Ask open-ended questions in the group.
- Empathize with group members.
- Confront members' behavior when necessary.
- Help members attribute meaning to their experience in the group.
- Help members integrate and apply their learning.
- Demonstrate the ability to apply the ASGW ethical standards in group practice.
- Keep the group on track in accomplishing its goals.

Training in Group Work. At a minimum, one group course should be included in a counselor-training program. This course should be structured to help students begin the process of acquiring the knowledge and skills described above. The ASGW standards state that skills in group work are best mastered through supervised practice. The practice component, which includes both observation and participation in a group experience, could occur in a classroom group. Although the minimum amount of supervised practice is 10 hours, the ASGW recommends 20 hours.

Advanced Competencies and Specializations. Once counselor trainees have mastered the core knowledge and skills outlined above, they can acquire advanced competencies in one or more of these four group specialties: (1) task/work groups, (2) guidance/psychoeducational groups, (3) counseling/interpersonal-problem-solving groups, and (4) psychotherapy/personality-reconstruction groups. The standards detail specific requirements of knowledge and skills for each of these four areas of specialization. Furthermore, they specify a minimum and a recommended number of hours of supervised training for each specialty.

The training for *task/work groups* involves courses in the broad area of organizational development and management and also in consultation. Furthermore, it includes a minimum of 30 hours of supervised experience beyond the 20 hours of training at the generalist level.

The training for *guidance/psychoeducational groups* involves courses in the broad area of community psychology, health promotion, marketing, consultation, and curriculum design. This specialty requires 30 hours of supervised experience beyond the 20 hours required for the generalist level.

The training for *counseling/interpersonal-problem-solving groups* should ideally include as much course work in group counseling as possible, but at least one course beyond the generalist level. In addition to the 20 hours of training at the generalist level, a minimum of 45 hours of supervised experience is required for this specialization.

The specialist training for *psychotherapy groups* consists of courses in abnormal psychology, psychopathology, and diagnostic assessment to ensure capabilities in working with more disturbed populations. In addition to the 20 hours of training at the generalist level, a minimum of 45 hours of supervised experience must be obtained in this specialty.

Training and Personal Experience

As is clear from our brief review of the ASGW's training standards, it is essential to prospective group leaders to undergo extensive training that is appropriate to the general type of group they intend to lead. We highly recommend three types of experience as adjuncts to a training program: personal (private) psychotherapy, group therapy, and participation in a supervised training group.

Personal Psychotherapy for Group Leaders. Should group leaders have individual therapy before or during their internship period? Should this experience be required or merely strongly recommended? What is the rationale for expecting leadership candidates to experience their own personal therapy? What are the possible values of such an experience?

We think that it is the ethical and professional responsibility of those who plan to become group therapists to seek private therapy before they attempt to become therapists for others. During the course of their sessions, we hope, they will come to a greater understanding of their motivation to become leaders of therapeutic groups. They can also explore the biases that might hamper their receptiveness to clients; any unfinished business that might lead to distortions in their perceptions of group members; their philosophy of life and view of human beings and the need they may have to impose this philosophy on clients; other needs that might either facilitate or inhibit the group process; current conflicts; and the impact that character traits such as courage, enthusiasm, integrity, honesty, and caring will have on others. In short, group therapists should demonstrate the courage to do for themselves what they expect members in their groups to do. Our rationale is that group counselors cannot effectively assist clients to explore conflicts that they have not recognized in themselves. We are not implying that therapists must have experienced every personal problem of the clients they work with, but they must have the courage to honestly search within themselves and face what they find.

Self-Exploration Groups for Group Leaders. We have discovered that participation in a self-exploration group (or some other type of therapeutic group) is an extremely valuable adjunct to a group leader's internship training experiences. Beginning group leaders typically experience some anxiety regarding their adequacy, and their interactions with group members frequently lead to a surfacing of unresolved past or current problems. It is generally inappropriate for group counselors to use the groups they lead to do their own extensive work. At times, there may be a fine line between being a leader and a member, but leaders who habitually "become members" of their groups should join a therapeutic group as a member and use that group for continuing their growth. Besides being of therapeutic value, such a group can be a powerful teaching tool for the intern. Leaders have said that exploring their own struggles in a group gives them the capacity to empathize with others. One of the best ways for leaders to learn how to assist members in their struggles is by working themselves as members of a group.

Training Groups for Group Leaders. In addition to participating in a therapeutic group as a member, the beginning group leader must, we believe, join a training group—that is, a group of leader trainees. The training group can lead to insights and awareness without becoming a therapy group. The interns can learn a great deal about their response to criticism, their competitiveness, their need for approval, their jealousies, their anxieties over being competent, their feelings about certain members of the group they lead, and their power struggles with co-leaders or members of their group. For example, leaders who have an exaggerated need for approval may avoid being confrontive in their groups, may asume a passive stance, or may become inappropriately supportive. Their need for approval thus hampers their potential effectiveness by preventing them from effectively encountering others. Another example is the person who is attracted to being a group leader primarily by the power inherent in this position. This person's exaggerated need to control and direct others may lead to mechanical use of techniques designed to impress the group participants with the therapist's prowess. Styles such as these can be detected and worked with in a training group.

Examples of questions that a supervisor might raise with the members of a training group are:

- How were you affected when your group sat silently for a few minutes? How did you deal with this silence? What do you suppose members were thinking but not saying?
- What were your reactions to Jim when he openly challenged you on your qualifications to lead his group of college students, some of whom are older than you are?
- Why did you keep pushing Sally to "work" after she had given several indications that she would rather be left alone?
- Do you think that there was adequate closure for your group today? Did you allow yourself enough time to summarize what had happened?
- Do you think you were confrontive enough with John when he continued with his storytelling? Why did you allow him to go on as long as you did?
- For several weeks you seem to have been quiet in your group, and your co-leader has been assuming most of the leadership responsibility. What thoughts run through your mind as you work with your co-leader? Are you satisfied with your participation level?
- How did you feel when you invited Sue to participate in an exercise and she flatly refused, saying "No, I won't role-play, because that seems phony to me"? Did you like your response to her?

Requiring Group Membership of Trainees in a Program

The issue of mandatory group participation, which will be taken up in the next section, becomes particularly thorny for students enrolled in programs designed to train counselors or paraprofessionals. Many universities that offer degrees in counseling and other human services are requiring participation in either individual or group therapy as an integral part of these programs. This practice raises a number of ethical issues. The rationale for requiring personal counseling, as we have said, is that the students need to be aware of their own motivations, needs, and problems before they attempt to counsel others. However, some faculty members and students oppose the requirement on the ground that any form of counseling should be initiated by the client. Some maintain that *mandatory counseling* is a contradiction in terms. In examining the ethics of requiring group participation for students in counseling programs, we think that another question should be asked: is it ethical for group leaders to consider themselves qualified to lead groups if they've never been group members themselves?

It appears that it is a common practice to include a group experience in counselor-education programs. Also, colleagues from graduate programs throughout the country report that they see a need for an experiential component to assist students in acquiring the skills necessary to function as effective group leaders. It is typical to combine the didactic and the experiential aspects of learning in many courses.

Faculty members who teach group courses often function in multiple roles as a facilitator of a group, a teacher, an evaluator, and a supervisor. There is the potential of dual-role conflicts when instructors who teach group courses also provide an experiential dimension that focuses on self-awareness and self-exploration. The *Ethical Standards* of the AACD (1988) caution against blending roles in training programs: "When the educational program offers a growth experience with an emphasis on self-disclosure or other relatively intimate or personal involvement, the member must have no administrative, supervisory, or evaluative authority regarding the participant." Some take exception to the restrictive nature of this guideline. Williams (1990) disagrees with the guideline's literal interpretation and maintains that counselor educators serve as role models to their students by participating in the various roles as teacher, supervisor, and group leader.

Lloyd (1990) has noted a conflict between the AACD guideline prohibiting dual relationships and a requirement of the Council for Accreditation of Counseling and Related Educational Programs (CACREP) that students be given the opportunity for small-group activity. He raises this question: if participating in group activities and supervision experiences, which may include elements of counseling, is the best method for training students, is it wise to deny them this opportunity because of the possibility of an ethical violation regarding dual relationships?

Pierce and Baldwin (1990) have also addressed the ethical issues involved in protecting student privacy and requiring personal-growth experiences. They contend that student participation in a growth experience is essential in the training of group counselors. At the same time, they address ways of coping with the ethical dilemma that group trainers and supervisors face as they evaluate their students' use of group-leadership skills. The key points of their position are:

- Students should be given information about what to expect before they enter a program. A written statement on the rationale for participation in personal-growth activities is likely to improve student participation.
- Students can be made aware that group participation is a basic part of the group course. It would help to provide guidelines to students regarding appropriate and useful self-disclosure.
- It is helpful to train students about the risks and benefits of self-disclosure. This process can best be done by a combination of didactic methods and modeling on the trainer's part.
- Trainers need to demonstrate sensitivity to the privacy needs of the students in their group courses. They might restrict certain

probing questions that are likely to open up highly personal material.

- Students can be involved in selecting topics or themes that they would be willing to explore in a group. In this way, they are enabled to protect their own privacy.

Forester-Miller and Duncan (1990) have identified guidelines that they contend will reduce the potential risks associated with combining a personal-growth experience with a group course:

- The personal-growth experience should not be related to the screening of students for entering or continuing in the program.
- No aspects of the student's personal life, value system, or group behavior may be considered in evaluating the student's academic performance in the group experience.
- Students should be evaluated only on their level of group skills.
- Students are not allowed to lead a personal-growth group of their peers without the presence of a professional staff member who supervises the group experience.

One way in which many educators attempt to minimize the conflict entailed in being both a professor and a counselor is to avoid grading students on their participation in the experiential activities that are part of the course (Forester-Miller & Duncan, 1990). This practice is consistent with an ASGW (1989) guideline: "Instructors of group counseling courses take steps to minimize the possible negative impact on students by separating course grades from participation in the group and by allowing students to decide what issues to explore and when to stop." In group courses that have an experiential component, we think that it does put students in a bind if their participation in the group is considered as a factor in determining their course grade. Doing this would seem to encourage "performances" by those striving to become "good group members."

There are several reasons for our stance of encouraging participation in a group as part of a leader's training. Struggling with trusting a group of strangers, risking vulnerability, receiving genuine support from others, feeling joy and closeness, and being confronted are all vital learning experiences for future group leaders. If for no reason other than because it provides an understanding of what clients face, we think that group experience for leaders is indispensable. However, students should be clearly informed before they enter a program of the specific nature of these requirements.

It is essential to keep in mind the primary purpose of a group-counseling course, which is teaching students the skills needed to effectively facilitate groups. Although the main aim of a group course is *not* to provide personal therapy for students, participating in such a group can and ought to be therapeutic. Students can make a decision about what personal concerns they are willing to share, and they can also determine the depth of their self-disclosures. A group course is not designed to be a substitute for an intensive self-exploration experience, but learning about how groups function can be enhanced through active and personal participation in the group process.

We have found that most serious students who are sincerely interested in becoming professionally qualified as group leaders are willing to invest themselves in membership in a therapeutic group. If a group is offered as a resource for the personal development of counselors and if students are given the freedom to determine their goals and the structure of the experience, most students will be eager for a group and will appreciate such a resource. Those who are highly defensive and antagonistic may need to reexamine their commitment to becoming counselors.

Ethical Issues in Group Membership

Involuntary Membership

Obviously, voluntary participation is an important beginning point for a successful group experience. Members will make significant changes only to the extent that they actively seek something for themselves. Unfortunately, all groups are not composed of clients who have chosen to be there. In some mental-health facilities the main therapeutic vehicle is group therapy. People from all wards may be required to attend these sessions, sometimes several times a week. This situation is somewhat akin to compulsory education: people can be forced to attend but not to learn.

For those leaders who work in institutions in which the policy is to require group treatment, the members should at least be given the opportunity to ventilate their feelings about this requirement. Perhaps many are reluctant to become involved because of misinformation or stereotyped views about the nature of therapy. They may not trust the group leaders or the process involved. They may think that group therapy is a form of indoctrination. Perhaps they view themselves as healthy and the other members of the group as ill. Most likely, many of them are frightened and have reservations about opening themselves up to others. They are likely to be very concerned about others' gossiping or maliciously using information against them. Perceptive leaders will deal with these issues openly, and although they may not be able to give the members the option of dropping out of the group, they can provide the support necessary to enable the members to fully come to grips with their fears and resistances. The members can also be given the freedom to decide how to use the session time. Group leaders can reassure members that the degree to which they participate is up to them—that they may remain silent if they wish and that it's up to them to decide what personal topics they will discuss and what areas they will keep private. In other words, they should be clearly informed that they have the same rights as the members of any other group, with the exception of the right not to attend.

Informed Consent

In general, participation in groups is voluntary in that people are not forced either to join a group or, once they are in the group, to participate in activities if they choose not to. As we have explained, however, this is not always the case. Providing adequate information to prospective group members so that they are able to make informed choices about their participation is essential for both voluntary and involuntary groups. Especially when group participation is mandatory, much effort needs to be directed toward clearly and fully informing members of the nature and goals of the group, procedures that will be used, the rights of members to decline certain activities, the limitations of confidentiality, and how active participation in the group may have an effect on them personally. For example, in a state mental hospital in which we served as consultants, groups were the basic form of treatment for "those incompetent to stand trial" and "mentally disordered sex offenders." Further, patients' release from the institution depended in part on their cooperation in treatment and rehabilitation, which included participation in regular group-therapy sessions. In cases such as these, getting the *informed consent* of members implies that leaders explore with the members during a screening or orientation session what the group process consists of and that they are careful to ascertain whether the members understand what may be involved. It would also be essential to inform sex offenders who were required to have group treatment about the consequences of noncompliance. For example, reporting a client's unwillingness to participate in a group program could result in revocation proceedings and eventual imprisonment. It is the therapist's responsibility to report noncompliance, because failure to do so misleads the courts and corrections authorities and may constitute a danger to the public (Aubrey & Dougher, 1990).

Informed consent involves leaders' making members aware of their rights (as well as their responsibilities) as group participants. Thus, in mandatory groups or in required groups that emphasize self-disclosure and personal involvement, leaders are advised to take special care in discussing what the members have a right to expect. The guidelines that follow, of course, apply equally to groups composed of voluntary participants. Those who join a group have a right to expect:

- a clear statement regarding the purpose of the group, the procedures to be used, and the leader's policies and ground rules
- a summary of the education and training of the leader

- clarification of what services can and cannot be provided within the group
- information about the leader's willingness to consult with them between group sessions
- entrance procedures and time limits for the group experience
- a clear statement about the leader's policies on fees and methods of payment (when appropriate)
- a discussion of the roles, rights, and responsibilities involved in being a group member
- reasonable safeguards to minimize the potential risks and hazards of the group
- respect for their privacy
- freedom from undue group pressure or coercion from either other members or leaders to participate in exercises or to disclose matters that they are unwilling to discuss
- protection against either verbal or physical assaults
- notice of any research involving the group, and observations of the group through one-way mirrors, or any audio or video taping of group sessions
- full discussion on the limitations of confidentiality, including a statement from the leader concerning how information acquired during group sessions will be used outside the group structure

Freedom to Withdraw from a Group

A difficult, and crucial, question is: Once members make a commitment to be a part of a time-limited and closed group, do they have the right to leave the group at any time they choose? The ASGW's (1989) position on this issue is that provisions should be made to assist a group member to terminate in an effective way. Procedures for leaving a group are explained to all members during the initial group session. Ideally, the leader and the member work in a cooperative fashion to determine whether a group experience is productive or counterproductive for each individual. Although members have a right to leave a group, it is important that they understand the importance of informing both the group leader and the members before making a final decision. It is a good policy for a leader to discuss the possible risks involved in leaving the group prematurely. Before leaving a group, members should generally discuss their reasons for wanting to stop attending. It is essential that the group leader intervene if other members use undue pressure to force any member to remain in the group. When all is said and done, members ultimately have a right to quit.

We are not in favor of forcing members to remain in a group regardless of the circumstances, but neither do we emphasize to prospective members that they have the freedom to leave whenever they choose. Instead, during the individual screening interview and the orientation session we take great care to inform prospective members about the nature of the group. In time-limited, closed groups we also stress to participants the importance of a careful commitment to carrying out their responsibilities. Our position is that anyone who decides to withdraw from a group has a responsibility to the other members and to the leader to at least explain his or her reasons for wanting to leave. The member can be encouraged to take time to consider whether to stay in the group as well as to think honestly about the factors that have led to the decision to leave.

If a person leaves without this careful consideration and explanation, the consequences could be negative to the members remaining as well as to the departing member. Some members may feel burdened with guilt and may blame themselves for saying or doing "the wrong thing" that contributed to an individual's decision to quit. The person who leaves may likewise be stuck with unexpressed and unresolved feelings that could have been worked through with some discussion. With a commitment to discuss the factors related to leaving, there is an opportunity for everyone concerned to express and explore unfinished business. It is critical, however, that the leader not subject the client to undue pressure to remain if the person ultimately chooses to leave.

Psychological Risks for Members

The forces at work in a therapeutic group are powerful ones. They can be constructive, bringing about positive change, but their unleashing always entails some risk. The *Ethical Guidelines for Group Counselors* (ASGW, 1989) specify that leaders have the responsibility to discuss some of the possible risks of participating in groups. It cannot be assumed that participants are aware of these risks. The guideline is: "Group counselors explore with group members the risks of potential life changes that may occur because of the group experience and help members explore their readiness to face these possibilities"(1.e.).* It is imperative that leaders consider ways of reducing these risks. Members of a group may be subjected to scapegoating, group pressure, breaches of confidence, inappropriate reassurance, and hostile confrontation. The group process may even precipitate a crisis in a member's life. A person may enter a group feeling relatively comfortable and leave feeling vulnerable and defenseless. Areas of personal conflict may be exposed for the first time, causing much pain and leading to a new self-awareness that is difficult to cope with. A person's outside life may be drastically affected, for family members may have adverse reactions to changes. Participants may be left, at the conclusion of a group, in no better condition than when they began the group; they may even feel less equipped than ever to cope with the demands of daily life.

*Citations refer to the ASGW guidelines, which appear at the end of Chapter 8.

These hazards should be discussed with the participants during the initial session, and the leader should examine with them how these dangers can be avoided. For example, a leader of a group for women who have been victims of incest might say: "As you begin to uncover painful memories of your childhood and the abuse that took place, you may feel more depressed and anxious for a time than before you entered this group. It is very important to talk about these feelings in the group, especially if you have thoughts about quitting." Group leaders should also help members explore the concerns they have about transferring what they are learning in the group to their everyday life. Some groups—short-term intensive workshops, in particular—may arouse strong, previously hidden feelings, and it is important that people be given the means of understanding, or even resolving, the issues that are behind these feelings. Participants sometimes leave a group with conflicting feelings, wanting to continue with individual or group counseling yet afraid of going further. In a follow-up session these members can get the support they need in order to be able to examine their ambivalence and decide what to do.

Sometimes, rather than being unaware of the dangers of participating in a group, members invent dangers of their own and are very fearful. For example, some members believe that if they allow themselves to feel their pain, they'll go crazy or sink into a depression so deep they won't be able to climb out of it. Some are convinced that if they give up their self-control, they won't be able to function. Others are frightened of letting others know them, because they think they'll be rejected. There are those who are reluctant to experience their anger, because they fear physically hurting another. Such fears should be explored early, so that the members can determine how realistic they are and try to put some of them to rest.

Not only do certain risks need to be identified and dealt with in the group, but safeguards against these risks also need to be established. The leader should stress that group members have the right to decide for themselves what to explore and how far to go. Counselors must be alert to group pressure and block any attempts by members to get others to do something they choose not to do.

Group members can be invited or asked, rather than ordered, to participate in certain exercises or techniques. Members should be reassured that they have the option of declining to participate in group activities that they find extremely threatening. Direct expression of aggression in an exercise could result in another person's being physically hurt. Therefore, we ask members to release feelings of anger in a symbolic way. Symbolic actions, such as beating a pillow, can have therapeutic value. It is essential that group leaders learn how to cope effectively with whatever may arise as the result of an exercise. It may be easy to provoke someone into experiencing rage, but it is another matter to know what to do when this person relaxes long-standing controls.

After an intense group experience participants may make rash decisions that affect not only their own lives but also the lives of members of their family. What the individual may see as the result of newfound spontaneity or decisiveness may be due merely to a burst of energy generated by the group. For example, a woman who has been married for 20 years and who becomes aware of her extreme alienation from her husband may leave the group with a resolve to get a divorce. The counselor should caution her of the danger of making decisions too soon after an intense group session. If this woman has changed in the group, she may be able to relate to her husband differently; if she acts too soon, she may not give this behavioral change a chance to happen. It is not the leader's responsibility to stand in the way of members' decisions, but the leader is responsible for warning members against acting on a "group high." It is also a good practice to caution members who have done significant cathartic work, such as role playing, to refrain from leaving a session and saying in person everything they may have symbolically said to a significant other in a therapeutic context. We find that members sometimes burden themselves with the notion that they are expected to unload everything they experienced in a therapeutic session. We caution them to be selective in what they express to other people in real-life situations. If members hope to enhance their relationships with those they love, they cannot afford to bombard them with the "psychological venom" that they may have released in a symbolic sense in the group. The group counselor can assist them in determining what they most want to communicate and also in finding ways to express their thoughts and feelings in a manner that shows concern and is most likely to lead to a successful encounter.

At this point we will summarize some of the other possible risks in therapeutic groups. Later in the book we will expand our treatment of the issue by developing guidelines for making participants aware of risks and for preparing the members in a way that will reduce the chances of their having a negative experience.

1. Self-disclosure is sometimes misused by group members. This issue will be dealt with at greater length in a later chapter, but we do want to mention that action needs to follow self-disclosure. The group ethic has sometimes been misunderstood to mean the more disclosure that takes place, the better. Privacy can be violated by indiscriminate sharing of one's personal life. Self-disclosure is an essential aspect of any working group, but it is a means to the end of fuller self-understanding and should not be glorified in its own right, at the expense of follow-through.

2. Some of the disclosures made during a session may not remain in the group. Leaders need to continually stress confidentiality in any group, but even when they do so, the possibility remains that members will talk about what they've heard in the group.

3. Scapegoating may occur in a group, particularly if leaders do not intervene when they see members "ganging up" on one particular client. When confrontation occurs, we find it useful to ask the member doing the confronting to state what reactions he or she is having to the person being confronted. This usually stops the member from merely throwing judgmental labels at another.

4. The danger of inadequate leadership is a by-product of the growth of the group movement. Some people attend a few weekend workshops as participants and then decide, with very little additional experience, to lead groups of their own. Because they experienced a "high," they decide that groups are the answer for any seeker of self-fulfillment. Lacking adequate training or experience, they hastily gather a group together without bothering to screen members or even prepare them for the particular group. Such leaders can do extensive damage and, in the process, cause participants to close themselves off from the possibility of seeking any type of therapy or counseling in the future.

As we've suggested, it is not realistic to expect that all personal risks can be eliminated, and to imply that they can is to mislead prospective members. What is essential is that members be made aware of the major risks, that they have an opportunity to discuss their willingness and ability to deal with them, and that as many safeguards as possible be built into the structure of the group. If members experience chronic depression, severe anxiety attacks, and periods of confusion and crisis, for example, and if they lack clarity regarding the effects of the group experience on them, they should have somewhere to turn for further professional assistance. This is true both during the course of the group and once the group has ended.

Often the "risks" and "terrible things" that some people associate with groups are really misconceptions about the purpose of groups. In conjunction with exploring potential risks, we make it a practice to separate facts from fantasy by discussing with members any preconceptions they may have brought with them to a group.

Confidentiality

One of the keystone conditions for effective group work is confidentiality. It is especially important because the group leader must not only keep the confidences of members but also get the members to keep one another's confidences. *Ethical Guidelines for Group Counselors* (ASGW, 1989) specifies that "group counselors protect members by defining clearly what confidentiality means, why it is important, and the difficulties involved in enforcement" (3.).

In certain group situations confidentiality becomes especially critical and also more difficult to maintain. This situation occurs in groups in institutions, agencies, and schools where the members know and have frequent contact with one another and with one another's associates outside of the group. In an adolescent group in a high school, for example, great care must be exerted to ensure that whatever is discussed in the sessions is not taken out of the group. If some members gossip about things that happened in the group, the group process will come to a halt. People are not going to reveal facts about their personal lives unless they feel quite sure that they can trust both the leader and the members to respect their confidences.

The group leader should emphasize at various stages of the group's evolution this importance of maintaining confidentiality (ASGW, 1989). This issue should be introduced during the individual screening interview, and it should be clarified at the initial group sessions. At appropriate times during the course of the group the leader should remind the members of the need for not discussing identities or specific situations. It is a good practice for group counselors to point out that confidences can be broken by carelessness as well as by malicious gossip. If at any time any member gives indications that confidentiality is not being respected, the leader should explore this matter with the group as soon as possible. Some practitioners recommend having members sign a contract in which they agree to honor confidentiality. Paradise and Kirby (1990) think that a contract reinforces the importance of confidentiality in groups and that it serves as a useful documentation when dropping a member from a group for violating confidentiality.

We do expect that members will want to talk about their group experiences with significant people in their lives. We caution them, however, about breaking others' confidences in this process. We tell them to be careful not to mention others who were in the group or to talk about what others said and did. Generally, members do not violate confidentiality when they talk about *what* they learned in group sessions. But they are likely to breach confidentiality when they talk about *how* they acquired insights or how they actually interacted in a group. For example, David becomes aware in a session that he invites women to take care of him, only to resent them for treating him like a child. He may want to say to his wife "I realize that I often resent you for the very thing that I expect you to do." It is not necessary that he describe the particular exercise, involving several women in the group, that led to his insight. If David talks about these details out of context, he runs the risk that his wife may misunderstand him and that he may inappropriately reveal other members' personal work. Group leaders not only need to establish clear guidelines for maintaining confidentiality but also to inform group members about the potential consequences of intentionally breaching confidentiality (ASGW, 1989).

Leaders may be tested by some members of the group. For instance, a counselor may tell the participants in a group in a juvenile correctional institution that whatever is discussed will remain in the group. The youths may not believe this and may in many subtle ways test the leader to discover whether in fact he or she will keep this promise. For this reason it is essential the group leaders not promise to keep within the group material that they may be required to disclose. Counselors owe it to their clients to specify at the outset the limits on confidentiality, and in mandatory groups they should inform members of any reporting procedures required of them (ASGW, 1989).

A counselor working with children may be expected to disclose some information to parents if they insist on it, or a leader of a group of parolees may be required to reveal to the members' parole officer any information acquired in the group concerning certain criminal offenses. It is a good policy for leaders to let members know that they may be required to testify against them in court. In general, licensed psychologists, psychiatrists, and licensed clinical social workers are legally entitled to privileged communication. This means that these professionals cannot break the confidence of clients unless (1) in their judgment, the clients are likely to do serious harm to themselves or to others; (2) the clients are gravely disabled; (3) abuse of children or the elderly is suspected; (4) they are ordered by a court to provide information; or (5) the clients give specific written permission.

A particularly delicate problem is safeguarding the confidentiality of minors in groups. Parents may inquire about what their child has discussed in a group, and it is the responsibility of the group leader to inform them in advance of the importance of confidentiality. Parents can be told about the purpose of the group, and they can be given some feedback concerning their child, but care must be taken not to reveal specific things that the child mentioned. One way to provide feedback to parents is through a session involving one or both parents, the child, and the group leader.

Group leaders have some general guidelines for what disclosures they should and should not make about what has occurred in group sessions. The AACD's (1988) caution to group counselors is that they must set a norm of confidentiality regarding all group participants' disclosures. However, the guideline does specify exceptions: "When the client's condition indicates that there is clear and imminent danger to the client or others, the counselor must take reasonable personal action or inform responsible authorities. Consultation with other professionals must be used where possible."

In basic agreement with the above position is the APA's 1989 code, which asserts that psychologists have a primary obligation to respect the confidentiality of information obtained in the course of their work. This position is qualified by the principle that psychologists "reveal such information to others only with the consent of the person or the person's legal representative, except in those unusual circumstances in which not to do so would result in clear danger to the person or to others. Where appropriate, psychologists inform their clients of the legal limits of confidentiality."

Group leaders would do well to consider some other ramifications of confidentiality. Following are guidelines concerning the issue of confidentiality:

- When working with minors or with clients who are unable to give voluntary and informed consent, it is essential that the professional exert special care to protect these persons' best interests (APA, 1989).
- When working with minors, leaders specify the limits of confidentiality (ASGW, 1989).
- It is a wise policy to ask participants to sign a contract in which they agree not to discuss or write about what transpires in the sessions or talk about who was present.
- Although confidentiality is crucial to the success of a group, the leader can do little to guarantee that it will be respected by all members (Paradise & Kirby, 1990). Leaders can ensure confidentiality only on their part, not on the part of members (ASGW, 1989).
- Professionals who obtain personal material during the course of their work and then use it in writing or in lectures do so after they have obtained prior consent or have adequately disguised all identifying information (AACD, 1988; AMHCA, 1980; APA, 1989).
- It is essential that group leaders become familiar with the local and state laws that have an impact on their practice. This is especially true in cases involving child molestation, neglect or abuse of the elderly and children, or incest.

Ethical and Legal Standards

Most professional organizations affirm that practitioners should be aware of the prevailing community standards and of the possible impact on their practice of deviation from these standards. Ethical and legal issues are frequently intertwined, which makes it imperative that group practitioners not only follow the ethical codes of their profession but also know their state's laws and their legal boundaries and responsibilities. Specifically, several guidelines can help ensure the ethical and legal practice of group work:

- Counselors do not misuse their professional role and power as group leaders to advance personal or social contacts with members throughout the duration of the group (ASGW, 1989).
- Sexual intimacies between group counselors and members are unethical (AACD, 1988; AMHCA, 1980; APA, 1989; ASGW, 1989).
- In providing psychological or counseling services to clients, professionals do not violate or diminish the legal and civil rights of their clients (AMHCA, 1980; APA, 1989).

The last guideline implies that professionals who work with children, adolescents, and certain involuntary populations are especially advised to learn the laws restricting group work. Issues such as confidentiality, parental consent, informed consent, protection of members' welfare, and the civil rights of institutionalized patients are a few areas in which group workers must be knowledgeable. It is a good idea to obtain legal information concerning group procedures and practices. Awareness of legal rights and responsibilities as they pertain to group work protects not only clients but also group leaders from needless lawsuits arising from negligence or ignorance.

Legal Liability and Malpractice

Group leaders who fail to exercise due care and to act in good faith are liable to a civil suit. Professionals are expected to practice within the code of ethics of their particular field and to abide by legal standards. Practitioners are subject to civil liability for not doing right or for doing wrong to another. If group members can prove that personal injury or psychological harm stems from a leader's failure to render proper service, either through negligence or ignorance, the leader is open to a malpractice suit. Negligence consists of departing from the standard and commonly accepted practices of others in the profession. In writing about the legal liability of group counselors in private practice, Paradise and Kirby (1990) contend that the three most important legal issues are confidentiality, the duty to protect the client and others, and billing practices.

The following are some of the bases for malpractice actions against mental-health professionals:

- engaging in sexual relations with a client
- breaching confidentiality inappropriately
- causing physical injury through the use of group exercises
- striking or physically assaulting a client as a treatment technique
- malicious infliction of emotional distress
- misrepresenting one's professional training and skills
- wrongful death
- violation of civil rights
- improper diagnosis
- the failure to consult
- the failure to refer a client when it becomes clear that the person needs intervention that is beyond the practitioner's level of competence
- a suit for fee collection
- providing birth-control or abortion information to a minor
- abandonment
- prescribing and administering drugs inappropriately
- failing to exercise reasonable care to avert a client's suicide

- failing to warn and protect a potential victim of a client who has made threats

Legal Safeguards for Group Practitioners

The key to a group leader's avoiding a malpractice suit is the maintaining of reasonable, ordinary, and prudent practices. Following are some guidelines for group leaders that are useful in translating the terms *reasonable, ordinary,* and *prudent* into concrete actions. Many of these suggestions are from the comprehensive textbook *The Law and the Practice of Human Services,* by Woody and his associates (1984). Other works that we have found of value are *Protecting Your Mental Health Practice: How to Minimize Legal and Financial Risk* (Woody, 1988), *Business Success in Mental Health Practice* (Woody, 1989), *Legal Liability in Psychotherapy* (Schutz, 1982), *The Counselor and the Law* (Hopkins & Anderson, 1990), *Ethical and Legal Issues in Counseling and Psychotherapy* (Van Hoose & Kottler, 1985), *Law and Ethics in Counseling* (Hummel, Talbutt, & Alexander, 1985), and *Professional Liability and Risk Management* (Bennett, Bryant, VandenBos, & Greenwood, 1990). As a group leader, you should:

- Take time and exercise care in screening candidates for a group experience. Many potential problems can be averted by effective screening and referral practices.
- Adequately inform group participants about the group process, including policies and procedures that govern your practice.
- Develop written informed-consent procedures at the outset of a group. Using contracts, signed by both the leader and the members, is an example of such a procedure.
- Obtain written parental consent when working with minors. This is generally a good practice, even if you are not required to do so by state law.
- Have a clear rationale for the techniques you employ in group sessions. Be able to intelligently and concisely discuss the theoretical underpinnings of your procedures.
- Have a clear standard of care that can be applied to your services, and communicate this standard to the members.
- Seek consultations with colleagues or supervisors in cases involving difficult legal and ethical issues.
- Avoid becoming entangled in social relationships with group members.
- Be aware of those situations in which you legally *must* break confidentiality.
- If you work for an agency or institution, have a contract that specifies the employer's legal liability for your professional functioning.
- Abide by the policies of the institution that employs you. If you disagree with certain policies, first attempt to find out the reasons

for them. Then see if it is possible to work within their framework. Realize that you do not always have to agree with such policies to be able to work effectively. If you strongly disagree with policies and if they interfere with your ability to do your job, do what you can to get them changed, or consider resigning.

- Practice within the boundaries of your local and state laws. (Several books in the reading list at the end of this chapter deal with the law and ethics of counseling.)
- Create reasonable expectations about what a group can and cannot do, and avoid promising members magical cures.
- Make it a practice to assess the general progress of a group, and teach members how to evaluate their individual progress toward their own goals.
- Be alert to when it is appropriate to refer a group member for another form of treatment as well as when group therapy might be inadvisable.
- Incorporate ethical standards in your practice of group work. You might want to give the members of your groups a copy of the ASGW's *Ethical Guidelines for Group Counselors* and discuss relevant guidelines at appropriate times during the course of a group.
- Take steps to keep up with theoretical and research developments that have a direct application to group work. Update your group-leadership skills. Compare your knowledge, skill, and supervised experiences in group work against the ASGW's *Professional Standards for the Training of Group Workers*, which we described earlier in this chapter.
- Carry malpractice insurance. Students are not protected against malpractice suits. (If students join the AACD, they not only receive the benefits of this professional organization but are also entitled to participate in the liability-insurance program.)

Uses and Abuses of Group Techniques

Some groups make use of nonverbal exercises to facilitate the therapeutic release of pent-up anger. In your role as a group leader you have a responsibility to exercise caution in using techniques, especially if these methods are likely to result in the venting of intense feelings. You should be prepared to intervene in cases where members attempt to act out aggression in a physical way that might harm themselves or others (ASGW, 1989). One way to deflect much aggression is to encourage clients to release anger on a symbolic object. It is important that you be equipped to cope with powerful feelings, including uncontrolled aggression, that can be triggered by certain role-playing activities. As a general rule, it is not a good idea to introduce a technique that will encourage the aggressive expression of anger unless you have confidence that you can handle the consequences, both physical and psychological. As we have elsewhere, the concern here is not simply for the physical safety of the group members. Those members who have held in emotions for many years, perhaps out of a fear of negative consequences if they expressed their feelings, would have their fears tragically reinforced if they were to lose control and harm themselves or someone else. We generally avoid involving the entire group in physical techniques, for reasons of safety. We employ such techniques, especially those that are likely to arouse strong emotions, with members with whom we have established a trusting relationship (G. Corey, M. Corey, Callanan, & Russell, 1992).

Concerning nonaggressive physical techniques, such as touching, the following precautions are suggested: First, it is important that members choose to participate in touching exercises and that those who have reservations retain the option of abstaining. People should be reminded, however, that forcing themselves to do something that makes them uncomfortable may be the only way of overcoming their discomfort. Second, it is important that you or the members avoid simulating affection. It should be expressed only when it is felt. For instance, if touching is done merely as a part of an exercise, members may come to distrust any affectionate gesture as a form of role playing.

As we said in Chapter 1, you should have a rationale for introducing nonverbal exercises, and it is critical that you use them appropriately and sensitively. It is also important to intervene if members attempt to coerce or pressure a reluctant member into participating. The participants should have an opportunity to share their reactions to the activities.

We use the following guidelines in our practice to avoid abusing techniques in a group:

- Techniques have a therapeutic purpose and are grounded in some framework.
- They are used to promote a client's further self-exploration.
- Techniques are not used to stir up emotions but, rather, to work therapeutically with emotional issues that the client initiates. Techniques can help members experience feelings that are hidden or merely beginning to emerge.
- Techniques are not used to cover up the group leader's discomfort or incompetence.
- They are introduced in a sensitive and timely manner.
- They are abandoned if they prove ineffective.
- Members are given the option of whether to participate in certain exercises; they are not ordered to participate, but invited.

It is important to use only techniques that you have some knowledge about, preferably those that you have experienced personally or have received supervision in using. The relevant ASGW (1989) guideline is: "Group counselors do not attempt any technique unless trained in its use or under supervision by a counselor familiar with the intervention. Depending upon the type of intervention, group counselors have training commensurate with the potential impact of a technique" (10.).

You need to be aware of what a technique might potentially lead to and to be able to deal with intense emotional outcomes. For example, we have observed student leaders with a reading knowledge of guided fantasy techniques who decided to introduce them in their groups. They were surprised and unprepared to work therapeutically with the emotions released in some members. It would be unrealistic for us to expect that leaders should always know *exactly* what will result from an intervention, but they should be able to cope with unexpected outcomes.

The Role of the Leader's Values in the Group

Your values are a fundamental part of who you are as a person. Thus, they cannot help but influence how you lead a therapeutic group. You can increase your effectiveness as a leader by becoming aware of the values you hold as well as the subtle and direct ways in which you might influence the people in your groups. The ASGW's (1989) guideline on the role of the leader's values is "Group counselors develop an awareness of their own values and needs and the potential impact upon the choice of the interventions likely to be made." (7.).

We see your function as a leader as challenging members to discover what is right for them, not persuading them to do what you think is right. You need not always express your personal views on value-laden situations during a session, but if members ask about your views, little is gained by refusing to express them. We are particularly inclined to tell members about our values in cases where there is a conflict, rather than blandly acceding or pretending that no difference of opinion exists. Expressed values are less likely to interfere with the progress of a group than values that are concealed. In certain cases it may be necessary to refer clients to someone else because the conflict is inhibiting the leader's objectivity.

We have heard leaders comment that they would not want to make known their personal values concerning religion, abortion, child rearing, extramarital affairs, and other such controversial issues because of the fear of swaying members to blindly accept their values. It is our position that leaders cannot simply remain neutral in value-laden areas. It is also important for group leaders to be aware that extremely needy and dependent members may feel pressure to please the leader at all costs and hence assume the leader's values automatically. This is a useful issue to explore in the sessions.

Consider for a moment the example of a man who is struggling with the decision of whether to file for a divorce. He tells the group that he is not sure he is willing to risk the loneliness he fears he'll experience as a divorced man, yet he feels stuck in an unsatisfying marriage and sees little hope that things will change for the better. Surely the values you have as a leader will influence how you relate to him. Nevertheless, it is one thing to challenge him to look at all his alternatives before making his decision and to use the group to help him explore these alternatives, and quite a different matter to persuade him (or to enlist the members to give him advice) to do what you (or they) think he should do. Your own values may dictate staying with a marriage at all costs, or they may include divorcing if one is unhappy. The key point is that it is not your role as leader to make this man's decision for him, even if he asks you to do so.

The basic function of a leader is to assist members in finding answers that are most congruent with their own values. The leader's role is to provide a context in which members can examine their feelings and values and eventually arrive at solutions that are in their best interests (G. Corey, M. Corey, & Callanan, 1990).

Summary of Ethical Principles for Group Leaders

A mark of professional group leadership is establishing a set of guiding principles. What follows is not a rigid set of policies but, rather, guidelines that we think will help you clarify your values and encourage you to take a position on basic professional issues pertaining to your role as a group practitioner. Many of these guidelines have already been discussed in this chapter; we repeat them here as a summary checklist for the purpose of review and for quick reference as you read the remainder of this book. We have struggled with these issues in our work with groups, and these guidelines make sense to us. You will have to develop principles that are appropriate for you. Our aim in presenting these guidelines is to stimulate you to think about a framework that will guide you in making sound decisions as a leader.

1. Make the time to reflect on your personal identity, especially as it is influenced by your professional work. Think about your needs and behavior styles and about the impact of these factors on group participants. It is essential for you to have a clear idea of what your roles and functions are in the group, so you can communicate them to the members.

2. Have a clear idea of the type of group you are designing. Be able to express the purpose of the group and the characteristics of the clients who will be admitted.

3. Develop a means of screening that will allow you to differentiate between suitable and unsuitable applicants.

4. Ask potential group members who are undergoing psychotherapy to consult their therapist before becoming involved in a group.

5. Tell prospective group members what is expected of them, and encourage them to develop a contract that will provide them with the impetus to obtain their personal goals. Tell members that they will be expected to make appropriate self-disclosures, experiment with new behaviors in the group, examine the impact of their interpersonal style on others, express their feelings and thoughts, actively listen to others and attempt to see the world through their eyes, show respect for others, offer genuine support, confront others as a way of developing an honest relationship with them, and try new behaviors outside of the group.

6. Make prospective participants aware of the techniques that will be employed and of the exercises that they may be asked to participate in. Give them the ground rules that will govern group activities.

7. Avoid undertaking a project that is beyond the scope of your training and experience. Make a written statement of your qualifications to conduct a particular group available to the participants. If an experienced clinician and a student intern are co-leading a group, this situation should be made clear to the members. Of course, it is essential that co-leaders meet regularly to discuss any problems that arise in their leading together.

8. Make clear at the outset of a group what the focus will be. For example, some groups have an educational focus, and so a didactic approach is used. Other groups have a therapeutic focus, and these take an emotive/experiential tack. Some groups have a developmental focus, with the aim of getting members to fully utilize their potential, whereas other groups are more remedial and stress treatment of disabling symptoms or elimination of faulty behavior patterns.

9. Protect the members' right to decide what to share with the group and what activities to participate in. Be sensitive to any form of group pressure that violates the self-determination of an individual and to any activity, such as scapegoating or stereotyping, that unfairly undermines a person's sense of self.

10. Develop a rationale for using group exercises, and be able to verbalize it. Use only those exercises that you are competent to employ. It is best if you have experienced as a member the techniques you use.

11. Relate practice to theory, and remain open to integrating multiple approaches into your practice. Keep yourself informed about research findings on group process, and use this information to increase the effectiveness of your practice. Be thoroughly grounded in a number of diverse theoretical orientations as a basis for creating a personalized style of leading groups. Unless you have a clear belief about the way to function in groups and about how groups work, you lack a basis for using appropriate methods.

12. Be aware of the danger of meeting your needs at the expense of the members' needs. Some members glorify and idealize the group leader and lessen their own power in the process. Do not take advantage of this tendency by forgetting that your primary job is as a group facilitator. Avoid dual relationships with group members, whether sexual or not.

13.   Point out to members the psychological risks involved in group participation both before they enter and also when it is appropriate throughout the life of the group.

14.   Emphasize the importance of confidentiality to members before they enter a group, during the group sessions when relevant, and before the group terminates. From the outset clearly present the limits of confidentiality, promising nothing that cannot be guaranteed.

15.   When it is appropriate, be open with the group about your values, but avoid imposing them on clients. Recognize the role that the members' culture and socialization play in the formulation of their values. Respect your clients' capacity to think for themselves, and be sure that members give one another the same respect. Members often impose their values on others by telling them what to do under the guise of being helpful. At these times you will need to intervene and remind members of the purpose of the group.

16.   Be alert for symptoms of psychological debilitation in group members, which may indicate that participation in the group should be discontinued. Make referral resources available to people who need or desire further psychological assistance.

17.   Encourage participants to discuss their experience in the group, and help them evaluate the degree to which they are meeting their personal goals. Time can be set aside at the end of each session for members to express their thoughts and feelings about that session.

18.   Do not expect the transfer of learning from the group to daily life to occur automatically. Assist members in applying what they are learning. Prepare them for the negative responses that they are likely to encounter when they try to transfer their group learning to their daily life. Such problems make useful material for exploration in the group, and members can learn specific ways of dealing with setbacks.

19.   Schedule follow-up sessions so that members are able to see how others in their group have done and so that you have a basis for evaluating the impact of the group experience. Individual sessions may sometimes be of value for members who feel a need to confer with you after a group has ended. These sessions can help members see the group as a beginning by getting involved in further growth experiences.

20.   Develop some method of evaluation to determine the effectiveness of the procedures you use. Through at least informal research efforts, you are in a better position to make informed judgments about how well your leadership style is working.

This chapter is not intended to increase your anxiety level or make you so careful that you avoid taking any risks. Leading groups is a risky as well as a professionally rewarding venture. You are bound to make mistakes from time to time. Making errors is not necessarily fatal, but what is essential is that you be willing to acknowledge mistakes and learn from them. It is a disservice to treat group members as though they were fragile and, thus, never to challenge them. We hope you won't be frozen with anxiety over needing to be all-knowing at all times. What we do encourage you to do is remain willing to ask yourself throughout your professional career *what* you are doing and *why* you are doing it. Ethical decision making is not a matter of seeking ready-made answers that are immune to questioning and revision. It is a never-ending process.

Where to Go from Here

This chapter is merely an introduction to the ethical issues that you will confront as a group practitioner. If you wish to do additional reading in the areas of training of group counselors, ethical standards, and legal issues, this section provides a resource guide.

Training of Group Leaders

For those interested in standards for the training and education of group leaders as well as basic issues relating to leader competence we recommend the following: *Professional Standards for the Training of Group Workers* (ASGW, 1990); *Guidelines for the Training of Group Psychotherapists* (American Group Psychotherapy Association, 1978); "Current Practice in the Training of Group Psychotherapists" (Dies, 1980); "Description of a Practicum Course in Group Leadership" (G. Corey, 1981); "In-Service Training for Group Leaders in a Prison Hospital: Problems and Prospects" (G. Corey, M. Corey, & Callanan, 1981); *Theory and Practice of Group Counseling* (G. Corey, 1990); "Experiential/Didactic Training and Supervision Workshop for Group Leaders" (M. Corey & G. Corey, 1986); "Group Ethics: A Multimodal Model for Training Knowledge and Skill Competencies" (Gumaer & Martin, 1990); "The Ethics of Dual Relationships in the Training of Group Counselors" (Forester-Miller & Duncan, 1990); "Ethical Dilemmas in Teaching a Group Leadership Course" (Williams, 1990); and *The Theory and Practice of Group Psychotherapy* (Yalom, 1985, chap. 17).

Ethical Issues

Concerning ethical standards in group work, we recommend the following: *Ethical Standards* (AACD, 1988); *Ethical Principles of Psychologists* (APA, 1989); *Ethical Guidelines for Group Counselors* (ASGW, 1989); *Code of Ethics for Certified Clinical Mental Health Counselors* (AMHCA, 1980); "Ethical Leader Practices in Sensitivity Training for Prospective Professional Psychologists" (Bass & Dole, 1977); *Group Procedures: Purposes, Processes, and Outcomes* (Diedrich & Dye, 1972, Part 5); *Group Counseling: A Developmental Approach* (Gazda, 1989); *Ethical and Legal Issues in Counseling and Psychotherapy* (Van Hoose & Kottler, 1985); "Professional Issues" (Zimpfer, 1976); *The Counselor and the Law* (Hopkins &

Anderson, 1990, chaps. 2 and 3); *Developmental Groups for Children* (Duncan & Gumaer, 1980, chap. 1); "Ethical and Legal Issues in Group Psychotherapy" (Pinney, 1983); "Ethical Problems of Group Psychotherapy" (Rosenbaum, 1982); and "Training Group Leaders in Ethical Decision Making" (Gumaer & Scott, 1985).

Issues and Ethics in the Helping Professions (G. Corey, M. Corey, & Callanan, 1988) contains many topics of relevance to the group worker. This book is a combination of textbook, manual, and resource guide, with open-ended cases and many situations relating to ethical and professional issues that affect the practice of group counseling. Chapter 8 deals with ethical issues special to group work. Two other sources that contain separate chapters on the ethics of group practice are *Theory and Practice of Group Counseling* (G. Corey, 1990) and *Group Techniques* (G. Corey, M. Corey, Callanan, & Russell, 1992). An excellent source is a special issue dealing with ethical and legal issues in group work in the *Journal for Specialists in Group Work* (Forester-Miller, 1990).

Legal Issues

Although we are not aware of any books that deal strictly with legal issues in group work, we highly recommend *Professional Liability and Risk Management* (Bennett et al., 1990), which is a comprehensive discussion of ethics, guidelines for practice, and professional liability. We also recommend that leaders consult books such as the following for some additional information: *The Law and the Practice of Human Services* (Woody & Associates, 1984); *Legal Liability in Psychotherapy* (Schutz, 1982); *Ethical and Legal Issues in Counseling and Psychotherapy* (Van Hoose & Kottler, 1985); *The Counselor and the Law* (Hopkins & Anderson, 1990); *School Law for Counselors, Psychologists, and Social Workers* (Fischer & Sorenson, 1985); and *Law and Ethics in Counseling* (Hummel et al., 1985). We also recommend the article "Some Perspectives on the Legal Liability of Group Counseling in Private Practice" (Paradise & Kirby, 1990).

Exercises

1. It comes to your attention that certain members have been gossiping about matters that came up in a high school group you're leading. Do you deal with the offenders privately or in the group? What do you say?

2. Assume that you are about to begin leading a high school counseling group and that the policy of the school is that any teacher or counselor who becomes aware that a student is using drugs is expected to report the student to the principal. How do you cope with this situation?

3. You are conducting a self-exploration group with children in a family clinic. The father of one of the children in your group meets with you to find out how his child is doing. What do you tell him? What do you not tell him? Would you be inclined to meet with the father and his child?

4. Assume that you are a private practitioner who wants to co-lead a weekend assertiveness-training workshop. How would you announce your workshop? How would you screen potential members? Whom might you exclude from your workshop, and why?

5. You are employed as a counselor in the adolescent ward of a county mental hospital. As one of your duties you lead a group for the young people, who are required to attend the sessions. You sense resistance on the part of the members. What are the ethical problems involved? How do you deal with the resistance?

6. Assume that you are asked to lead a group composed of involuntary clients. Because their participation is mandatory, you want to take steps to clearly and fully inform them of procedures to be used, their rights and responsibilities as members, your expectations of them, and matters such as confidentiality. If you were to write up an "informed-consent document," what would you most want to put into this brief letter?

7. A member in a group you are leading comes to you after one of the group sessions, saying: "I don't want to come back next week. It doesn't seem as if we're getting anywhere in here, because all that ever goes on is people putting each other down. I just don't trust anyone in here!" She has not said any of this in the sessions, and the group has been meeting for five weeks. What might you say or do? Would you attempt to persuade her to stay in the group? Why or why not?

8. Consider some of the following areas in which your values and those of the members might clash. Consider how you might respond in each of these situations that could arise in your group:
- A woman discloses how excited she is over a current affair and then wonders if she should continue staying with her husband.
- Same situation as above, only the client is a man.
- A woman whose cultural background is different from yours and that of the other members in the group says that she is having difficulty expressing what she wants and in behaving assertively (both in the group and at home). She says she has been taught to think of the interests of others and not be concerned about what she wants.
- An adolescent relates that his life feels bland without drugs.
- A pregnant 16-year-old is struggling to decide whether to have an abortion or give up her baby to an adoption agency.
- A chronically depressed man talks about suicide as his way out of a hopeless situation.

- A man says he is very unhappy in his marriage but is unwilling to get a divorce because he is afraid of being alone.
- Same situation as above, only the client is a woman.
- A member who is from a different culture than the other members says he is having difficulty in the group because he is not used to speaking so freely or openly about family problems.

9. Consult the section "Where to Go from Here," which precedes these exercises. Several students can form a panel and, after doing some reading on a particular ethical or professional issue of interest, present ideas to the class.

10. Carefully review the *Ethical Guidelines for Group Counselors* (ASGW, 1989), which are found at the end of Chapter 8. Identify any of the guidelines that you tend to disagree with or would like to argue about. Which guidelines do you think are the most important? Are there any guidelines that you think should be added? In small groups in class, discuss both the values and the limitations of these guidelines for the practitioner. Select a few specific guidelines that you'd most like to discuss, and bring them to your discussion group.

PART TWO

GROUP PROCESS:
Stages of Development

The stages in the life of a group do not generally flow neatly and predictably in the order described in the chapters to follow. In actuality, there is considerable overlap between stages, and once a group moves to an advanced stage, it is not uncommon for it to stay at a plateau for a time or to temporarily regress to an earlier stage. Similarly, the fact that certain tasks have been accomplished in a group, such as working through conflicts, does not mean that new conflicts will not erupt. Groups ebb and flow, and both members and leaders need to pay attention to the factors that affect the direction a group takes.

Knowing about typical patterns in the evolution of a group will give you a valuable perspective. You will be better able to predict problems and to intervene in appropriate and timely ways. Knowledge of the critical turning points in a group lets you help the participants mobilize their resources so that they can successfully meet the tasks facing them at each stage.

CHAPTER 3

Forming a Group

FOCUS QUESTIONS

1. What issues do you think leaders should consider in organizing a group?
2. How would you go about drafting a written proposal for a group, and how would you "sell" your idea to the agency or institution where you work?
3. How would you announce your group and recruit members? What are some practical ways you can think of to get a group started?
4. What criteria would you use to screen and select members for a group? If you decided to exclude someone who had applied, how would you handle this matter?
5. If you were conducting individual interviews to select group participants, what are some questions you would most want to ask?
6. How would you explain to a potential member the risks and benefits involved in groups? What are some ways of minimizing the psychological risks?
7. What are some misconceptions that you think people have concerning the nature and functioning of groups?
8. What are some advantages of a preliminary session in which potential members can determine whether a given group is for them? How would you want to make use of this first meeting?
9. What are the major ethical considerations in organizing and forming a group?
10. Do you have different attitudes about forming a voluntary group than you do regarding an involuntary one?

Introduction: Where to Begin

We cannot overemphasize the importance of the preparatory period during which a group is organized. Careful attention to forming a group is crucial to its outcome. You will spend time wisely by thinking about what kind of group you want and by getting yourself psychologically ready for your leadership role and functions. The more clearly you can state your expectations, the better you will be able to plan and the more meaningful the experience will be for the participants. A lack of careful thought and planning will show up later in a variety of problems that lead to confusion and floundering among the participants. In planning a group, an initial step is clarifying the rationale for it, which entails drafting a detailed proposal.

Developing a Proposal for a Group

Many good ideas for groups are never put into practice because they are not developed into a clear and convincing plan. If you are going to create a group under the auspices of an agency, you will probably have to explain your proposed goals and methods. The following questions are the kind you should consider in preparing your proposal:

- What type of group are you forming? Will it be a personal-growth group or one designed to treat people with certain disorders? Will it be long term or short term?
- Whom is the group for? Is it for a particular population, such as college students or married couples? for children who are learning to cope with interpersonal problems? for people seeking something specific, such as help with a personal problem?
- What are the general goals and purposes of this group? That is, what will members gain from participating in it?
- Why is there a need for such a group?
- What are the basic assumptions underlying this project?
- What are your qualifications to lead this group?
- What screening and selection procedures will be used? What is your rationale for using these particular procedures?
- How many members will be in the group? Where will the group meet? How often will it meet? How long will each meeting last? Will new people be allowed to join the group once it has started?
- How will the members be prepared for the group experience? What ground rules will you establish at the outset?
- What structure will your group have? What techniques will be used? Why are these techniques appropriate? In what ways can you employ your techniques in a flexible manner to meet the needs of culturally diverse client populations?
- How will you handle the fact that people will be taking some risks by participating in the group? What will you tell the members about these dangers, and what will you do to safeguard members from unnecessary risks? Will you take any special precautions with participants who are minors?
- What evaluation procedures do you plan? What follow-up procedures?
- What topics will be explored in this group? To what degree will they be determined by the group members and to what degree by you?
- What do you expect to be the characteristics of the various stages of the group? What might the problems be at each stage, and how will you cope with them?

Summary Checklist for a Proposal. Five general areas form the basis of a sound and practical proposal.

1. **Rationale.** Do you have a clear and convincing rationale for your group? Are you able to answer questions that might be raised?
2. **Objectives.** Are you clear about what you most want to attain and how you will go about doing so? Are your objectives specific, measurable, and attainable within the specified time?

3. **Practical considerations.** Is the membership defined? Are the meeting time, frequency of meetings, and duration of the group reasonable?
4. **Procedures.** Have you selected specific procedures to meet the stated objectives? Are these procedures appropriate and realistic for the given population?
5. **Evaluation.** Does your proposal contain strategies for evaluating how well the stated objectives were met? Are your evaluation methods objective, practical, and relevant?

Working within the System

If you hope to have your proposal accepted both by your supervisors in an agency and by the potential members, you will need to develop the skills necessary to work within a system. In order to get a group off the ground, you must use awareness and sensitivity in negotiating with the staff of the institution involved. In all clinics, agencies, and hospitals, power issues and political realities play a role. You may become excited about organizing groups only to encounter resistance from your co-workers or your administrators. You may be told, for example, that only psychologists, social workers, and psychiatrists are qualified to lead groups. The rest of the staff may be as cynical as you are inspired about the prospects of doing groups in your setting. Some of your colleagues may be jealous of your efforts, especially if you have successful groups. They may feel that you are taking "their" clients away from them.

The representatives of institutions need to be educated about the potential value, as well as realistic limitations, of groups for their clients. It is helpful to be able to predict some of the major concerns that administrators and agency directors are likely to have about the proposal you submit. For example, if you are attempting to organize a group in a public high school, the administrators may be anxious about parental complaints and potential lawsuits. If you are able to appreciate their concerns and speak directly to ethical and legal issues, you stand a better chance of getting your proposal accepted. If you are not clear in your own mind about what you hope to accomplish through group work or how you will conduct the meetings, the chances are slim that a responsible administrator will endorse your program. If you have not thought through some questions that you are likely to be asked about your proposal, you are setting yourself up for defeat. Here are a few examples of questions that we've been asked as we were presenting a group proposal:

- How will this institution be covered legally in the event of a lawsuit?
- Will the program be voluntary, and will the parents of minors give written consent?

- What will you do in the event that this group proves psychologically disruptive to some of the members?
- Are you prepared to deal with potential confrontations from parents or from community members?

At the various stages of our professional development we have prepared group proposals for such diverse situations as elementary and secondary schools; community colleges; teacher-training and counselor-training departments of universities; church-related groups; mental hospitals for elderly and psychotic patients; a state mental hospital for mentally disordered sex offenders; a mountain resort community operated through the continuing-education programs of several universities; and a variety of groups in private practice. With all the above examples except for private practice, we have found that a clear and organized written proposal (followed up by a person-to-person presentation) is the key to getting our ideas translated into the reality of a group in action. To make the matter of written proposals more concrete, there are a variety of sample proposals in Chapters 9–12. As you review these proposals for various age groups, it is a good idea to think of the specific groups that would be appropriate to the population you serve and the setting in which you work.

Attracting and Screening Members

Assuming that you have been successful in getting a proposal accepted, the next step is to find a practical way to announce your group to prospective participants. How a group is announced influences both the way it will be received by potential members and the kind of people who will join. Although professional standards should prevail over a commercialized approach, we have found that making personal contact with potential members is one of the best methods of recruiting.

Guidelines for Announcing a Group and Recruiting Members

Professional issues are involved in publicizing a group and recruiting members. The *Ethical Guidelines for Group Counselors* (ASGW, 1989) state that prospective members should have access to the following information (preferably in writing):*

- a statement of the goals and purposes of the group
- entrance procedures, time limits of the group experience, and termination procedures.

---

*Refer to the end of Chapter 8, where these guidelines are reproduced. See guideline 1.

- the rights and responsibilities of both group members and the group leader
- the techniques and procedures that may be used, especially any specialized or experimental activities in which members may be expected to participate
- the education, training, and qualifications of the group leader
- the fees and any other related expenses
- a statement of whether follow-up service is included in the fee
- a realistic statement of what services can and cannot be provided within a particular group structure
- the personal risks involved in the group
- the use of any recording of sessions

In writing announcements, it is best to give an accurate picture of the group and to avoid making promises about the outcomes of the group and raising unrealistic expectations. As we've indicated, making direct contact with the population that is most likely to benefit from the group is an excellent way to follow up printed announcements. These personal contacts, which can include distributing printed information to those interested, lessen the chances that people will misunderstand the purposes and functioning of the group.

Another effective method of announcing and recruiting for a group is to inform your agency colleagues. They can then refer clients to you who are appropriate for the particular group. It is possible that they can also do the preliminary screening, including giving written information on the group to potential members with whom they have contact. Involve your co-workers as much as possible in every phase of organizing your group.

Practical Procedures for Announcements and Recruitment

A specific example of identifying and recruiting a target population is provided by Deborah Lambert and Nancy Ceraso English, at North Allegheny Senior High School in Pennsylvania. They find that some groups are more popular than others with high school students. Groups that tend to have relatively low enrollment because of their nature or the stigma attached to them include those for children of alcoholics and those for clients needing follow-up care after a drug-treatment program. On the other hand, groups with a high appeal are those for dealing with parents and for dealing with sexual relationships. Below is a description of practical strategies and considerations that they find helpful in overcoming student identification and recruitment difficulties:

Classroom Presentations. Presenting the information to individual classrooms or to homerooms may be one of the most effective means of announcing and recruiting potential group members. Films, lectures, and discussions naturally increase knowledge and sensitivity among the student body.

Hallway Posters. Place signs in well-attended areas such as the lunchroom, hallways, and bathrooms. Attractive and eye-catching phrases increase the likelihood of a response. "Tear-off" phone numbers or "take-one" business cards allow for discretion and future reference. Remove the signs after three to four weeks, but post new ones at regular intervals (four or five times a year).

PA Announcements. Public-address announcements have limited effectiveness, because students often miss them or tune them out. But they can be made at different times of the day. Give a room number and a main office contact for easy student access.

Newspaper Articles. Advertise in the school paper. Include registration information and key phrases to describe your groups. Supply articles written by past or present members or by facilitators.

Teacher Contacts. Keep the faculty members informed of the groups you are running. Provide them with a brief description of the types of students you hope will participate. Familiarize teachers with the characteristics and behavior that typify the populations you are hoping to reach. Provide homeroom teachers with an announcement to be read to their classes describing the groups and the names of the group facilitators.

Parent Letter or Bulletin. Inform parents of the groups available and the benefits of participating. Provide them with the name of the student-assistance coordinator or counselor who is running the group.

Peer Referrals. Friends are an excellent resource. Follow your school policy on peer referrals. Take steps to ensure that peer reporting does not take on a "narc" quality. At designated "open-house" meetings invite students to bring their friends.

Student Handbook. Include in the school handbook a description of your program and the various groups that will be held.

Counselor Staffing. Meet with the counselors, the school nurse, and administrators to let them know the groups you will be offering. They may be able to identify appropriate candidates.

    The main point is that Lambert and English do not wait passively for students to come in and sign up for the groups they offer. Instead, they use multiple approaches to contact students directly (giving talks in the classrooms) and indirectly (meeting with counselors, teachers, and other school personnel). Because of their own enthusiasm for their groups, they are more likely to attract students who could profit. In Chapter 10 there is a description of two groups that English and Lambert offer at North Allegheny Senior High School: a group for children of alcoholics and one for students who are coming out of drug rehabilitation.

Screening and Selection Procedures

After announcing a group and recruiting members, the next crucial step is arranging for screening and selecting the members who will make up the group. The ASGW *Ethical Guidelines for Group Counselors* (1989) state: "Insofar as possible, the leader screens and selects group members whose needs and goals are compatible with the goals of the group, who will not impede the group process, and whose well-being will not be jeopardized by the group experience" (2.).

The above guideline raises several questions: What screening method should be used? How can you determine who would be best suited for the group, who might have a negative impact on the group process, or who might be jeopardized by the experience? How can you therapeutically deal with those candidates who, for whatever reason, are not included in the group?

The type of group should determine the kind of members accepted. A person who can work well in a structured, short-term group designed to teach social skills or to cope with stress might not be ready for an intensive therapy group. Psychotic individuals would probably be excluded from a personal-growth workshop yet might benefit from a weekly group for outpatients at a mental-health center. The question that needs to be considered is: Should *this* particular person be included in *this* particular group at *this* time with *this* group leader?

Preliminary Screening Sessions. We endorse screening procedures that include a private session between the candidate and the leader. During the private session the leader might look for evidence that the group will be beneficial to the candidate. Some questions to consider are: Is this person motivated to change? Is this a choice of the individual or of someone else? Why this particular type of group? Does he or she understand what the purposes of the group are? Are there any indications that group counseling is contraindicated for this person at this time?

Group applicants should be given the opportunity, at their private sessions, to interview the group leader. They should be invited to ask questions, concerning the procedures, basic purposes, and any other aspect of the group. This questioning is important as a means not only of getting information but also of developing a feeling of confidence in the group leader, which is necessary if productive work is to take place. In other words, we believe that screening should be a two-way process and that potential members should be encouraged to form a judgment about the group and the leader. Given enough information about the group, a member can make a better informed decision about whether to enter it.

In addition to the private screening session, a pregroup session for all of the candidates is extremely valuable. At a preliminary session the leader can outline the reason for the group and the topics that might be explored. This introduction can be most helpful for people who are uncertain whether they want to invest themselves in this group. Potential members can meet one another and begin to explore the potential of the group.

We admit that screening and selection procedures are subjective and that ultimately the intuition and judgment of the leader are crucial. We are concerned that candidates benefit from a group but even more concerned that they might be psychologically hurt by it or might drain the group's energies excessively. Certain members, while remaining unaffected by a group, sap its energy for productive work. This is particularly true of hostile people, people who monopolize, extremely aggressive people, and people who act out. The potential gains of including certain of these members must be weighed against the probable losses to the group as a whole. We also believe that group counseling is contraindicated for individuals who are suicidal, extremely fragmented or acutely psychotic, sociopathic, facing extreme crises, highly paranoid, or extremely self-centered.

A leader needs to develop a system for assessing the likelihood that a candidate will benefit from a group experience. Factors that must be taken into consideration are the level of training of the leader, the proposed makeup of the group, the setting, and the basic nature of the group. For example, it might be best not to accept a highly defensive individual into an ongoing adolescent group, for several reasons. A group may be too threatening for a person so vulnerable and may lead to increased defensiveness and rigidity, or such a person may have a counterproductive effect on group members who want to do serious work.

In some cases it may not be practical and realistic to conduct individual interviews, and alternatives will have to be relied on. One alternative is group screening sessions. This method saves time and also has the advantage of providing an idea of how each person reacts to a group situation. Once members meet one another in a group situation, they can better decide if they want to make a commitment to the group.

Personal contact is always best. For example, we offered a personal-growth group in Europe in which it was unrealistic to screen members privately on a personal basis. We did provide the person who had agreed to organize this group with a detailed letter that described relevant information about the workshop. In several personal contacts with the sponsor we discussed our philosophy of group work, the central purposes of the workshop, and who would most benefit from it. In spite of our efforts to spell out the nature of the group and to prepare those who would attend, we met with considerable opposition from some members, who asserted that the group was not what they had envisioned. This experience reinforced our belief in the value of screening and detailed preparation done in a personal way.

There are other instances when screening may not be practical or even possible. If you work in a county facility or a state hospital, the chances are that you will simply be assigned a group. The basis for assigning members could be their diagnosis or the ward they are on. Even if you are not able to select members for your group, you can make at least brief individual contact with them to prepare them. You will also have to devote part of the initial sessions to preparation, for many of the members may not have the faintest idea why they are in the group or how the group might be of any value to them. In open groups, whose membership changes as some clients leave and new ones are added, it is a good practice to meet individually with incoming members so that you can orient them.

Assessing and Choosing Members. We are often asked the questions "How do you decide who will best fit into the group, who will most benefit from it, and who is likely to be harmed by the experience?" "If you decide to exclude a person from the group, how do you handle this in a tactful and therapeutic manner?" As a group leader you must make the ultimate decision to include or exclude certain clients. Because the groups that we typically offer are voluntary, one factor we look for during the interview is the degree to which a candidate wants to make changes and is willing to expend the necessary effort. We consider whether a group seems the appropriate method of intervention to accomplish the desired changes. We also weigh heavily how much the candidate seems to want to become a member of this group, especially after he or she is given information about it.

We sometimes find ourselves reluctant to let certain people into a group in spite of their desire to join. As we've mentioned, we do pay attention to our intuitions concerning a person, so in the last analysis our screening and selection process is a subjective one. There can be a variety of reasons that would lead us to exclude a person, but whatever our reservations might be, we generally discuss them with the prospective member. At times, after we've discussed our concerns, we see matters differently. At other times we simply cannot with a clear conscience admit a person.

If we do not accept people, we tend to stress how the group might not be appropriate for them and, in some cases, how they would not be appropriate for the group. We strive to break the news in a manner that is honest, direct, and sensitive and that helps those who are being rejected remain open to other options. For example, we might determine that a highly defensive and extremely anxious person who is very frightened in interpersonal relationships is likely to benefit from a series of individual counseling sessions before being placed in a group situation.

We would explain our rationale and encourage the person to consider accepting a referral for an appropriate type of intervention. In other words, we do not close the door on people we exclude from a group with no explanation, nor do we convey that there is something intrinsically wrong with them because they were not included in this particular group.

When we do in-service training workshops for group leaders in various agencies and institutions, many leaders tell us that they don't screen people for their groups. They cite any number of reasons: they don't have the time; they don't have much voice in choosing group members, because people are simply assigned to a group; they don't really know how to determine who will or will not benefit or will be negatively influenced by a group experience; they cannot see why screening is really important; they don't want to play the role of expert in deciding who will be included or excluded; or they don't want to make a mistake by turning away people who might gain from a group. In response, we emphasize that we see screening not as a highly objective and scientific process but as a rough device for getting together the best clientele for a given group. As we mentioned earlier, our view of screening entails a dialogue with the prospective members. It is an opportunity to give information to them and to orient them to the group, and it is a way to help them share in the decision of whether it is appropriate for *them* to become involved.

How to Help Clients Choose Which Group to Join

During the screening and selection interviews, as well as in your announcements for groups, it is well to educate the public on how best to select a group. If people are to make an informed decision about a group, they need information and guidelines. Because people often wonder what to look for in selecting a group, we've prepared this section. Although there are no guarantees that the group one picks will be the right one, a consumer can make a wise choice by considering the following suggestions:

1. Do not join a group just because someone you know thinks you should. Decide for yourself whether you want to be a member of a particular kind of group.

2. Check with others who know the group leader before you make your decision. Although some reports may be biased (either positively or negatively), feedback from people who have participated in one of the leader's groups can be particularly valuable.

3. Before you join a group, interview the group leader. Many leaders will want a private session with a prospective client to determine the person's readiness for a group. By the same token, it is reasonable for the prospective client to want to know about the personal and professional qualifications of the person who leads the group. If the therapist

is indignant over such a request, you should probably avoid this leader's group. If you do speak to the leader, try to decide whether he or she inspires your trust.

4. Questions such as the following can be asked of a group leader:

- What is the purpose of your group?
- What are the responsibilities of the leader and of the members?
- What do you see as the risks of participation, and what safeguards do you take to minimize the risks?
- What results do you see in your groups?
- What techniques do you use?
- Is there an opportunity for individual sessions?
- What is your background and training?
- What experience do you have in leading groups?
- Are you licensed as a therapist? If not, what are your qualifications as a group practitioner?
- What theoretical model do you use?

5. Ask the leader about matters such as fees, the structure of the group, the method of deciding when a member should quit the group or when the group should be terminated, and follow-up procedures.

6. Be cautious about responding to advertisements or to brochures and pamphlets circulated in the mail. Referrals from agencies, from professionals, and most of all from clients who have been in the leader's groups should guide you in selecting a group.

7. The size of the group is another factor to consider. Groups of more than 16 or fewer than 5 members are best avoided (except for children's groups, which may have fewer than 5 members). If a group is very small, there are not enough interaction possibilities. If a group is very large, group cohesion is hard to establish, and even a highly qualified leader may have trouble monitoring the interaction. For a group as large as 16, there should be at least two leaders.

Practical Considerations in Forming a Group

Group Composition

Whether a group should have a homogeneous membership or a heterogeneous one depends on the group's goals. In general, for a specific target population with given needs, a group composed entirely of members of that population is more appropriate than a heterogeneous group. Consider a group composed entirely of elderly people. It can focus exclusively on the specific problems that characterize their developmental period, such as loneliness, isolation, lack of meaning, rejection, deterioration of the body, and so forth. The similarity of the members can lead to a great degree of cohesion, which in turn allows for an open and intense exploration of their life crises. Members can express feelings that have been kept private, and their life circumstances can give them a bond with one another.

Examples of other homogeneous groups are Alcoholics Anonymous, Recovery Inc., Parents without Partners, and Weight Watchers. It is common to hear people claim that, unless one has actually experienced what it is like to be, for example, an alcoholic, one cannot fully understand, and thus cannot help with, an alcoholic's unique problems. We don't accept the premise that the group leader must have experienced every problem of the client. It is important only that group leaders be able to identify with the feelings of clients—their loneliness, fear, and anxiety. When a specific problem exists, however, group cohesion can help, and so homogeneity is appropriate.

A case can sometimes be made, however, for combining people from different populations in a single group. In one of her "Death and Dying" seminars, Dr. Elisabeth Kubler-Ross shared her dream of having children on every hospital ward for the elderly. She maintained that this would give the elderly a chance to share their life and experiences with children and to get the meaning from life that comes from taking care of children. The children would benefit by getting the opportunity to experience older people. Thus, a combination of these two age groups could have some unique therapeutic results for members of both.

Sometimes a microcosm of the outside social structure is desired, and in that case a heterogeneous group is, of course, called for. Personal-growth groups and certain therapy groups tend to be heterogeneous. Members can experiment with new behavior and develop interpersonal skills with the help of feedback from a rich variety of people in an environment that represents out-of-group reality.

Group Size

What is a desirable size for a group? The answer depends on several factors: the age of the clients, the experience of the leader, the type of group, and the problems to be explored. For instance, a group composed of elementary schoolchildren might be kept to three or four, whereas a group of adolescents might be made up of six to eight people. For a weekly ongoing group of adults, about eight people with one leader may be ideal. A group of this size is big enough to give ample opportunity for interaction and small enough for everyone to be involved and to feel a sense of "group."

Frequency and Duration of Meetings

How often should a group meet? For how long? Should a group meet twice weekly for one-hour sessions? Or is an hour and a half to two hours once a week preferable? With children and adolescents it may be better to meet more frequently and for a shorter period, to suit their attention span. If the group is taking place in a school setting, the meeting times can correspond to regularly scheduled class periods. For groups of college students or relatively well-functioning adults, a two-hour weekly session might be preferable. This two-hour period is long enough to allow some intensive work yet not so long that fatigue sets in. You can choose any frequency and duration that suit your style of leadership and the type of people in your group. For an inpatient group composed of lower-functioning members, it is desirable to meet on a daily basis for 45 minutes. Because of the members' psychological impairments it may not be realistic to hold their attention for a longer peiod. Even for higher-functioning inpatient groups it is a good practice to meet several times a week, but these groups might be scheduled for 90 minutes. (An excellent description of inpatient therapy groups for both higher-level and lower-functioning clients is provided by Irvin Yalom in his 1983 book *Inpatient Group Psychotherapy*.)

Length of a Group

What should the duration of a group be, and is it wise to set a termination date? We believe that with most groups a termination date should be announced at the outset, so that members will have a clear idea of the time limits under which they are working. Our college groups typically run about 15 weeks—the length of a semester. With high school students the same length seems ideal, for it is long enough for trust to develop and for work toward behavioral changes to take place but not so long that the group seems to be dragging on interminably. One of our colleagues has several closed groups in his private practice that last 16 weeks. After a few meetings he schedules an all-day session for these groups, which he finds adds greatly to their cohesion. When the group comes to an end, those who wish to join a new group have that option. The advantages of such an arrangement are that the time span allows for cohesion and productive work and that members can then continue practicing newly acquired interpersonal skills with a new group of people. Perhaps a major value of this type of time-limited group is that members are forced to realize that they do not have forever to attain their personal goals. At different points in this 16-week group the members are challenged to review their progress, both individually and as a group. If they are dissatisfied with their own participation or with the direction the group is taking, they have the responsibility to do something to change the situation.

Of course, some groups composed of the same members meet for years. Such a time structure allows them to work through issues in some depth and to offer support and challenge in making life changes. These ongoing groups do have the potential for fostering dependency, and thus it is important that both the leader and members evaluate the impact of the group on the clients' daily living.

Place for Group Meetings

Where should the group hold its meetings? Many places will do, but privacy is essential; the members must feel that they will not be overheard by people in adjoining rooms. Groups often fail because of their physical setting. If they are held in a day hall or ward full of distractions, productive group work will not occur. We like a group room that is not cluttered up with chairs and tables and that allows for a comfortable seating arrangement. We prefer a setting that enables the group to sit in a circle. This arrangement lets all the participants see one another and allows enough freedom of movement that the members can spontaneously make physical contact. It is a good idea for co-leaders to sit across from each other. In this way the nonverbal language of all members can be observed by one leader or the other, and "we-versus-them" atmosphere can be avoided.

Voluntary versus Involuntary Membership

Obviously, the most desirable group is composed of clients who are motivated to change and committed to working. Realistically, some of your groups will be made up of people who are sent to you. In such cases, providing members with information about the group, teaching them how to participate, and orienting them to the basic procedures of group process are essential. It is usually helpful to let the members know that although they don't have much choice about attending, they *can* decide how they will spend their time in the group. Discussing with members various ways in which they can use their time profitably increases the chances that the group will be meaningful.

Open versus Closed Groups

Open groups are characterized by changing membership. The group continues, and as certain members are ready to leave, new members are admitted. *Closed groups* typically have some time limitation, and members are expected to remain in the group until it ends; new members are not added. The question of whether a group should be open or closed depends on a number of variables. There are some advantages to incorporating new members as others leave, for this change can provide stimulation. There can be a lack of cohesion, however, particularly if too many clients leave or too many new ones are introduced at once. Therefore, it may be better to bring in new members one at a time as an opening occurs. One colleague who co-leads open groups in an agency stresses reviewing of the ground rules with each incoming member. Rather than taking group time whenever a new person is included, he covers the rules with the new member as part of the intake interview. He also asks other members to teach the new member about a few of the guidelines in an attempt to have them take more responsibility for their own group. If members are dropped and added sensitively, these changes do not necessarily interfere with the cohesiveness of the group.

In some settings, such as mental-health wards in state hospitals or certain day-treatment centers, group leaders do not have a choice between an open and a closed group. Because the membership of the group changes almost from week to week, continuity between sessions and cohesion within the group become difficult to achieve. Nevertheless, cohesion is possible, even in cases where members attend only once or a few times. However, a high level of activity is demanded of inpatient group therapists, for at times the life of the group may be only a single session. These leaders must structure and activate the group. They need to call on certain members, they must actively support members, and they need to interact personally with the participants (Yalom, 1983).

If you are forming an open group, it is essential that you have some idea about the rate of turnover of the members. How long a given member can participate in the group may be unpredictable. Therefore, your interventions need to be designed with the idea in mind that many members may attend for only one or two sessions. In conducting an open group, it is good to remind all the members that this may be the only time they have with one another. The interventions that you make need to have closure within each session. For example, you would not want to facilitate a member's exploration of a painful concern that could not be satisfactorily addressed in that session. You also have a responsibility to facilitate member interactions that can lead to some form of resolution within a given session. This involves leaving enough time to explore with members what they have learned in a session and how they feel about leaving each session.

One of our colleagues regularly conducts several open groups in a community mental-health agency. He finds that trust and cohesion do develop in most of these groups, for even though the membership does change somewhat over a period of time, there is a stable core of members. When new members join, they agree to attend for at least six sessions. Also, members who miss two consecutive meetings without a valid excuse are not allowed to continue. These practices increase the chances for continuity.

The Uses of a Pregroup Meeting

We suggested earlier that a preliminary meeting of all those who were thinking of joining the group was a good follow-up to screening and orientation interviews as well as a useful device when individual interviews were impractical. We think that such a pregroup session provides an excellent way to prepare members and to get them acquainted with one another. This session also provides the members with more information to help them decide if they are willing to commit themselves to what would be expected of them. Busy practitioners sometimes do not make the time for a separate preparation period but, instead, incorporate an orientation to group participation as a part of the initial stage of a group's life. If an individual interview or a pregroup session with all members is impractical, the first group meeting can be used to cover the issues we are discussing in this chapter. Our preference is for a separate individual orientation interview (which is part of the individual screening interview), followed up by a pregroup meeting for all participants.

At this initial session or the pregroup meeting the leader can explore the members' expectations, clarify the goals and objectives of the group, discuss procedural details, impart some information about group process, and answer members' questions. This is an ideal time to focus on the clients' perceptions, expectations, and concerns. This process does not have to consist of a lecture to the members; it can involve the members and encourage them to interact with one another and the leader from the onset. This interactive model of preparation can reveal interesting information about both the dynamics of the individuals and the "personality of the group" as well. Patterns begin to take shape from the moment a group convenes. The structuring of the group, including the specification of procedures and norms, should be accomplished early in the group's history. Some of this structuring should have been done during the individual intake session, but a continuation of it should be the focus of the first session. Group counselors should either establish ground rules or ask the group to do so. Ideally, group rules can be cooperatively developed by the leader and the members as a part of the group process.

Clarifying Leader and Member Expectations

The pregroup session is the appropriate time to encourage members to express the expectations they are bringing with them to the group. We typically begin by asking: "What are your expectations for this group? What did you have in mind when you signed up?" The replies usually give us a frame of reference for how the members are approaching the group, what they want from it, and what they are willing to give to it to make it a success.

We also share *our* expectations by giving the members an idea of why we designed the group, what we hope will be accomplished, and what we expect of ourselves as leaders and them as members. This is a good time for you to reemphasize and clarify what you see as your responsibilities to the group and to further discuss the members' rights and responsibilities. You can explain what services you can and cannot realistically provide within the particular structure offered—for example, private consultations or follow-up sessions.

If you are forming groups in a community agency, it is likely that their members will be culturally diverse. Depending on a member's specific heritage, you will need to deal with a variety of expectations about you as a group leader. Some participants may look to you as an authority figure who will direct them, some will view you as an expert, and some may expect you to do most of the talking while they mainly listen. In working with culturally diverse groups, it is essential that you do not make assumptions based on race, ethnicity, or culture without checking out your assumptions with individual members. Never assume that because people give the appearance of being ethnically different, they are indeed culturally different. If a person with Asian features applies for your group, do not assume that he or she necessarily adheres to Asian cultural values. It is also a mistake to conclude that merely because certain clients have lived in the United States for a period of time, they have become acculturated into the mainstream society. What is important is that you invite the members of your groups to verbally state *their* expectations and that you be willing to explore these expectations during the initial session.

By having members identify and express their expectations and by clarifying your expectations as a group leader, you will help members function successfully in the group. You can do a great deal to prevent the unnecessary anxiety that results when members are thrown into a group without any idea of what to expect from the situation. You can alleviate members' anxiety by helping them clarify their goals and the methods they can use to achieve these goals. It also helps to explain what you expect of them as members and give them at least a general idea of what they can expect from you and from the group.

Setting Up Basic Ground Rules

The pregroup session is the appropriate place to establish some procedures that will facilitate the group process. Some leaders prefer to present their own policies and procedures, in a nonauthoritarian manner, whereas other leaders tend to place the major responsibility on the group members to come up with procedures that will assist them in attaining their ends. Whatever approach is taken, some discussion of ground rules will be necessary.

Ethical Guidelines for Group Counselors (ASGW, 1989) can help group leaders establish minimum ground rules and ethical standards. Some of these guidelines state, for example, that group leaders:

- protect members by defining clearly what confidentiality means, why it is important, and what difficulties are involved in enforcing it
- protect members against physical threats, intimidation, coercion, and undue peer pressure
- discuss with members the risks involved in group participation, especially regarding life changes, and help them explore their readiness to face these risks
- take steps to ensure informed-consent procedures in both voluntary and involuntary groups

- tell members what will be expected of them
- give members a general idea of the techniques and activities that are part of the group process

As you saw in Chapter 2, confidentiality is a crucial issue in groups. Ideally, this issue is discussed during the individual interview, but because it is so important to the functioning of a group, you cannot stress it too often. At the pregroup session it is a good idea to make it clear that confidentiality is not an absolute and what the restrictions are. Depending on the type of group and the setting, leaders may not be able to guarantee that all of the members' disclosures will be kept within the group. In cases of incest and child abuse, for example, and in cases when clients pose a danger to themselves or to others, confidentiality must be breached. Limitations to confidentiality apply especially to groups of children and adolescents, groups of parolees, groups composed of involuntary populations such as criminals and sex offenders in an institution, and groups of psychiatric patients in a hospital or clinic. These clients should be told that certain things they say in the group may go into their hospital chart, which may be available for other staff members to read. It is a good practice to let them know what information may be recorded, as well as who will have access to it. Leaders should specify what they can and cannot promise to their clients. The members then have a basis for deciding what and how much they will disclose. This kind of honesty about confidentiality will go a long way toward establishing the trust that is absolutely necessary for a working group. You are referred to Chapter 2 for a further discussion of confidentiality.

There are other issues to explore with your group at the first (or another early) session. These include policies about attendance; tardiness; smoking and eating during sessions; bringing friends to a session; getting written parental permission, in the case of minors; socializing outside of the group with other members; getting involved intimately with other members; and members' rights and responsibilities. You will not be able to fully discuss all of the policies and procedures that you deem essential to the smooth functioning of your group in one or two sessions, but establishing your position on these matters will be an asset when they arise at some point in the development of the group.

Preventing Surprises

Holding a pregroup meeting helps ensure that group procedures will not take members by surprise. In the 1960s, for example, some leaders included nudity as a part of the group experience. In this case, obviously, it would be essential that members be given full information in advance. The assumption of these "nude encounter groups" was that the shedding of one's clothes paralleled the shedding of masks. In some cases, the experience of being nude with others is thought to be useful in correcting distorted pictures of one's body and dispelling shame.

Although nude groups are no longer as popular as they once were, they raise some interesting ethical issues. Certain risks are associated with the practice of nudity in group work. Certainly, some cautions need to be voiced. The appropriateness of nudity depends largely on the type of group, the setting, and the nature of the participants.

One of our colleagues attended a week-long residential group and had no idea that nudity would be a part of the group process. In the middle of the week the group leader announced that in the afternoon he wanted the participants to shed their clothes and talk about how they felt about their bodies. Our colleague was totally surprised, and a couple of the other participants voiced strong objections to disrobing. They said that doing so would violate their sense of decency and their cultural upbringing. The leader replied: "Trust me. I've done this exercise many times before, and it always brings the group closer together. Most of us have hang-ups about our bodies, and it helps to confront our fears in this way." In spite of some members' objections to being nude in front of others, the leader forcefully persuaded them to go along with his plan. In a situation such as this, there might also be some group pressure to abide by the decision of the majority to disrobe. This is an example of an area where members should be given advance notice, before they sign up for a group, so that they can make an informed decision whether they want to take the risk of baring both their soul and their body. At this point, ask yourself what you would say or do if you attended a group or a workshop and, without previous notice, the leader asked the group to disrobe.

Exploring the Advantages of and Misconceptions about Groups

We typically devote some time at the pregroup session to a discussion of both the advantages of therapeutic groups and certain misconceptions about the group process.

Advantages. Therapeutic groups have certain distinct advantages over other intervention strategies:

▪ Participants are able to explore their style of relating to others and to learn more effective social skills.

▪ The group setting offers support for new behavior and encourages experimentation. Members can try out new behaviors and decide whether they want to incorporate them into their outside life.

▪ There is a re-creation of the everyday world in some groups, particularly if the membership is diverse with respect to age, interests, race, cultural background, socioeconomic status, and type of problem. When this heterogeneity occurs, a member has the advantage of interacting with a wide range of personalities, and the feedback received can be richer and more diverse than that available in a one-to-one setting.

- Certain factors that foster personal growth are more likely to be present in groups. For instance, members have the opportunity to learn about themselves through the experience of others; to experience emotional closeness and caring, which encourage them to be open; and to identify with the struggles of other members. The group setting provides an optimal arena for participants to discover how they affect others. A member (Susan) may complain that she feels isolated from people. Through interaction with members in the group, she is likely to become aware of what she is doing to create her loneliness and isolation. If she typically sits apart from the group, rarely says much, and often appears critical, other members may respond to her by saying that they are afraid of her and that they are staying away from her. She may be rejecting others before they have a chance to reject her.

Misconceptions. Some misconceptions about groups need to be critically appraised at the pregroup meeting:

- "Groups are for everyone." Not all people are suited to groups. Some clients are too suspicious, too hostile, or too fragile to benefit from a group experience. Some can be psychologically damaged by attending certain groups. Before a person is accepted into a group, such factors need to be carefully weighed by both the counselor and the client to increase the chances that the person will benefit from such an experience.
- "Working out my problems in the group will automatically solve my problems at home." Participants need to be aware that acquiring insights and skills in handling their concerns within the group does not mean that they can apply this learning to their everyday life without facing some obstacles. In the group they may have received positive feedback and support for daring to change. When they return home, they may well meet with resistance and antagonism when they deviate from old and familiar ways. Others may have an investment in keeping them as they were, because that way they're more predictable and more easily controlled. The depression that so often follows the feeling of being able to conquer the world is a reality that participants need to examine.
- "The goal of a group is that members will leave it feeling close and loving toward everyone in the group." The genuine closeness that can be achieved in an intensive group can be the result of shared struggles, and the worth of this emotional bond is not to be discounted. However, the basic purpose of a group is *not* to create a loving bond among all the members. Rather, intimacy should be considered a by-product of meaningful work in a group that leads to increased intimacy in one's outside life. Unfortunately, some members use groups as a vehicle for expressing their problems, in the hope that they will be understood and totally accepted, and make little or no attempt to do what is necessary to substantially change their life. It is important to remember that a group experience is not an end in itself.

- "Groups are places where people are attacked and defenses are torn down." We frequently hear people express the fear that they will leave the group defenseless and emotionally wounded. Leaders must respect necessary defenses and not strip them away. Our hope is that people can learn that rigid defenses are not always necessary and that they can safely remove unnecessary walls that separate them from others. When people become more authentic, even though they may be vulnerable, they discover a core of strength within themselves. We certainly don't support the approach of some groups, in which ruthless attacks are seen as a desirable way of stripping away a person's defenses.

- "Groups make people more miserable and unhappy, because their problems surface." To some extent this statement is true. When people face the truth about their life, pain and conflict may be the result. However, people need not remain fixated in this unhappy condition. Once people recognize those aspects of themselves or their environment that are contributing to this misery, they can take some decisive steps to change. Continued group counseling or individual therapy can be useful in assisting people to work through the personal conflicts that surface in the group.

- "Groups tell people how to be." Instead of merely accepting the dictates or suggestions of others, successful group members acquire an increased ability to look within themselves for their own answers to the present and future problems that life poses. Groups are neither places to dispense advice nor means of indoctrinating people into agreement with a particular philosophy of life. The group experience can challenge members to reexamine their philosophy and make the modifications they desire.

- "Group pressure forces people to lose a sense of identity." Although it is true that group pressure can be used in destructive ways, it can also be used constructively. Some pressure is almost inevitable, for there are expectations to be honest, to get involved personally, to interact with people in the group in direct and open ways, and to reveal oneself. What is important is how leaders and members deal with the basic pressure that is part of a group experience. Pressure does not have to be viewed as something that "cracks" a person and forces submission. Instead, it can be the impetus for members to face and work through conflicts they might otherwise avoid.

- "Only people who are emotionally disturbed join groups." There is a misconception that all therapy or counseling, either individual or group, is designed to cure people of mental and emotional illness. It is true that some groups are aimed at helping a disturbed population find some relief; but there are also many groups for developmental purposes —groups designed to help people recognize their potential and remove blocks to personal growth. Healthy people can use the group experience as an aid in viewing themselves more honestly and critically and seeing themselves as others see them. Many groups focus on a well population and use therapy for preventive as well as remedial purposes.

- "Groups are artificial and unreal." Some criticize groups on the ground that they operate in an unrealistic context. We believe that a group setting can be more real than so-called real life, in the sense that people shed many of the pretenses that characterize their everyday interactions. Certain aspects of this experience may seem artificial, but if the participants can discover ways of putting into practice what was learned in the group, the real value of their experience is undeniable. That some groups never transcend an artificial level does not necessarily mean that what is experienced in all groups is artificial.

For his long-term outpatient groups, Yalom (1985) provides an overview of the interpersonal theory of therapy and shows members that many of their current problems are linked with past personal relationships. He also clears up misconceptions about group therapy by teaching members how to involve themselves in active and responsible ways in the group sessions. In sum, he shows them how group therapy can be a rich arena for learning more about their interpersonal style and how they can use the group as a place to acquire and practice more effective interpersonal skills. For his short-term inpatient groups, Yalom (1983) modifies his approach to preparation, because most hospital stays are too short to allow for much pretraining. Instead, he does this preparation as an initial part of the therapy group. He invites members who have been in the group for a time to join him in the orientation process for newcomers.

The Values and Limitations of Pregroup Preparation

As can be seen by the emphasis we give to the preparation of individuals for group membership, we endorse this type of orientation. Some practitioners, in contrast, promote ambiguity and view pregroup structuring as counterproductive to the evolution of the group. For instance, psychoanalytic practitioners believe that ambiguity among clients leads to anxiety, so that the group provides a natural setting in which to observe and work with the defenses that the members develop as a way of coping with their anxiety. Also, many T-groups, or laboratory groups, emphasize studying the group process that unfolds as a result of minimal structuring or leadership on the part of the counselor. The interactions that occur within these groups, such as members' assuming of leadership functions or dealing with conflict and the struggle for control, produce material for discussion and exploration by the group. Some practitioners believe that too much advance preparation "pollutes" the process and prevents members from creating their own structure.

The pregroup preparation that we advocate is a form of structuring aimed at helping the members focus and express whatever thoughts and feelings they are having about the here-and-now interactions at the beginning of a group experience. This preparation assists members in deciding what they want from a group and gives them some tools to attain their goals. The basic aim of this preparation is to increase the chances that the group will become a cohesive, productive, and autonomous unit that will let members engage in productive work.

Research Findings

Practitioners often give positive reports of their particular approach to pregroup preparation. Reviews of the literature are generally favorable concerning the benefits of advance preparation. There are studies suggesting that members who understand what behaviors are expected of them tend to be more successful. Preparatory training increases the chances of successful outcomes because it reduces the anxiety that participants often experience during the initial sessions and provides a framework for understanding the group process, according to these studies (Bednar, Melnick, & Kaul, 1974; Borgers & Tyndall, 1982; Burlingame & Fuhriman, 1990; Fuhriman & Burlingame, 1990; Meadow, 1988; Piper & Perrault, 1989; Stockton & Morran, 1982).

Borgers and Tyndall (1982) describe three ways of preparing members for a group experience: cognitive learning, vicarious experiencing, and behavioral practice. With cognitive methods, members acquire basic factual information and performance information. Vicarious experiencing includes the use of tape recordings, videotapes, and films to model desired group behavior. Behavioral practice involves members' engaging in structured activities. Borgers and Tyndall conclude that perhaps the most useful form of pregroup preparation consists of a combination of these approaches, fitting the methods to the characteristics of the clients. Their conclusions have some research support. Studies have consistently shown that groups receiving both instruction and modeling do better than those receiving only one treatment or neither (Stockton & Morran, 1982).

A good deal of research has been conducted into the value of pretherapy preparation for both individual and group psychotherapy. The overwhelming consensus of reviewers in both cases is that role preparation appears to affect early therapeutic processes positively and also seems to be linked to clients' later improvement (Fuhriman & Burlingame, 1990). Pregroup orientation appears to be a standard practice for members of short-term therapy groups. A number of factors make such orientation sessions necessary for these clients: the diversity of members in a typical group, the range of personal concerns, the different settings, the time-limited framework, and the unfamiliarity of the group format. The content of this pregroup orientation reflects the perspective of leaders who conduct short-term group therapy. It sets the stage for the later development of the leader/member and member/member therapeutic relationships. The preparation activities in short-term groups are directed toward facilitating the most effective use of the time that is available (Burlingame & Fuhriman, 1990).

Meadow (1981) contends that preparing clients for a group before the first meeting is essential. She stresses that this preparatory activity should include informing clients about the purpose, process, and rules of the group and clarifying any inaccurate expectations that potential clients may have about being members. Meadow (1988) conducted an empirical test to assess the theoretical assumptions underlying the preparation of members by a series of pregroup interviews. Her study tested three hypotheses. The first was that clients who had participated in the interviews would have more realistic expectations and perceptions of group membership. The second hypothesis was that clients who had had the interviews would demonstrate a clearer understanding of the group's purpose than those who had not. Both of these hypotheses were supported by her tests. The third hypothesis was that clients who had had pregroup interviews would identify personal goals that were more compatible with the purpose of the group as it was defined by the group leader. This hypothesis was not supported. One of the implications of this study is that a method can be devised for helping group leaders structure pregroup interviews in ways that are consistent with the theoretical literature and with the principles of social work.

In their review of the literature on pretherapy preparation for group members, Piper and Perrault (1989) found that practitioners had a core of long-term objectives. These goals included maintaining attendance, enhancing the process and outcome of a group, and increasing the level of satisfaction within a group. To obtain these objectives of pregroup preparation, leaders used a variety of cognitive, affective, and behavioral strategies. The cognitive procedures involved creating accurate expectations about desirable behavior by members, customary roles of therapists, typical events in therapy, and realistic outcomes. The affective strategies had the aim of reducing anxiety and establishing positive interpersonal bonds. Increasing clients' participation, self-disclosure, and interpersonal feedback are examples of behavioral strategies.

Piper and Perrault's review involved 20 studies during the period from 1962 to 1987. Despite the widespread positive endorsement found in the clinical literature, their survey did *not* show impressive benefits in process and outcome stemming from such preparation. They concluded that there were not enough methodologically strong research studies to clearly answer questions about the relationship between particular forms of pretraining and specific process and outcome effects. Although they assert that the effects of pretherapy preparation on outcome have been overstated, they concede that there is evidence to suggest that there are benefits with respect to promoting regular attendance, increasing the number of clients who remain in the group, and enhancing the therapy process.

In concluding this discussion of pretherapy preparation, let us caution against bombarding the members with too much information at the preliminary meeting. Many of the topics that relate to participation in the group can be handed out in written form, and clients can be encouraged to raise any questions or concerns they have after they have read this material.

It should be emphasized that the theoretical and research literature *generally* supports the value of systematically preparing members for a group experience (Meadow, 1988). Many groups that get stuck at an early developmental stage do so because the foundations were poorly laid. What is labeled as "resistance" on the part of group members is often the result of a failure on the leader's part to adequately explain what groups are about, how they function, and how members can become actively involved.

Building Evaluation into Group Work

If you do group work in a community agency or an institution, you may be required to demonstrate the efficacy of your treatment approach. Federal and state grants typically stipulate measures for accountability. Thus, it is essential in most settings that you devise procedures for assessing the degree to which clients benefit from the group experience, much as some of the studies just described did. In your proposals for groups, we suggest that you include the procedures you intend to use to evaluate both the progress of individual members and the outcomes of the group as a unit.

There is no need to be intimidated by the idea of incorporating a research spirit into your practice. Nor do you have to think exclusively in terms of rigorous empirical research. One alternative to traditional scientific methods is evaluation research, which aims at gathering data that can be useful in making improvements within the structure of a group. *Member-specific measures* are used to assess changes in attitudes and behaviors of individual clients. It is possible to develop your own devices for evaluating the degree to which members attain their goals. *Group-specific measures* assess the changes that are common to all members of the group, such as increased self-awareness, decreased anxiety, and improved personal relationships. Many of these measures are available in standardized form, or you can adapt them to suit your needs. The practice of building evaluation into your group programs is not only a useful procedure for accountability purposes, but it can also help you sharpen your leadership skills and see more clearly changes that you might want to make in the format for future groups. (The problems of combining research and practice are addressed in some detail in Chapter 8.)

Co-Leader Issues at the Pregroup Stage

If you are co-leading a group, the central issue at this early stage is that you and your co-leader have equal responsibility in forming the group and getting it going. Both of you need to be clear about the purpose of the group, what you hope to accomplish with the time you have, and how you will meet your objectives. Cooperation and basic agreement between you and your co-leader will be essential in getting your group off to a good start.

This cooperative effort might well start with your meeting to develop a proposal, and ideally both of you will present it to the appropriate authority. This practice ensures that designing and originating the group are not solely one leader's responsibility. This shared responsibility for organizing the group continues with the various tasks that we've outlined in this chapter. You and your co-leader will be a team when it comes to matters such as announcing and recruiting for membership; conducting screening interviews and agreeing on whom to include and exclude; agreeing on basic ground rules, policies, and procedures and presenting them to the members; preparing members and orienting them to the group process; and sharing in the practical matters that must be handled to form a group.

It may not always be possible to share equally in all the responsibilities. Although it is *ideal* that both leaders interview the applicants, time constraints may make this impractical. Tasks may have to be divided, but both leaders should be involved as much as possible in making the group a reality. If one leader does a disproportionate share of the work, the other can easily develop a passive role in the leadership of the group once it begins.

If co-leaders do not know each other or if they don't have much sense of how the other works professionally, they are likely to get off to a poor start. Simply walking into a group unprepared, without any initial planning or acquaintance with your co-leader, is to invite future problems. Just as it is critical that members be prepared for entering a group, the leaders must be psychologically prepared and oriented to each other's style. We have a few suggestions that co-leaders can consider before the initial session:

- Make the time to at least get to know something about each other personally and professionally before you begin leading together.
- Talk about your theoretical orientations and how each of you perceives groups. What kind of group work has each of you experienced? In what ways will your theory and leadership styles influence the direction the group takes?
- Is either of you concerned or having reservations about leading with the other? What might get in your way in your dealings with each other? How can you use your separate talents productively as a team? How can your differences in leadership style have a complementary effect and actually enhance the group?
- Each of you can talk about your own strengths and weaknesses, with implications for how they will affect your leading together. With this knowledge you may be able to forestall some potential problems.

- For the two of you to work together well as team, you should be in agreement on the ethical aspects of group work. What does each of you consider to be unethical practice, and are there differences? The ethical issues touched on both in this chapter and in the preceding chapter need to be discussed.

Although these suggestions do not represent all the possible areas that co-leaders can explore in getting to know each other, they do provide a basis for focusing on significant topics.

How We Prepare for Groups

Because we believe that involvement, enthusiasm, inventiveness, and caring are important in group leaders, we try to be physically and psychologically ready for every new group or workshop we lead. We have found that in order to avoid becoming programmed group leaders, we must spend some time away from our daily routines thinking about the group that will shortly be convening.

Whether the group is a weekend workshop of skills training for counselors and teachers, a couples group, or a weeklong, intensive personal-growth group, we generally arrange to spend a day or at least several hours together before we begin. Not only is it important for us to reflect on the goals and structure that we would like a particular workshop to have, it is also important for us to talk about ourselves with each other. How are things between us? Are there any sources of friction between us that might interfere with the progress of the group? Do we feel good enough about ourselves and each other to devote our energy to the demanding tasks of group leadership, or will our unspoken conflicts drain off our vitality and energy? Are we feeling nurtured by each other and excited by the prospect of working together?

Our summer residential workshops come after a busy school year, and so we feel a need to shift gears and become psychologically ready for them. Sometimes at the end of spring we realize that we've both been so involved with the demands of our separate projects that we've neglected to make contact with each other or failed to resolve certain grievances between us. Even though we may not work through all of our conflicts, we do attempt to air our grievances so that our needs will be known to each other.

We don't want to give the impression that a husband and wife who lead groups together must present an ideal image of togetherness and self-actualization. We find that being ourselves, with our individual problems and interpersonal differences, doesn't necessarily block our effectiveness in leading groups. In fact, by being honest with each other and our groups about our strengths and limitations, we're able to provide a model of behavior that facilitates group movement. However, we do mean to emphasize that our job is taxing; it requires our full attention.

We can't afford to divert energy to an unspoken resentment between us. If there were a crisis in our relationship, it would be very difficult for us to function effectively and be there fully for the group. And we don't believe we would be justified in using the group time for our therapy. To bring our unfinished business into a group we were leading and attempt to work it through would be to unfairly burden the group. If there are major difficulties or differences between us, we evaluate the wisdom of attempting to co-lead at that particular time.

We believe not only that our relationship should be in good shape but also that we must feel in good psychological shape as individuals. If we're feeling ineffectual, overworked, overtired, unappreciated, depressed, highly anxious, or in a state of personal crisis, then our effectiveness as leaders will be seriously diminished. We know how much physical and emotional energy leading an intensive group workshop generally takes, and if we're not personally nourished before the group, the danger exists that we'll only use the group to satisfy our own needs. But if we feel ready when we enter a group, we derive additional energy from our giving and receiving. The questions we ask ourselves before we begin a new group are:

- Am I really looking forward to beginning this group?
- Do I feel alive and enthusiastic?
- How personally effective have I been feeling lately?
- Have my projects been rewarding?
- Are there certain internal conflicts that are haunting me and that need to be resolved before I attempt to work therapeutically with others?
- Am I liking the quality of my own life and the direction it's taking, or am I dissatisfied with the choices I've made?
- Am I willing to do for myself what I might be encouraging group members to do?
- Am I willing to face myself honestly, accept what I see, make decisions to change, and act on my decisions?

Before most of the groups for adults that we do, we ask the members to write a paper telling about significant aspects of themselves, about their personal goals for the group, and about the nature of the personal struggles that they hope to explore in the group. This writing exercise not only helps the group members get a clear focus on the areas they most want to understand and change but also provides us with their subjective view of what they want for themselves from this group. As we read these papers, we look for common themes and give some thought to how we might work with these topics. We do not bring up specific issues or break confidentiality as we are working in the group by saying "In your paper you wrote . . . " Instead, we encourage members to initiate the kind of work they want to do; they take responsibility for what they will explore.

Most of all, we want to be looking forward to the experience at the initial session. We hope to direct our full attention to effectively and creatively leading a group, and we find that preparing ourselves pays off for both the group and ourselves.

Pregroup Stage: Summary

Member Functions and Possible Problems

It is important that members joining a group possess the knowledge necessary for making an informed decision concerning their participation. Members should be active in the process of deciding if a group is right for them. Following are some issues that pertain to the role of members at this stage:

- Members should know all the specifics about a group that might have an impact on them.
- Members need to learn how to screen the group leader to determine if this group with this particular leader is appropriate for them at this time.
- Members need to be involved in the decision to include or exclude them from the group.
- Members need to prepare themselves for the upcoming group by thinking about what they want from the experience and how they can attain their goals.
- Members can be given pretests, which can be either standardized instruments or devices designed by the leader, to assess values, perceptions, attitudes, and personal problems.

  Problems can arise if potential members:

- are coerced into a group
- do not have adequate information about the nature of the group and thus do not know what they are getting themselves into
- are passive and give no thought to what they want or expect from the group

Leader Functions

The main tasks of group leaders during the formation of a group include:

- developing a clearly written proposal for the formation of a group
- presenting the proposal to the proper authorities and getting the idea accepted
- announcing the group in such a way as to inform prospective participants
- conducting pregroup interviews for screening and orientation purposes

- making decisions concerning selection of members and composing the group
- organizing the practical details necessary to launch a successful group
- getting parental permission, if necessary
- preparing psychologically for leadership tasks, and meeting with the co-leader (if any)
- arranging for a preliminary group session for the purposes of getting acquainted, orientation to ground rules, and preparation of the members for a successful group experience

Exercises

Exercise in Group Planning

Select a particular type of group (personal-growth, counseling, or other) and a target population (children, adolescents, or adults). Keeping in mind the group you've selected, answer the following questions. The purpose of the exercise is to give you an idea of the questions you need to ask yourself while planning your group.

1. What is your role in this group?
2. What do you most want to occur in your group? State your purposes simply and concretely.
3. Would you form a contract with your group, and, if so, what would be the essence of the contract? Would you expect each member to develop a contract?
4. Mention a few ground rules or policies you feel would be essential for your group.
5. How can you determine whether you have the skills necessary to lead this particular type of group?
6. What is the focus of your group? (Is it didactic? experiential? remedial? developmental?)
7. Would you accept only volunteer group members? Why or why not?
8. What characteristics would people have to have to be included? What is the rationale?
9. What procedures and techniques would you use in your group? Are your procedures practical? Are they related to the goals and the population of the group?
10. What evaluation methods might you use to determine the effectiveness of your approaches? Are your evaluation procedures appropriate to the purposes of your group?

Interviewing Exercises

1. Screening-Interview Exercise. One person in the class volunteers to play the role of a group leader conducting a screening interview for members for a particular type of group. The group leader conducts a ten-minute interview with a potential member, played by another member. Then the prospective client tells the group leader how he or she felt and what impact the group leader made. The group leader shares his or her observations about the prospective group member and tells whether the person would have been accepted into the group and why or why not. This exercise can be repeated with another client so that the group leader can benefit from the feedback and try some new ideas. Several students can experience the role of the interviewer and the role of the interviewee. It is essential that feedback be given so that people can improve their skills in conducting screening interviews. The rest of the class can offer feedback and suggestions for improvement after each interview.

2. Group-Member Interview. We have recommended that prospective group members examine the leader somewhat critically before joining a group. This exercise is just like the preceding one, except that the group members asks the questions of the leader, trying to learn things about the leader and the group that will allow a wise decision about whether to join. After ten minutes the leader shares observations and reactions, and then the member tells whether he or she would join this leader's group and explains any reservations. Again, the class is invited to make observations.

CHAPTER 4

Initial Stage of a Group

FOCUS QUESTIONS

1. What guidelines might you offer to help members get the most from a group experience?
2. What ways can you think of to assist members in creating trust in the leader and among themselves? What role do you see yourself as having in establishing trust during the initial stage of a group?
3. What are some specific ways to help members identify and clarify their goals for group participation?
4. If you were meeting with your co-leader during the early stage of a new group, what are some topics you'd most want to discuss?
5. What sort of resistance behaviors might you encounter during the first few sessions?
6. What group norms, or standards, would you most want to establish?
7. What are some ways to help a group develop cohesion at the first few meetings?
8. What are a few things you would attend to in opening each group session?
9. What ideas do you have for effectively bringing each session to closure?
10. How much structuring do you think is helpful for a group to accomplish its tasks? To what degree might you assume the responsibility for providing structure in a group you lead or co-lead?

Introduction

This chapter contains many examples of teaching members about how groups function. We describe the characteristics of a group in its early stage, explore the topic of establishing goals for the group, and discuss the formation of group norms and the beginnings of group cohesion. Also treated are the roles of the leader and members in creating trust, the leader's skills in opening and closing group meetings, and the leader's responsibility for providing a structure that will help members attain their goals.

Helping Members Get the Most from a Group Experience

Some behaviors and attitudes promote a cohesive and productive group —that is, a group in which meaningful self-exploration takes place and in which honest and appropriate feedback is given and received. We begin orienting and preparing members during the preliminary session, but we typically find that time allows only an introduction to the ways in which clients can get the most from their group experience. Consequently, during the initial phase of the group's evolution we devote some time to teaching members the basics of group process, especially how they can involve themselves as active participants. We emphasize that they will benefit from the experience in direct proportion to how much they invest of themselves, both in the group and in practicing on the outside what they are learning in the sessions.

We do not present the following guidelines as a lecture in one sitting. We begin by giving members written information about their participation in the group. We also allocate time to discuss these topics as they occur naturally within the sessions, which increases the odds that members will be receptive to thinking about how they can best participate.

We encourage you to use these guidelines as a catalyst for thinking about your own approach to preparing members. Reflecting on this material may help you develop an approach that suits your own personality and leadership style and that is appropriate for the groups you lead. The following suggestions are written from the leader's point of view and directed to the members.

Guidelines for Members

Learn to Help Establish Trust. Participants often wait for some other person to take the first risk or to make some gesture of trust. Members can enhance their experience in the group by helping to create a trusting climate. They can do this, paradoxically, by revealing their lack of trust. Members can gain from initiating a discussion that will allow genuine trust to develop.

Example: Harold was older than most of the other group members, and he was afraid that they would not be able to empathize with him, that they would exclude him from activities, that they would view him as an outsider—a parent figure—and that he would not be able to open up. After he disclosed these fears, many members gave Harold praise for his willingness to reveal his mistrust. His disclosure, and the response to it, stimulated others to express some of their concerns. This sharing stimulated trust in the entire group by making it clear that it was appropriate to express fears. Instead of being rejected, Harold was accepted and appreciated, for he was willing to make a significant part of himself known to the rest of the group.

Express Persistent Feelings. There are times when members keep their feelings of boredom, anger, or disappointment a secret from the rest of the group. It is most important that persistent feelings related to the group process be aired. We often make statements to members such as "If you are feeling detached and withdrawn, let it be known" or "If you are experiencing chronic anger or irritation toward others in this group, don't keep these feelings to yourself."

Example: In a group of adolescents that met once a week for ten weeks, Margaret waited until the third session to disclose that she didn't trust either the members or the leader, that she was angry because she felt pressured to participate, that she was scared to express what she felt because she might look foolish, and that she really didn't know what was expected of her as a group member. She had experienced these feelings since the initial session but had withheld them from the group. The leader let Margaret know how important it was for her to reveal these persistent feelings of distrust in order for them to be explored and resolved.

Beware of Misusing Jargon.   It is unfortunate that the group movement offers another way of being dishonest. Some people learn a new language that can remove them from their direct experiences. Take, for example, phrases such as "I can really relate to you," "I want to get closer to my feelings," "I get good vibes from you," "I'd like to stop playing all these games with myself," "Let me be in the present moment," and "I have to be spontaneous." If terms such as *relate to, get closer to,* and *vibes* aren't clearly defined and reserved for certain circumstances, the quality of communication will be poor. People who learn to use this vague language may deceive themselves into thinking that they are self-actualized. What a refreshing experience it is to talk with people who have had no group experience and who are able to say in plain English what it is they want and why they decided to get involved in a group.

We encourage members to use descriptive language by asking them what they mean by "really relating to that " or by asking them to clarify what feelings they want to express. When members speak in hazy terms and use jargon, we are likely to ask them to imagine that they are talking to a foreigner who has little command of English or to repeat what they said in terms that a 10-year-old child could understand.

Related to misusing jargon is the way in which members' use of language sometimes distances them from themselves and from others. For example, when people say "I can't" instead of "I won't" or when they use many qualifiers in their speech ("maybe," "perhaps," "but," "I guess"), we ask them to be aware of how they are contributing to their powerlessness by their choice of words. This practice also applies to the use of a generalized "you" or "people" when "I" is what is meant. The more members can assume responsibility for their speech, the more they can reclaim some of that power they have lost through impersonal modes of expression.

Example: "People are usually afraid to talk openly in the group," Valerie said. "They feel threatened and scared." The leader intervened by asking Valerie to repeat everything she had just said but to substitute "I" for the general impersonal words "people" and "they." The leader asked her whether using "I" was closer to the truth of what she really wanted to convey. After all, she could speak with authority about her own feelings, but she could not be an expert about others' feelings.

Decide for Yourself How Much to Disclose. Group members are sometimes led to believe that the more they disclose about themselves, the better. They are asked not to think about the need for privacy. Though self-disclosure is an important tool in the group process, it is up to each participant to decide what aspects of his or her life to reveal. This principle cannot be stressed too much, for the idea that members will have to "tell everything" contributes to the resistance of many people to becoming participants in a group.

The most useful kind of disclosure is unrehearsed. It expresses present concern and may entail some risk. As participants open up to a group, they have fears about how other people will receive what they reveal. If a member shares that he is shy, often quiet, and afraid to speak up in the group, the other members will have a frame of reference for more accurately interpreting and reacting to his lack of participation. Had he not spoken up, both the leader and other members would have been more likely to misinterpret his behavior.

Members should be cautioned, however, about the dangers of "paying membership dues" by striving to reveal the biggest secret. Self-disclosure is not a process of "letting everything hang out" and of making oneself psychologically naked. Let members know time and again that they are responsible for deciding what, how much, and when they will share personal conflicts pertaining to their everyday life.

Example: In a weekly group in an agency, Luis, a minority client, did not want to talk about his sexual relationship with his wife. One of the cultural values he grew up with was to keep such personal concerns private. He did talk about how difficult it was for him to identify what he felt, let alone express feelings to others. Although he did not feel comfortable in discussing sexuality, he was willing to share with the group his difficulties in letting himself experience feelings of sadness, compassion, jealousy, and fright. Luis did not want to go through life as an unfeeling person. Other group members respected him for his willingness to tell them why he was not ready to talk about his sexual relationship. Because of this understanding that he felt from other members, he was encouraged to share more of his feelings of fear and sadness.

Be an Active Participant, Not an Observer. A participant might say: "I'm not the talkative type. It's hard for me to formulate my thoughts, and I'm afraid I don't express myself well. So I usually don't say anything in the group. But I listen to what others are saying, and I learn by observing. I really don't think I have to be talking all the time to get something out of these sessions." Although it is true that members can learn by observing interactions and reacting nonverbally, their learning will tend to be limited. If they assume the stance of not contributing, others will never come to know them, and they can easily feel cheated and angry at being the object of others' perhaps flawed observations.

Another way in which some members keep themselves passively on the fringe of group activity is by continually saying "I have no real problems in my life at this time, so I don't have much to contribute to the group." We attempt to teach these members to share their reactions to their experience in the group as well as to let others know how they are being affected. Members who choose to share little about events outside of the group can actively participate by keeping themselves open to being affected by other clients. Leaders can contribute to group cohesion by helping those members who feel that they have nothing to contribute recognize that they are depriving fellow members if they do not at least share how they are reacting to what others are saying.

Example: When Thelma was asked what she wanted from the group, she replied: "I haven't really given it that much thought. I figured I'd just be spontaneous and wait to see what happens." The leader let Thelma know that sometimes other people's work might indeed evoke some of her own issues and that she might spontaneously react. However, the leader taught her that it was important for her to think about and to bring up the concerns that initially brought her to the group. As the sessions progressed, Thelma did learn to let the other members know what she wanted from them. Instead of being a passive observer without any clear goals, who would be content to wait for things to happen to her, she began to take the initiative. She showed that she wanted to talk about how lonely she was, how desperate and inadequate she frequently felt, how fearful she was of being weak with men, and how she dreaded facing her world every morning. As she learned to focus on her wants, she found that she could benefit from her weekly sessions.

Expect Some Disruption of Your Life. Participants in therapeutic groups should be given the warning that their involvement may complicate their outside life for a time. As a result of group experiences, members tend to assume that the people in their life will be both ready and willing to make significant changes. It can be shocking for members to discover that others thought they were "just fine" the way they were, and the friction that results may make it more difficult than ever to modify familiar patterns. Therefore, it is important for members to be prepared for the fact that not everyone will like or accept some of the changes they want to make. Perhaps some relationships will be discontinued and some new ones formed.

Example: Ron came away from his group with the awareness that he was frightened of his wife, that he consistently refrained from expressing his wants to her, and that he related to her as he would to a protective mother. He feared that if he asserted himself with her, she would leave. In the group he not only became disgusted with his dependent style but also decided that he would treat his wife as an equal and give up his hope of having her become his mother. Ron's wife did not cooperate with his valiant efforts to change the nature of their relationship. The more assertive he became, the more disharmony there was in his home. While he was trying to become independent, his wife was struggling to to keep their relationship the way it was; she was not willing to respond differently to him.

Realize That You Don't Have to Be Sick to Benefit from a Group. It is not uncommon to find members questioning the value of the group and being somewhat skeptical about its ability to help them. Some people shy away from counseling groups because they believe that groups are only for people with severe emotional problems. Members should be taught that a minor "tune-up" is possible without a major overhaul. Groups can offer the opportunity to examine how past decisions are influencing one's present life. Effective groups provide both the support and the challenge necessary for evaluating one's direction and for making changes if desired.

    Example: Sid was embarrassed over having joined a group. He accepted the notion that any kind of therapy was for people with serious emotional and mental disorders. Gradually, through the example of fellow group members, he found that struggling for change was not sick but, rather, courageous. He then felt freer to use the group as a place to try out new behavior, and he became open to working with internal blocks that were preventing him from forming close ties with those he cared about.

Expect to Discover Positive Aspects of Yourself. A common fear about therapy is that one will discover how unlovable, how empty, how hopeless, or how powerless one is. More often than not, though, people in groups begin to realize that they're lovable, that they can control their own destiny, and that they have talents they never knew about. Members often explore intense feelings of pain in a group. Unrecognized and unexpressed pain is blocking them from living a truly joyous life. It is through releasing and working through these painful experiences that they begin to reclaim a joyful dimension of themselves. For instance, many participants experience an inner strength, discover a real wit and sense of humor, create moving poetry or songs, or dare for the first time to show a creative side of themselves that they have kept hidden from others and from themselves. A group experience, then, can show people a positive and creative side of themselves.

    Example: Frank expressed the positive side of the group experience rather poetically when he said: "I have learned that there are lots of beautiful rose bushes with pretty flowers, and on those bushes are thorns. I'd never trade the struggle and pain I had to go through to appreciate the joy of smelling and touching those roses. Both the roses and the thorns are a part of life."

Listen Closely and Discriminatingly. Group members should listen carefully to what the other members say about them, neither accepting it wholesale nor rejecting it outright. Members should listen discriminatingly, deciding for themselves what does and what doesn't apply to them. Before they respond, they can be asked to quiet down, to let what is being said to them sink in, and to take note of how it is affecting them. Members are sometimes busy formulating responses while others are still speaking to them. They cannot fully comprehend what is being communicated to them if they are not totally engaged in listening.

Example: In an adolescent group, members told Jack that it was hard for them to listen to his many stories. Although some of his stories were interesting, they gave no clue to the nature of his struggles, which were why he was in the group. Other members told him that it was easier to hear what he was saying when he talked about himself. When Jack became defensive and angry and denied that he had been acting that way, he could have been asked by the leader or members to think over the feedback before he so rigorously rejected it.

Pay Attention to Consistent Feedback. A person may get similar feedback from many people in different groups yet may still dismiss it as invalid. Although it is important to discriminate, it is also important to realize that a message that has been received from a variety of people is likely to have a degree of validity.

Example: In several groups Dan heard people tell him that he didn't seem interested in what they had to say and that he appeared distant and detached. The members said that although he was physically in the room, he often looked at the ceiling and sighed, moved his chair away from the circle, yawned, and sometimes even took a short nap. In short, they felt that he had no interest in them and that it was difficult for them to get close to him. Dan was surprised by this feedback and insisted that his behavior in the group was very different from his behavior in his outside life—that on the outside he felt close to people and was interested and involved. It seems unlikely that someone could be so different in the two areas, however, and the leader intervened with: "You may be different in here than you are on the outside. But would you be willing to monitor how people respond to you away from here and be open to noticing if any of the feedback given to you might indeed fit you?" The leader's response eliminated unnecessary argumentation and debates over who was right.

Don't Categorize Yourself. During the initial stage of a group, members often present themselves to the other clients in terms of a role, one that they dislike but at the same time appear to cling to. For instance, we've heard people introduce themselves as "the group mother," "the walled-off and impenetrable one," "the fragile person who can't stand confrontation," and "the one in this group whom nobody will like." There are times when a person who views himself or herself as a "walled off" would like to be different. What is important is for people not to fatalistically pin labels on themselves and for the group not to fulfill the expectations and thereby even further convince members that they are what they fear. It may be helpful for group leaders to remind themselves and the members of how certain participants can be pegged with labels such as "the monopolist," "the storyteller," "the intellectualizer," "the withdrawn one," "the obsessive/compulsive one," and so on. People may exhibit behaviors that characterize them in one way or another, and it is appropriate to confront them with these actions during the group. But this confronting can be done without cementing people into rigid molds that become very difficult to shatter.

Example: Roz presented herself to the group as withdrawn and fragile. When she was asked how she would like to be different, she said she would like to speak out more often and more forcefully. She was willing to make a contract that required her to speak out and at least act as if she were strong. In this way she was able to challenge an old image that she had clung to and was able to experiment with a different type of behavior.

Other Suggestions for Group Members. Some additional guidelines that we bring up early in a group as they seem appropriate are briefly listed below:

- Be willing to do work both before and after a group. Consider keeping a journal as a supplement to the group experience. Create homework assignments as a way of putting your group learning into practice in everyday living.
- Develop self-evaluation skills as a way of assessing your progress in the group. Examples of questions you might ask are "Am I contributing to the group?" "Am I satisfied with what is occurring in the sessions? If not, what am I doing about it?" "Am I using in my life what I'm learning in my group?"
- Spend time in clarifying your own goals by reviewing specific issues you want to explore during the sessions. This can best be done by thinking about specific changes you want to make in your life and by deciding what you are willing to do both in and out of the group to bring about these changes.
- Concentrate on making personal and direct statements to others in your group, as opposed to giving advice, making interpretations, and asking impersonal questions. Instead of telling others how they are, let them know how they are affecting you.
- Realize that the real work consists of what you actually do outside of your group. Consider the group a means to an end, and give some time to thinking about what you will do with what you are learning. Expect some setbacks, and be aware that change may be slow and subtle. Do not expect one group alone to renovate your entire life.

Avoiding Too Much Teaching

As much as we've been stressing the value of preparing members about how groups function, we want to add that too much emphasis on teaching the group process can have a negative influence. All the spontaneous learning can be taken out of the group experience if members have been told too much of what to expect and have not been allowed to learn for themselves. Moreover, it is possible to foster a dependency on the structure and direction provided by the leader.

Our hope, as the group progresses, is that members will increasingly be able to function with less intervention from the leader. There is a delicate balance between providing too much structuring and failing to give enough structure and information, which results in confusion. Especially important, perhaps, is that the leader be aware of factors such as group cohesion, group norms, and group interactions at any given point. With this awareness the leader can decide when it is timely and useful to suggest a discussion of certain behavior that is occurring in the here and now.

We mentioned earlier that the stages in the life of a group are not rigidly defined but, rather, fluid and somewhat overlapping. What we teach and how we teach members about the group process have a lot to do with the level to which the group has evolved. Burlingame and Fuhriman (1990) have identified particular therapeutic characteristics that are primarily linked to the various stages of a group. During the beginning phase the most crucial factors are identification, universality, hope, and cohesion. During the middle phase, catharsis, cohesion, interpersonal learning, and insight are essential. As termination approaches, existential factors surface. Conceptualizing a group in this way provides an understanding of the group's dynamics and suggests appropriate strategies for intervention.

Group Characteristics at the Initial Stage

The central process during the early stage of a group is orientation and exploration. Members are getting acquainted, learning how the group functions, developing spoken and unspoken norms that will govern group behavior, exploring their feelings about the group, clarifying their expectations, identifying personal goals, and determining whether this group is a safe place. This stage is characterized by members' expressing fears and hesitations as well as hopes and expectations. The manner in which the leader deals with these reactions determines the degree of trust that can be established in the group.

Some Early Concerns

It is common at the initial sessions for the participants to be tentative and vague about what they hope to get from a group experience. Most members are uncertain about group norms and expected behavior; thus, there are moments of silence and awkwardness. Some may be impatient to "get things moving" and say that they feel like an airplane on the runway ready to take off. If your leadership style involves very little structure, the level of anxiety is likely to be high because of the ambiguity of the situation. In this case there will probably be considerable floundering and requests from members for direction. Members will say: "What are we supposed to be doing in here?" "Why don't we get down to business?" "I really don't know what we should be talking about."

If someone does volunteer a problem for discussion, chances are that other members will be oriented toward problem solving. Rather than encouraging the person to fully explore a struggle, some members are likely to offer suggestions and what they consider to be helpful advice. Though this process may at first appear to some as progress, participants will soon tire of ready-made solutions to every problem posed.

Eventually, conflict and anger may surface over a number of situations: some are angry at the lack of direction and at being allowed to simply "waste time"; some are growing impatient with those who are quick to tell others what to do; some are bored with social chit chat; some are resentful that a few are "doing all the talking" while others "say nothing"; and some are irritated over seemingly trivial matters. Regardless of what is triggering any intense feelings, it is crucial that you be sensitive to these reactions and encourage members to express them openly. If you react defensively or cut off the exploration of feelings that are expressed, a norm is being established that only certain feelings are acceptable. Trust can be lost or gained by the manner in which the leader handles the initial expression of any negative reactions. A member's internal dialogue might go thusly: "I'll take a chance and say what I'm thinking, and then I'll see how this leader and the others in here respond. If they're willing to listen to what I don't like, perhaps I can trust them with some deeper feelings."

Initial Resistance

During the initial phase of a group the members typically appear rather hesitant to get involved. In some cases the participants are highly suspicious of the group leader, fearing being manipulated. The participants may doubt that counseling groups can be of any real value in helping them solve their problems. Some clients will not believe that they have the freedom to talk about personally significant matters, and they may sit back and wait, almost expecting to listen to a lecture.

You need to be aware of cultural factors and how they influence clients' readiness to participate in a group. You may see members as "resistant" when they are only being true to their cultural heritage. Such members may believe that it is distasteful to talk publicly about private matters such as sexuality, family problems, and religious convictions. Those members who have cultural injunctions against talking about their family in a group may be reluctant to take part in role playing involving symbolically talking to their parents. You would do well to explore with these members how they could work with personal concerns in a way that would not violate their cultural norms. You can help such members by being aware of their cultural context and at the same time respectfully challenging them to consider modifying their values enough to allow them to explore personal issues. An important leadership function is assisting members in understanding how some of their initial resistance to self-disclosure relates to their cultural conditioning.

Regardless of the type of group, some initial resistance is to be expected in the early stage, even if people are eager to join in. This resistance can be manifested by complaints about the place of meeting or about what appear to be inconsequential matters. What members do talk about is likely to be less important than what they keep hidden inside them: their real fears about being in this group at this moment. Because resistance often arises from fearful expectations, identifying and discussing these fears at the early stage will benefit the whole group.

The following are some common fears that participants identify:

- Will I be accepted or rejected in here?
- Can I really say what I feel, or do I have to couch my words carefully so that others won't be offended?
- How will this group be any different from my interactions in daily situations?
- I'm afraid that others will judge me.
- Am I like other people in here?
- Will I feel pressured and pushed to perform?
- Will I be able to take risks in here?
- I'm afraid I'll look stupid.
- What if I find I'm abnormal?
- Will I tell too much about myself?
- I'm afraid I'll be withdrawn and passive.
- I fear being hurt.
- What if the group attacks me?
- I'm afraid of seeing my problems magnified.
- I'm afraid I'll become dependent on the group.
- What if I find out things about myself that I can't cope with?
- Will I physically hurt someone if I'm really open to my feelings?
- What if I go crazy?
- What will happen if I open up Pandora's box in the group?
- I'm afraid that I'll change and that those I'm close to won't like my changes.
- What if I'm asked to do something I don't want to do?

Because we recognize that such anxieties exist, we begin by encouraging the members to share and explore them. It sometimes helps in the building of a trusting atmosphere to ask people to split up into pairs and then to join to make groups of four. In this way members can choose others with whom to share their expectations, get acquainted, and talk about their fears or reservations. For some reason, talking with one other person and then merging with others is far less threatening to most participants than talking to the entire group. This subgroup approach seems to be an excellent icebreaker, and when the entire group gets together again, there is generally a greater willingness to interact.

Members are testing the waters at the early sessions to see if their concerns are being taken seriously and if the group is a safe place to express what they think and feel. If their reactions, positive or negative, are listened to with respect and acceptance, they have a basis to begin dealing with deeper aspects of themselves. A good way for you to start dealing with members' resistance is by listening to their fears and encouraging full expression of them. It is not helpful to say to an anxious member: "You don't need to be afraid in here. Nobody will hurt you." You cannot honestly make such promises, because some members may very well feel hurt by someone's response to them. What is far more important is that members know that you want them to say when they feel hurt and that you will not abandon them but will help them deal with whatever they are feeling.

Hidden Agendas

A common form of resistance in the group relates to the presence of a hidden agenda (an issue that affects the way the group is progressing but is not openly discussed). If encouragement to face these issues is lacking, the group process gets bogged down because the norm of being closed, cautious, and defensive replaces the norm of being open. We find that when there are unspoken reactions (by one member, several members, or the entire group), a common set of features emerges: trust is low, hostility emerges, people are guarded and are unwilling to take risks, we feel that we are working harder than the members, and there is a vague feeling that something just does not make sense.

In one group a member said "There's someone in this room I don't like." The entire group was affected by this comment, and several members later disclosed that they had wondered if they were the disliked person. It wasn't until the member was willing to deal directly with the conflict that he was having with another participant that the atmosphere in the room cleared up.

One group-counseling class, which we conducted as an experiential training workshop, was made up of graduate students in the military. These students held different ranks and included both officers and enlisted personnel. One participant discovered that his wife was working with the wife of another person in the group. The hidden agenda in this group class consisted of reactions related to the two men's different ranks and concerns over repercussions of what might be said in the group and how it might be used outside of the group. Others wondered if confidentiality would be honored. The concerns that members had were not initially discussed, in spite of our invitations. The polite and hesitant interactions eventually led to a high level of frustration among the participants. Not until one member took the risk of disclosing her real fears did others acknowledge what was really going on in the room.

Another group, of adolescents, displayed a great unwillingness to talk. The hidden agenda was the concern over rumors that some gossiping was taking place. The members who had the concern over confidentiality were reluctant to express their feelings because of a fear that others might condemn them for their lack of trust.

In our training and supervision workshops we have sometimes made an erroneous assumption that all the participants were there voluntarily. In several cases in various agencies, resistance was initially high because some members felt pressured by their superiors to attend. We encouraged them to express their grievances, after which they were more willing to become involved. Even though we were not able to remove the pressure they felt over having to attend, our willingness to nondefensively hear what they had to say did help them overcome their reluctance to participate. If we had not facilitated an exploration of their feelings, little learning would have occurred.

We continue to find that groups do not move forward unless hidden agendas are uncovered and fully discussed. This process often requires patience on our part and a willingness to continually check with members to find out if they are saying what they need to say. We point out to them that what bogs groups down is not what people *are* saying, but what they are *not* saying. It is not comfortable for us to deal with these undercurrents, yet we continue to learn about the value of respectfully, yet firmly, challenging members to express persistent thoughts and feelings about what is emerging in the group.

Self-Focus versus Focus on Others

One characteristic we observe in members of most beginning groups is a tendency to talk about others and to focus on people and situations outside of the group. Storytelling participants will at times deceive themselves into believing that they are really working, when in fact they are resisting speaking about and dealing with their own feelings. They may talk about life situations, but they have a tendency to focus on what other people in their life are doing to cause them difficulties. Skilled group leaders help such members examine their own reactions to others.

During the initial phase of a group the demanding job is to get the group members to focus on themselves. Of course, trust is a prerequisite for this openness. When members use a focus on others as a method of resisting deeper exploration of themselves, your leadership task is to steer them back. You need to learn to confront members who are using this defense in such a manner that they will not defensively reject what you or other members are saying. For example, you might say: "I'm aware that you're talking a lot about several important people in your life. They're not here, and we won't be able to work with them. But we *are* able to work with your feelings and reactions toward them and how their behavior affects you." An awareness of proper timing is essential. The readiness of a client to accept certain interpretations or observations must be considered. You must be skilled not only in helping people recognize that their focus on others can be defensive but also in giving them the courage to work through their resistance.

Here-and-Now Focus versus There-and-Then Focus

Some groups have a primary focus on what is occurring at the time in the room. The predominant theme that such groups explore is present member/member interactions. The material for discussion emerges from these encounters. Other groups focus largely on outside problems that members bring to the session, as well as problems associated with past experiences.

We have both a here-and-now focus and a there-and-then focus. We find that members are not ready to deal with significant issues pertaining to their life away from the group until they first deal with their reactions to one another in the room. In order to meaningfully explore personal problems, they must first feel safe and trusting. During the initial sessions we ask members to make connections between personal problems they are facing in their world and their experience in the group. If a member discloses that she feels isolated in her life, for instance, we ask her to be aware of how she may be isolating herself in the group setting.

Trust versus Mistrust

If a basic sense of trust and security is not established at the outset of a group, serious problems can be predicted. People can be said to be developing trust in one another when they can express any feelings without fear of censure; when they are willing to decide for themselves specific goals and personal areas to explore; when they focus on themselves, not on others; and when they are willing to risk disclosing personal aspects of themselves.

In contrast, a lack of trust is indicated by an undercurrent of hostility and suspicion and an unwillingness to talk about these feelings. Other manifestations of lack of trust are participants' taking refuge in being abstract or overly intellectual and being vague about what they expect from the therapeutic group. Before a climate of trust is established, people tend to wait for the leader to decide for them what they need to examine. Any disclosures that are made tend to be superficial and rehearsed, and risk taking is at a low level.

Identifying and Clarifying Goals at the Initial Stage

One of the major tasks of the initial stage is to establish both group goals and individual goals. Examples of general group goals include creating a climate of trust and acceptance, promoting self-disclosure in significant ways, and encouraging the taking of risks. It is essential that these goals (and norms, which we will discuss later) be explicitly stated, understood, and accepted by the members early in the group. Otherwise, considerable conflict and confusion are certain to occur at a later stage. What follows are some general goals that are common to most therapeutic groups and some examples of goals for specialized groups.

General Goals for Group Members

Although the members must decide for themselves the specific aims of a group experience, there are some broad goals:

- to increase self-esteem
- to accept the reality of one's limitations
- to reduce behavior that prevents intimacy
- to learn how to trust oneself and others
- to become freer and less bound by external "shoulds" and "musts"
- to increase self-awareness and thereby increase the possibilities for choice and action
- to learn the distinction between having feelings and acting on them
- to free oneself from the inappropriate early decisions that keep one less than the person one would like to be
- to recognize that others struggle, too
- to clarify the values one has and to decide whether and how to modify them
- to learn to make choices in a world where nothing is guaranteed
- to find ways to resolve personal problems
- to increase one's capacity to care for others
- to become more open and honest with selected others
- to deal with other members in a direct manner in the here-and-now group situation
- to support and challenge others
- to confront others with care and concern
- to learn how to ask others for what one wants
- to become sensitive to the needs and feelings of others
- to provide others with useful feedback

These goals are only general ones, and they must be narrowed down to apply to what each member expects to gain from group participation. What follows are a few examples of member goals for specialized groups:

- **Goals for an incest group** are to assist people in talking about incidences of incest; to discover common feelings of anger, hurt, shame, and guilt; and to work through unfinished business with the perpetrator.
- **Goals for disabled people** are to express anger, grief, and resentment about their disability; to learn to deal with the reduced privacy caused by the disability; to learn to work within the limitations imposed by the handicap; and to establish a support system.
- **Goals for a substance-abuse group** are to help the abuser confront difficult issues and learn to cope with life stresses more effectively; to provide a supportive network; and to learn more appropriate social skills.
- **Goals for elderly people** are to review life experiences; to express feelings over losses; to improve members' self-image; and to continue finding meaning in life.
- **Goals for acting-out children** are to accept feelings and at the same time learn ways of constructively expressing them and dealing with them; to develop skills in making friends; and to channel impulses into constructive behavior.

Regardless of the type of therapeutic group, it is important to consider some methods of assisting participants in developing concrete goals that will give them direction. Participants in groups do not automatically formulate clear goals. It is the responsibility of group leaders to use their skills to help members make their goals specific so that others present in the group will understand them (ASGW, 1989).

Helping Members Define Personal Goals

Participants are typically able to state only in broad terms what they expect to get from a group. For instance, Carol, who says that she'd like to "relate to others better," needs to specify with whom and under what conditions she encounters difficulties in her interpersonal relationships. She also needs to learn to state concretely what part of her behavior she needs to change. The leader's questions should help her become more specific. With whom is she having difficulties? If the answer is her parents, then what specifically is causing her problems with them? How is she affected by these problems? How does she want to be different with her parents? With all this information the leader has a clearer idea of how to proceed with Carol.

What follows are some examples of how leaders can intervene to help members make a global goal more specific:

Member: "I want to get in touch with my feelings."
Leader: "What kind of feelings are you having difficulty with?"

Member: "I want to work on my anger."

Leader: "With whom in your life are you angry? What do you most want to say?"

Member: "I have very low self-esteem."

Leader: "List some of the ways in which you put yourself down."

Member: "I have trouble with intimacy."

Leader: "Whom in your life are you having trouble getting close to, and what might you be doing to prevent the intimacy you want?"

Defining goals is an ongoing process, not something that is done once and for all. Throughout the course of a group it is important to help members assess the degree to which their personal goals are being met and, if appropriate, to help them revise any of their goals (ASGW, 1989). As members gain more experience, they are in a better position to know what they want from a group, and they also come to recognize additional goals that can guide their participation. Their involvement in the work of other members can act as a catalyst in getting them to think about ways in which they can profit from the group experience.

Once members have a general idea of what they want to get from being a group member, establishing a contract is one excellent way for them to be more precise in their personal goals. Basically, a contract is a statement by participants of what problems they want to explore and what behaviors they are willing to change. It is a way of encouraging clients to think about the group and about their role in it. In the contract method group members assume an active and responsible stance. Of course, contracts can be open-ended, in that they can be modified or replaced as appropriate. Contracts can be used in most of the groups discussed in this book.

Contracts and homework assignments can be combined fruitfully. In Carol's case a beginning contract could commit her to observe and write down each time she experiences difficulties with her parents. If she discovers that she usually walks away at times of conflict with them, she might pledge in a follow-up contract to stay in one of these situations rather than avoiding it.

As another example, consider a man in an assertiveness-training group who decides that he would like to spend more time on activities that interest him. He might make a contract that calls for him to do more of the things he would like to do for himself, and he might assign himself certain activities to be carried out during the week as experiments. At the next group session he would report the results. Partly on the basis of these results, he could decide how much and in what ways he really wanted to change. Then he could do further work in the group toward his chosen ends.

Group-Process Concepts at the Initial Stage

The group process, as we have said, involves the stages that groups tend to go through, each characterized by certain feelings and behaviors.

Initially, as the members get to know one another, there is a feeling of anxiety. Each waits for someone else to begin the work. Tension, hostility, or even boredom build up. If things go well, however, the members learn to trust one another and the leader, and they begin to openly express feelings, thoughts, and reactions. Thus, included under the rubric *group process* are activities such as establishing norms and group cohesion, learning to work cooperatively, establishing ways of solving problems, and learning to express conflict openly. We'll now discuss in depth two of these group-process concepts—group norms and group cohesion —that are especially important during the initial stage. *Group norms* are the shared beliefs about expected behaviors that are aimed at making groups function effectively. *Group cohesion* is a sense of togetherness, or community, within a group. A cohesive group is one in which members have incentives for remaining in the group and share a feeling of belongingness and relatedness.

Group Norms

Norms and procedures that will help the group attain its goals can be developed during the early stage. If the norms—standards that govern behavior in the group—are vague, valuable time will be lost, and tensions will arise over what is appropriate and inappropriate. There are, however, implicit (or unspoken) norms as well as those that are explicitly stated.

Implicit norms may develop because of preconceived ideas about what takes place in a group. Members may assume, for example, that a group is a place where everything must be said, with no room for privacy. Unless the leader calls attention to the possibility that members can be self-disclosing and still retain a measure of privacy, members may misinterpret the norm of openness and honesty as a policy of complete candor, with no secrets. Another example of an implicit norm that we sometimes see in our groups is pressure to experience catharsis and crying. In most of our intensive therapeutic groups, there is a fair amount of crying and expression of pent-up feelings. Certain members wrongly assume that we judge the quality of their personal work by the volume of tears shed or the intensity of catharsis.

Implicit norms may also develop because of modeling by the leader. If a leader curses and uses abrasive language, members are more likely to adopt this pattern of speech in their group interactions, even though the leader has never expressly encouraged people to talk in such a manner. Another example of an implicit norm pertains to changes in members' everyday life. If an unassertive member reports that she is being perceived as more assertive at work, she may receive applause from the group. Even though behavior change outside of the group is not specifically stated as a norm, this implicit norm can have a powerful effect on shaping the members' responses and behaviors. Implicit norms do affect the group. They are less likely to have an adverse influence if they are made explicit.

The following explicit norms are examples of standards of behavior that are common in many groups:

- Members are expected to attend regularly and show up on time. When they attend sessions only sporadically, the entire group suffers. Members who regularly attend will resent the lack of commitment of those who miss sessions.
- Members are encouraged to be personal and share meaningful aspects of themselves, communicating directly with others in the group and, in general, becoming active participants.
- Members are expected to give feedback to one another. They can evaluate the effects of their behavior on others only if the others are willing to say how they have been affected. It is important for members not to withhold their perceptions and reactions but, rather, to let others know what they perceive.
- Members should focus on feelings and express them, rather than talking about problems in a detached and intellectual manner.
- Members are encouraged to focus on here-and-now interactions within the group. Immediacy refers to being genuine in one's relationships. Members focus on being immediate by expressing and exploring conflicts within the group. Immediacy is called for when there are unverbalized thoughts and feelings about what is happening in a session, particularly if these reactions are having a detrimental effect on the group process. There is little need to dwell in the group on the details of how members behave in various social situations, because this behavior becomes apparent in the here and now of group interaction. Thus, one of your leadership functions is to ask questions such as "How is it for you to be in this group now?" "With whom do you identify the most in here?" "What are some of the things that you might be rehearsing to yourself silently?" "Whom in this room are you most aware of?" You can also steer members into the here and now by asking them to reveal what they think and feel about what is going on in the group.
- Members are expected to bring into the group personal problems and concerns that they are willing to discuss. They can be expected to spend some time before the sessions thinking about the matters they want to work on. This is an area in which unspoken norms frequently function. In some groups, for example, the participants may get the idea that they are not good group members unless they bring personal issues from everyday life to work on during the sessions. Members may get the impression that it is not acceptable to focus on here-and-now matters within the group itself and that they should be willing to work on other problems.
- Members are encouraged to provide therapeutic support. Ideally, this support facilitates both an individual's work and the group process, rather than distracting members from self-exploration. But some leaders can implicitly "teach" being overly supportive or, by their modeling, can demonstrate a type of support that has the effect of short-circuiting pain-

ful experiences that a member is attempting to work through. Leaders who are uncomfortable with intense emotions (such as anger or the pain associated with past memories) can actually collude with members by fostering a pseudosupportive climate that prevents members from fully experiencing and expressing intense feelings of any kind. Some groups are so supportive that challenge and confrontation are ruled out. An unverbalized norm in this area is the focus on expressing only positive feelings and favorable reactions. If this practice becomes a pattern, members can get the idea that it is not acceptable to express any criticism, even if it is constructive.

- The other side of the norm of support is providing members with challenges to look at themselves. Confrontation is the process that involves expressing in a direct and caring manner a challenge for members (or leaders) to look at some discrepancy between what they are saying and doing. Members need to learn how to confront others without arousing defensiveness. Early in our group, for example, we establish a norm that it is not acceptable to dismiss another in a hostile and labeling way, such as by saying "You're an idiot!" Instead, we teach members to directly and cleanly express the anger they are feeling, avoiding name calling. Members are asked to express the source of their anger, including what led up to their feelings. For example, if Ann says to Rudy "You're an idiot," the leader can ask her to let Rudy know how she has been affected by him. She can also be encouraged to express the stored-up reactions that led her to label him. In contrast, some leaders model harsh confrontations, and members soon pick up the unexpressed norm that the appropriate way to relate to others in this group is with attacks. Some groups even specialize in confrontation, on the assumption that the only way people change is by having their defenses stripped away through unrelenting verbal attacks.

- Groups can operate under either a norm of exploring personal problems or a norm of problem solving. In some groups, for example, as soon as members bring up situations that they'd like to understand better, they are bombarded by suggestions for how they can "solve" these problems. The fact of the matter is that solutions are often not possible, and what members most need is an opportunity to talk about what they are feeling. Of course, problem-solving strategies are of use in teaching members new ways of coping with their difficulties. But it is important that clients have an opportunity to explore their concerns before suggested solutions are presented.

- Members can be taught the norm of listening without thinking of a quick rebuttal and without becoming overly defensive. Although we don't expect people to merely accept all the feedback they receive, we do ask them to really hear what others are saying to them and to seriously consider these messages—particularly ones that are repeated consistently.

The above are merely a few examples of norms. The important point is that the group's norms be discussed as the group unfolds and develops.

Many groups become bogged down because members are unsure of what is expected of them. This is a further rationale for the importance of preparing members to assume an active role in attaining their personal goals (which we emphasized in Chapter 3). For instance, a member may want to intervene and share her perceptions while a leader is working with another client, but she may be inhibited because she is not sure whether she should interrupt the group leader at work. Another member may feel an inclination to support a fellow group member at the time when that member is experiencing some pain or sadness but may refrain because he is uncertain whether his support will detract from the other's experience. Another member who is bored, session after session, may keep this feeling to herself because she is not sure of the appropriateness of revealing it. Perhaps if she were told that it was permissible to experience her boredom and valuable to express it, she might be more open with her group and, consequently, less bored.

If group norms are clearly presented and if the members see the value of them and cooperatively decide on some of them, they will be potent forces in the shaping of the group. Part of the orientation process consists of identifying and discussing norms that are aimed at the development of a cohesive and productive group.

Group Cohesion

During the early stage of a group the members do not know one another well enough for a true sense of community to be formed. There is an awkwardness and a period of becoming acquainted. Though participants talk about themselves, it is likely that they are presenting more of their public self rather than deeper aspects of their private self. Genuine cohesion typically comes after groups have struggled with conflict, have shared pain, and have committed themselves to taking significant risks. But the foundations of cohesion can begin to take shape at the initial stage.

Some indicators of this initial degree of cohesion are cooperation among members; a willingness to show up for the meetings and be punctual; an effort to make the group a safe place, including talking about any feelings of lack of trust or fears of trusting; support and caring, as evidenced by being willing to listen to others and accept them for who they are; and a willingness to express reactions to and perceptions of others in the here-and-now context of the group interactions. Genuine cohesion is not a fixed condition arrived at automatically. Instead, it is an ongoing process of solidarity that members earn through the risks they take with one another. Group cohesion can be developed, maintained, and increased in a number of ways, some of which are described below:

▪ Trust must be developed during the early stage of a group. One of the best ways of building trust is to create a group climate characterized by respect for the opinions and feelings of the members. It is essential that members openly express their feelings concerning the degree of trust they are experiencing. An opportunity can be provided at the outset for members to share their reservations, and this open sharing of concerns will pave the way for productive work. (The creating of trust will be discussed in detail in the next section.)

- If group members share meaningful aspects of themselves, they both learn to take risks and increase group cohesiveness. By modeling— for instance, by sharing their own reactions to what is occurring within the group—leaders can encourage risk-taking behavior. When group members do take risks, they can be reinforced with sincere recognition and support, which will increase their sense of closeness to the others.

- Group goals and individual goals can be jointly determined by the group members and the leader. If a group is without clearly stated goals, animosity can build up that will tend to lead to the fragmentation of the group.

- Cohesion can be increased by inviting (but not forcing) all members to become active participants. Members who appear to be passive or withdrawn can be invited to express their feelings toward the group. These members may be silent observers for a number of reasons, and these reasons ought to be examined openly in the group.

- Cohesion can be built by sharing the leadership role with the members of the group. In autocratic groups all the decisions are made by the leader. A cooperative group is more likely to develop if members are encouraged to initiate discussion of issues they want to explore. Also, instead of fostering a leader-to-member style of interaction, group leaders can promote member-to-member interactions. This can be done by inviting the members to respond to one another, by encouraging feedback and sharing, and by searching for ways to involve as many members as possible in group interactions.

- Conflict is inevitable in groups. It is desirable for group members to recognize sources of conflict and to deal openly with them when they arise. A group can be strengthened by acceptance of conflict and by the honest working through of differences.

- Group attractiveness and cohesion are related. It is generally accepted that the greater the degree of attractiveness of a group to its members, the greater the level of cohesion. If the group deals with matters that interest the members, if the members feel that they are respected, and if the atmosphere is supportive, the chances are good that the group will be perceived as attractive.

- Members can be encouraged to disclose their ideas, feelings, and reactions to what occurs within their group. The expression of both positive and negative reactions should be encouraged. If this is done, an honest exchange can take place, which is essential if a sense of group belongingness is to develop.

Creating Trust: Leader and Member Roles

The Importance of Modeling

We've alluded to the establishment of trust as a central task for the initial stage of a group. It is not possible to overemphasize the significance of the leader's modeling and the attitudes expressed through the leader's behavior in these early sessions. In thinking about your role as a leader, ask yourself questions such as these: Do you feel energetic and enthusiastic as you approach your group? Do you trust yourself in your leadership, and are you able to inspire confidence? To what degree do you trust the group members to work effectively with one another? Are you able to be psychologically present in the sessions, and are you willing to be open about your own reactions to what is going on in the group?

Your success in creating a climate of trust within a group has much to do with how well you've prepared both yourself and the members. If you've given careful thought to why you are organizing the group, what you hope to accomplish, and how you'll go about meeting your objectives, the chances are greatly increased that you'll inspire confidence. The members will see your willingness to think about the group as a sign that you care about them. Furthermore, if you've done a good job with the pregroup issues (such as informing members of their rights and responsibilities, giving some time to teaching the group process, and preparing the members for a successful experience), the members will realize that you are taking your work seriously and that you are interested in their welfare. Such attention can go a long way toward the establishment of trust.

The person who you are, and especially the attitudes about group work and clients that you demonstrate by the way you behave in the sessions, may be the most crucial factor in building a trusting community. (Refer to our discussion of the personal characteristics of the effective leader in Chapter 1.) You teach most effectively through your example. If you trust in the group process and have faith in the members' capacity to make significant changes in themselves, they are likely to see value in their group as a pathway to personal growth. If you listen nondefensively and respectfully and convey that you value members' subjective experience, they are likely to see the power in active listening. If you are genuinely willing to engage in appropriate self-disclosure, you will foster honesty and disclosure among the members. If you are truly able to accept others for who they are and avoid imposing your values on them, your members will learn valuable lessons about accepting people's right to differ and to be themselves. In short, what you model through what you do in the group is one of the most powerful ways of teaching members how to relate to one another constructively.

If you are co-leading a group, you and your colleague have ample opportunities to model a behavioral style that will promote trust. If the two of you function harmoniously with a spontaneous give and take, for example, members will feel more trusting in your presence. If your relationship with your co-leader is characterized by respect, authenticity, sensitivity, and directness, the members will learn about the value of such attitudes and behaviors. Furthermore, the way in which the two of you interact with the members obviously contributes to or detracts from the level of trust. If one co-leader's typical manner of speaking with members is sharp, short, and sarcastic, for example, the members are likely to quickly pick up this leader's lack of respect for them and tend to become closed or resistant. Therefore, it is wise for co-leaders to examine each other's style of interacting.

It is a mistake to assume that as a leader or a co-leader you have sole responsibility for the development and maintenance of trust. The level of trust is engendered by your attitudes and actions, yet it also depends to a large degree on the level of investment of the members. If they want very little for themselves, if they are unwilling to share enough of themselves so that they can be known, if they simply wait passively for you to "make trust happen," and if they are unwilling to take risks in the sessions, trust will be slow to develop. In the last analysis, however, the tone set by your leadership will influence their willingness to disclose themselves and to take those steps necessary to establish trust.

Attitudes and Actions Leading to Trust

We value Carl Rogers's (1987) emphasis on the "facilitative dimensions of the therapeutic relationship," and we see certain attitudes and actions as enhancing the level of trust in a group:

Attending and Listening. Careful attending to the verbal and nonverbal messages of others is necessary for trust to occur. If genuine listening and understanding are absent, there is no basis for connection between members. If members feel that they are being heard and deeply understood, they are likely to trust that others care about them.

There are numerous ways in which both leaders and members may demonstrate a lack of attending, including not focusing on the speaker but thinking of what to say next, asking many closed questions that have the effect of probing for information, doing too much talking and not enough listening, giving advice readily instead of encouraging the speaker to explore a struggle, paying attention only to what people say explicitly and thus missing what they express nonverbally, and engaging in selective listening (hearing only what one wants to hear).

We don't think that most group members possess natural listening skills, nor do they have the ability to respond effectively to what they perceive. Therefore, teaching basic listening and responding skills is a part of the trust process. Pay attention to whether members feel that they are being listened to with understanding. If they don't feel that they are, why should they speak about matters that are deeply personal? Why should they reveal themselves to those who do not care?

Understanding Nonverbal Behavior. Inexperienced group workers frequently make the error of focusing exclusively on what members are saying and miss the more powerful nonverbal messages. People often express themselves more honestly nonverbally than they do through their words. Detecting discrepancies between verbal and nonverbal behavior is an art. Examples of clients displaying these discrepancies include a member who is talking about a painful experience while smiling; a client who is verbally expressing positive feelings yet is hitting the floor with clenched fists; a person who says that she really wants to work and to have group time but consistently waits until the end of a session before bringing up her concerns; a participant who claims that she feels comfortable in the group and really likes the members yet sits with her arms crossed tightly and tends to face away from the group; and a member who displays facial expressions and gestures but denies having any reactions.

What are some guidelines for understanding and dealing with nonverbal behavior? Even though you may have a clear idea what a nonverbal behavior means, it is crucial not to confront the client with an interpretation. It is best to describe the behavior: "I notice that you're smiling, yet you're talking about painful memories, and there are tears in your eyes. What do you want me to believe, your words or your body?" After describing what you are seeing, invite the participant to offer the meaning of the nonverbal behavior. At times you may misunderstand nonverbal information and even label it as resistance. The behavior may well be a manifestation of a cultural injunction. For example, a leader is role-playing Javier's father and asks Javier to make eye contact with him as he is talking. In spite of many invitations, Javier continues to look away or at the floor as he talks to his symbolic father. The leader is unaware that Javier would have felt disrespectful if he looked directly at his father or another authority.

In summary, it is essential that you avoid making assumptions about what members are experiencing and, instead, assist members to recognize and explore the possible meanings of their nonverbal behavior. If you misread or ignore nonverbal messages or if you abrasively confront certain behavior, the level of trust in the group will surely suffer.

Empathy. Empathy is the ability to tune in to what others are subjectively experiencing and to see their world through their eyes. When people experience this understanding without critical judgment, they are most likely to reveal their real concerns, for they believe that others are understanding and accepting them as they are. This kind of non-judgmental understanding is vitally related to trust.

One of your leadership functions is to help members develop greater empathy by pointing out behaviors that block this understanding. Examples of these counterproductive behaviors include responding to others with pat statements, not responding to others at all, questioning inappropriately, telling others how they should be or should feel, re-sponding with critical judgments, and being defensive.

Empathy is an avenue of demonstrating support. For example, Judy benefits when others are able to understand her. If she talks about going through an extremely painful divorce, Clyde can let her know the ways in which he identifies with and understands her pain. Though their cir-cumstances are different, he empathizes with her pain and is willing to share with her his feelings of rejection and abandonment when his wife left him. What helps Judy is Clyde's willingness to tell her about his struggles rather than providing her with quick answers. Instead of giv-ing her ready-made solutions or offering her reassurance, he helps her most by sharing his life with her. Our colleague, Patrick Callanan, often says that people learn more from hearing how others are engaged in a struggle than from hearing their solutions to their problems.

Genuineness and Self-Disclosure. Genuineness implies a congruence between a person's inner experience and what he or she projects exter-nally. Applied to your role as a leader, genuineness means that you don't pretend to be accepting when internally you are not feeling accepting, you don't give out dishonest responses, you don't rely on behaviors that are aimed at winning approval, and you avoid hiding behind a profes-sional role as a leader. Through your own authenticity, you offer a model to members that inspires them to be real in their interactions.

Consider a couple of examples in which you might be challenged to provide authentic responses rather than expected ones. A member who is new to your group might spontaneously ask you "What do you think of me?" You could politely respond with "I think you're a very nice per-son." A more honest response could be: "I don't know you well enough to have strong reactions to you. I'm sure that as I get to know you better, I'll share my perceptions with you." You might want to ask this person what prompted her question and discover that she is intimidated by your position in the group and needs quick reassurance. By helping her iden-tify the reason for her question, you can help her be more authentic with you. In another case a member says to you in the middle of a conflict with him "Oh, give me a hug; I don't like this tension between us." Chances are that you don't really feel like hugging him at this moment. It is nevertheless important that you give an honest reply to his request. You could say, "I'm very much struggling with you right now, and I'm willing to continue working this through. I'm not willing to hug you now, but that doesn't mean that at some later point, when we've resolved our conflict, I won't feel close enough to hug you. I don't think a hug now will alleviate the tension between us."

Related to being real is the matter of self-disclosure. As a leader you can invite members to make themselves known by letting others in the group know you. As we have pointed out before, this openness does not have to entail an indiscriminate sharing of your private life with the participants. You can reveal your thoughts and feelings that are related to what is going on within the group. If you are authentic and appropriately self-disclosing and if you avoid hiding behind defenses, you will encourage the rest of the group to be open about their concerns. Sometimes group participants will challenge you by saying "We tell you all of our problems, but we don't know any of yours." You could surrender to this pressure to prove that you are "genuine" and end up with a problem. A genuine disclosure is: "Yes, in this group, due to my role, I'm likely to learn more about the nature of your problems than you will learn about my personal concerns, but this doesn't mean that I don't have difficulties in my life. If you and I were members in another group, I expect that you'd learn more about me. While I'm not likely to bring my outside problems into this group, I'm very willing to let you know how I'm being affected in these sessions."

Respect. Respect is shown by what the leader and the members actually do, not simply by what they say. Attitudes and actions that demonstrate respect include avoiding critical judgments, avoiding labeling, looking beyond self-imposed or other-imposed labels, expressing warmth and support that is honestly felt, being genuine and risking being yourself, and recognizing the rights of others to be different from you. If people receive this type of respect, they are supported in their attempts to talk about themselves in open and meaningful ways.

Nancy may express her fear of being judged by others and talk about how she is reluctant to speak because of this fear of criticism. Members are not offering her respect when they too quickly reassure her that they like her just as she is and that they would not judge her. It would be more helpful to encourage her to explore her fear of being judged, both in past situations and in the group. It is important to let her feelings stand and to work with them, rather than discounting them. Most likely her feelings of being judged reside within her and are projected onto others. If the leader allows the members to reassure Nancy, she may momentarily feel reassured. However, as soon as she is away from the group, her internal judge will speak up again.

Caring Confrontation. A crucial factor in the development of trust is the way in which confrontations are handled in the sessions. A confrontation can be an act of caring that takes the form of an invitation for members to examine some discrepancy between what they are saying and what they are doing or between what they are saying and some nonverbal cues they are manifesting. If confrontations are made in an abrasive, "hit-and-run" fashion and if the leader allows people to be verbally abusive, trust is greatly inhibited. You can teach members directness coupled with sensitivity, which results in their seeing that confrontation can be handled in a caring yet honest manner. Challenging members is just as important as supporting them, for a timely challenge can inspire them to look at aspects of themselves that they have been avoiding. Whereas hostile attacks have the result of closing people up by making them defensive, caring confrontations can actually increase the trust in a group. Members learn that they can express even negative reactions in a way that respects those they are confronting.

An example of a caring confrontation follows. Claire is very willing to speak on everything and constantly brings herself in on others' work. An ineffective confrontation is "I want you to be quiet and let others in here talk." An effective confrontation is: "Claire, I appreciate your willingness to participate and talk about yourself. However, I'm concerned that I have heard very little from several others in the group, and I want to hear from them, too."

The attitudes and behaviors described above have an important bearing on the level of trust that is established within a group. Although trust is the major task to be accomplished at the initial stage of a group's development, it is a mistake to assume that once trust has been established, it is ensured for the duration of that group. We want to emphasize that it ebbs and flows, and new levels of trust must be established as the group progresses toward a deeper level of intimacy. A basic sense of safety is essential for the movement of a group beyond the initial stage, but this trust will be tested time and again and take on new facets in later stages.

Leader Issues at the Initial Stage

Early in the history of a group it is especially important to think about the balance of responsibility between members and the leader (or co-leaders) as well as the degree of structuring that is optimal for the group. If you are working with a co-leader, discussing these issues is essential, for divergent views are bound to hurt the group. If you assume the majority of the responsibility for keeping the group moving, for example, and your co-leader assumes almost no responsibility on the ground that the members must decide for themselves what to do with group time, the members will sense this division and are bound to be confused by it. Similarly, if you function best with a high degree of structure in groups and your co-leader believes that any structuring should come from the members, this difference of opinion will have a detrimental effect on the group.

For these reasons, it is wise to select a co-leader who has a philosophy of leadership that is compatible with yours, though this does not mean that both of you need to have the same style of leading. You can have differences that complement each other.

The Division of Responsibility

A basic issue that you will have to consider is responsibility for the direction and outcome of the group. If a group proves to be nonproductive, will this failure stem from your lack of leadership skills, or does the responsibility rest with the group members?

One way of conceptualizing the issue of responsibility is to think of it in terms of a continuum. At one end is the leader who assumes a great share of the responsibility for the direction and outcomes of the group. Such leaders tend to have the outlook that unless they are highly directive, the group will flounder. They tend to see their role as that of the expert, and they actively intervene to keep the group moving in ways they deem productive. A disadvantage of this form of leadership is that it robs the members of the responsibility that is rightfully theirs; if members are perceived by the leader as not having the capacity to take care of themselves, they soon begin to live up to this expectation by being irresponsible, at least in the group.

Leaders who assume an inordinate degree of responsibility not only undermine members' independence but also burden themselves. If people leave unchanged, such leaders see it as their fault. If members remain separate, never forming a cohesive unit, these leaders view this outcome as a reflection of their lack of skill. If the group is disappointed, they feel disappointed and tend to blame themselves, believing that they didn't do enough to create a dynamic group. This style of leadership is draining, and leaders who use it may eventually lose the energy required to lead groups.

At the other end of the responsibility continuum is the leader who proclaims: "I am responsible for me, and you are responsible for you. If you want to leave this group with anything of value, it is strictly up to you. I can't do anything for you—make you feel something or take away any of your defenses—unless you allow me to."

Ideally, you will develop a leadership style that entails a balance between accepting your share of the responsibility and usurping the members' share. This issue is central, because your approach to other issues (such as structuring and self-disclosure) hinges on your approach to it.

The Degree of Structuring

The issue is not *whether* a group leader should provide structure but, rather, *what degree* of structure. Like responsibility, structuring exists on a continuum. The leader's theoretical orientation, the type of group, and the membership population are some of the factors that determine the amount and type of structuring employed.

Balance at the Initial Stage. Providing therapeutic structuring is particularly important during the initial stage of a group, when members are typically unclear about what behavior is expected and are therefore anxious. Structure can be both useful and inhibiting in a group's development. Too little structure results in members' becoming unduly anxious, and although some anxiety is productive, too much can inhibit spontaneity.

Although you may be particularly active during the early phase of a group, it is important that you encourage members to assume an increasing role. Too much structuring and direction can foster leader-dependent attitudes and behavior. The members may wait for the leader to "make something happen" instead of acting themselves.

Yalom (1983, 1985) sees the basic task of the group leader as providing enough structure to give a general direction to the members yet avoiding the pitfalls of fostering dependency. His message for leaders is to structure the group in a fashion that facilitates each member's autonomous functioning. An example of fostering dependency on the leader would be encouraging members to speak only when they are invited to do so. Instead, the leader can encourage members to bring themselves into the interactions without being called on.

We do not subscribe to a passive style of group leadership, for we do not simply wait and let the group take any direction it happens to go in. By providing some structure we give group members the opportunity to experiment with new levels of awareness and to build new forms of behavior from this awareness. During the initial stage our structure is aimed at helping members identify and express their fears, expectations, and personal goals. For example, we often use dyads, go-arounds, and open-ended questions as ways of making it easier for members to talk to one another about current issues in their lives. After talking to several people on a one-to-one basis, as you have seen, members find it easier to talk openly in the entire group. The leadership activity that we provide is designed to help members focus on themselves and the issues they most want to explore in the group.

Many short-term groups are structured around a series of topics. In a group for learning effective parenting skills, for example, the sessions are guided by topics such as listening well, setting limits, learning to convey respect, and providing discipline without punishment. Group leaders sometimes rigidly adhere to a structured exercise or a discussion of a topic when another pressing matter demands attention. If there is conflict in the group, it is more important to suspend the topic or exercise until the conflict has been attended to. If the conflict is brushed aside, there is a greater likelihood that discussion of the topic will be superficial. At other times, members spontaneously bring up unrelated concerns, and leaders have difficulty in keeping them focused on the topic in a meaningful way. The leader and members of the group need to explore whether the shift in the topic is due to their discomfort with the issue or to the fact that a more relevant subject has surfaced. If the shift is an avoidance tactic, the facilitator might point out the dynamics of what is occurring.

We often supervise leaders who are facilitating structured growth groups. These groups are focused on different themes for each session. Some of these topics are sex roles, body image, meaning and values, work and leisure, love and sexuality, loneliness, intimacy, and death and dying. We try to teach the group facilitators how to balance a discussion of group-process concerns (trust, confrontation, unfinished business, subgrouping) with an exploration of the particular topic. Process issues among members (such as clients' feeling isolated in the group) generally take precedence over dealing with the topic. It is not a matter of either focusing on a member's particular concern or dealing with a topic. The art consists of learning how to help members relate topics to themselves in significant ways so that group interaction and group learning can occur.

Research on Structuring. Research indicates the value of an initial structure that builds supportive group norms and highlights positive interactions among members. Leaders must carefully monitor this therapeutic structure throughout the life of a group, rather than limiting the evaluation process to the final stage. Structuring that offers a coherent framework for understanding the experiences of individuals and the group process will be of the most value. When goals are clear, when appropriate member behaviors are identified, and when the process provides a framework for change, members tend to engage in therapeutic work more quickly (Dies, 1983b). Moreover, leader direction during the early phase of a group tends to facilitate the development of cohesion and the willingness of members to take risks by making themselves known to others and by giving others feedback (Stockton & Morran, 1982).

Bednar, Melnick, and Kaul (1974) developed a group model that shows the value of structure for group process and outcome. In their formulation, as group cohesion increases, members gradually begin to feel safer in sharing themselves in meaningful ways, in giving feedback, and in providing support and challenge to others. Their general model specifies the following sequence: initial ambiguity and anxiety, increased structure through specific instructions, increased risk taking, increased group cohesion, and increased personal responsibility.

Research-Based Guidelines for Leaders. Here are some guidelines for providing therapeutic structure in your groups; they underscore many of the major points that we have developed in this chapter and the previous one. What follows is an adaptation of some of the conclusions of research on short-term groups, as summarized by Dies (1983b):

- Be aware that direct instruction, or teaching, tends to facilitate a group's development during the early stages.
- Introduce an initial structure to build supportive group norms and foster the establishment of trust.

- Once the basic norms are established and the therapeutic potential of the group is developed, the degree of structure can be lessened. A less-directive structure is appropriate during the later stages as the members assume increased direction of their group.
- Use more-structured interventions with clients whose level of personal functioning restricts their capacity to interact in socially competent ways.
- Employ active leadership, yet at the same time use interventions that encourage members to assume increased responsibility.
- Develop and maintain a task-oriented focus by helping members develop and stick to clear goals.
- Help members understand the value of disclosing themselves, of providing feedback to one another, and of providing a balance between support and confrontation. You can do this by giving them a clear rationale for such group behaviors.
- Acknowledge what members do by providing positive reinforcement. Make statements to members more often than asking them questions. Provide concrete feedback that describes specific behavioral characteristics, and teach members to do the same.
- Model directness by speaking *to* members instead of talking *about* them.
- Structure initial sessions in a way that will help members acquire a clear framework for understanding experiences within the group.
- Use interpretations that help members generalize from how they behave in the here and now of the group situation to their problems in everyday living. Discuss with them the value of experimenting outside of the group with new interpersonal behaviors.

In summary, some degree of structuring exists in all groups. It is not possible to have an "unstructured" group, for even this is a form of structure. The art is to provide structuring that is not so tight that it robs the group members of the responsibility for finding their own structure.

Opening and Closing Group Sessions

An important aspect of structuring involves the procedures that leaders use in opening and closing group sessions. Such skills are very important throughout the group process; we discuss them here because you need to be aware of this essential aspect of group leadership from the very beginning. We suggest that you refer to this discussion as you read about subsequent stages.

Guidelines for Opening Sessions. We have observed that many leader trainees do not pay attention to how they open group sessions. Such leaders are all too ready to focus on the first person who speaks, staying with this person for an inappropriate length of time because at least someone is speaking. They often make no attempt to link the coming session with the last session, and they do not check with each client to determine how the members want to use the time for this particular session. If you begin a session abruptly, you may find it difficult to involve many of the members in productive work. Some kind of warmup is essential before plunging into work on problems.

We've emphasized in our workshops the value of learning the skills necessary for introducing each session in an effective way. For groups that meet on a regular basis, such as once a week, we suggest some of the following procedures to open each session:

- We find it useful to have all of the members briefly say what they want from the upcoming session. A quick go-around is all that is needed for the members to identify issues that they are interested in pursuing; in this way an agenda can be developed that is based on some common concerns. If several members say that they are having difficulties in talking with their spouse, for example, you can then bring the group together in working on communication problems. If you do not check out what issues the members have brought to a particular session and if you stay with the first member who speaks, much important material is lost.

- Give members at least a brief opportunity to share what they have done in the way of practice outside of the group since the previous session. Some may want to talk about problems they are experiencing in transferring their learning from the group to everyday situations. This difficulty can then be the basis for work in that session.

- The participants may have unresolved feelings about the previous session, or they may have given thought to that session during the week. If members don't have a chance to mention these concerns, hidden agendas will probably develop and block effective work.

- As a leader, you may also have afterthoughts about the previous session. You can begin some sessions by letting the group know what you have been thinking during the week about how the group is progressing. This practice is especially appropriate when you see certain problems emerging or when you think the group is getting stuck. Your self-disclosure can lead the way for members to be open with their reactions to what is or is not going on in the sessions.

- In an open group (in which the membership changes somewhat from week to week), introduce any new members. Rather than putting the spotlight on the incoming member, you can ask some of the clients who have been a part of the group for a time to briefly reflect on what they have been learning about themselves in the group. You can point out that some members may be attending for only a few sessions and can also ask them how they expect to get the most from the brief time that they may have in the group. A question we sometimes ask is "If this were the only session you had, what would you most want to accomplish?"

Although we don't want to suggest that you memorize certain lines to open a session, we'd like to suggest some comments that convey the spirit of eliciting important material for leading into a session. Let these lines serve as catalysts that can be a part of your own leadership style. At different times we've opened a session with remarks such as:

- "How is each of you feeling about being here today?"
- "Before we begin today's session, I'd like to ask each of you to take a few minutes to silently review your week and think about anything you want to tell us."
- "Are you here because you want to be?"
- "Did anyone have any afterthoughts about last week's session?"
- "As a way of beginning tonight, let's have a brief go-around. Each of you say what you'd most like to be able to say by the end of this session."
- "Could each of you briefly complete this sentence: 'Today I'd like to get actively involved by . . .'"
- "What are you willing to do to get what you say you want?"
- "What were you thinking and feeling before coming to the group?"
- "Whom are you most aware of in this room right now, and why?"

Guidelines for Closing Sessions. Just as important as how you open a session is the way in which you bring a meeting to closure. Too often a leader will simply announce that "time is up for today," with no attempt to summarize and integrate and with no encouragement for members to practice certain skills. Some time, if even only ten minutes, should be set aside to give participants an opportunity to reflect on what they liked or did not like about the session, to mention what they hope to do outside of the group during the week, and so forth. Attention to closing ensures that consolidation of learning will take place.

For groups that meet weekly, it is important to summarize what occurred in that session. At times, it is useful to stop the group halfway through the session and say: "I notice that we have about an hour left today, and I'd like to check out how each of you feels about what you've done so far today. Have you been as involved as you want to be? Are there some issues you'd like to explore before this session ends?" This does not need to be done routinely, but sometimes such an assessment during the session can help the members focus their attention on problem areas, especially if you sense that they are not doing and saying what they need to.

In closing a weekly group session, consider the following guidelines.

- It is good for clients to leave a session with some unanswered questions. We think it's a mistake to try to ensure that everyone leaves feeling comfortable. If clients leave feeling that everything is nicely closed, they will probably spend very little time during the week reflecting on matters raised in the group.

- Some statement from the members concerning their level of investment of energy is useful. If clients report feeling bored, you can ask them
what they're willing to do to relieve their boredom: "Is your boredom
all right, or is this something that you want to change?"
- You can ask members to tell the group briefly what they're learning
about themselves through their relationships with other members. The
participants can briefly indicate some ways in which they've changed
their behavior in response to these insights. If participants find that they
would like to change their behavior even more, they can be encouraged
to develop specific plans or homework assignments to complete before
the next session.
- Ask members whether there are any topics, questions, or problems
they would like to explore in the next session. This request creates a link
between one session and the next. Prompting the members to think about
the upcoming session also indirectly encourages them to stick to their
contracts during the week.
- You can ask members to give one another feedback. Especially helpful
are members' positive reactions concerning what they have actually
observed. For instance, if Doug's voice is a lot more secure, others may
let him know that they perceive this change. Of course, feedback on what
members are doing to block their strengths is also very helpful.
- If your group is one with changing membership, you need to be especially alert to reminding members a week before certain participants
will be leaving the group. Not only do the terminating members need
to talk about what they have learned from the group, but other members
are also likely to want to share their feelings. It is essential that time
be allotted for any unfinished business.

As we did for opening sessions, we present some comments for you
to consider in closing a session. Of course, not all of them need to be
asked at any one time.

- "What was it like for you to be in this group today?"
- "What affected you the most, and what did you learn?"
- "What would each of you be willing to do outside of the group this
week to practice some of the new skills you are acquiring?"
- "I'd like a quick go-around to have everyone say a few words on how
this group is progressing so far and make any suggestions for change."
- "Are you getting what you want from this group?"
- "If you are not satisfied with what is happening in this group, what
do you see that you can do to change things?"
- "Before we close tonight, I'd like to share with you some of my reactions and observations of this session."

By developing skills in opening and closing sessions, you increase
the possibility of continuity from meeting to meeting. Such continuity
can help members transfer insights and new behaviors from the group

into daily life and, along with encouragement and direction from your leadership, can facilitate the participants' ongoing assessment of their level of investment for each session.

If you work with a co-leader, the matter of how the sessions are opened and closed should be a topic for discussion. A few questions for exploration are: Who typically opens the sessions? Do the two of you agree on when and how to bring a session to closure? With five minutes left in the sessions, does one leader want to continue working, whereas the other wants to attempt some summary of the meeting? Do both of you pay attention to unfinished business that might be left hanging toward the ending of a session? Although we are not suggesting a mechanical division of time and functions when you begin and end sessions, we think it is worth noting who tends to assume this responsibility. If one leader typically opens the session, members may be likely to direct their talk to this person. In our groups, one of us may open the session while the other elaborates and makes additional remarks. In this way spontaneous give-and-take between co-leaders can replace an approach characterized by "Now it's your turn to make a remark."

Initial Stage: Summary

Stage Characteristics

The early phase of a group is a time for orientation and determining the structure of the group. At this stage:

- Participants test the atmosphere and get acquainted.
- Members learn what is expected, how the group functions, and how to participate in a group.
- Risk taking is relatively low, and exploration is tentative.
- Group cohesion and trust are gradually established if members are willing to express what they are thinking and feeling.
- Members are concerned with whether they are included or excluded, and they are beginning to define their place in the group.
- Negative feelings may surface as members test to determine if all feelings are acceptable.
- A central issue is trust versus mistrust.
- There are periods of silence and awkwardness; members may look for direction and wonder what the group is about.
- Members are deciding whom they can trust, how much they will disclose, how safe the group is, whom they like and dislike, and how much to get involved.
- Members are learning the basic attitudes of respect, empathy, acceptance, caring, and responding—all attitudes that facilitate the building of trust.

Member Functions and Possible Problems

Early in the course of the group some specific member roles and tasks are critical to the shaping of the group:

- taking active steps to create a trusting climate
- learning to express one's feelings and thoughts, especially as they pertain to interactions in the group
- being willing to express fears, hopes, concerns, reservations, and expectations concerning the group
- being willing to make oneself known to the others in the group
- being involved in the creation of group norms
- establishing personal and specific goals that will govern group participation
- learning the basics of group process, especially how to be involved in group interactions

Some possible problems that can arise are:

- Members may wait passively for "something to happen."
- Members may keep to themselves feelings of distrust or fears pertaining to the group and thus entrench their own resistance.
- Members may keep themselves vague and unknown, making meaningful interaction difficult.
- Members may slip into a problem-solving and advice-giving stance with other members.

Leader Functions

The major tasks of group leaders during the orientation and exploration phase of a group are:

- teaching participants some general guidelines and ways to participate actively that will increase their chances of having a productive group
- developing ground rules and setting norms
- teaching the basics of group process
- assisting members in expressing their fears and expectations, and working toward the development of trust
- modeling the facilitative dimensions of therapeutic behavior
- being open with the members and being psychologically present for them
- clarifying the division of responsibility
- helping members establish concrete personal goals
- dealing openly with members' concerns and questions
- providing a degree of structuring that will neither increase members' dependence nor result in floundering
- assisting members to share what they are thinking and feeling about what is occurring within the group

- teaching members basic interpersonal skills such as active listening and responding
- assessing the needs of the group and leading in such a way that these needs are met

Exercises

1. Initial-Session Exercise. For this exercise, ten students volunteer to play group members at an initial group session, and two volunteer to play co-leaders. We suggest that the co-leaders begin by giving a brief orientation explaining the group's purpose, the role of the leader, the rights and responsibilities of the members, the ground rules, group-process procedures, and any other pertinent information they might actually give in the first session of a group. The members then express their expectations and fears, and the leaders try to deal with them. This lasts for approximately half an hour, and the class members then describe what they saw occurring in the group. The group members describe how they felt during the session and offer suggestions for the co-leaders. The co-leaders can discuss with each other the nature of their experience and how well they feel they did, either before any of the feedback or afterward.

2. Introducing-Yourself Exercise. This exercise consists of telling the class what you would tell a group about yourself if you were the group leader. About four people volunteer, and each person is given five minutes. When this is completed, the four talk among themselves first, and then the class offers input regarding the impact made by each person.

3. Exercise for the Beginning Stage of a Group. This exercise can be used to get group members acquainted with one another, but you can practice it in class to see how it works. The class breaks into dyads. Select a new partner every ten minutes, and each time you change partners, consider a new question or issue. The main purpose of the exercise is to get members to contact all of the other members of the group and to begin to reveal themselves to others. We encourage you to add your own questions or statements to our list of issues:

- Discuss your reservations about the value of groups.
- What do you fear about groups?
- What do you most want from a group experience?
- Discuss how much trust you have in your group. Do you feel like getting involved? What are some things that contribute to your trust or mistrust?
- Decide which of the two of you is dominant. Does each of you feel satisfied with his or her position?

- Tell your partner how you imagine you would feel if you were to co-lead a group with him or her.

4. Exercise in Meeting with Your Co-Leader. Select a person in your class with whom you might like to co-lead a group. Explore with your partner some of the following dimensions of a group during the initial stage:

- How would both of you assist the members in getting the most from this group? Would you be inclined to discuss any guidelines that would help them be active members?
- How would the two of you attempt to build trust during the initial phase of this group?
- How much structuring would each of you be inclined to do early in a group? Do both of you agree on the degree of structure that would help a group function effectively?
- Whose responsibility is it if the group flounders? What might you do if the group seemed to be lost at the first session?
- What are some specific procedures that each of you might use to help the members define what they want to get from their group?

5. Brainstorming about Ways of Creating Trust. In small groups, explore as many ideas and ways you can think of that might facilitate the establishment of trust in your group. What factors do you think are likely to lead to trust? What would it take for *you* to feel a sense of trust in a group? What do you see as the major barriers to the development of trust?

CHAPTER 5

Transition Stage of a Group

FOCUS QUESTIONS

1. If your group consisted of members much like yourself, what do you imagine it would be like to lead it?
2. What reasons can you think of for a lack of participation by group members? Have you been a nonparticipating member in any group?
3. Have you been in a group with people who monopolize? What was the effect on you?
4. What might you say (as a group leader or a member) to a person who told anecdotes about his or her past?
5. What guidelines can you think of for effectively confronting others in a group? How can you challenge them in a caring way and not increase their defensiveness?
6. What is the distinction between giving advice and giving feedback? Do you think giving advice is ever warranted? If so, when?
7. What is the difference between smoothing things over and giving genuine support?
8. How might you, as a leader, deal with a member's hostility?
9. What member behavior would you find most difficult to deal with as a leader?
10. If you have been in a group before, did you experience any resistance in either yourself or others? How was it handled? Did conflicts surface in the group? If so, how were they managed?

Introduction

Before groups progress to a working stage, they typically go through a transitional phase. A group in this phase is generally characterized by anxiety, defensiveness, resistance, a struggle for control, conflicts among members, challenges to the leader, and various other problem behaviors. In order for a group to move to a working stage, these problems must be recognized and dealt with effectively. Some groups remain stuck at a transitional phase because they bypass resistance or smooth over conflict and leave it as an undercurrent that destroys open group interaction.

Because a group's ability to move forward is dependent on the ability and willingness of both the members and the leader to face and work with various forms of resistance, leaders must fully understand the dynamics of a group during the transition period. What follows is a discussion of typical characteristics of a group during the transition stage.

Characteristics of the Transition Stage

Anxiety

During the transition stage anxiety is high. The sources of this anxiety are found within individuals and within the group itself. For example,

Christie's anxiety stems primarily from internal factors: "I'm really afraid to go any further for fear of what I'll find out about myself." But when Sunny says "I'm afraid to speak in here because several people are so judgmental," her anxiety arises from external factors as well as internal ones: she is inhibited by what others in the group think of her and how they may judge her.

Anxiety also relates to one's fears of looking foolish, of losing control, of being misunderstood, of being rejected, and of not knowing what is expected. As the participants come to more fully trust one another and the leader, they become increasingly able to share their concerns, and this openness lessens their anxiety about letting others see them as they are.

Defensiveness and Resistance

Group participants need to test the leader and other members before the group can move from the transition phase to the working phase. It is essential that the leader encourage an openness in which the members express their hesitations and anxieties.

Participants are torn during the transition phase between wanting to stay safe and wanting to risk getting involved. Often they are wise to show some resistance. It is foolish for a leader to think that a group will gather and effortlessly begin intensive work. Resistance needs to be respected, which means that the leader does not chastise a reluctant member but explores the source of the resistance. Both leader and members must understand the meaning of resistance.

If leaders do not respect the members' resistances, they are really not respecting the members themselves. For example, Betty revealed some painful material and then suddenly stopped and said that she did not want to go on. In "going with" the resistance, the leader asked her what was stopping her. She indicated that she was afraid of losing people's respect. The issue now became her lack of trust in the group, rather than a painful personal problem. By proceeding in this manner, the leader helped Betty to eventually talk openly about personal matters. If the leader had ignored her initial resistance by pushing her to open up, she would probably have become increasingly defensive and resistant.

Not every instance of a member's unwillingness to participate fully can be accurately labeled "resistance." Sometimes members' unwillingness to cooperate is the result of factors such as an unqualified leader, an aggressive and uncaring leadership style, or a failure to prepare members to participate in the group. One of the key tasks of leadership is for you to accurately appraise whether the source of resistance is members' fears or your ineffective leadership. Simply labeling a member "resistant" is to entrench this resistance even more deeply. If you show a willingness to explore and understand members' resistive behavior, the likelihood of cooperation and risk taking is increased.

If group members keep their fears inside, all sorts of avoidances are bound to occur. Although you cannot pry open members and force them to discuss the worries that could inhibit their participation, you can sensitively invite them to recognize that they may be suffering from fears they share with others. Below are brief descriptions of common fears that manifest themselves during the transition stage, along with possible interventions you might make to help members.

The Fear of Making a Fool of Oneself. People often worry about looking foolish if they step out of roles that are familiar to them. Mike disclosed that he had held back from saying much because he did not want to take the chance of being seen as a fool. Therefore, he decided to enter in only when he was extremely sure of himself. At other times he found it safer to take the course of censoring and endlessly rehearsing his "performances." The leader asked Mike: "Next time you become aware of sitting here quietly rehearsing, would you be willing to do so out loud?" The leader was operating on the assumption that Mike's internal critic was far harsher on him than others in the room would be. As Mike rehearsed out loud, others had a better appreciation of the nature of his struggle.

The Fear of Rejection. We often hear participants say that they are reluctant to get involved with others in the group because of their fear of being rejected. Stephen repeatedly came back to his fears that people would not want anything to do with him. He frequently said that he had erected walls to protect himself from the pain of rejection, and he made the assumption that nobody in the group would like what they might discover about him. The leader asked: "Are you willing to look around the room and see if indeed you feel that every person in here would surely reject you?" Stephen took some time to look around the room and discovered that out of ten, he was convinced that four of them would reject him, and he was not sure of two of them. If Stephen agreed to continue working, he could be asked to "own" his projections by addressing those whom he had decided might reject him. He could do this by completing the sentence "I'm afraid that you will reject me by . . ." He could also talk to the people whom he saw as more accepting by letting them know what it was about him that they would accept. After Stephen did his work, others could react to him in a sensitive way. Some in the group might say that they were afraid of him and that they found it difficult to penetrate his walls. Through this exploration, Stephen could learn about his part in creating a sense of rejection.

The Fear of Emptiness. Members sometimes fear that if they do get involved and explore issues that they've kept tucked away, they'll discover that they are merely hollow and empty, that there is nothing in them that anyone could like or value. Janice expressed this fear, yet she continued in spite of her fears. She realized that even if she did find that she was empty, she could begin a process of creating a different kind of existence for herself. She chose not to let her fear prevent her from looking at her life.

The Fear of Losing Control. Debbie expressed her fear that she might open up some potentially painful areas and then be left without closure. She was anxious about "opening up Pandora's box," as she put it. She wondered: "Will I be able to stand the pain? Maybe it would be best if things were just left alone. If I started crying, I might never stop! Even though I might get support in the group, what will I do when I'm on my own if I'm stuck with this pain?" The leader responded: "I'm sure you've been alone and have found it painful. What do you normally do when this happens?" Debbie replied that "I lock myself in the room, I don't talk to anyone, and I just cry by myself and then get depressed." The leader asked her to pick two or three people in the room who she thought would be most able to understand her pain and tell them about some of the distress in her life. As she did this, she would be likely to discover the difference between isolating herself with her pain and sharing it with others and experiencing their support. She could also come to the realization that she was not condemned to dealing with her pain in isolation, unless she chose to do so. She could be challenged to identify a few people in the group and in her outside life whom she could reach out to in time of need.

The Fear of Self-Disclosure. Members often fear self-disclosure, thinking that they will be pressured to open up too far as part of the "admission dues" for being in the group. It often helps to reinforce emphatically to members that they can make themselves known to others and at the same time retain their privacy. Consider this example: "I can't imagine myself talking about my parents in the negative ways that others are doing in here," Charlene said. "If I were to talk this way about my parents, I would be overcome with shame and disloyalty." Because the leader was aware of certain cultural values that Charlene held, he let her know that he respected her deep-seated injunctions. He did not push her to do something that she would later regret. But he did encourage her to think of ways in which she could participate in the group that would be meaningful to her. There is a delicate balance between reluctance because of cultural injunctions and resistance over moving into frightening territory. As we explained in Chapter 4, it is the choice of members to determine what and how much they share. When they recognize that they are responsible for what they tell others about themselves, participants tend to be less fearful of self-disclosure.

Some Other Fears. A variety of other fears are often expressed by members:

- "The leaders and members intimidate me, making me want to retreat."
- "If I tell people about some of the things that I've done in the past, I worry about their judging me."
- "I'm afraid I'll get too dependent on the group and rely on others to solve my problems for me."
- "I'm afraid that if I let my anger out, I'll lose control and hurt somebody.
- "I'm uncomfortable with physical contact, and I'm afraid I'll be expected to touch and be touched even though I don't want to."
- "I'm worried that I'll take too much group time by talking about my problems, that I'll bore people, and that they'll just tune me out."
- "I'm afraid I'll get close to people in here and then I'll never see them again once the group ends."

Though it is not realistic to expect that all these fears can be eliminated, we do think that members can be encouraged to face their fears. Through what you model as a leader, you can help create a trusting climate in which members will feel free enough to test their fears and put the unrealistic ones to rest. If members decide to be open about the fears that are keeping them from talking about themselves and if this decision can be made relatively early in a group, a good foundation of trust is created that will enable them to deal constructively with other personal issues as the group evolves.

The Struggle for Control

Struggles over control are common at the transition stage. Some characteristic group behaviors include competition, rivalry, jockeying for position, jealousies, challenges to the leadership (or lack of it), and discussions about the division of responsibility and decision-making procedures. Participants' main anxieties relate to having too much or too little responsibility. In order to deal constructively with these control issues, members must bring them to the surface and talk about them. If the here-and-now problems are ignored, the group will be inhibited by a hidden agenda. Below are some comments we have heard members make that illustrate control issues:

- "I don't want to talk just because you want me to talk. I learn just as much by listening and observing."
- "There are several people in here who always get the attention. No matter what I do, I just don't seem to get recognized, especially by the leaders."
- "You leaders should pay more attention to Paul. He's been crying several times, and you haven't been taking care of him."
- "How come when I cried you didn't hold me the way you're holding Harold right now?"

- "No matter what I say, you leaders never seem to think I'm doing it right. Why can't I just do it my way?"

In response to any one of these members' statements, it is imperative that the leader not assume a defensive stance. The leader's task is to help members understand that their struggle for control may be a form of resistance. Assume that Brenda says: "No matter what I say, you leaders never seem to think I'm doing it right. Why can't I just do it my way?" The leader might respond with: "I'm not looking at what you're doing in terms of right or wrong. I'm more concerned that what you do in here will help you achieve the goals you set for yourself. I've noticed that you sometimes avoid talking about difficult areas in your life." Another intervention would be to ask Brenda "What would your way be of using time in this group?" Or the leader could say "Tell me more about what is helpful to you in this group and what is not helpful."

Conflict

Conflict often carries a negative connotation. People sometimes assume that it is a sign of something intrinsically wrong and should be avoided at all costs. When there are conflicts within a group, both the leader and the members often want to avoid them rather than spend the time necessary to work through them. However, because conflict is inevitable in all relationships, including groups, it is the avoidance of conflict that makes it destructive. Unexplored conflict is typically expressed in defensive behavior, hostility, indirectness, and a general lack of trust. It is especially crucial in the transition stage that conflict be managed effectively, so that the level of trust will increase. Thus, a primary task of leaders is to teach members the value of working through conflicts in a constructive way.

Diane expressed a conflict within one group: "There are some people in here who never say anything." Jeff immediately replied, defensively, "Not everybody has to be as talkative as you." Sylvia joined in, sarcastically, "Well, Diane, you talk so much you don't give me a *chance* to participate!" Bert's contribution was: "I wish you would be nicer to one another and stop this arguing. This isn't getting us anywhere."

Unproductive interventions by the leader would have been: "I agree with you, Bert, and I wish people would knock it off!" Or "Diane, you're right. There are too many people in here who blend into the woodwork. I wish everyone would take as many risks as you do!" Such remarks increase the members' defensiveness and entrench resistance.

The emerging conflict was dealt with constructively when the leader took the tack of exploring the underlying dynamics of what had been said and what was *not* being said: "I agree with you, Bert, that right now we're not getting anywhere. But I don't want people to stop talking, because we need to get to the bottom of what all this means." Turning to Diane, the leader asked her: "How are you affected by all these reactions? Whom in particular do you want to hear from? What does it do to you when people don't say anything? What do you imagine that these people may be saying about you to themselves?"

Diane's original statement was a defensive and chastising remark to the group in general. The group reacted with appropriate defensiveness. The leader was refocusing on Diane's difficulty with the group and trying to get her to be more specific about how she was affected by people whom she saw as being silent. The conflict found resolution when she let people know that she was afraid that they were judging her when they said very little and that she was interested in how they perceived her. The chances are that this conflict would not have come about if Diane had made such statements to begin with. For example, she might have said to Sylvia: "I notice that you're quiet, and I often wonder what you think of me. I don't like it when you don't say much, because I'm really interested in what you have to say." Such a statement would have reflected more accurately what was going on inside Diane than did her punitive remark. It is important for the leader not to cut off the expression of conflict but to facilitate more direct expression of feeling and thinking among the members.

Cohesion within a group typically increases after conflict and anger are recognized and expressed, for venting such feelings is one way of testing the freedom and trustworthiness of the group. The participants soon discover whether this group is a safe place in which to disagree openly and whether they will be accepted in spite of the intensity of their feelings. When conflict is constructively dealt with, the participants learn that their relationships are strong enough to withstand an honest level of challenge.

Challenges to the Group Leader

Although leaders may be challenged throughout a group, they are more often confronted both personally and professionally during the transition stage. For example, several members may complain about not getting the "right" type of leadership, thereby challenging the leader's competence. It is a mistake for leaders to assume that every confrontation is an attack on their integrity. Instead, they need to nondefensively examine what is being said in order to differentiate between a *challenge* and an *attack*. How they respond to members' confrontations has a bearing on how trustingly the participants will approach them in the future.

If Art says to the leader "I'm bored in here, and I wish you'd do more to make this a better group," a nontherapeutic reply is "Do you think you could do it better yourself?" By contrast, therapeutic replies might include: "Tell me more about what you'd like from me or what you'd like me to do differently." "Say more about what's missing for you in this group." "What could you continue to do to make this a more meaningful group for you?" (By saying what he does, Art has already taken the first step in changing the situation for himself.) It is not necessary that the leader quickly comply with Art's demand to conduct the group differently. What is essential is that she listen nondefensively and promote a full expression of his dissatisfaction. The leader is not willing to assume total responsibility for his boredom. She explores with him their mutual responsibility to make this a meaningful and productive group, and she invites others to express their reactions to what she has said.

Though challenges may never be comfortable to the leader, it is important to recognize that these confrontations are often the members' significant first steps toward testing the leader and thus becoming less dependent on the leader's approval. The way the group leader responds to challenges such as Art's has a powerful effect on the members' willingness to continue to take risks and to trust. Leaders can be good role models if they respond openly and avoid becoming defensive.

Confrontation

As we have mentioned before, our view of a therapeutic group includes both support and challenge. In Chapter 4 we noted that people sometimes see confrontation as a negative act with destructive potential. Because of this connotation, they sometimes avoid it at all costs. In contrast, we think that people cease being effective catalysts to others' growth if all they offer is support and empathy. If carried to excess, such an "understanding" attitude can be counterproductive. Groups that focus almost exclusively on positive feedback and strengths do not challenge participants to take a deeper look at themselves. If members limit their responses to supportive ones, they fail to provide people with information on the way they are perceived and how they affect others.

We think leaders have a responsibility to teach members what confrontation is and how to challenge others in constructive ways. We see confrontation *not* as (1) tearing others down carelessly, (2) hitting others with negative feedback and then retreating, (3) committing an act of hostility aimed at hurting others, (4) telling others what is basically wrong with them, or (5) assaulting others' integrity. Ideally, we see confrontation as an invitation for participants to look at some aspect of their interpersonal style or their life to determine if they want to make changes. Caring confrontation is designed to help members make an honest assessment of themselves or speak more about their own reactions, rather than talking about others.

Our approach to group practice entails providing members with guidelines for appropriate and responsible confrontation:

- Members and leaders should know why they are confronting.
- Confrontations should not be dogmatic statements concerning who or what a person is.

- The person being confronted is likely to be less defensive if told what effect he or she has on others rather than simply branded with a label or judgment.
- Confrontations are more effective if, instead of being global generalizations about a person, they focus on specific, observable behaviors.
- One of the purposes of confrontation is to develop a closer and more genuine relationship with others.
- Sensitivity is an important element of effective confrontation; it is useful for the person doing the confronting to imagine being the recipient of what is said.
- Confrontation should give others the opportunity to reflect on the feedback they receive before they are expected to respond or to act on this feedback.
- Those confronting would be wise to ask themselves if they are willing themselves to do what they are asking others to do.

The quality of the confrontations that occur in a group is an index of how effective the group is. The more cohesive a group is, the more challenging and daring the members and leaders can be. Groups that disintegrate under challenge are based on a false sense of cohesion.

To make the issue of confrontation more concrete, we present the following examples. The first statements illustrate ineffective confrontation; they are followed by effective confrontations.

- "You're always so judgmental, and you make me feel inadequate." This could be changed to: "I feel uncomfortable with you because I'm afraid of what you think of me. Your opinion is important to me. I don't like it that I often feel inadequate when I'm with you."
- "You're a phony! You're always smiling, and that's not real." An effective confrontation is: "I find it difficult to trust you, because often when you say you're angry, you're smiling. That makes it hard for me to get close to you."
- "You aren't getting anything from this group. All you ever do is sit and observe. We're just interesting cases for you." An effective challenge would be: "I'd like to get to know you. I'm interested in what you think and feel, and sometimes I worry that you see me as an interesting case. I'd like to change the way I feel around you."
- "If I were your husband, I'd leave you. You're full of venom, and you'll poison any relationship." A more effective statement is: "I find it hard to be open with you. Many of the things you say really hurt me, and I want to strike back. It would be difficult for me to be involved in an intimate relationship with you."
- "You do nothing but play games." A more concrete and effective statement is: "When you cry, I'm bothered, because it's not easy for me to feel compassionate. I'd like to talk to you more about this."

In each of the ineffective statements, the people being confronted are being told how they are, and in some way they are being discounted. In the effective statements the members doing the confronting are revealing their perceptions and feelings about the other members and how they are being affected by them.

The Leader's Reactions to Resistance

As we have stressed, a central characteristic of the transition stage is resistance, which manifests itself in many forms of member behavior. It is essential that you not only learn to recognize and deal with the members' resistance but also become aware of your own reactions to resistance. A mistake that we commonly observe when we supervise group leaders is their tendency to focus on "problem members" or difficult situations, rather than on their own dynamics and how they are affected personally when they encounter a "resistant group." Typically, leaders have a range of feelings: being threatened by what they perceive as a challenge to their leadership role; anger over the members' lack of cooperation and enthusiasm; feelings of inadequacy to the point of wondering if they are qualified to lead groups; resentment toward several of the members, whom they label as some type of problem; and anxiety over the slow pace of the group, with a desire to stir things up so that there is some action.

One of the most powerful ways to intervene when you are experiencing strong feelings over what you perceive to be resistance is to deal with your own feelings and possible defensive reactions to the situation. If you ignore your reactions, you are leaving yourself out of the interactions that occur in the group. Furthermore, by giving the members your reactions, you are modeling a direct style of dealing with conflict and resistance, rather than bypassing it. Your own thoughts, feelings, and observations can be the most powerful resource you have in dealing with defensive behavior. When you share what you are feeling and thinking about what is going on in the group—in such a way as not to blame and criticize the members for deficiencies—you are letting the members experience an honest and constructive interaction with you.

We hope that you will keep these thoughts in mind as you read the next section, which deals with problem behaviors and difficult group members. Although it is understandable that you will want to learn how to handle problem members and the disruption of the group that they can cause, the emphasis should be on actual *behaviors* rather than labels. It is helpful to consider problem behaviors as manifestations of resistance that most participants display at one time or another during the history of a group.

Problem Behaviors and Difficult Group Members

We think it is important to describe specific behaviors that interfere with the establishment of a cohesive and productive group, but as we have said, we want to resist the temptation to characterize any member as "the monopolist," "the group nurse," "the assistant therapist," "the calculator," and so on. Certain problems inherent in such labeling have already been discussed. In addition, placing a fixed label on a participant represents a failure to take into account what the person is besides that behavior. Although a man may exhibit overly supportive behavior, he is surely more than a "group nurse." And even though a woman is prone to intellectualizing and storytelling, she is surely more than just an "avoider." With this caution, we will now describe member behaviors that are counterproductive to group functioning.

Silence and Lack of Participation

Silence and withdrawal are two forms of behavior that most group leaders must eventually learn to deal with. Even though the silent and withdrawn member does not interfere verbally with group functioning, this behavior may constitute a problem for both the member and the group. The danger is that quiet or withdrawn members will go unnoticed and that their pattern of silence may indicate a problem.

Some silent group members may argue that their lack of verbal participation is not an index of their involvement. They may maintain that they are learning by listening and by identifying with others' problems. These members may say that "I don't feel like talking just to hear myself talk" or that when they have something important to contribute, they'll do so. Group leaders should encourage these members to discuss their silence in the group. There are many reasons for nonparticipating behavior, and these should be explored. Some of the reasons are:

- the feeling that one doesn't have anything worthwhile to say
- the feeling that one shouldn't talk about oneself or that one should be seen and not heard
- the fear of looking foolish; not knowing the appropriate thing to say or do
- the fear of certain members in the group or of the authority of the group leader
- resistance, particularly if the person doesn't really want to be a member of the group
- uncertainty about how the group process works
- fear of being rejected or of being accepted
- lack of trust in the group; fear of leaks of confidentiality

It is important that members not be attacked for their silence but instead be invited to participate. Also, group leaders must be careful to avoid consistently calling on a silent person, for in this way the member is relieved of the responsibility of initiating interaction. A "game" can be made of drawing out the person, and this can lead to resentment on the part of both the rest of the group and the silent member and frustration on the part of the leader who perpetuates this behavior.

Silent members can be invited to explore what their silence means. For example, are they this way outside of the group as well? How does it feel for them to be in this group? Do they want to do anything about becoming verbally active participants? The rest of the group can participate in this discussion, for group members generally do have reactions to nonparticipating members. They may feel cheated that they know so little of that person, or they may resent that the person is observing them as they risk and reveal themselves. If there are several silent members in a group, the verbally active members may become less revealing because they don't trust those who aren't revealing also.

Silent members can be taught that others will not know of their involvement unless they express it in words. The leader may ask such members to make a contract to speak at every session, sharing with the group at some point how they responded to the session that day. Another way for the leader to handle this behavior is to ask the relatively silent members at the end of a session whether they got from the session what they had wanted. If they indicate that there were some things they wanted to talk about but that time ran out before they got a chance, they can make a contract to be the first on the agenda at the next group meeting.

A useful group technique is to ask people who feel that they are not active participants to form an inner circle within the group. Those who identify themselves as active participants sit in an outer circle. The members of the inner circle are then instructed to talk among themselves about how they feel in the group, what their fears and concerns are, and in what ways they want to change their behavior. After a time, the members of the outer group can take the inner circle and react to what they've heard. In this way the entire group is involved in the discussion of the issue of participation.

Monopolistic Behavior

At the other end of the participation continuum is the person who exhibits a high degree of self-centeredness by monopolizing the activities of the group. This member is continually "identifying with others"— that is, taking others' statements as openings for detailed stories about his or her own life. Because of a great need to talk, this person prevents others from getting their share of group time. People sometimes operate under the assumption that a good group member is one who talks a lot. Leaders need to help such members explore the possible dynamics of their behavior. They may be talking excessively out of anxiety, they may be accustomed to being ignored, or they may be attempting to keep control of the group.

During the beginning stage of a group, members as well as some leaders may be relieved that someone else is going first, and no one will intervene to stop the person from taking center stage. It is most likely that as time goes on, both leaders and members will tire of this behavior and will become increasingly frustrated. As meetings continue, the group generally becomes less tolerant of the person who monopolizes, and unless these feelings of annoyance are dealt with early, they may be bottled up and then released in an explosive way.

For both ethical and practical reasons it is essential that the monopolizing person be gently challenged to look at the effects of such behavior on the group. Ethical practice dictates that group leaders acquire intervention skills necessary to block rambling. The relevant ASGW (1989) guideline is: "Group counselors ensure equitable use of group time for each member by inviting silent members to become involved, acknowledging nonverbal attempts to communicate, and discouraging rambling and monopolizing of time by members" (8. c.). It is desirable that the leader intervene before the members react out of frustration and make a hostile remark such as "Shut up!" Some possible leader interventions are:

- "Tanya, you talk often. I notice that you typically identify with every problem that is raised. You tell stories, and I get lost in the details. I'm confused about what you want to say. In one sentence, what do you most want me to hear?"
- "Tanya, you seem to have a lot to say. I wonder if you're willing to go around the room to different members and finish the following sentence: 'What I most want you to hear about me is ...'"
- Other possible incomplete sentences that could lead to fruitful exploration are:
  "If I didn't talk ..."
  "If I let others talk ..."
  "I have a lot to say because ..."
  "When people don't listen to me I feel ..."
  "I want you to listen to me because ..."

Tanya can be asked to make the rounds by addressing each person in the group through the process of completing any one of these sentences. It is important for her not to elaborate or explain but to say the first thing that comes to her mind. It is best to instruct members not to respond during the time that she is going around. Through such exercises we usually discover crucial information that helps everyone get a better sense of the function served by the monopolizing behavior.

Assume that another member, Vance, confronts Tanya in a hostile manner before the leader has said anything about her behavior. Vance asks Tanya: "Why don't you shut up for a change? Do you think you're the only one who has a right to speak in here?" An appropriate leader intervention could be: "Vance, I'd like you to say more to Tanya. Tell her how her talking gets in your way of understanding her. What all had you been feeling and thinking before it ended in your feeling this frustrated?"

We can dismiss Tanya's behavior as simply a nuisance, or we can see it as a defense and encourage her to explore the price she is paying for her defenses. Consider that she initially appeared to be a motivated member. She seemed to reveal personal aspects of herself, she readily made suggestions to others, she could identify with most who spoke, she became an "assistant therapist" by questioning and interpreting, she told detailed stories of her past, and most of her behavior was an expression of the message "Please notice me and like me." In her own mind she felt that she was doing what was expected of her and viewed herself as an eager participant. One of the issues that she had initially said she wanted to look at was her difficulty in getting close to people. She acknowledged that she had few friends and that people were typically annoyed with her, which she found perplexing. By confronting Tanya in an honest and sensitive manner, the leader can help her learn what she is doing that prevents her from getting what she says she wants in her relations with people. She may discover that during her childhood she was often ignored and not listened to. She had to fight to be heard by her family then, and she is still behaving in some of the same ways. She may have decided that if she didn't talk a lot, she would be ignored. The fact is that her familiar behavior is not getting her what she wants, either inside or outside of the group. The group experience offers her the possibility of behaving in other ways that can satisfy her wants.

You can approach difficult members like Tanya with a sense of interest and ask questions such as: "How is it that Tanya is working so hard at getting me to pay attention to her, yet I feel that I want to ignore her? How is it that she can get a whole group of people to be angry with her? How is she replicating, in this group, behavior that is problematic on the outside?" You cannot afford to stop at the tendency to remain annoyed with people like Tanya. Instead, you can explore the context in which her behavior makes sense.

Storytelling

Self-disclosure is frequently misunderstood by some group members to mean a lengthy recitation about their life, past and present. If they are confronted about continually relating their detailed history, they sometimes express resentment, maintaining that they are risking disclosing themselves. In teaching group process, leaders need to differentiate between pseudodisclosure, which is merely talking about oneself or about others and life situations, and disclosure of what a person is thinking and feeling now. During the beginning stages of a group the leader may allow some storytelling, for people who are new to groups frequently need to hear facts about others or to share some of their own past. However, if storytelling behavior becomes a familiar style (either for the whole group or for one member), the leader should recognize this problem and deal with it. The following examples illustrate how storytelling can be handled.

Richard would, almost predictably, bring the group up to date each week on developments in his marriage. He focused on details of his wife's behavior during the week, but he rarely described his own feelings or behavior. Since Richard was the spouse who was in the group, the leader pointed out, it was him the group was interested in. As Richard and the group looked more at this behavior, it became obvious to him that this was his way of avoiding talking about himself. He thus made a contract to talk about his reactions and not to talk about his wife in the group each week.

Sandra typically told every detail of her earlier experiences, but even though the group knew a lot about the events in her past, they knew very little about how she felt about what she had experienced. Like Richard, she felt that she was open in sharing her private life with the group; and, like Richard's group, her group wanted to know more about how she responded to her life situations. The group leader told her that he was "losing Sandra" in all of the details. He let her know that he was indeed interested in knowing her but that the information she was offering was not helping him do so.

Storytelling can be any form of talking about out-of-group life that leaves the person telling the story unknown. Feedback from the group given directly, without judgment, can assist the person to speak in personal terms and keep the focus on feelings, thoughts, and reactions.

Questioning

Another counterproductive form of behavior in the group is interrogation. Some members develop a style of relating that involves questioning others, and they intervene at inappropriate times, asking why a person feels a certain way. People who habitually ask questions should be helped to see that this behavior may be a way of hiding, of remaining safe and unknown in a group. And they should be taught that the people to whom the questions are addressed typically lose the intensity of any emotion they may have been experiencing; questions tend to direct people toward thinking and away from feeling.

If members can be made to understand that questions not only intrude on others but also keep the questioner's feelings about others disguised, there is a good chance that they will change. Practice for behavior change might consist of trying to make only direct statements. For example, Marie could be invited to say what had prompted her to ask a question. If she had asked another member why he was so quiet, the leader could encourage her to say what had been going on in her mind before she asked the question. She may tell the leader "I noticed that Jim hardly says anything in here, and I'm interested in him and would like to get to know him." In such a statement Marie discloses her investment in her question without putting Jim on the spot. Questions often arouse defensiveness, whereas personal statements are less likely to do so.

Because questions do not tell the entire story, we typically ask members who raise them to fill in the details. We might say: "What prompted you to ask . . .?" "How come you want to know?" "What are you aware of right now that makes you want to ask that question?" Or "Tell [the person] what led up to your question." Following are some examples of questions and the possible hidden messages they contain:

- "How old are you?" ("I'm much older than you, and I wonder if I'll be able to identify with you.")
- "Why did you make Shirley cry?" ("I don't trust you, and I would never open myself up to you the way she did.")
- "Why do you push people so hard?" ("I'm scared, and I don't know how far I want to go.")
- "Why are you laughing?" ("I'm irritated at you, and I don't think you take seriously what goes on in this group.")
- "What do you think of me?" ("I like and respect you, and your view of me matters.")
- "Why don't you leave your husband?" ("I care about you and the way you struggle, and I worry over how long you can keep going.")
- "Why do people in here always criticize their parents?" ("I'm a parent, and I wonder if my kids are that angry at me.")

Giving Advice

A problem behavior that is related to questioning is giving advice. It is one thing to offer a perception or opinion to other members and quite another to tell people what they should feel or what they should or shouldn't do. The advice giving may be subtle: "You shouldn't feel guilty that your parents divorced, because that was their decision and not something you made them do." Although this is true, the point is that the young woman does feel guilty and believes that if it had not been for her, her parents might still be married. It does not serve the best interest of the woman to advise her not to feel guilty. She has to resolve this feeling for herself. The man who had a need to tell her that she shouldn't feel guilty could profit from examining his own motives for wanting to remove the guilt. What does this mean about him? At this point the focus might be shifted to the advice giver, and the meaning of his giving such advice might be explored.

Advice giving can be less subtle. Pam has been considering not only leaving her husband but also leaving her two teenage daughters with him. She is confused, and though she thinks she wants to live alone, she feels somewhat guilty. Robin intervenes: "Pam, you owe it to yourself to do what you want to do. Why should you be stuck with your kids? Why not let him take them? If I were you, I'd leave both my kids and my husband, get an apartment, and take that job as an interior decorator." This type of behavior raises a lot of questions about Robin. What are her values and possible unresolved problems? Why does she feel a need to straighten Pam out? Wouldn't it be better for Robin to talk about herself instead of trying to be helpful by deciding what is best for Pam? The group might now focus on Robin's need to provide others with a pat solution. Robin might learn about what she is getting from giving others advice.

Advice giving has the tendency to interrupt the expression of thoughts and feelings and to increase dependency. If Pam were given enough time to explore her conflict more fully, she would be better able to make her own decision. In essence, an abundance of advice tells her that she is not capable of finding her own way, and it conditions her to become more dependent on others for direction. In our opinion, this is not a positive outcome of a therapeutic group. Even if the advice given is helpful and sound, in the long run it does not teach Pam the process of finding her own solutions to new problems as they occur.

A related behavior is displayed by members who want to assist the leader. They ask questions, probe for information, freely give advice, and focus more on others in the group than on themselves. This issue must be dealt with, because it will create resentment among the other members as well as the leader. Recognizing this behavior as a possible defense, or form of resistance, the leader can sensitively block it by pointing out to such members that they are depriving themselves of maximum benefit from the group by paying more attention to others than to themselves.

Band-Aiding

Related to the advice-giving style is the style of trying to soothe wounds, lessen pain, and keep people cheerful. This behavior is sometimes manifested by a person who complains of how negative the group is and who wants to focus more on the positive side. The following are two examples of such "Band-Aiding":

Jack was finally able to feel his sadness over the distance between his sons and himself, and he sobbed in the group as he talked about how much he wanted to be a better father. Before Jack could have a cathartic cry, Randy put his hands on Jack's shoulders and tried to reassure him that he was not such a bad father, because at least he lived with his kids. Randy might have wanted to make Jack feel better so that he himself would feel more comfortable.

Jan revealed her memories of the loneliness, rejection, and fright she had felt when she had an abortion as an adolescent. She was reliving the emotions that she had felt earlier. Louise moved across the room, held Jan, and tried her best to take Jan's lonely feelings away. What had Jan provoked in Louise? Why did Louise need to protect her from the intensity of her pain? Far too often, people fail to see the therapeutic value in the release of pain.

There is a real difference between behavior that is Band-Aiding and behavior that is a genuine expression of care, concern, and empathy.

When there is real caring, the interests of the people who are experiencing the pain are given paramount importance. Sometimes it is best to allow them to experience the depths of their pain; ultimately, they may be better off for having done so. They can be supported after they've had the chance to intensely experience their pain. Band-Aiding is pseudo-support, designed primarily to aid the one who is supporting. Finding it too difficult to witness another's pain, the supportive one attempts to distract the other. Like questioning and giving advice, Band-Aiding needs to be examined at some point for its meaning to the person who performs it.

We want to emphasize that we are not opposed to members' touching others who are experiencing pain. It is the motivation behind the touch that is crucial. Does the person want to communicate "I can't tolerate seeing you in pain, and I want you to stop"? Or is the person saying "I know how hard this is for you, and I want you to know that you don't have to cry alone"? It is surprising to us how often people who are in pain accurately pick up the message of the touch. An important lesson for those who are uncomfortable in witnessing or experiencing pain is that the release of pain is often the first necessary step toward healing.

Hostile Behavior

Hostility is difficult to deal with in a group, because the person who is expressing it often works indirectly. Hostility can take the form of caustic remarks, jokes, sarcasm, and other "hit-and-run" tactics. Members can express it by missing group sessions, by coming late, by acting obviously bored and detached, by leaving the group, by being overly polite, and the like. Extremely hostile people are not generally good candidates for a group, because they are so defensive that they will not acknowledge their fears. In addition, extreme hostility can have a devastating effect on the group climate. People are not going to make themselves vulnerable if there is a good chance that they will be ridiculed or in some other way devalued.

One way to deal with the person who behaves in a hostile way is to request that he or she listen without responding while the group members tell how they are being affected by that individual. It is important that the members not be allowed to dump their own feelings of hostility, however. Instead, they can describe how they feel in the group with the hostile person and what they would like the person to do differently. Then it should be ascertained what the hostile individual wants from the group. Hostile behavior may be a manifestation of fear of getting intimate or of a limited capacity for vulnerability. If the fears underneath the hostility can be brought to the surface and dealt with, the hostility may decrease.

One notable manifestation of hostility is passive/aggressive behavior. This behavior characteristically involves the element of surprise: the person confronts and then quickly retreats. The confrontation has a sharp and cutting quality, and the person attacking withdraws, leaving the attacked person stunned.

For example, Karl, who has a good relationship in the group with Linda, suddenly calls her a "castrating female." Before she has a chance to express her surprise, hurt, and anger, he tells her that he sees his wife in her, and it isn't really her he is upset with. Karl has attempted to take back what he said, yet Linda is still stuck with her hurt feelings. On an intellectual level she may understand that he is transferring his reactions to her, but on an emotional level she is hurt and has become distrustful of him. Even though it makes sense on an intellectual level, she needs some time to recover emotionally. Eventually, Karl acknowledges that he indeed had some negative feelings toward her personally, not just as his symbolic wife. He quickly wanted to retreat when he saw that she had responded strongly.

Dependency

Group members who are excessively dependent typically look either to the group leader or to the other members to direct them and take care of them. Dependency is manifested in a variety of behaviors in the group, such as exclaiming that one couldn't live without one's wife (or husband, or parents, or children), presenting oneself as stupid so that others will provide one with answers, and playing helpless.

A special variety of the dependency syndrome is the "yes, but" style of interaction. The person requests help, and the group gives feedback, perhaps pointing out options that the person had not considered. Without even allowing this input to register, the individual replies with a "Yes, but . . ." Consider Donald, 25 years old and living with his mother. He has been complaining that his mother constantly harasses him, treating him like a child, reminding him to take his vitamins, telling him to do his homework, admonishing him that he should not stay out too late, and on and on. The group members soon tire of listening to his litany of complaints, and the following exchanges occur:

> **Maria:** If things are as bad as you say, why do you stay at home? Wouldn't it be a good idea to leave?
> **Donald:** Yes, but I don't have a job, and I'm broke.
>
> **Jim:** If you don't like the way your mother treats you, wouldn't it help to let her know?
> **Donald:** Yes, but my mother would just disintegrate if I were to confront her.

The essential point is that dependent people are not helped by being allowed to lure others into the trap of giving pity. They can't use advice, because no matter what is suggested, they can show why it will fail. The starting point for helping dependent people is to refuse to reinforce the helpless position by refusing to fill the dependency needs. At the same time, the leader should help such people realize the means they are using to keep themselves dependent.

In confronting Donald with his dependent behavior, the leader could work toward getting him to recognize the ways in which he is continuing his dependency. She might say: "Donald, I've noticed in several sessions now that you seem to provoke people into helping you. You complain that your mother is treating you like a child, but I wonder whether you solicit this kind of response from your mother also." As an alternative, she might say: "Do you really want to change, or do you think you're waiting for your mother to change? When will *you* begin to be different with your mother?" Or the leader could ask Donald to list all the possible reasons for being afraid of leaving home.

Leaders sometimes foster dependency in their clients. They have an exaggerated need to be wanted and needed, and they feel a sense of importance when participants rely on them. This is an example of the leader's unmet psychological needs interfering with the therapeutic outcome of a group. There are many other reasons that leaders collude with members to form a dependent alliance, some of which are:

- The leader may need the economic rewards from the members' attendance.
- The group may be filling the leader's unmet needs for a social life.
- Some leaders have a need to be parental in the sense of directing others' lives.
- Leaders may rely on their groups as the sole source of feeling appreciated and recognized.
- Leaders may feel useful when participants tell them how much they need them.
- Leaders may attempt to work through their own unresolved conflicts by using the group.

These examples show how the personality of the leader cannot be separated from what sometimes appears as problem behavior within the group. The behaviors of leader and members have a reciprocal effect.

Acting Superior

Some group members take on a superior attitude. They may be moralistic and find ways to judge or criticize others for their behavior. Such people are unable to identify any pressing problems in their lives. Their attitude and behavior tend to have the same effect on a group as hostility. Participants freeze up, for they are more hesitant to expose their weaknesses to someone who projects an image of being perfect. Take the example of Eliseo, who says: "My problems are nothing compared to yours. I feel sorry that so many of you had such terrible childhoods, and I feel fortunate that my parents really loved me." Eliseo is likely to respond to someone who is sharing a problem with "I used to have your problem, but I don't anymore." He will antagonize others with comments such as "I can identify with you, because at one time I was where you are." In his condescending tone is the message "I really don't need anything for myself, and there are no problems in my life; I'm perfectly content now."

You can challenge such comments by asking Eliseo what he wants from the group. A possible intervention is: "You're comparing your problems with those of others in here. You're saying that you feel pressured to come up with problems so that you can be accepted. What is it that you'd like to get from this group? How is it for you to be here? How are you being affected personally by what you're hearing? How does it feel that people are annoyed with you and don't believe that you're problem-free?" This intervention lessens the chances of pressuring Eliseo to come up with problems that he is likely to deny having. Instead, it gives him some room to talk and respond without having to defend a position of being without problems. Taking an argumentative stance generally leads to a fruitless and frustrating debate. Instead, your focus needs to be on the reasons that Eliseo continues attending this group. However, if he insists that his primary reason for attending is to observe others and learn about how people function, you may have made a mistake in initially not screening him out. You may now be stuck with the difficult task of recommending that he leave, for the purpose of the group is not to learn by merely observing others.

Seductive Behavior

The person using seduction is attempting to manipulate others in the group in order to avoid any genuine encounter. Seductive behavior can take many forms, including some of the behaviors already mentioned. There are four types of seductive behavior:

1. **Quiet seduction.** Some clients try to get others to draw them out. The game element consists of the client's underlying belief that "if people really care about me, they'll come and reach out to me first." An intervention that could challenge this behavior is: "I notice that you're often quiet throughout an entire session. I wonder if you're waiting for me or others to draw you out. I hope you're willing to bring yourself in and not rely on others."

2. **Active seduction.** Some members try to get intimacy instantly, to get acceptance without earning it. These clients tell others what they want to hear, touch others a lot, and are afraid of genuine intimacy. For example, Antonio says during the very first group meeting, to a leader whom he doesn't know, "I really think you're powerful, and I'm sure I'll learn a lot from you." A possible reply is: "I hope you'll learn something

from me, but at this moment I'm a bit uncomfortable with your adula-
tion because you don't know much about me yet."

3. **Playing fragile.** Clients may pretend that they're so fragile that
if anyone confronts them, they'll be devastated. They often talk with a
soft voice and are quickly frightened by any emotional intensity. For instance, Connie says: "I'd die if anyone hurt my feelings in here. I'm very
sensitive and scared of being attacked." She may well be setting up the
group not to react to her or challenge her. One example of the way a
leader might begin working with her is: "Connie, I certainly can empathize with the fact that it's uncomfortable when people hurt your feelings. It might well happen that someone in here will hurt your feelings.
I doubt that you will die. I'm asking you to consider contracting with
me to let us know when you feel hurt and not to withdraw."

4. **Sexual seduction.** Members may be sexually provocative and then
be angry and hurt when others respond to them in a like manner. For
example, much of what Jerome talks about in the group has sexual
undertones. He actively flirts with other members and sends many
double messages. One of his major complaints is that people don't see
him for who he really is but, rather, typically notice his physical attractiveness. You could ask him: "Are you willing to explore some of the ways
in which you have invited us in this group to react to you in a way that
you find offensive?"

Socializing

When members socialize outside of these sessions, group cohesion can
be increased. They can extend what they are learning in their group to
the informal gatherings. Such meetings can also be useful in challenging members to follow through with their plans and commitments. For
some populations, such as an inpatient group for the elderly, this can
be the only network of support.

Meetings outside the group can also be a form of resistance, however,
and can therefore work against cohesion. This is especially true when
participants talk about group matters but refuse to discuss these issues
in the group. Other signs that indicate counterproductive socializing include the forming of cliques and excluding of certain members from such
gatherings, the forming of romantic involvements without a willingness
to share them in the group, a refusal to challenge one another in the
group because of a fear of jeopardizing friendships, and an exclusive
reliance on the group as the source of social life.

When socializing outside of the sessions hampers group progress,
it is essential that the issue be openly examined by the group. You can
ask the members if they are genuinely concerned about developing the
kind of group that will function effectively. You can help them see that
forming cliques and making pacts to keep information out of the regular
sessions do not lead to a productive and cohesive group.

Intellectualizing

Some cognitive work is a necessary part of the group process, but it should be integrated with members' feelings. When members discuss, in a very detached way as though out of intellectual interest, topics that for most people are emotionally loaded, they can be said to be intellectualizing. Intellectualizing is a defense against feelings. Most people use this defense at times; it is when it comes to characterize a person's behavior that it becomes a problem.

It is important for people who intellectualize to be made aware of what they're doing. A question that you might raise with people who rely heavily on their intellect is: "Does what you are doing get you what you want most of the time? Is this something that you want to change?" Some Gestalt awareness techniques can be useful in helping such people more directly experience the emotions associated with the events they talk about. Clients can be directed to reexperience events, perhaps by role playing. You need to be alert, however, when dealing with intellectualizing. As with other counterproductive styles, there is obviously some defensive purpose being served. You ought to ask yourself whether you're competent to deal with what would be revealed should the defenses be stripped away. It is good to avoid making quick judgments about people who do not readily display intense emotions and labeling them as "removed from their feelings" or "detached."

Emotionalizing

Although groups provide an opportunity for members to focus on expressing a range of their emotions, some individuals dwell on "getting in touch with their feelings" to the extent that it can be a resistance. Lori is triggered by everyone's emotions, and her responses manage to draw attention to herself. Perhaps she believes that the only way to be productive in the group is to be highly cathartic and, consequently, to be seen by the leader as a "good" member. She can be deceiving herself in thinking that she is "really working" when she cries so easily and frequently. This behavior can also serve as a defense, because others are likely to hesitate in confronting her. In Lori's case it is not so much a matter of her being sad. Instead, her issues are wanting attention from people—wanting to be liked, accepted, and approved of. Her fear may be that if she does not display emotions most of the time, she will be ignored. In some ways, she may be clinging to her problems so that she can keep being emotionally reactive. Her emotionalism is an indirect way of getting what she wants. You need to be sensitive in determining when catharsis is an expression of a genuine struggle and when it is a form of resistance and, therefore, counterproductive.

Interventions for Dealing with Resistance Therapeutically

In addition to the descriptions we have given of ways to deal with various forms of resistive behavior, we also list interventions that can facilitate work *with* resistance, rather than against it. The statements below often help members get beyond their resistance. First we give examples of comments that illustrate resistance. These are followed by several simple responses that usually result in helping clients get unstuck. Of course, not all these responses are made simultaneously to each member comment.

Member: "I don't know."
Leader: "Pretend you knew." "And if you did know, what might you say?" "What *do* you know?" "What are you aware of as you look at me or at others in the room?" "Say the first thing that comes to your mind."

Member (during a role play): "I don't know what to say to my father."
Leader: "That's a good place to start. Tell him that." "If this is the last chance you have to speak to him, what do you want to tell him?" "If you were your father, what would you want to say?" "If you were your father, what do you fear you would say?" "Tell your father what stops you from talking to him."

Member: "I try so hard to say things the right way."
Leader: "Say it the wrong way." "What I would say if I knew how to say it right would be . . ." "Rehearse out loud."

Member: "I don't want to be here."
Leader: "Where would you rather be?" "What or who made you come here?" "You *are* here, so how can you make the most of it?" "What makes it difficult for you to be here?" "Why are you here if you didn't want to come today?"

Member (after an intense piece of work): "I feel like withdrawing."
Leader: "What or whom do you want to get away from?" "Go to a few people and finish the sentence 'I want to get away from you because. . .'" "Say more about your feelings."

Member (to the leader, sarcastically): "You think you're so high and mighty!"
Leader: "What do you really want to say to me?" "Tell me all the ways I've put myself above you." "Tell me the ways you put yourself down."

Member: "I'm afraid to talk more about this."
Leader: "What's stopping you?" "What do you fear would happen if you said more?" "What do you imagine will happen if you don't talk about it?" "What would it take for you to feel safer in here?" "I hope you'll say more about your fears of talking."

Several Members: "It's far easier to talk in the coffee shop to other group members than it is to express ourselves here."

Leader: "Form an inner circle. Imagine you're out having coffee. What are you saying?" "Say at least two things to several members about your difficulty in talking in here." Some possibilities for incomplete sentences to be completed by a client are: "I find it hard to talk in here because . . ." "I'm afraid to talk in here because . . ." "When I stop myself from talking, I'm most aware of . . ."

Member: "I'm very uncomfortable with the anger in here."

Leader: "Tell those who are angry how you're affected by them." "What happens [happened] when people express [expressed] their anger in your life?" Some possibilities for incomplete sentences to be completed by the client are: "I'm afraid to get angry like this because . . ." "When you're angry with me, I . . ." "I'm afraid of my anger because . . ." "When I witness anger, I want to . . ."

Member (who typically engages in storytelling): "But you don't understand. I need to tell you all the details so that you'll understand me."

Leader: "Give me the topic of your story." "I get lost in your words. In one sentence, what do you most want me to hear?" "What's it like not to feel understood in here?" "What's it like to discover that people don't want to hear your stories?" "How does this story relate to the way you're struggling now in your life?" "What makes it important that I listen to your story?"

Member: "I feel that my problems are insignificant."

Leader: "Whose problems in here are more important?" "If you didn't compare your problems with those of others, what could you tell us about yourself?" "How are you affected by hearing all these problems?" "Tell us about one of your insignificant problems."

Member (who has been feeling close to others in the group): "I'm afraid of this closeness, because I'm sure it won't last."

Leader: "What did you do to get close to people?" "Tell a few people what scares you about remaining close to them." "Tell us how you can get close in here but not in your life." "What will it be like for you if people don't stop feeling close to you?" "What is one thing that keeps you from maintaining the closeness you felt?" "If nothing changed for you, how might this be?" "Tell us all the advantages of isolating yourself."

Member (who is typically silent): "I don't think I need to be talking all the time. I learn a lot by observing."

Leader: "So, tell us some things you've been observing but keeping to yourself." "Are you satisfied with the way you are in this group, or would you like to change?" "What are some of the things that make it difficult to speak out more?" "Would you be willing to select two people you've been observing and tell them how they have affected you?" "Does this behavior get you what you want, both in here and on the outside?" "I'm interested in knowing what you have to say, and I'd like to hear more from you." "When you

observe me and quietly make assumptions about me, I feel uncomfortable. I'd like to be included in the conclusions you're drawing
about me. I hope you'll check out your assumptions with me." "If
you don't talk about yourself, people are likely to project onto you,
and there's a good chance you'll be misunderstood."

Member (who tends to give people advice): "I think you should stop
criticizing yourself, because you're a wonderful person."

Leader: "For several weeks now, you've observed people in this
room. Give each person an important piece of advice." "What advice would you like to give to yourself?" "When you give advice, do
you sound like anyone you know?" "How is it for you when others
reject your advice?" "How are you affected by the person you're
ready to give advice to?" "How do people in your life respond to
you when you give them advice?"

Most of these suggestions for responses by the leader provide encouragement for members to say more rather than stopping at the point
of initial resistance. The questions are open-ended and are presented in
an invitational manner. The interventions all grow out of clues provided
by members, and they are designed to offer directions that clients might
pursue in becoming unstuck.

Interventions for Dealing with
Resistance by the Whole Group

We have been focusing on ways of dealing therapeutically with the resistive behaviors of individuals. At times an entire group colludes and
presents a profile of resistance. In this section we describe one of our
experiences when this was the case. In the interest of maintaining the
anonymity of a particular group, we are changing some of the details,
and we are including themes that have been characteristic of a number
of groups that we have co-led. Our main purpose is to demonstrate how
group resistance affects us as co-leaders and how we deal with the
phenomenon of group resistance. We also describe some of the ways in
which this group resistance affects the members as individuals and the
group as a whole.

At one of our weeklong residential training workshops for group
counselors, it was not possible to individually screen candidates. In lieu
of screening, we provided all who were interested with a detailed letter
describing the workshop and outlining our expectations of participants.
We repeated this information at the first session, and participants had
an opportunity to raise questions. It was especially crucial to us that
they understand that they were to become personally involved and would
function both as members and as co-leaders during different sessions.
The full group was divided into two groups of eight. Each two-hour
period was co-led by two different trainees, so that they all had an equal

opportunity to function both as members and leaders. As supervisors, we changed groups each two-hour session. This change presented problems for some of the trainees, who said they were inhibited because the same supervisor was not continually in their group.

One of the groups (Group 1) was formed by people who got up and actively chose to be with one another. By contrast, the other group (Group 2) was largely formed by one member who remained seated and said: "I'm staying here. Anyone who wants to join my group can come over here." As the week progressed, some interesting differences arose between the two groups. Group 2 was characterized by a series of resistive moves on the part of most members. Many of them complained that they had not understood that they were to become personally invested in the group process. They said they had expected to learn about groups by observing us do the work, rather than by getting actively involved. Although a few of the members disclosed readily, others refused to share and did very little interacting, which eventually led to an increased sense of withholding on the part of all members.

The participants in Group 2 were apparently feeling many things that they refused to express. Some of them said that they were enjoying the group time, yet they spoke little and appeared bored. There was considerable subgrouping. During the breaks the members talked about difficulties they were experiencing in the sessions, yet they did not bring this information back to their group. Two members ended a session with an unresolved conflict and decided to clear the air during the break, but they did not inform the group of the outcome. During a subsequent session, one of us observed that the group seemed to have a hard time interacting and wondered if there was anything that was not being said. At first, the entire group accused the supervisor of being "too picky" and asserted that everything was "just fine." Only after some probing by the supervisor did the members eventually acknowledge that they were preoccupied and concerned about the two people who had had the conflict. The supervisor attempted to teach again how subgrouping can be deleterious to a group's attaining its purpose.

Several women in Group 2 often confronted one of the male members in a harsh manner. When a supervisor asked how he was affected by the confrontations, he quickly insisted that he was not fazed in the least. After several sessions, however, he blew up at everyone in the group (including the supervisor) and let them know how angry he was. He declared that he was ready to leave. The group mood was again one of hesitancy, and members very tentatively interacted.

During one of the sessions a cat wandered into the group room and defecated in a corner. Although the odor was undeniably strong, people attempted to ignore the obvious. Finally, one of the supervisors (Jerry) exclaimed "There's cat shit in this room, and I find it distracting to go on as though nothing has happened!" Symbolically, this pattern expressed this group's tendency to deny interpersonal conflict and to pretend that all was well. As a group, it preferred to ignore dealing directly with uncomfortable situations.

Another pattern that emerged was a tendency of Group 2 to judge itself against the performance of the other group. The members compared themselves unfavorably to those in Group 1 at those times when the two groups joined to discuss the day's progress. At a later point, people in Group 2 revealed the jealousy they had felt over the intensity and closeness that seemed to characterize the other group.

On the next to last day, Group 2's level of trust continued at a low ebb. The members showed great reluctance to be personal and to interact with one another. One of the supervisors (Jerry) told them before the lunch break: "I hope each one of you will spend some time in determining if you are getting what you wanted. This workshop is almost over. If today were the end, how would that be for you? If you aren't satisfied, what do you see that you can do to change the situation?"

The members of Group 2 decided to have lunch together for the first time. The group sessions were scheduled to resume promptly at 1 o'clock. What follows are the comments of the supervisor (Marianne) about what occurred:

"I arrived at the group I was to supervise shortly before 1:00, and at 1:20 I was still sitting impatiently in a hot and stuffy room with empty chairs. At 1:25 the group members finally sauntered into the room laughing and joking, telling me what a 'wonderful, intimate lunch' they had had. As they sat down, they let me know that they had felt much more comfortable and cohesive than they did in the group room. Even though I suspected what was occurring with them as a group, I would not have felt very honest if I had not let them know of my annoyance over their being late and not even apologizing.

"Once I had taken care of my feelings with them, I was able to explore the dynamics of what was occurring. I confronted them by saying: 'You say that talking at lunch was very easy and that you felt close to one another. You also say that when you come into this room, you feel stifled. What do you think is different?' Of course, the most obvious variable was the presence of the supervisor. As they began to open up, they initially lashed out at both supervisors. They perceived us as demanding too much, expecting them to be personal and academic at the same time, wanting them to perform, and demanding that they have problems (even if they didn't). They insisted that we had been unclear with them about our expectations. I listened to their grievances, attempting not to be defensive, which was not easy with the degree of hostility that was directed toward me. I did acknowledge that it was a difficult workshop and that indeed much was demanded of them, but I was not apologetic about my standards.

"Finally, as a group, they admitted their envy over the intimacy the other group seemed to have, and they said they had tried to replicate this closeness at lunch. It was then that I challenged them again, as had

Jerry before lunch, to reflect and begin to verbalize what they were rehearsing internally and what they were keeping from one another. Furthermore, I told them that I had a difficult time in trusting the sincerity of the intimacy they supposedly had had at lunch if they could not be more direct with one another in the session a few minutes later."

The next session took place the following morning, which also was the last full day of the workshop. At that session the members finally displayed more honesty. They had taken our challenges seriously and had given thought during the night to their behavior during the workshop. They were willing to take personal responsibility for their actions in the group, and there was no blaming. They achieved more closeness in this final session because of their willingness to say what was on their mind. They learned in an experiential way that what they had not expressed during much of the week had kept them from having genuine cohesiveness. They also learned that they could not have the true intimacy that they envied in Group 1 because of their decision to interact at a relatively superficial level. Yet neither they nor we thought that their group had been a failure, because they realized how their behavior had thwarted their progress as a group. Most of them were able to see some of the ways in which their low level of risking had inhibited the flow of their group. They all agreed that they were sorry that the group was ending, for they were just beginning to establish the trust necessary to significantly encounter one another. Since they were willing to talk in honest ways about their group, they learned some important lessons about themselves as persons as well as about the group process.

When the two of us conferred privately, we made some comparisons between the two groups. Our comparisons did not focus on labeling one group as a success and the other as a failure. Rather, we were acutely aware of the different dynamics that had characterized each group. Supervising and facilitating each group was demanding work, yet the main difference was Group 1's willingness to at least talk about its difficulties, whereas Group 2 continually withheld important reactions. In the follow-up papers that the participants wrote, our hunches were confirmed, for many members of Group 2 wrote about many of their reactions during the week that they had never mentioned in the sessions. Had they chosen to express them at the time, we are quite certain that their experience as a group and their individual experience would have been greatly different.

As supervisors, we felt that we had worked diligently with both groups, yet at times we had wondered what the participants in Group 2 were really gaining from the workshop. We experienced how draining it can be to work with a group that has a number of hidden agendas. Not only did Group 2 display resistance, but there were times when we also felt discouraged and resistant. It was necessary to remind ourselves that this was not the first time we had worked with a difficult group. Our experience has taught us the importance of making a commitment to face what is going on, to bring to the surface the hidden agendas, and to refuse to give up. In spite of our belief in the natural process of a group, our patience was tested. It often seemed that we were doing most of the work. As has been true with other groups, our patience paid off, for the members of this group eventually developed the trust necessary to explore the ways in which they had become stuck and learned what was necessary to move forward. Even though this group did not become cohesive, the members did learn important lessons about what had held them back as individuals and how this impasse at the transition stage had stalled their efforts to become a working group.

Dealing with Transference and Countertransference

As we've emphasized, it is essential when leading groups to recognize how your unresolved personal issues can feed into problematic behaviors in members. This interplay often involves transference and countertransference. *Transference* consists of feelings that clients project onto the therapist. These feelings usually have to do with past relationships, and when they're transferred to the therapist, they're not realistic. *Countertransference* refers to feelings that are aroused in the therapist by clients, feelings that, again, have more to do with unresolved conflict in a past relationship than with any feature of the present relationship. In a group context there is the potential for multiple transferences. Members project not only onto the leaders but also onto other members. Depending on the kind of group being conducted, members may find people who elicit feeings in them that are reminiscent of those they had for their parents and siblings. Again, depending on the purpose of the group, these feelings can be productively explored so that members become aware of how they are keeping old patterns functional in many of their present relationships. The group itself provides an ideal place to become aware of certain patterns of dysfunctional behavior.

How Members May View the Leader

Regardless of the value you may place on exploring transferences, you should be aware of the expectations that members are likely to have of you as their group leader. Unless their feelings about you are dealt with in the group, meaningful work may never occur. Participants have an image of the group leader, and sometimes they harbor unrealistic notions. We'll now describe some of the more common ways in which clients may initially perceive you in your leadership role.

The Expert. Some members enter a group because they are seeking direction and help. They hope that the answers to their problems rest with the therapist, who is empowered to show them how they should live. They want to increase their self-confidence, to know themselves better, to become more assertive, to feel more intensely, to lose their fears, and to gain courage. If they don't move in this direction, they may tend to resent you for not doing your job.

Some clients, because of their cultural conditioning, will perceive of and react to you as the expert. Indeed, they often present their problems and then expect you as an expert in human relations to provide them with advice, direction, and solutions. At least initially, these clients are unaware that counseling is a collaborative effort. Their perceptions of you may not be a transference reaction but more of a response to their cultural conditioning. For both clients who come from mainstream society and the clients from a minority group, you need to sensitively explain the role that both they and you will play in the group process.

The Authority Figure. It is not uncommon for members, during the transition phase of a group, to feel embarrassed about disclosing that they feel awkward and self-conscious in your presence. They say that they feel judged, that they feel inferior and insignificant, and that they don't see themselves as able to measure up to your standards. These people may be psychologically bringing their parents (or other significant authority figures) with them into the group; how they feel toward you is much the way they've always felt toward the significant people in their lives. By elevating you to a superior place, they discount their own worth. They cannot really enjoy, like, or respect you as a person, for they are too intimidated. It is often said that those who are placed on a pedestal can go only one way: down.

In culturally diverse groups, some clients may treat counselors as authority figures because they have been encouraged and taught to show respect and deference for all types of authority. We are reminded of a group member who made it a point never to sit next to either of us. To our surprise, we found out from him that indeed he was deliberately avoiding sitting next to us. From his cultural perspective, doing so would have been a sign of disrespect for us. He also had trouble respecting Jerry and questioned his level of expertise because of his use of humor. Our client was not sure that he could take Jerry as a serious professional.

The Superperson. Clients often view the group leader as infallible. It is inconceivable to them that leaders may feel inadequate at times, that their marriage may not be perfect, or that they do not have all the answers to human suffering. These clients are amazed if they discover that you are not a perfectly adjusted, self-actualizing being. Perhaps they need to believe that you have actually reached perfection and that, therefore, they can also hope to do so. One danger is that you will actually believe these grandiose perceptions of some of your clients. You may engage in self-deception and convince yourself that you do have the superpowers that some clients attribute to you.

The Friend. Some clients resent the professional aspects of a client/ therapist relationship. Others feel jealous over having to share "their" therapist. Some say that the office structure—appointments, fees, waiting room, and so on—interferes with the spontaneity they would like. It is not realistic for members to expect you, as their therapist, to be their friend, the kind with whom they would have a social relationship. If clients rely too heavily on this therapeutic relationship for friendship, they may fail to develop friendships on the outside. The dynamics of making you their friend are similar to the dynamics of reacting to you as one or both of their parents. Clients hope that you will care for them in a special way, that you will approve of and even love them unconditionally, and that you will see them as desirable. From an ethical perspective, you are cautioned to avoid dual relationships: "Group counselors do not misuse their professional role and power as group leader to advance personal or social contacts with members throughout the duration of the group" (ASGW, 1989, 9.a.).

The Lover. Some group members want to convert the therapeutic relationship into a romantic one. They may attempt in many ways to attract and seduce you. They may feel that if they succeed in getting your intimate attention, they will hold a special place in the group. No matter how seductive a client may be with you, it is always your professional and ethical responsibility to set appropriate boundaries and to avoid romantic entanglements with members: "Sexual intimacies between group counselors and members are unethical" (9.c.). Of course, seductive behavior often generates countertransference, which you will have to deal with in a therapeutic way for both your own and your clients' sake. This is true of all the projections, whether you are made into the expert, the authority figure, the superperson, the friend, or the lover. Unless you are well aware of your own motivations and unresolved conflicts, there is a likelihood that the member/leader relationship will be countertherapeutic.

Guidelines for Leaders

As a group leader, how can you deal with members' transference reactions toward you? The answer is complex and depends on the circumstances under which the relationship develops. Following are some general guidelines:

Do not quickly discount members' reactions to you as transference. Be willing to explore the possibility that members have genuine reactions to the ways in which you have dealt with them. It takes courage on your part to acknowledge that you have indeed been insensitive to a client and are now receiving warranted reactions. Often, however, members will treat you as if you were a significant figure in their life. This is especially likely to be true if members have intense feelings toward you when they have had very little contact with you.

Even if you strongly suspect transference feelings, you would be discounting the person if you said: "You are having a transference reaction toward me. This is not my problem, it's your problem." A less defensive response is "Tell me more about how you see me." This intervention elicits additional information about how the client developed a set of reactions to you. After both you and the client express your reactions, you could acknowledge that the client does have some real perceptions of your behavior by saying: "I think you have a point. I was preoccupied, and I didn't notice that you wanted to talk to me." Or you might say: "I'm surprised at the reactions you're having to me. I wonder if I remind you of anyone for whom you have similar feelings?"

When clients identify you as an object of transference, there is the potential for rich therapeutic work. You can take on a symbolic role and allow the client to talk to you and work through unfinished business. Additionally, you and the client can engage in role reversal as a way to explore feelings and to gain insight. Assume that a member, Mark, becomes aware that he is behaving around you much as he does with his father. During a role play, in which he is talking to you as his father, he says: "I don't feel important in your life. You're too busy and never have time for me. No matter what I do, it's never enough for you. I just don't know how to go about getting your approval." Because you don't know how Mark's father relates to him, you could ask him to take on the role of his father by responding as he imagines that his father would respond. After Mark has several interchanges in which he is both himself and his father, you will have a clearer sense of how he struggles with his father. Armed with this information, you can help him work through his unresolved issues with both his father and with you. Through the process of his therapeutic work, he may be able to see you as the person who you are, rather than as the father with whom he is struggling. These are but a few illustrations of how transference problems can be worked out. The important elements are that (1) the feelings be recognized and expressed and (2) the feelings then be dealt with therapeutically.

A more delicate issue is how the leader can best deal with feelings toward a group member. Even in the Freudian tradition, which dictates that therapists spend years in analysis in order to understand and resolve blocked areas, countertransference is a potential problem. So it can be a big problem for the beginning group leader. Some people are attracted to this profession because, on some level, they imagine that as a helper they will be respected, needed, admired, looked to as an expert, and even loved. Perhaps they have never experienced the acceptance and self-confidence in their ordinary life that they feel while helping others. Such leaders are using groups to fulfill needs that would otherwise go unmet.

The issue of power is germane here, for as group members elevate the leader to the level of expert, perfect person, or demanding parent, they also give away most of their power. A self-aware therapist who is interested primarily in the client's welfare will not encourage the member to remain in an inferior position. The insecure leader who depends on clients' subordinate position for a sense of adequacy and power will tend to keep the group members powerless.

We do not want to convey the impression that it is inappropriate for you to meet your needs through your work. Nor are we suggesting that you should not feel powerful. In fact, we think that if you are not meeting your needs through your work, you are in danger of losing your enthusiasm. What is crucial is that you do not exploit the members as a way of fulfilling yourself. The problem occurs when you put your own needs first or fail to be sensitive to those of the members.

Countertransference feelings are likely to develop in the romantic/sexual realm, particularly when an attractive group member indicates an interest in a group leader. Group leaders may never have felt desirable before assuming their professional role. Now that they do, there is the danger that they will depend on group members for this feedback.

Dealing with countertransference openly can compound the complexities of the group process by generating critical feelings and reactions toward the leader. Nevertheless, you may at times have to do so. One of the advantages of working with a co-leader is that the partner can offer valuable feedback from an objective viewpoint and can help the other partner see things that he or she had been blocking from awareness.

Through your training, you may have the opportunity to explore with a supervisor feelings of attraction or repulsion toward certain members. If you are conducting groups independently and become aware of a pattern that indicates possible countertransference problems, you should seek consultation with another therapist or become a member of a group to work through these problems.

Three additional points need to be emphasized:

1. Don't be gullible and believe uncritically whatever group members tell you, particularly initially. It's easy to become enamored with feedback that tells you how helpful, wise, perceptive, attractive, powerful, and dynamic you are; don't be swept away by the unrealistic attributions of group members.

2. Don't be overly critical and thus discount genuine positive feedback. All members who see a leader as helpful or wise are not suffering from "transference disorders." Members can feel genuine affection and respect for group leaders. By the same token, just because participants become angry with you does not mean that they are transferring anger toward their parents onto you. Clients can feel genuine anger and have negative reactions toward you personally. It may be true that certain leaders radiate a distant, know-it-all manner, manipulate the group toward their own ends, or are seductive with certain members. In short, all feelings that members direct toward the group leader should not be "analyzed" as transferences to be "worked through" for the client's good. A useful rule of thumb that we apply to ourselves is that if we hear a

consistent pattern of feedback, it is imperative that we seriously examine what is being told to us. If we see validity in this feedback, we are likely to make some changes in our behavior.

3. Recognize that not all of your feelings toward members can be classified as countertransference. You may be operating under the misconception that you should remain objective and care for all members equally. One of your unrealistic beliefs could be your expectation that you should be superhuman and be all things to all members. Countertransference is indicated by exaggerated and persistent feelings that tend to recur with various clients in various groups. You can expect to enjoy some members more than others and to be sexually attracted to some members. Again, this is not some disease to be cured. What is important is that you recognize your own feelings for what they are and that you avoid emotional entanglements that are countertherapeutic.

Effective Leadership: Research Findings

Research has yielded considerable evidence of the importance of a positive therapist/client relationship. A consistent empirical finding in the literature of psychotherapy is the role of a favorable therapeutic relationship as a contributing factor to positive changes in clients (Fuhriman & Burlingame, 1990). As the relationship between the leader and the members worsens, the amount of group tension increases, and the potential for therapeutic gain diminishes (Lieberman, Yalom, & Miles, 1973). Thus, it is not surprising that most articles on short-term group therapy emphasize the significance of the leader's role in fostering an interactive climate among the members that encourages feedback and participation as key group norms. Indeed, such a climate is often viewed as the basic therapeutic factor in group treatment. A high degree of interaction is thought to foster cohesion and group identity, reality testing, and the development of coping skills (Burlingame & Fuhriman, 1990).

The group leader's relationship with the members, in addition to facilitating a high level of client interaction, is also seen as a crucial determinant of the process and outcomes of a group. The leader's interpersonal skills, genuineness, empathy, and warmth are significant variables associated with effective group work. Some of the literature focuses on the therapist's contributions to the therapeutic enterprise. The specific personality characteristics that have frequently been mentioned in the literature include empathy, competence, responsiveness and attentiveness, presence, and engagement. The reviews of the literature identify the leader's personal development and awareness of personal style as influential aspects of the therapeutic relationship (Fuhriman & Burlingame, 1990). Not only is therapist style a significant factor, but the leader's awareness of how his or her behavior affects the group is crucial.

As we discussed in Chapter 1, however, these relationship variables and other personal characteristics are not by themselves sufficient to ensure effective group outcomes. Simply because group leaders possess desirable personal attributes does not necessarily mean that they will be successful. Certainly it is essential that leaders possess the knowledge of how groups best function and the skills to intervene in timely and effective ways. As we have mentioned, one of the leader's tasks is to promote good working relationships among the members and to teach them how to work productively in a group. Dies (1983b) maintains that the quality of interpersonal relationships *among group members* is more crucial to therapeutic change than the leader's relationship to individual members. Thus, the leader's central task is to create interpersonal norms such as openness, directness, respect, and concern for one another that will lead to therapeutic interactions among members.

Support versus Confrontation

Forging an effective group requires achieving an appropriate balance between support and challenge. In our opinion, groups having either explicit or implicit norms that limit group interactions to supportive ones do not have the power to help people challenge themselves to take significant risks. We further think that those groups that stress confrontation as a requisite for peeling away the defensive maneuvers of members are characterized by hostile and increasingly defensive interactions. The reviews of research that describe negative outcomes in groups consistently cite aggressive confrontation as the leadership style with the highest risks (Lieberman et al., 1973; Yalom, 1985). Based on research findings, Dies (1983b) suggests that leaders should not engage in highly confrontational interventions until they have earned that right by building a trusting relationship with the members. Once the foundation of interpersonal trust is established, group members tend to be more open to challenge. Dies recommends that because it takes time to create a supportive atmosphere, confrontational interactions are probably most appropriate at a later stage of a group's development.

We agree that there are dangers in confronting too soon and that leaders must earn the right to challenge. The attacking of defenses can lead to an entrenchment of resistance and tends to breed hostility and mistrust within the group. But we think that confrontation is appropriate even during the initial stages of a group if it is done with sensitivity and respect. In fact, the foundations of trust are often solidified by caring confrontations on the leader's part. Beginning with the early phase of the group, the leader needs to model ways of providing appropriate support and challenge. To avoid challenging a group in its early phase, when this is what the group needs, is to treat the group members as though they were fragile. How leaders deal with conflict, resistance, anxiety, and defensiveness does much to set the tone of the group. In our view, members have a tendency to follow the leader's manner of confronting.

Guidelines for Creating Therapeutic Relationships with Members

In this section we present an adaptation of further guidelines for group leadership practice based on research summaries done by Dies (1983b), Fuhriman and Burlingame (1990), Burlingame and Fuhriman (1990), Stockton and Morran (1982), and Bednar and Kaul (1978):

- Strive for positive involvement in the group through genuine, empathic, and caring interactions with the members. Impersonal, detached, and judgmental leadership styles can create resistance and can thwart the development of trust and cohesion.
- Develop a reasonably open therapeutic style characterized by appropriate and facilitative self-disclosure, but do not make it a practice to use the group you lead as a therapy group for yourself. Be willing to share your own reactions and emotional experiences, especially as they relate to events and relationships within the group.
- Keep in mind that leader self-disclosure can have either a constructive or a detrimental effect on the group process and outcome, depending on specific factors such as the type of group, the stage of its development, and the content and manner of the disclosure.
- Help members make maximum use of effective role models, especially those members who demonstrate desirable behavior. Members can be encouraged to learn from one another. If you have a co-leader, model openness with your partner.
- Provide opportunities for all members to make maximum use of the resources within the group by teaching them skills of active participation in the group process.
- Take an active role in teaching members the importance of developing an interactive climate, and model ways in which members can use in their interpersonal behavior in the group.
- Demonstrate your caring by being willing to confront members when that is called for, but do so in a manner that provides the members with good modeling of ways to confront decently.
- Intervene when a member is preventing others from using the group's resources by engaging in nonconstructive confrontations, hostility, and indirect exchanges. Help members deal with one another in direct and constructive ways.

We want to underscore our belief that you can do much to encourage members to give up some of their defensiveness by reacting to them with directness, honesty, and respect. Members are more likely to develop a stance of openness in a group that they perceive as being safe for them, and your modeling has a lot to do with creating this therapeutic atmosphere.

Co-Leader Issues at the Transition Stage

As you can see, the transition stage is a critical period in the history of the group. Depending on how conflict and resistance are handled, the group can take a turn for the better or for the worse. If you are working with a co-leader, you can efficiently use the time you have for meeting before and after sessions to focus on your own reactions to what is occurring in the group. Here are a few problems that can develop between leaders at this time:

Negative Reactions toward One Leader. If members direct a challenge or express negative reactions toward your co-leader, it is important to avoid either taking sides with your colleague in attacking clients or siding with the members in ganging up against the co-leader. Instead, nondefensively (and as objectively as possible) continue your leadership by facilitating a constructive exploration of the situation.

Challenges to Both Leaders. Assume that several members direct criticism to both you and your co-leader, saying: "You leaders expect us to be personal in here, but we don't know anything about you that's personal. You should be willing to talk about your problems if that's what you expect us to do." In such a case, difficulties can develop if one of you responds defensively while the other is willing to deal with this confrontation from the members. Ideally, both leaders should talk about the confrontation objectively. If not, this disagreement would surely be a vital topic to discuss in the co-leaders' meeting outside of the group or during a supervision session. We don't want to convey the impression that all difficulties should be reserved for a private discussion between the co-leaders. As much as possible, matters that pertain to what is happening during sessions should be discussed with the entire group. The failure to do so can easily lead to a you-versus-them split within the group.

Dealing with Problem Behaviors. We have discussed a variety of difficult members that you and your co-leader might have to confront. We want to caution against the tendency of co-leaders to chronically discuss what such members are doing or not doing and never to explore how such behavior affects them as leaders. It is a mistake to dwell almost exclusively on strategies for "curing" problem members while ignoring your own personal reactions to such problematic behaviors.

Dealing with Countertransference. It is not realistic to expect a leader to work equally effectively with every member. At times, ineffectiveness results from countertransference reactions on the part of one of the leaders. For example, a male leader could have strong and irrational negative reactions to one of the women in the group. It may be that he is seeing his ex-wife in this member and responding to her in cutting ways because of his own unresolved issues over the divorce. When this situation occurs, the co-leader can be therapeutic for both the member and the leader who is not being professional. The colleague can intervene during the session itself as well as explore these inappropriate reactions with the other leader outside the session. Co-leaders who are willing to be objective and honest with each other can have a positive impact through this process of mutual confrontation.

Transition Stage: Summary

Stage Characteristics

The transitional phase of a group's development is marked by feelings of anxiety and defenses in the form of various resistances. At this time members are:

- concerned about what they will think of themselves if they increase their self-awareness, and concerned about others' acceptance or rejection of them
- testing the leader and other members to determine how safe the environment is
- struggling between wanting to play it safe and wanting to risk getting involved
- experiencing some struggle for control and power and some conflict with other members or the leader
- observing the leader to determine if he or she is trustworthy
- learning how to express themselves so that others will listen to them

Member Functions and Possible Problems

A central role of members at this time is to recognize and deal with the many forms of resistance. Tasks include:

- recognizing and expressing any negative feelings
- respecting one's own resistances but working with them
- moving from dependence to independence
- learning how to confront others in a constructive manner
- being willing to face and deal with reactions toward what is occurring in the group
- being willing to work through conflicts, rather than avoiding them

  Some of the problems that can arise with members at this time are:

- Members may be categorized according to "problem types," or they may limit themselves with some self-imposed label.
- Members may refuse to express persistent negative feelings, thus contributing to the climate of distrust.

- If confrontations are poorly handled, members may retreat into defensive postures, and issues will remain hidden.
- Members may form subgroups and cliques, expressing negative reactions outside of the group but remaining silent in the group.

Leader Functions

The major challenge facing leaders during the transition period is the need to intervene in the group in a sensitive and timely manner. The major task is to provide the encouragement and the challenge necessary for members to face and resolve conflicts and negative feelings that exist within the group and the resistances that stem from their defenses against anxiety. Groups need to move from a stage of conflict and confrontation to an effective level of relating. To meet this challenge, leaders have the following tasks:

- teaching members the value of recognizing and dealing fully with conflict situations
- assisting members to recognize their own patterns of defensiveness
- teaching members to respect resistance and to work constructively with the many forms it takes
- providing a model for members by dealing directly and tactfully with any challenges, either personal or professional
- avoiding labeling members but learning how to understand certain problem behaviors
- assisting members to become autonomous and independent
- encouraging members to express reactions that pertain to here-and-now happenings in the sessions

Exercises

Self-Assessment Scale

Use the following scale to determine your strengths and weaknesses as a group member. Rate yourself as you see yourself at this time. This inventory assumes that you have had some type of group experience. If you have not, you might rate yourself in terms of your behavior in the class you're now in. This exercise can help you determine the degree to which you may be either a resistive or a productive member in a group. If you identify specific problem areas, you can decide to work on them in your group.

After everyone has completed the inventory, the class should break into small groups, each person trying to join the people he or she knows best. Members of the groups should then assess one another's self-ratings.

Rate yourself from 1 to 5 on each of the following self-descriptions, using these extremes:

1 = This is almost never true of me.
5 = This is almost always true of me.

_____ 1. I'm readily able to trust others in a group.
_____ 2. Others tend to trust me in a group situation.
_____ 3. I disclose personal and meaningful material.
_____ 4. I'm willing to formulate specific goals and contracts.
_____ 5. I'm generally an active participant, as opposed to an observer.
_____ 6. I'm willing to openly express my feelings about and reactions to what is occurring within a group.
_____ 7. I listen attentively to what others are saying, and I'm able to discern more than the mere content of what is said.
_____ 8. I don't give in to group pressure by doing or saying things that don't seem right to me.
_____ 9. I'm able to give direct and honest feedback to others, and I'm open to receiving feedback about my behavior from others.
____ 10. I prepare myself for a given group by thinking of what I want from that experience and what I'm willing to do to achieve my goals.
____ 11. I avoid monopolizing the group time.
____ 12. I avoid storytelling by describing what I'm experiencing now.
____ 13. I avoid questioning other group members and instead make direct statements to them.
____ 14. I'm able to be supportive of others when it is appropriate without giving pseudosupport.
____ 15. I'm able to confront others in a direct and caring manner by letting them know how I'm affected by them.

Exercises and Questions for Exploration

Many of the following exercises are ideally suited for small-group interaction and discussion. Explore these questions from the vantage point of a group leader.

1. Assume that various members make these statements:
   - "I'm afraid of looking like a fool in the group."
   - "My greatest fear is that the other members will reject me."
   - "I'm afraid to look at myself, because if I do, I might discover that I'm empty."
   - "I'm reluctant to let others know who I really am, because I've never done it before."

With each of the preceding statements, what might you say or do? Can you think of any ways in which to work with members who express these fears?

2. Imagine that you are leading a group that does not seem to want to get beyond the stage of "playing it safe." Members' disclosures are superficial, their risk taking is minimal, and they display a variety of resistances. What might you do in such a situation? How do you imagine you'd feel if you were leading such a group?

3. Assume that there is a good deal of conflict in a group you are leading. When you point this discord out to members and encourage them to deal with it, most of them tell you that they don't see any point in talking about the conflicts because "things won't change." What might be your response? How would you deal with a group that seemed to want to avoid facing and working with conflicts?

4. In a group that you are co-leading, several members attack your competence. In essence, they give you the message that you are not working professionally and that they favor the other leader. How do you imagine you'd feel in such a situation? What do you think you'd do or say?

5. In one of your groups there is a member, Betty, who rarely speaks, even if encouraged to do so. What are your reactions to the following leader interventions? (a) Ignore her. (b) Ask others in the group how they react to her silence. (c) Remind her of her contract detailing her responsibility to participate. (d) Ask her what is keeping her from contributing. (e) Frequently attempt to draw her out. What are some interventions you would be likely to make?

6. One client, Herb, continually gives unsolicited advice every time a member brings up an issue for exploration. Other members finally confront him for playing "assistant therapist" and express their impatience with his ready-made answers for every problem. What intervention would you be inclined to make? What would you want to say to Herb? to the others who had confronted him?

7. Larry has a style of asking many questions of fellow group members. You notice that his questioning has the effect of distracting members and interfering with their expression of feelings. What are some things you might say to him?

8. Jill has a habit of going into great detail in telling stories when she speaks. She typically focuses on details about others in her life, saying little about how she is affected by them. Eventually, another member says to her: "I'm really having trouble staying with you. I get bored and impatient with you when you go into such detail about others. I want to hear more about you and less about others." Jill responds: "That really upsets me. I feel I've been risking a lot by telling you about problems in my life. Now I feel like not saying any more!" What interventions would you make at this point?

9. How do you think you'd react in situations characterized by transference toward you? How might you react if certain members responded to you as an expert? as an authority figure? as a superperson? as a friend? as a lover? as a parent?

10. From what you know of yourself, in what area(s) are you most likely to experience countertransference? If you found your objectivity seriously hampered in a group because of your own personal issues, what might you do?

CHAPTER 6

Working Stage of a Group

FOCUS QUESTIONS

1. What do you think are the major differences between a working and a nonworking group? between a working and a nonworking member?
2. How can a client who has gained insight into the reasons for a problem be helped to act on this awareness?
3. What is your position on the values and limitations of catharsis in groups?
4. As a group leader, what do you think you can do to assist participants in making constructive choices about their behavior in the group?
5. What is your position on the use of techniques and exercises to facilitate communication and interaction?
6. What is your view of the "ideal" group member?
7. What are three major factors that you think bring about change in clients?
8. What specific guidelines can you come up with to determine whether self-disclosure would be appropriate and facilitative for you as a leader?
9. What would you want to teach members during the working stage about giving and receiving feedback?
10. What are several factors that prevent a group from reaching a working stage?

Introduction

As we've mentioned, there are no arbitrary dividing lines between the phases of a group. This is especially true of the movement from the transition stage to the working stage, for there is often a thin line between expressing conflicts and resistance, which is so characteristic of the transition stage, and working them through, which moves the group into a more advanced stage of development.

Many groups never reach a true working level. There are several reasons for this failure. Some open groups with a rapidly changing membership may not have the opportunity to develop trust, cohesion, and continuity. Some closed groups that cannot master the major tasks of conflict management and dealing with resistance do not establish enough trust to allow members to do what they (or the leader) consider productive work. However, clients may still benefit from a group even if it does not reach a working stage.

As we discussed earlier, conflict, resistance, and feelings of mistrust must be expressed, and a commitment must be made to face and work through barriers that interfere with a group's progress. In this chapter we examine the following questions:

- What are the characteristics of the working stage?
- How does a leader facilitate a group's movement from the transition stage to the working stage?
- What therapeutic factors operate in the working stage? What factors influence changes within an individual and a group, and how are these changes brought about?
- How does cohesion foster a spirit of productivity among the members?
- Why are disclosures by the leader and members particularly important during the working stage?
- What kind of feedback is especially valuable to members during the working stage? What are some guidelines for giving and receiving feedback?
- What are some issues for co-leaders to consider at this stage?

Progressing from the Transition Stage to the Working Stage

In Chapter 5 we described the difficulties facing a group in its transition stage. With a few examples, we now show how a leader's intervention can assist a group in transition to become a working one.

EXAMPLE 1

Frank and Judy complain that not enough is happening in the group and that they are getting impatient. They are likely to back off if the leader responds defensively. Therapeutic interventions could be any of the following statements:

- "What would you like to see happening?"
- "I suggest that you tell each member one thing you'd like him or her to do to improve this group."
- "You might have some reactions to the way I'm leading. Is there anything you need to say to me?"

These interventions can help Frank and Judy go beyond complaining, explore the source of their dissatisfaction, and express what they would like to see happen. When Joe, another member, makes a hostile remark ("If you don't like it, leave the group"), the leader can bring it into this interaction. This could be accomplished by asking Joe to make some direct statements to Frank and Judy, instead of dismissing them. If the leader does not address hostile remarks, they will have a negative impact on the group.

EXAMPLE 2

Sunny's saying that she is afraid of talking about herself in the group is another opportunity for productive work. A good place to begin is her admission that she feels judged; the leader can further her work by intervening in any of these ways:

- "Would you be willing to talk to one person in here who you think would judge you the most harshly? Why not tell that person all the things you imagine he or she would think about you?"
- "Perhaps you can go around the group and finish this sentence: 'If I let you know me, I'm afraid you would judge me by . . .'"
- "Sunny, would you be willing to go around and make some judgmental comment to each person in the group?"
- "If you would be willing, I'd like to have you close your eyes and imagine all the judgments that people in here could possibly make about you. You don't need to verbalize what you imagine, but do let yourself feel what it's like to be judged by everyone in the group."

In each of these interventions is the potential for further exploration, which can help Sunny learn how she allows herself to be inhibited by her fear of others' judgments. If she follows any of these suggestions, she has a basis for actually working through her fears.

EXAMPLE 3

Jennifer says that she never gets any attention in her group and that the leader gives everyone else priority over her. The leader does not waste time trying to persuade her that she is indeed important to him; rather, he listens to her perceptions and feelings. He then asks her to talk directly to the members whom she sees as getting more of his attention. She talks about her feelings about being pushed aside. The leader intervenes with: "I wonder if being in this group is anything like being in your family. Are there any ways in which you felt that you were not given attention at home, and are the feelings you are experiencing in here familiar to you?" This intervention can encourage Jennifer to work in greater depth on connecting her outside life, past and present, with reactions she is having in the here-and-now context of her group.

Characteristics of the Working Stage

After the tentativeness of the initial stage and the expression of feelings and difficulties in the transition stage, the working stage is characterized by the commitment of members to explore significant problems they bring to the sessions and their attention to the dynamics within the group. At this time in a group's evolution, we find that our degree of structuring and intervention is lower than during the initial and transition stages. By the working stage, participants have learned how to involve themselves in group interactions, rather than waiting to be invited into an interaction. In a sense there is a sharing of the group-leadership functions, for the members are able to assume greater responsibility for the work that occurs. This does not mean that the members become co-leaders. It does imply that they initiate work more readily, bring themselves into the work of others without waiting for the leader to call on them, and offer personal feedback to others.

Group Norms and Behavior

During the working stage there is a further development and solidification of group norms that were formed in the earlier stages. Members are more aware of facilitative behaviors, and unspoken norms become more explicit. At this time the following group behaviors tend to be manifested:

- Members are provided with both support and challenge; they are reinforced for making behavioral changes both inside and outside of the sessions.
- The leader employs a variety of therapeutic interventions, designed to further self-exploration, that lead to experimentation with new behavior.
- Members increasingly interact with one another in more direct ways; there is less dependence on the leader for direction and less eye contact directed toward the leader as the members talk.
- Control issues, power struggles, and interpersonal conflicts within the group are frequently the basis of discussion and tend to be explored on a deeper level. Members learn about how they deal with conflict in everyday situations by paying attention to how they interact with one another in the group.
- A healing capacity develops within the group as members increasingly experience acceptance of who they are. There is less need to put up facades, for members are learning that they are respected for showing deeper facets of themselves.

Group cohesion, which is a primary characteristic of a well-functioning group, actually fosters action-oriented behaviors such as self-disclosure, the giving and receiving of feedback, discussion of here-and-now interactions, confrontation, and the translation of insight into action.

Though cohesion is necessary for effective group work, it is not sufficient. Some groups make an implicit decision to stop at the level of comfort and security and do not push ahead to new levels. Groups can reach a plateau unless members are willing to confront one another. In an effective group the cohesion that has developed marks the beginning of a lengthy working process.

In the next section we provide a further discussion of the factors that differentiate a working group from a nonworking one.

Contrasts between a Working Group and a Nonworking Group

The following lists represent our view of some basic differences between productive and nonproductive groups. As you study the lists, think of any other factors you could add. If you are or have been in a group, think about how these characteristics apply to your group experience.

Working Group

Members trust other members and the leaders, or at least they openly express any lack of trust. There is a willingness to take risks by sharing meaningful here-and-now reactions.

Goals are clear and specific and are determined jointly by the members and the leader. There is a willingness to direct group behavior toward realizing these goals.

Most members feel a sense of inclusion, and excluded members are invited to become more active. Communication among most members is open and involves accurate expression of what is being experienced.

There is a focus on the here and now, and participants talk directly to one another about what they're experiencing.

The leadership functions are shared by the group; people feel free to initiate activities or to suggest exploring particular areas.

There is a willingness to risk disclosing threatening material; people become known.

Nonworking Group

Mistrust is evidenced by an undercurrent of unexpressed hostility. Members withhold themselves, refusing to express feelings and thoughts.

Goals are fuzzy, abstract, and general. Members have unclear personal goals or no goals at all.

Many members feel excluded or cannot identify with other members. Cliques are formed that tend to lead to fragmentation. There is fear of expressing feelings of being left out.

People tend to focus on others and not on themselves, and storytelling is typical. There is a resistance to dealing with reactions to one another.

Members lean on the leaders for all direction. There are power conflicts among members as well as between members and the leader.

Participants hold back, and disclosure is at a minimum.

Working Group

Cohesion is high; there is a close emotional bond among people, based on sharing of universal human experiences. Members identify with one another. People are willing to risk experimental behavior because of the closeness and support for new ways of being.

Conflict among members or with the leader is recognized, discussed, and often resolved.

Members accept the responsibility for deciding what action they will take to solve their problems.

Feedback is given freely and accepted without defensiveness. There is a willingness to seriously reflect on the accuracy of the feedback.

Members feel hopeful; they feel that constructive change is possible—that people can become what they want to become.

Confrontation occurs in such a way that the confronter shares his or her reactions to the person being confronted. Confrontation is accepted as a challenge to examine one's behavior and not as an uncaring attack.

Communication is clear and direct.

Group members use one another as a resource and show interest in one another.

Members feel powerful and share this power *with* one another.

There is an awareness of group process, and members know what makes the group productive or nonproductive.

Nonworking Group

Fragmentation exists; people feel distant from one another. There is a lack of caring or empathy. Members don't encourage one another to engage in new and risky behavior, so familiar ways of being are rigidly maintained.

Conflicts or negative feelings are ignored, denied, or avoided.

Members blame others for their personal difficulties and aren't willing to take action to change.

What little feedback is given is rejected defensively. Feedback is given without care or compassion.

Members feel despairing, helpless, trapped, and victimized.

Confrontation is done in a hostile, attacking way; the confronted one feels judged and rejected. At times the members gang up on a member, using this person as a scapegoat.

Communication is unclear and indirect.

Members are interested only in themselves.

Members or leaders use power and control *over* others.

There is an indifference or lack of awareness of what is going on within the group, and group dynamics are rarely discussed.

Working Group

Diversity is encouraged, and there is a respect for individual and cultural differences.

Nonworking Group

Conformity is prized, and individual and cultural differences are devalued.

Group norms are developed cooperatively by the members and the leader. Norms are clear and are designed to help the members attain their goals.

Norms are merely imposed by the leader. They may not be clear.

There is an emphasis on combining the feeling and thinking functions. Catharsis and expression of feeling occur, but so does thinking about the meaning of various emotional experiences.

The group relies heavily on cathartic experiences but makes little or no effort to understand them.

Group members use out-of-group time to work on problems raised in the group.

Group members think about group activity very little when they're outside the group.

The Nonworking Group Member

Having described the characteristics of a working and nonworking group in general, we now move to specifics. In the previous chapter we examined a variety of problem behaviors, and what follows is a composite picture of a nonworking group member.

Barney has joined a weekly ongoing group because his wife thinks he needs such an experience. Although he agreed to sign up for the group, he had many doubts that it would help him. He was convinced that groups do more harm than good.

Barney keeps all his reservations to himself. For several group sessions he either says nothing or reacts in a hostile manner to many of the women. When several of them let him know that they are feeling distant and are having difficulties with him, he reacts sarcastically and defensively by saying: "Well, aren't you supposed to be honest in here? What's wrong with my saying that you girls are all alike?"

At one point, tears come to Barney's eyes, and he looks very scared. When the leader checks with him about what he is feeling, he replies: "Stop pushing me, and leave me alone. All you ever do is make people cry." After that he storms out of the room.

Barney often talks about his wife, blaming her for most of his misery. When the leader suggests a role-playing exercise in which he could talk directly to his "wife" in this room, Barney refuses by saying: "That's silly. I can't talk to Bertha [a group member], because she's not my wife." At times he comes late to sessions or misses a session, either having a "good" excuse or simply not giving any reason.

Several times, toward the end of a session, Barney begins what could become some meaningful work. The leader lets him know of her concern that time is running out and makes the observation that his waiting until the end seems to be a pattern. He brusquely responds: "You don't care about me the way you do about the rest of the people. I can't program my feelings."

Although in some sessions Barney says almost nothing and expects to be drawn out, at other times he interrupts others' work by giving them unsolicited advice and solutions to their problems. He then rambles on with stories about himself. When confronted on his behavior, Barney replies, aggressively, "When I don't talk, you criticize me, and when I do talk, you want to shut me up!" He makes no attempt to listen to any constructive feedback given to him, and he is always quick to take a defensive stance.

When conflict arises in the group, Barney is quick to note: "See, I was right. All groups ever do is tear people down." He is very able to stir up conflict in his group, yet he quickly retreats in a hit-and-run fashion. At one point he admits that he feels isolated in this group, as well as in his outside life. But he is unable to see how his behavior contributes to his feelings of isolation.

In considering Barney's case, how might you deal with him? Which of his behaviors would cause you the most difficulty? Would you have let him into the group to begin with? On what basis would you have included or excluded him at the outset? Would you have excluded him later, after he had joined the group?

The Working Group Member

Now we describe the combination of traits that we think makes for a working and productive group member. We encourage you to create your own profile of the ideal group participant. Our ideal member is a woman we'll call Sandy.

Sandy wants to participate in a weekly, ongoing counseling group. She wants to take a good look at herself, her marriage, her career goals, and her relationship with her son, and she wants to discover more ways of feeling alive. She has sought group counseling voluntarily. She is motivated to work, as evidenced by her willingness to spend time thinking about what she wants from her group sessions. She eventually forms a contract that guides her work in the group. She is specific about what she wants, and she is willing to explore her problems with the group.

Sandy is sometimes scared by her feelings, and she expresses these fears. For example, she sometimes doubts that she wants to stay with her husband, and she's willing to face this issue squarely. She has never told anyone of her need to control her sexual relationship, yet in her group she deals with this need and considers relinquishing the control.

Sandy says what she feels, not what others in her group (including the therapist) might expect of her. She confronts both leader and members when she feels that something needs to be challenged, and she does so by bringing her own reactions into the confrontation. She avoids labeling or judging and instead speaks of how she is affected by what others are doing in the group. Sandy gives feedback when she has something to offer and gives support or affection when she genuinely feels this toward another member. She resists participating in activities that don't seem right for her, and she is not pressured into doing or saying something to please anyone but herself. During the group sessions she listens undefensively to what others tell her, and when she is given feedback, she doesn't try to rationalize her behavior. Instead, she considers the feedback seriously. Then she decides for herself how accurate others' perceptions of her are and what she will do with this information.

Sandy devotes time between sessions to reflecting on her involvement in the group, and she eventually makes decisions to change her behavior. She not only tries out new behavior in her group but also risks applying what she has learned in the group to her daily affairs. In between sessions she reads books dealing with areas of struggle for her and keeps a daily journal. She brings into therapy any insights she has about herself or about the group. She commits herself to doing things actively outside her group, yet at times she doesn't live up to these contracts. If she feels that she's backsliding, she mentions this in her sessions. At this point she evaluates her contract and determines how realistic her expectations are. Sandy realizes that she's not perfect, yet she accepts herself.

Group Process during the Working Stage

Even if groups reach a high level of productivity during the working stage, this achievement does not imply that the group will always remain at that level. The group may stay on a plateau for a time and then regress to an earlier developmental phase characterized by issues faced during the initial and transition stages. For example, trust can become an issue again, and it may need to be reestablished. Some members may have the tendency to close off and withdraw. The reasons for this lack of trust may be that intensive work threatens them, that they have doubts about the validity of what they have experienced, that they have second thoughts about how involved they want to remain, that they are frightened by the display of anger between members or the expression of painful experiences, or that they are anticipating the eventual ending of the group and are prematurely winding down.

As is the case with personal relationships in daily life, groups ebb and flow. Periods of stagnation can be expected, but if they are recognized, they can be challenged. Because groups are not static entities, both the leader and the members have the task of accurately assessing a group's ever-changing character, as well as its effectiveness.

The reality of the changing character of trust within a group is illustrated in the following example of an adolescent group. Members had done some productive work, both with individuals outside of the group and with one another during the sessions. At one previous meeting, several members experienced intense emotional catharsis. Felix, who had initially identified his worst fear as "breaking down and crying in front of everyone," did cry and released some stored-up pain over being denied his father's acceptance. In role playing with his "father," Felix became angry and told him how hurt he felt because of his seeming indifference. Later in this scenario, he cried and told his "father" that he really loved him. Before he left the session, Felix said that he felt relieved.

The particular session just described was characterized by a high level of trust, risk taking, caring, and cohesion. At the subsequent session, however, the group leader was surprised at how difficult it was to draw people out. Members were hesitant to speak. Felix, other than saying "Hello," said little else. The leader described what she saw in the room and asked the members why it seemed so hard to talk, especially in light of the fact that the previous session had gone so well. At first, several members expressed annoyance by making comments such as: "Do we always have to bring up problems in here?" "Can't we talk about something other than problems?" "Do we need to cry to show that we're good members?" "I think you're pushing people too hard." Felix finally admitted that he had felt very embarrassed over "breaking down" and that during the week he had convinced himself that others saw him as weak and foolish. Some others admitted that although they saw value in what Felix had done, they would not want to go through what he had out of fear of what others might think of them. Again, the task of this group was to deal with the lack of trust that members had in one another ("I'm afraid of what others will think of me"). Several of the members' statements implied a lack of trust in the leader, which made it imperative that she encourage the members to discuss this dynamic.

In retrospect, what could the leader have done differently? It is possible that Felix might have felt less embarrassed had the leader remembered his original fear and dealt with it. She might have said: "Felix, I remember that one of your fears was crying in the presence of others. You just did. How was it for you to have done this?" She could also have invited others to tell him how they had been affected by his work. Assume that Felix had said "I feel good, and I got a lot from what I did." Then, she might have replied: "Imagine two days from now, when you think about what you did this morning. Could it be possible that you might regret what you've done or that you might be critical of yourself?" If Felix had replied with a smile, saying "You may be right," she could have suggested that if he caught himself discounting his work, it would be helpful to remember the support he had felt from everyone in the room and how they had acknowledged his courage.

On the other hand, assume that Felix had responded to the leader's inquiry by saying "I feel embarrassed" and looking down at the floor. She might have replied: "I know how hard it was for you to express yourself in this way. I really hope you won't run away. Look at different people in this room, especially the ones whom you feel most embarrassed with. What do you imagine they're saying about you right now?" After Felix told others what he imagined they were thinking of him, they could be invited to give their honest reactions. Typically, members do not have disparaging remarks after someone has done significant work.

As this example shows, it is not uncommon for the issue of trust to resurface in an intense and productive session. After times like this, members may be frightened and may have a tendency to retreat. Leaders who are aware of this tendency can take some preventive measures, as we have described. When a group does appear to regress, the most critical intervention is for the leader to describe what is happening and to get members to express what they are thinking and feeling.

Choices to Be Made during the Working Stage

In discussing the initial stages of a group's evolution, we described several critical issues, such as trust versus mistrust, the struggle for power, and self-focus versus focus on others. During the more intensive, working period of a group, certain other key issues are at stake, and again the group as a whole must resolve the issues for better or worse. We now discuss each of the choices that the group must make at this stage. Remember that a group's identity is shaped by the way its members resolve these critical issues.

Disclosure versus Anonymity. Clients can decide to disclose themselves in a significant and appropriate way, or they can choose to remain hidden out of fear that if they were to reveal themselves to others, they would be rejected. People may protect themselves through anonymity, yet the very reason that many become involved in a therapeutic group is that they want to make themselves known to others and to come to know others in a deeper way. If the group process is to work effectively, the participants must be willing to reveal themselves, for it is through self-disclosure that they begin to learn about themselves.

Honesty versus Game Playing. Some believe that in order to survive in the real world, they must sacrifice their honesty and substitute deceit, game playing, and manipulation. They may say that to get ahead, they have to suppress what they really think and feel, figure out what others expect from them, and then meet those expectations.

It is fundamental to the success of a therapeutic group that honesty prevail and that a person not have to be dishonest to win acceptance. If these conditions hold, participants can both be themselves and learn to accept the true selves of others. If they don't, group interaction can deteriorate into another form of game playing. However, honesty does not mean saying anything and everything to another person (or about oneself). Saying "I hate the sight of you" is not honest, it is cruel. As one of our colleagues says, "Honesty without caring is cruelty."

Spontaneity versus Control. We hope that group participants will make the choice to relinquish some of their controlled and rehearsed ways and allow themselves to respond more spontaneously to events of the moment. We encourage spontaneity indirectly, by making clients feel that it's all right to say and do many of the things they've been preventing themselves from saying or doing. This does not mean that members "do their own thing" at the expense of others. Members sometimes stifle themselves by rehearsing endlessly everything they say. As a result, they often sit quietly and rehearse internally. We generally make contracts with clients like this. We get them to agree to rehearse out loud and to speak more freely, even at the risk of not making sense.

Acceptance versus Rejection. Throughout the course of a group the members frequently deal with the acceptance/rejection polarity. We sometimes hear a member say "I'd like to reveal more of myself, but I'm afraid that if I'm me in here, I'll be rejected." The basis of this fear can be explored, which often results in challenging unrealistic fears. Members are likely to find that they reject themselves more often than others reject them. These members may also discover that they are frightened about the prospects of being accepted, as well as of being rejected. Although they do not enjoy rejection, it has often become a familiar feeling. Therefore, feelings of acceptance can be unsettling. It's as though some say "If you accept me or love me or care for me, I won't know how to respond."

The group setting offers people opportunities to learn some of these ways in which they are setting themselves up to be rejected by behaving in certain ways. We hope that group members will recognize their own role and responsibility in the creation of an accepting climate and come to understand that by contributing to a climate either of acceptance or of rejection, they can help determine whether they as individuals will be accepted or rejected.

Cohesion versus Fragmentation. Our conviction is that cohesion is largely the result of the group's choice to work actively at developing unifying bonds. Members do this mainly by choosing to make themselves known to others, by sharing their pain, by allowing caring to develop, by initiating meaningful work, and by giving honest feedback to others.

If a group chooses to remain comfortable or to stick with superficial interactions, there will be little group togetherness. There are times when members choose not to express their fears, suspicions, disappointments, and doubts. When they do bury their reactions, fragmentation typically results. Cohesion comes from working with meaningful, painful problems as well as from the intimate sharing of humorous and joyous moments.

Responsibility versus Blaming. In any form of therapy, clients must accept responsibility for their behavior if any significant behavior changes are to take place. Thus, group members must stop viewing themselves as victims of external factors.

At some point in group work, clients usually focus their anger on others, whom they blame for their unhappiness. But during the more intensive phases of a group, clients generally come to accept the fact that a blaming style will get them nowhere. What they need to realize is that they can change only themselves. If they do succeed in changing, others may change in response. When members stop blaming others, they find that they are in control and are more able to make changes in their life.

Consider a mother, Christie, who complains endlessly how her husband and her children take advantage of her. She often exclaims "If only they were different, my life would be so much better!" She could be challenged to consider the reality that her family is not likely to change. If she focuses on blaming others and getting them to be different, she will keep herself in a powerless position. Christie is the one who will have to be different. She will need to say no, set firm limits, follow through with consequences, and learn to live with the fact that she may not always be liked by her family.

Therapeutic Factors That Operate in Groups

In this section we give attention to the special forces within groups that produce constructive changes. We've come to believe that a variety of forces within groups can be healing, or therapeutic, and that these forces are interrelated. We came up with the therapeutic factors listed below by reflecting on our experiences in leading groups and by reading the reports of hundreds of people who have participated in our groups. (We've always had the participants in our groups write follow-up reaction papers telling what factors they think were related to their changes in attitudes and behavior.) We are also indebted to other writers in the field of group work, especially Yalom (1983, 1985).

Self-Disclosure

The willingness to make oneself known to others is a part of each stage of a group, but at the working stage self-disclosure is more frequent and more personal. Although disclosure is not an end in itself, it is the means by which open communication occurs within the group. Through this process, the participants experience a healing force and gain new insights that often lead to desired life changes. If disclosures are limited to safe topics, the group does not progress beyond a superficial level.

SELF-DISCLOSURE AND THE GROUP MEMBER

Group members are able to deepen their self-knowledge through disclosing themselves to others. They develop a richer and more integrated picture of who they are, and they are better able to recognize the impact they have on others.

We tell the members of our groups that it is essential to let others know about them. Otherwise, they are likely to be misunderstood, because people tend to project their own feeling onto members who are mysterious. For example, Andrea thinks that Hal is very critical and judgmental of her. When Hal finally talks, he discloses that he is both attracted to and fearful of Andrea. Self-disclosure entails revealing current struggles, unresolved personal issues; goals and aspirations; fears and expectations; hopes, pains, and joys; strengths and weaknesses; and personal experiences. If members keep themselves anonymous and say little about themselves that is personal, it is difficult for others to care for them, because genuine concern implies knowledge of the person. This disclosure is not limited to revealing personal concerns; it is equally important to disclose ongoing persistent reactions toward other members and the leader.

What Disclosure Is Not. We've found that group participants frequently misunderstand what it means to be a self-disclosing person, equating disclosure with "letting it all hang out" without any discrimination. They may believe that the more they can dig up hidden secrets and display them in the group, the more they are being disclosing. Below are some observations on what self-disclosure is *not*.

- Self-disclosure is not merely telling stories about one's past in a rehearsed and mechanical manner. It is not a mere reporting of there-and-then events. A client needs to ask the question "How is what I reveal related to my present conflicts?"
- In the name of being open and honest and as a result of the pressure of other group members, people often say more than is necessary for others to understand them. They confuse being self-disclosing with being open to the extent that nothing remains private, and as a result they may feel exposed in front of others.
- Dumping every fleeting feeling or reaction on others is not to be confused with self-disclosure. Judgment is needed in deciding how appropriate it is to share certain reactions. However, persistent reactions are generally best shared. People can be honest without being tactless and insensitive.

Guidelines for Appropriate Member Self-Disclosure. In our groups we suggest the following five guidelines as a way of assisting participants in determining *what* and *when* self-disclosure is both appropriate and facilitative:

1. Disclosure needs to be related to the purposes and goals of the group.
2. If members have persistent reactions to certain people in the group, we encourage them to bring them out into the open, especially if these reactions are inhibiting their level of participation.
3. Members must determine what and how much they want others to know about them. They also have to decide what they are willing to risk and how far they are willing to go.
4. Reasonable risks can be expected to accompany self-disclosure. If groups are limited by overly safe disclosures, the interactions become boring.
5. The stage of group development has some bearing on the appropriateness of self-disclosure. Certain disclosures may be too deep for an initial session but quite appropriate during the working stage.

Related to the issue of member self-disclosure is the role of self-disclosures by the leader. We now turn to some guidelines designed to assist leaders in thinking about what disclosures can have a facilitative effect on a group.

SELF-DISCLOSURE AND THE GROUP LEADER

The key question is not whether leaders should disclose themselves to the group but, rather, how much and when. What are the effects of leaders' disclosures on the group? What are the effects on the leader?

Some group leaders keep themselves mysterious. They're careful not to make themselves pesonally known to the group, and they strive to keep their personal involvement in the group to a minimum. Some do this because of a theoretical preference. They view their role as one of a "transference figure" on whom their "patients" can project feelings that they've experienced toward parents and other "authority figures." By remaining anonymous, the leader tends to limit the reactions of group members to projections. Through this re-creation of an earlier relationship, unresolved conflicts can be exposed and worked through.

Other reasons why some group leaders don't reveal themselves personally are that they don't want to incur the risk of losing their "professional" image and that they don't want to be uncomfortable. They may also operate on the assumption that personal disclosure would contaminate the therapeutic relationship. Some leaders, in addition to keeping their personal life a secret, disclose very little about how they feel in the group or how they feel toward different members. Instead of sharing these reactions, they intervene, making interpretations and suggestions, clarifying issues, acting as a moderator or coordinator, evaluating, and imposing structured exercises to keep the group moving. Admittedly, all of these functions are necessary at various times, but it is both possible and desirable for leaders to get involved in these activities by revealing what they are experiencing in this process.

What about the leaders at the other end of the continuum, whose ethic is the more disclosure, the better? Inexperienced group leaders tend to make the mistake of trying too hard to prove that they're just as human as the members. They freely disclose details of their personal life and explore their current problems in the groups they lead. There are several rationales for such an approach. These leaders may have submitted to group pressure to stop acting like a leader and become more of a group member. They may also feel that it is unfair to expect members to disclose and risk unless they are also willing to do so. Although this reasoning has merit, it is important that group leaders not fall into the trap of pretending that there are no differences between the roles and functions of leaders and members. Even though group leaders can function as participants at times, their primary reason for being in the group is to initiate, facilitate, direct, and evaluate the process of interaction among members. If leaders are uncomfortable in their role, perhaps this is an indication that they should be participating in a group as a full-fledged member.

Following are four guidelines for your consideration in determining your own position on the issue of leader self-disclosure:

1. If you determine that you have problems you wish to explore, consider finding your own therapeutic group. This would allow you to be a fully participating member without the concern of how your personal work would affect the group. You have a demanding job and shouldn't make it even more difficult by confusing your role with that of the participants.

2. Ask yourself why you're disclosing certain personal material. Is it to be seen as a "regular person," no different from the members? Is it to model disclosing behavior for others? Is it because you genuinely want to show private dimensions to the members? It may be therapeutic for group members to know you and your struggles, but they don't need to know in elaborate detail. For instance, if a member is exploring her fear of not being loved unless she is perfect, you might reveal in a few words that you also wrestle with this fear, if indeed you do. Your sharing makes it possible for your client to feel a sense of identification with you. At another time it may be appropriate for you to talk at greater length about how this fear is manifested in the way you lead groups, particularly if it is revealed in your feeling pressured to be a good therapist and feeling afraid of not being loved if you do not help the group. Again, the timing is crucial, as is being true to yourself and doing what is compatible with your personal therapeutic style. Although this disclosure may be appropriate in the advanced stages of a group, sharing it initially may

burden the participants with the feeling that they should help you or should take your pain away.

3. Disclosure that is related to what is going on in the group is the most productive. For instance, any persistent feelings you have about a member or about what is happening (or not happening) is generally best revealed. If you feel annoyed at a member's behavior, it is usually advisable to let the member know your reaction. If you sense a general resistance in the group, it is best to talk openly about the resistance and about how it feels to experience it. Disclosure related to how you feel in the group is generally more appropriate than disclosure of personal material that is not relevant to the ongoing interaction of the group.

4. Ask yourself how much you want to reveal about your private life to the many people with whom you will come into contact. In our workshops, other groups, and classes we want to feel the freedom to function openly as people, but at the same time we want to preserve a measure of our privacy. If we made it a pattern to give detailed accounts about ourselves, moreover, we would lose spontaneity, for it would probably be impossible with this kind of repetition to maintain a fresh and unrehearsed style. Having said this, we hasten to add that we see ourselves as generally being personal in our groups. We are not overly concerned when people in our groups come to know about us as individuals and as a couple. We also usually decide to disclose worries or preoccupations we have that could interfere with our ability to be present and to listen effectively to the members.

Confrontation

As was discussed in both Chapters 4 and 5, constructive confrontation is a basic part of a productive group. A lack of confrontation results in stagnation. It is through acts of caring confrontation that members are invited to examine discrepancies between what they say and do, to become aware of potentials that are dormant, and to find ways of putting their insights into action. Done with sensitivity, confrontation by others ultimately assists members to develop the capacity for the self-confrontation that they will need in applying what they have learned to the problems they face in their daily life.

Example: Rich complained of feeling tired and drained. He asserted that everyone in his life was too demanding. In the group, his style of interacting involved being a helper. He was attentive to what others needed, yet he rarely asked anything for himself. In one session he finally admitted that he was not getting what he wanted from the group and that he did not feel like returning again. The leader confronted Rich with: "Many times I have seen you do in this group what you say that you typically do with people in your life. I see you as being very helpful, yet you rarely ask for anything for yourself. I'm not surprised about your resistance over coming back to this group. You've created the same environment in here as the one at home. I'm glad you're finally talking about this, and I hope you'll continue talking."

Feedback

One of the most important ways by which learning takes place in a group is through the willingness of members to give and to receive feedback. If feedback is given honestly and with sensitivity, members are able to understand the impact they have on others and decide what, if anything, they want to change about their interpersonal style. The process of interpersonal feedback teaches members that they are responsible for creating favorable and unfavorable outcomes and for changing the style in which they relate to others (Rothke, 1986).

Although feedback as a process in groups is given further consideration in the next chapter, we want to discuss some guidelines for effective feedback during the working stage. Below are some ideas that are modified from Rothke's (1986) article on the role of interpersonal feedback in group psychotherapy, as well as some of the key points that we emphasize in teaching members how to give and receive feedback:

- Concise feedback given in a clear and straightforward manner is more helpful than statements with qualifiers. For instance, Brenda is being quite clear and direct with Brian when she tells him: "I feel uncomfortable when I'm sharing very personal things about myself and I see you smiling. It makes me wonder if you're taking me seriously."
- Give others feedback throughout the course of a group. In doing so, share with them how they affect you, rather than giving them advice or judging them. In the example above, Brenda is speaking about her own discomfort and how she is affected by Brian's smiling, rather than telling Brian how he is.
- Avoid giving global feedback, for it is of little value. Feedback that relates to specific behavior exhibited in the group provides members with helpful information that they can consider using. Feedback that is particularly helpful deals with immediate events in the group. With this kind of here-and-now feedback, others in the group can confirm the message that is being sent, or they can offer a different perception.
- Feedback must be timed well and given in a nonjudgmental way, or else the person receiving it is likely to become defensive and reject it. In Brenda's case, her feedback to Brian is focused on her feelings, and it represents a risky self-disclosure. She is not judging Brian, which increases the chance that he will be able to consider what she is telling him.
- The most meaningful kind of feedback deals with the relationship between the sender and the receiver. For instance, in giving feedback to Brian, Brenda might add: "I really do want your acceptance, and I'd like to feel closer to you. But I'm aware that I'm careful of what I say when I'm around you, because I'm afraid that you might be judging me. When

you look away and either smile or frown when I talk, I'm left wondering how what I'm saying affects you. I'd like not to feel so cautious around you, and this is why I'm telling you this." With this kind of statement, Brenda is talking about her feelings of fear and uncertainty, but she is also letting Brian know that she would like a different kind of relationship with him.

- In giving feedback, concentrate on what you like about a person and on the person's strengths as well as the difficulties you might be experiencing with this person. This is not to imply that you should sugarcoat your message, but it is also a good idea to focus on strengths and how people might be blocking them.

Examples: Members sometimes make a sweeping declaration such as Florian's comment: "I'd like to know what you think of me, and I'd like some feedback!" His spontaneous request puts people in the group on the spot. He has hit the ball into their court. If we were to hear this, we would probably say to the group "Before any of you give Florian feedback, we'd like him to say more about what prompted him to ask for your reactions." This intervention puts the ball back into Florian's court, for he will be making significant disclosures about himself rather than insisting that others disclose themselves to him first. Members are more likely to respond to him when they know more about his needs for their feedback. Behind his question may well be any of these statements: "I'm afraid in here, and I don't know if I'm liked." "I'm afraid people in here are judging me." "I don't have many friends in my life, and it's important that people like me." If Florian has said very little about himself, it is difficult to give him many reactions. To find out how others perceive him, it is necessary that he let himself be known. After he has explored his need for feedback, the group leader can ask members if they want to react to him. However, the leader should not pressure everyone in the group to give him their comments. When people do offer their reactions, the leader can ask Florian to listen nondefensively, to hear what others have to say to him, and to consider what, if anything, he may want to do with this information. As the group progresses to a working stage, we typically see a willingness of members to freely give one another their reactions. Feedback is at its best when members spontaneously let others know how they are affected by them and their work. The norm of asking for, receiving, and giving feedback is one that needs to be established early in a group. Furthermore, it is the leader's task to teach members how to give useful feedback, which can be done by giving examples of both appropriate and inappropriate feedback.

Joseph's situation is an example of how feedback can be helpful in teaching a member about specific behaviors that others are reacting to negatively. Joseph joined a group because he found himself isolated from people. Soon he found that he felt isolated in the group also. He was sarcastic with everyone in his group, a trait that quickly alienated others.

Because the members were willing to tell him in a caring way that they felt put off and distanced by his sarcastic style, he was able to examine and eventually assume responsibility for creating the distance and lack of intimacy he typically experienced. With the encouragement of his group, he sought out his son, toward whom he felt much anger. He found that when he let go of his sarcasm and talked honestly with his son, they felt closer to each other.

Cohesion and Universality

A central characteristic of the working stage is group cohesion, which has resulted from members' willingness to let others know them in meaningful ways. If they have faced the conflicts of the earlier stages, the deep level of trust they have developed allows for a working-through process.

At the working stage the members are able to see commonalities, and they are struck by the universality of their life issues. For example, our growth groups are composed of a very wide mixture of people. The clients come from all walks of life, their age range is from 18 to 65 years, they represent various social and cultural backgrounds, and they have a variety of careers. Although in the earlier stages members are likely to be aware of their differences and at times feel separated, as the group achieves increased cohesion, these differences recede into the background. Members comment more on how they are alike than on how they are different. A woman in her early 50s discovers that she is still striving for parental approval, just as is a man in his early 20s. A man learns that his struggles with masculinity are not that different from a woman's concern about her femininity.

The circumstances leading to hurt and disappointment may be very different from person to person or from culture to culture. But the resulting emotions have a universal quality. Although we may not speak the same language or come from the same society, we are connected through our feelings of joy and pain. It is when group members no longer get lost in the details of daily experiences and instead share their deeper struggles with these universal human themes that a group is most cohesive. The leader can help the group achieve this level of cohesion by focusing on the underlying issues, feelings, and needs that the members seem to share.

This bonding provides the group with the impetus to move forward, for participants gain courage by discovering that they are not alone in their feelings. A woman experiences a great sense of relief when she discovers, through statements by other women, that she is not strange for feeling resentment over the many demands her family makes on her. Men find that they can share their tears and affection with other men without being robbed of their masculinity. Other common themes evolving in this stage that lead to increased cohesion and trust are members' fears of rejection, feelings of loneliness and abandonment, feelings of inferiority and failure to live up to others' expectations, painful memories, guilt and remorse over what they have and have not done, discovery that their worst enemy lives within them, need for and fear of intimacy, feelings about sexual identity and sexual performance, and unfinished business with their parents. This list is not exhaustive but merely a sample of the universal human issues that participants recognize and explore with one another as the group progresses. Earlier we discussed group cohesion as an achievement of the initial stage of a group. The cohesion that is characteristic of the working stage is a deeper intimacy that develops with time and commitment. This bonding is a form of affection and genuine caring that often results from sharing the expression of painful experiences.

Hope

Hope is the belief that change is possible—that one is not a victim of the past and can make new decisions. Hope is therapeutic in itself, for it gives members confidence that they have the power to choose to be different. Some people approach a group convinced that they are victims of external circumstances over which they have no control. In the group, however, they may encounter others who have struggled and found ways to assume effective control over their life. Seeing and being associated with such people can inspire a new sense of optimism that their life can be different.

Example: Pete, who was left paralyzed as a result of a motorcycle accident, spent most of his energies thinking about all that he could no longer do. With the encouragement of his physician, he joined a rehabilitation group, where he met several people who had at one time felt as he was feeling. By listening to their struggles and the ways in which they had effectively coped with their disability, he found hope that he, too, could discover more effective ways of living his life.

Willingness to Risk and Trust

Risking involves opening one's self to others, being vulnerable, and actively doing in a group what is necessary for change. Taking risks involves letting go of what is known and secure and moving toward uncertain terrain. This willingness to reveal one's self is largely a function of how much one trusts the other group members and the leader. Trust is therapeutic, for it allows people to show the many facets of themselves, encourages experimental behavior, and allows people to look at themselves in new ways.

Example: Jane expressed considerable resentment and hostility to the men in her group. Eventually, she took the risk of disclosing that as a child she had been sexually exploited by her stepfather. As she explored ways in which she had generalized her distrust of getting close to men in everyday life and in her group, she began to see how she was keeping men at a distance so that they would never again have the chance to exploit her. Finally, she made a new decision that all men would not necessarily hurt her if she allowed herself to get close to them. Had she been unwilling to risk making the disclosure in her group, it is unlikely that she would have made this attitudinal and behavioral change.

Caring and Acceptance

Caring is demonstrated by listening and involvement. It can be expressed by tenderness, compassion, support, and even confrontation. If members sense a lack of caring, either from other members or from the leader, their willingness to drop their masks will be reduced. Members are able to risk being vulnerable if they sense that their concerns are important to others and that they are valued as people.

Caring implies acceptance, a genuine support from others that says, in effect: "We will accept all of your feelings. You do count here. It's acceptable to be yourself. You don't have to strive to please everyone." Acceptance involves affirming each person's right to have and express feelings and values.

Caring and acceptance develop into empathy, a deep understanding of another's struggles. Commonalities emerge that unite the members. The realization that certain problems are universal—loneliness, the need for acceptance, the fear of rejection, the fear of intimacy, hurt over past experiences—lessens the feeling that one is alone. Through identification with others, moreover, one is able to see oneself more clearly.

Example: Bobby, who was in a group for children of divorce, finally began to talk about his sadness over not having his father at home anymore. Other children were very attentive. When Bobby said that he was embarrassed by his crying, two other boys told him that they also cried. This sharing of loneliness and hurt bonded the children, who learned that what they were feeling was normal.

Power

A feeling of power emerges from the recognition that one has untapped internal reserves of spontaneity, creativity, courage, and strength. This strength is not a power over others; rather, it is the sense that one has the resources necessary to direct the course of one's life. In groups, personal power can be experienced in ways that were formerly denied, and people can discover ways in which they are blocking their strengths. Some people enter groups feeling victimized, and they cannot see any power to choose their destiny. Indeed, some of them *were* victimized by people in their lives, yet they may live with the untested assumption that the rest of the world is bent on bringing them harm. They become empowered when they realize that they can take certain steps in their current situation to make life more rewarding.

Example: As a child, Ethyl usually got hit by her parents if she made herself visible. She made an early decision to keep a low profile to avoid being abused physically and psychologically. Through her participation in a group she discovered that she was still behaving as if everyone was out to get her, even though her defensive ways were no longer warranted. Because she chose not to make her presence known in her group, people saw her as distant, cold, and aloof. Ethyl gradually discovered that she was no longer a helpless child who could not protect herself in a cruel adult world. By challenging her assumptions and by taking risks with people in her group, she also assumed more power over how she felt about herself and how she allowed herself to be treated by others.

Another case shows how a person can learn skills that will lead to empowerment. Carl, a recovering alcoholic, admitted that he felt powerful only when he drank. In addition to his Alcoholics Anonymous group he joined an assertion-training group, where he learned social skills that helped him to deal effectively with situations in which he had felt powerless. He found the courage to ask people directly for what he wanted from them, and he learned how to nonaggressively deny unreasonable requests made of him.

Catharsis

The expression of pent-up emotions can be therapeutic, because clients release energy that has been tied up in withholding threatening feelings. This type of emotional release plays an important part in many kinds of groups, and the expression of feeling can facilitate trust and cohesion. However, both group leaders and members sometimes make the mistake of concluding that mere catharsis implies "real work." Some disappointed members who do not have an emotional release are convinced that they are not really getting involved. Although it is often healing, catharsis by itself is limited in terms of producing long-lasting changes. Members need to learn how to make sense of their emotional experiences, and one way of doing so is by putting words to their intense emotions and attempting to undertand them.

Example: Susan learned that she could experience both love and hate toward her mother. For years she had buried her resentment over what she saw as her mother's continual attempts to control her life. In one session Susan allowed herself to feel and to fully express her resentment to her mother in a symbolic way. The group leader assisted her in telling her mother, in role playing, many of the things that had contributed to her feelings of resentment. She felt a great sense of relief after having expressed these pent-up emotions. The leader cautioned her about the dangers of repeating in real life everything that she had just said in the therapy session. It would not be necessary to harshly confront her mother and to expose the full range of her pain and anger. Instead, Susan learned that it was important to understand how her resentment toward her mother was continuing to affect her now, both in her present dealings with her mother and in her relationship to others. It was essential that Susan become clear about what she really wanted with her mother and what was still keeping her from getting closer to her. Susan can choose what she wants to tell her mother, and she can also deal with her in more direct and honest ways than she has in the past. She can be aware of and sensitive to her mother and at the same time can behave differently with her.

The Cognitive Component

As mentioned above, catharsis is even more useful if a person attempts to find words to explain the feelings expressed. Some conceptualization of the meaning of the intense feelings associated with certain experiences can give members the tools to make significant changes. Members who simply *experience* feelings often have difficulty in integrating what they learn from these experiences. Yalom (1983, 1985) cites substantial research evidence demonstrating that to profit from a group experience, the members require a cognitive framework that will allow them to put their here-and-now experiencing into perspective.

Example: Earlier we described the case of Felix, an adolescent who expressed pent-up hurt. As you recall, he initially felt better after an outburst of crying, but he soon discounted the experience. Felix needed to put into words the meaning of his emotional interchange. He may have learned any of the following: that he was storing up feelings of anger toward his father, that he had a mixture of resentment and love for his father, that he had made a decision that his father would never change, that there were many things he could say to his father, or that there were numerous ways that he could act differently with his father. It was therapeutically important for him to release his bottled-up emotions. It was also essential that he clarify his insights and discover ways to use them to improve his relationship with his father.

Commitment to Change

A resolution to change is also therapeutic in itself. If one is motivated to the point of becoming an active group participant, the chances are good that change will occur. But for this change to occur, participants need to formulate action plans and strategies that they can employ in their day-to-day existence. Once they have developed a plan, it is crucial that they commit themselves to carrying it out. This commitment to change involves a willingness to make use of the tools offered by the group process to explore ways of modifying their behavior.

Example: Pearl discovered her tendency to wait until the session was almost over to bring up her concerns. She described many situations in her life when she did not get what she wanted. She insisted that she wanted to make some changes and behave differently. The leader issued the following challenge: "Pearl, would you be willing to be the first to speak at the next group session? I'd like you to also think of at least one situation this week in which your needs are not being met because you are holding yourself back. What could you do to bring about a more positive outcome for yourself?" Thus, the leader provided Pearl with alternatives for taking the initiative to try new ways of acting, both in real life and in the group sessions. If she continued to sabotage meeting her needs by not doing what she said she would do, the leader would certainly need to confront her with her lack of commitment.

Freedom to Experiment

The group situation provides a safe place for experimentation with new behavior. Members are able to show facets of themselves that they often keep hidden in everyday situations. In the accepting environment of a group, a shy member can exhibit spontaneous behavior and be outgoing. A person who typically is very quiet may experiment with being more verbal. After trying new behaviors, members can gauge how much they want to change their existing behavior.

Example: Myrtle said she was tired of being so shy all of the time and would like to let people know her better. The leader responded "Myrtle, would you be willing to pick out a person in this group who is the opposite of you?" Myrtle identified Patti. After getting Patti's approval, the leader suggested to Myrtle: "Go around to each person in the room, and act in a way that you have seen Patti behave. Assume her body posture, her gestures, and her tone of voice. Then, tell each person something that you would want them to know about you." As a variation, Myrtle could have been asked to share with all of the members her observations and reactions to them. Yet another variation would have included asking Patti to be Myrtle's coach and assist her in carrying out this task. It can be surprising how outgoing members are when they pretend to be in someone else's skin. What Myrtle gained from this experiment was the recognition that she did possess the capacity to be outgoing and that she could practice being different by being herself.

Humor

Not everything that goes on in a group has to be heavy and serious. Effective feedback can sometimes be given in a humorous way. Laughing at oneself can be extremely therapeutic, because it requires seeing one's problems in a new perspective. The power of humor as a therapeutic tool is often underrated, but timing is crucial. A level of trust must be established before taking too many liberties with humor. The leader and members should be sure not to laugh *at* people but to laugh *with* them, out of a sense of affection and caring.

Example: Sarah, who dressed seductively and was sexually provocative, expressed pain over the fact that men saw her only as a sexual object. A male member spontaneously dressed up as a woman and moved about in a seductive way in the group, saying "All you ever see is my body!" Everyone, including Sarah, broke into hysterical laughter. As silly as this behavior may seem, it was powerful feedback to Sarah. She realized that her seductive ways were distracting others from seeing other dimensions of her.

Research Implications for the Working Stage

In their comparative analysis of research into individual and group psychotherapy, Fuhriman and Burlingame (1990) conclude that the two forms of treatment share many therapeutic factors. Some of the common factors they identify are insight, catharsis, reality testing, hope for change, disclosure, and identification.

- **Insight** is thought to be a central therapeutic factor in fostering clients' improvement. There appears to be unanimity concerning the importance of insight for both forms of treatment.
- **Catharsis,** or emotional ventilation, is valued as a therapeutic process of both individual and group therapy from a conceptual perspective. However, empirical reviews of individual therapy do not show a consensus supporting the relationship between catharsis and clients' improvement.
- **Reality testing** is provided in a group by both the leader and the members through feedback. There is a great deal of conceptual support for the importance of this therapeutic factor for both individual and group therapy.
- **Hope for change,** or the expectation of improvement, has both conceptual and empirical support in both individual and group therapy and has been shown to be related to clients' improvement.
- **Disclosure** can be divided into two categories: therapist self-disclosure and client self-disclosure. In group therapy, there is a considerable amount of evidence suggesting that client disclosure facilitates the development of other therapeutic factors.
- **Identification** is the process by which a client can relate to others. The group-therapy literature suggests that clients who identify with both the therapist and with other group members tend to improve more than with those who do not. The group process affords opportunities for members to form multiple identifications.

In addition to this brief review of findings about therapeutic factors, we consider below in more detail research into three group-process variables as they are related to the working stage. We have selected *cohesion, self-disclosure,* and *feedback* because these factors have a central role in determining group productivity.

Research into Cohesion

Perhaps no other construct in group therapy has received as extensive and intensive study as cohesion. Nevertheless, it is difficult to demonstrate a clear relationship between cohesion and the outcomes of a group because cohesion is a multidimensional, interactive factor that can be studied from various perspectives (Fuhriman & Burlingame, 1990). Although cohesion has been defined in a variety of ways, common phrases are often used: a climate of support, bonding, attractiveness, sharing of experiences, mutuality within a group, the togetherness that unites members, a sense of belonging, warmth and closeness, and caring and acceptance. A group high in cohesiveness provides a climate in which members feel free enough to do meaningful work. Under these conditions, the members are likely to express what they feel and think, engage in significant self-exploration, and relate more deeply to others (Bednar & Kaul, 1978).

Yalom (1985) maintains that research evidence shows cohesion to be a strong determinant of a positive group outcome. If members experience little sense of belonging or attraction to the group, there is little likelihood that they will benefit, and they may well experience negative outcomes (Lieberman, Yalom, & Miles, 1973). Yalom has summarized research showing that highly cohesive groups tend to be characterized by better attendance and less turnover. The evidence indicates that this stability increases cohesiveness and leads to more self-disclosure and risk taking and the constructive expression of conflicts in the group.

How, then, is group cohesion developed? If a group is to be cohesive, its members must perceive it as a means to helping them achieve their personal goals. According to Yalom (1983, 1985), groups with a here-and-now focus are almost invariably vital and cohesive. By contrast, groups in which members engage in much "talking about" with a "there-and-then" focus rarely develop much cohesiveness.

Although cohesion is thought to be one of the most crucial factors related to group process and outcomes and in spite of the vast amount of research on it, the literature provides some conflicting conclusions. Rather than being a stable factor, group cohesion is a complex process (Kaul & Bednar, 1986; Stockton & Hulse, 1981). Kaul and Bednar imply that research on cohesion could be improved by giving specific information about the members and the leaders, the nature of the treatment, and the stage in the group at which cohesion is assessed.

Research into Self-Disclosure

Like cohesion, self-disclosure cannot be studied and discussed in a simple way. The empirical base for self-disclosure in group counseling is somewhat limited, but it suggests a complex, multidimensional interaction between frequency of disclosure and other factors such as type of group and population, level of disclosure, and timing (Morran, 1982; Stockton & Morran, 1982).

Although research and clinical evidence clearly point toward the desirability of encouraging the norm of member self-disclosure, these findings do not imply that more disclosure is always better. There is a curvilinear relationship between self-disclosure and optimal group functioning, with either too little or too much disclosure being counterproductive. Although self-disclosure should be encouraged, there needs to be a balance so that a single member does not lead the others by too great a gap in terms of frequency and depth of disclosure (Yalom, 1985).

After surveying the literature on leader self-disclosure, Dies (1983b) suggests that this behavior may have either a constructive or detrimental effect on group process and outcome, depending on specific factors such as the type of group, the stage of group development, and the content of disclosure. Dies concludes that therapist self-disclosure is less appropriate with client populations that are psychologically impaired. Group leaders who are willing to be open about their own reactions to what is going on within the group are more likely to foster the development of positive interpersonal relationships. But Dies adds the cautionary note that clients tend to expect the group leader to possess confidence and competence and to provide some initial structuring and direction. Clients may not want leaders to be too revealing of their feelings, experiences, or conflicts early in the course of a group. Leaders who disclose more to meet their own needs than to meet the needs of the members may tend to be manipulative and thus to cause members to question their capabilities. But leaders can facilitate interaction within the group by disclosing some of their personal reactions related to the here and now, because this type of information generally pertains directly to members' opportunities for interpersonal learning (Morran, 1982).

Yalom (1983) stresses that leader self-disclosure must be instrumental in helping the *members* attain their goals. He calls for selective therapist disclosure that provides members with acceptance, support, and encouragement. For Yalom, group leaders who disclose here-and-now reactions, rather than detailed personal events from their past, facilitate the movement of the group.

Jourard (1968) suggests that the group leader is a strong determiner of how open and trusting the client will become. He maintains that the therapist is the leader in the therapeutic dance and that the client follows the leader. Jourard's studies (1971a, 1971b) led him to conclude that therapist self-disclosure begets client self-disclosure and that therapist manipulation begets countermanipulation on the client's part.

Research into Feedback

Some researchers consider interpersonal feedback to be one of the major therapeutic factors in group therapy (Kaul & Bednar, 1978). However, little has been done empirically to investigate the degree to which it is effective as a curative factor or the nature of its effectiveness (Morran, Robison, & Stockton, 1985).

Kaul and Bednar (1986) suggest that feedback can be considered along a number of dimensions, including its *valence* (the positive or negative nature of the message); *content* (either behavioral, which describes another member's behavior, or emotional, which describes the feelings of the person giving the feedback); *source* (public or anonymous); *form of delivery* (written or spoken); and *time reference* (here and now or there and then). Some research findings on these specific dimensions of feedback are listed below:

- Positive feedback by the leader is almost invariably rated as being more desirable, having greater impact, and leading to greater intention to change than negative feedback (Dies, 1983b; Morran et al., 1985; Morran & Stockton, 1980).
- Feedback that describes specific behaviors is rated by group members as more effective than interpretive or mixed feedback (Stockton & Morran, 1980).
- Negative feedback seems to be more credible and helpful if it comes at a later phase of the group; it is more likely to be accepted when it has been preceded by positive feedback (Stockton & Morran, 1981).
- Leader feedback is generally of higher quality than member feedback, but it is not more readily accepted; feedback tends to be of higher quality and to be more accepted in later sessions than in earlier ones; and positive feedback is more accepted and of higher quality than negative feedback (Morran et al., 1985).
- The feedback offered by both members and the leader are useful in reality testing. A group offers opportunities for members to check out some of the assumptions underlying their behavior, and feedback can add a realistic and objective perspective (Fuhriman & Burlingame, 1990). One of the main goals of feedback is to provide individuals with information to correct their distortions and past errors. When reality testing is considered in this light, research shows that there is a relationship between feedback and other therapeutic factors in groups, such as cohesion (Kaul & Bednar, 1986).
- The impact of the feedback offered in a group is a reflection of the progress the group has made (Rothke, 1986). In a sense, if feedback is honest, personal, and risky and deals with the interpersonal

relationships within the group, this in itself is a sign that cohesion and trust have been established. This quality of feedback is one of the indications that the group is at least moving toward a working stage.

In summarizing the research findings, Morran, Robison, and Stockton (1985) report that feedback is most effective and most readily accepted when it focuses on observable behaviors, is unqualified, refers to specific and concrete situations, and describes the giver's reactions rather than being evaluative or judgmental. These findings are very consistent with those of Rothke.

Co-Leader Issues during the Working Stage

Our Leadership Style

When we co-lead groups or intensive workshops, we become energized if the group is motivated to work. In effective groups the members do the bulk of the work, for they bring up subjects they want to talk about and demonstrate a willingness to be known. Between group sessions we devote time to discussing our reactions to group members, to thinking of ways of involving the various members in transactions with one another, and to exploring possible ways of helping participants understand their behavior in the group and resolve some of their conflicts. We also look critically at what we are doing as leaders and examine the impact of our behavior on the group. Toward this end we reflect on the patterns of feedback that we have received from the members about how our behavior has affected them. We also talk about the process and dynamics of the group. If we find that we have differing perceptions of the group process, we discuss our differences. In this way we challenge each other, and we grow.

When a group seems very resistant and when productive work seems to emerge very slowly, we may wonder whether we want to continue doing group work. At times like this we experience a sapping of our energies. If we have persistent feelings that the group is avoiding doing meaningful work, we will express these feelings and the perceptions they're based on to the group. We try to disclose honestly what we see occurring and how we are feeling about being in the group, but we avoid chastising the members and telling them that they're not meeting our expectations. At the same time, we challenge the group to assess its own processes. If resistance is the general rule in a group, it is imperative that we challenge the members to recognize the barriers that are standing in the way of effective work. For a concrete example of this process, refer to our description of a group in resistance, in Chapter 5.

Topics for Co-Leader Meetings

We cannot overemphasize the importance of meeting with one's co-leader throughout the duration of the group. Much of what we have suggested in earlier chapters as issues for discussion at these meetings also applies to the working stage. We will briefly consider a few other issues that are particularly relevant to the working stage.

Ongoing Evaluation of the Group. Co-leaders can make it a practice to devote some time to appraising the direction the group is taking and its level of productivity. If the group is a closed one with a predetermined termination date (say, 20 weeks), co-leaders would do well to evaluate the group's progress around the 10th week. This evaluation can be a topic of discussion both privately and in the group itself. If both leaders agree that the group seems to be bogging down and that members are losing interest, for example, they should surely bring these perceptions into the group so that the members can look at their degree of satisfaction with their direction and progress.

Discussion of Techniques. It is useful to discuss techniques and leadership styles with a co-leader. One of the leaders might be hesitant to try any technique because of a fear of making a mistake, because of not knowing where to go next, or because of passively waiting for permission from the co-leader to introduce techniques. Such issues, along with any stylistic differences between leaders, are topics for exploration.

Theoretical Orientations. As we've mentioned earlier, it is not essential that co-leaders share the same theory of group work, for sometimes differing theoretical preferences can blend nicely. You can learn a lot from discussing theory as it applies to practice. Therefore, we encourage you to read, attend workshops and special seminars, and then discuss with your co-leader what you are learning. Doing so can result in bringing to the group sessions some new and interesting variations.

Self-Disclosure Issues. Co-leaders should explore their sense of appropriate and therapeutic self-disclosure. For example, if you are willing to share with members your reactions that pertain to group issues yet are reserved in disclosing personal outside issues, whereas your co-leader freely and fully talks about her marital situation, members may perceive you as holding back. This issue, too, can be discussed both in the group and privately with your co-leader.

Confrontation Issues. What we have just said about self-disclosure also applies to confrontation. You can imagine the problems that could ensue from your co-leader's practice of harsh and unrelenting confrontations to get members to open up, if you believe in providing support to the exclusion of any confrontation. You might easily be labeled as the "good guy" and your co-leader as the "bad guy." If such differences in style exist, the two of you surely need to talk about them at length if the group is not to suffer.

Working Stage: Summary

Stage Characteristics

When a group reaches the working stage, its central characteristics include the following:

- The level of trust and cohesion is high.
- Communication within the group is open and involves an accurate expression of what is being experienced.
- Leadership functions are likely to be shared by the group, in that members interact with one another freely and directly.
- There is a willingness to risk threatening material and to make oneself known to others; members bring to the group personal topics they want to discuss and understand better.
- Conflict among members is recognized and dealt with directly and effectively.
- Feedback is given freely and accepted and considered nondefensively.
- Confrontation occurs in a way in which those doing the challenging avoid slapping judgmental labels on others.
- Members are willing to work outside the group to achieve behavioral changes.
- Participants feel supported in their attempts to change and are willing to risk new behavior.
- Members feel hopeful that they can change if they are willing to take action; they do not feel helpless.

Member Functions and Possible Problems

The working stage is characterized by the exploration of personally meaningful material. To reach this stage, members have certain tasks and roles, which include:

- bringing into group sessions issues that they are willing to discuss
- offering feedback and being open to feedback from others
- assuming some leadership functions, especially by sharing their personal reactions of how they are affected by others' presence and work in the group
- being willing to practice new skills and behaviors in daily life and to bring the results to the sessions
- offering both challenge and support to others and engaging in self-confrontation

- continually assessing their level of satisfaction with the group and actively taking steps to change their level of involvement in the sessions if necessary

Some problems that can arise with members at this time are:

- Members may form a collusion to relax and enjoy the comfort of familiar relationships and avoid challenging one another.
- Members may gain insights in the sessions but not see the necessity of action outside of the group to bring about change.
- Members may withdraw because of anxiety over others' intensity.

Leader Functions

Some of the central leadership functions at this stage are:

- continuing to model appropriate behavior, especially caring confrontation, and disclosing ongoing reactions to the group
- providing a balance between support and confrontation
- supporting the members' willingness to take risks and assisting them in carrying this into their daily living
- interpreting the meaning of behavior patterns at appropriate times so that members will be able to engage in a deeper level of self-exploration and consider alternative behaviors
- assisting members to pay attention to and ask clearly for what they want from the group
- exploring common themes that provide for some universality and linking one or more members' work with that of others in the group
- focusing on the importance of translating insight into action; encouraging members to practice new skills
- promoting those behaviors that will increase the level of cohesion
- paying attention to the intensification and further development of group norms
- being aware of the therapeutic factors that operate to produce change and intervening in such a way as to help members make desired changes in feelings, thoughts, and actions

Exercises

1. What signs do you look for to determine whether a group has attained the working stage? Identify specific characteristics you see as especially related to this stage.

2. Assume that you are leading a group with a changing membership. Although there is a core of members who attend consistently, clients eventually terminate, and new members join the group. What obstacles will the members have to deal with if this group is to reach a working

stage? What are your ideas on ways in which to increase cohesion in this type of group? How would you handle the reality of members' terminating and new members' being assimilated into the group?

3. What guidelines would you offer to members on appropriate self-disclosure? How might you respond to the following statement made by a member, Carol? "I don't see why there is so much emphasis on telling others what I think and feel. I've always been a private person, and all this personal talk makes me feel uncomfortable." How might you deal with Carol if she were in a voluntary group? an involuntary group?

4. There are important differences between effective and ineffective confrontation. How would you explain this difference to group members? Think about how you might respond to a person who had been in your group for some time and who said: "I don't see why we focus so much on problems and on confronting people with negative feelings. All this makes me want to retreat. I'm afraid to say much, because I'd rather hear positive feedback."

CHAPTER 7

Ending a Group

FOCUS QUESTIONS

1. If a member wants to leave a closed group before its termination, how should the leader handle the situation?
2. What activities are important during the closing phase of a group?
3. What questions might you as a leader ask members in order to determine how the group had affected them?
4. How might you deal with members' requests to continue a time-limited group that is approaching termination?
5. How important do you think it is to hold some type of follow-up session? What might you want the group to discuss at such a session?
6. How might you handle an individual's leaving an open group? How would you work a new member into the group?
7. What personal characteristics of yours could get in the way of helping members in your groups deal fully with separation and termination issues?
8. What specific methods and procedures would you use to help members review the group experience and make plans for using what they had learned in the group in everyday life?
9. What assessment techniques might you use at both the beginning and the end of a group? How can you build evaluation research into your group design?
10. What issues might you explore with your co-leader after a group terminates?

Introduction

The initial phase of a group's development is crucial, for participants are getting acquainted, basic trust is being established, norms are being determined that will govern later intensive work, and a unique group identity is taking shape. The final stage of a group's evolution is just as vital, for members have an opportunity to clarify the meaning of their experiences in the group, to consolidate the gains they've made, and to decide what newly acquired behaviors they want to transfer to their everyday life.

In this chapter we discuss ways of terminating the group experience. We show how you can help members evaluate the meaning of their behavior in the group. Questions we explore are these: How can the members be encouraged to evaluate the degree of their satisfaction with each session? How can a group complete its unfinished business? How can the members best be prepared for leaving the group and carrying their learning into the real world? What are the difficulties in saying good-bye, and are they avoidable? How can you prepare the members to cope with their tendency to regress to old ways or to discount the meaning of their experience in the face of the outside world's pressures and skepticism? Are follow-ups necessary? If so, how should they be designed? How can you get participants to actively prepare themselves for a follow-up session? How can you and the members evaluate the group experience?

We describe many tasks that need to be accomplished in the final stage of a group's history. The number of sessions devoted to reviewing and integrating the group experience is dependent on how long the group has been in existence. A group that has been meeting weekly for two years will need more time for closure than one that has met for only ten weeks. Whatever the type of group, adequate time should be set aside for integrating and evaluating the experience. There is a danger of attempting to cover too much in one final meeting, which can have the effect of fragmenting the group instead of leading to closure.

Tasks of the Final Stage: Consolidation of Learning

During the final stage of a group, members need to be asked certain questions: "What has this experience meant to you?" "You have shared your struggles and emotions, but is that enough in itself?" "What does all of this work mean in terms of your living in the world?" "Where can you go from here?"

The final phase in the life of a group is critical, for this is when members must consolidate their learning. It is a difficult time, because the members are aware that their community is about to dissolve, and they are mourning the loss of it in advance. Sometimes the intensity of work tapers off during the final sessions, because participants are reluctant to bring up new business to explore. It is important that you focus on the feelings of loss that may permeate the atmosphere. These feelings need to be identified and explored, although they probably cannot be alleviated. Members must face the reality of termination and learn how to say good-bye. If the group has been truly therapeutic, they will be able to extend and continue their learning outside, even though they may well experience a sense of sadness and loss.

As members realize that their group is ending, there is a danger that they will begin to distance themselves from the group experience and thus fail to closely examine the ways in which their learning in the group might affect their out-of-group behavior. For this reason you need to learn to help members put what has occurred in the group in a meaningful perspective. Typically, this is the phase of group work that leaders handle most ineptly, partly owing to their lack of training and partly because of their own resistance to termination. Avoiding acknowledgment of a group's termination may reflect discomfort on the leader's part in dealing with endings and separations. Therapists may unconsciously resist ending their treatment of clients who provide much gratification for them, particularly if they do not have meaningful lives themselves (Kramer, 1990). When termination is not dealt with, the group misses an opportunity to explore concerns that may affect many members, and the clients' therapy is jeopardized. Kramer nicely captures the main tasks of termination:

> The termination stage is characterized by a mixture of feelings, among them sadness, confusion, and joy. The tasks are numerous and difficult. They include understanding endings as a psychological experience, recapitulating the treatment experience, obtaining closure and letting go, and finally, the ultimate freedom of experiencing new beginnings. No other stage in treatment or in life, for that matter, challenges us more [1990, p. 25].

The potential for learning permanent lessons is likely to be lost if the leader does not provide a structure that helps members review and integrate what they have learned. This discussion on the consolidation and termination phase applies to both closed groups (those with the same membership for the group's history) and to open groups (those with a turnover of members). In a closed group, leaders can help the members review their individual work and the evolving patterns from the first to the final session. Of particular value is having the members give one another feedback on specific changes they have made. The tasks to be accomplished with a person who is terminating membership in an *open group* include:

- announcing in advance the person's intended departure, to ensure the clearing up of any potential unfinished business
- allowing time for the person to prepare for termination
- giving others an opportunity to say good-bye and to share their own reactions and give feedback
- assisting the member who is leaving to review what has been learned in the group and, specifically, what to do with this learning
- making referrals, when appropriate, such as couple therapy, family therapy, individual therapy, or another type of group therapy or a support group

At times, members may want to leave a group prematurely. As you will recall from Chapter 2, there are ethical guidelines for dealing with matters such as leaving a group, exerting pressure for members to remain in a group, and ways of dealing with premature termination. We find that members rarely leave a group prematurely when they are encouraged in a nonthreatening way to fully explore their reasons for wanting to leave. Yet there are times when it is wise that clients discontinue membership. When it becomes clear that the needs of a member cannot be met within a particular group, there is an ethical responsibility to suggest appropriate referrals (ASGW, 1989, 15.). It is essential that group counselors know about local community resources for further professional assistance.

Termination of the Group Experience

Dealing with Feelings of Separation

In discussing the initial phase of a group, we commented on the importance of leaders' encouraging members to express their fears and expectations so that trust would not be inhibited. As members approach the ending of the group, it is equally essential that they be encouraged to express their reactions. They may have fears or concerns about separating, and leaving the group may be as threatening for some as entering it. Some members are likely to be convinced that the trust they now feel in the group will not be replicated outside. A central task of the leader at this time is to remind the participants that the cohesion they now have is the result of active steps they took. They need to be reminded that close relationships don't happen by accident; rather, they are the product of considerable struggle and commitment to work through personal conflicts.

Even if the participants realize that they can create meaningful relationships and build a support system outside of the group, they still may experience a sense of loss and sadness over the ending of this particular community. The members are likely to need encouragement in facing the fact that their group is terminating, and some mourning over this separation can be expected if the group has become a cohesive one. If this mourning is avoided, the members are deprived of a valuable experience in learning how to cope with feelings of grief and loss. In order to be able to facilitate members' expressions of their feelings over separation, it is important for you, as the facilitator, to recognize and be able to deal with your own feelings about the ending of the group. If you avoid dealing with feelings of sadness, the members will probably follow this example.

In many of the groups that we lead, we typically ask members at the first session to spend a few minutes looking quietly around the room. We say: "As you are looking at different people, be aware of your reactions. Are you already drawn to certain people more than others? Are there some in here whom you already feel intimidated by? Are you catching yourself making judgments about people?" After a few minutes of this silent scanning of the room, we tell them to refrain from sharing anything that they have just thought or felt. Generally, we let the members know that we'll ask them to repeat this exercise at the final group session. When this time arrives, we tell them: "Check out the room again, being aware of each person in here. Do you remember the reactions you had to anyone at that first meeting? How have your reactions changed toward anyone, if at all? How does it feel to be in here now compared with what it was like for you when the group began?" A main task the members have during the final session is to be able to put into words what has transpired from the first to the final session and what they have learned about others and themselves. If the group appears different at this final meeting than it did initially, they are asked to think about how this change came about. We point out to them that this transformation was not magic, nor was it something that we did to the group. It largely stemmed from their commitment to hard work.

Dealing with Unfinished Business

During the final phase of a group, time needs to be allotted for expressing and working through any unfinished business relating to transactions between members or to the group process and goals. Some members may not get their issues fully resolved, but they should be encouraged to discuss them. For example, Wanda may say that she has held back because of reservations about the leader. Though there may not be enough time to work through her concern completely, it is still important to identify this unfinished issue and to attempt to resolve it within the limitations of the remaining time.

Edward may have unfinished business with another member (or members) or with the leader. It may well be his responsibility for having waited too long to bring up such matters, and he can be assisted in looking at some of the ways in which he got into the situation. Members like Edward may need help in bringing some closure to deeply personal issues they have raised and explored. It is not realistic to assume that all of the issues that were explored will have been worked through. If members are given this reminder a few sessions before the final meeting, they can be motivated to use the remaining time to complete their own personal agenda. We often ask the question "If this were the last session of this group, how would you feel about what you have done, and what would you wish you had done differently?" In addition, the group may point out many areas on which people could productively focus once they leave the group. In this way members can be prepared to continue working with these issues in further groups or in individual counseling. One index of a successful group is that members do not get "turned off" by the experience and would consider seeking this kind of help (or another avenue of personal growth) at other phases in their development.

Reviewing the Group Experience

At the final stage of a group we place value on reviewing what members have learned throughout the sessions and how they learned these lessons. For example, Ralph learned that keeping his anger inside had contributed to his feelings of depression and to many psychosomatic ailments. In the sessions he practiced expressing his anger, instead of smiling and denying those feelings, and he acquired important skills. It is helpful for

Ralph to recall what he actually did to get others to take him seriously, for he could easily forget these hard-earned lessons.

Part of our practice for ending groups involves setting aside time for all the participants to discuss matters such as what they've learned in the group, turning points for them, what they liked and did not like about the group, ways that the sessions could have had a greater impact, and the entire history of the group seen in some perspective. To make this evaluation meaningful, we encourage participants to be concrete. When members make global statements such as "This group has been fantastic, and I grew a lot from it" or "I don't think I'll ever forget all the things I learned in here," we assist them in being more specific. We might ask some of these questions: *"How* has this group been important for you?" "In what ways has it been fantastic?" "What are a few of the things you've learned that you'd most want to remember?" "When you say that you've grown a lot, what are some of the changes you've seen in yourself?"

One way to help members review concrete highlights of their experience is to ask them to take a few minutes to spontaneously recall moments they shared together. Members can be helped to briefly relive their initial reactions to being in the group and to recall specific events. Each member can take several turns in completing the sentence "I remember the time when . . ." Recalling incidents of conflict and pain in the group as well as moments of closeness, warmth, humor, and joy can contribute to putting the group experience into perspective. Such turning points can provide a conceptual framework needed to make sense of what has taken place. We frequently emphasize to members the importance of putting what they have learned into specific language and stating the ways in which they have translated their insights into action.

Practice for Behavioral Change

In groups that meet weekly there are many opportunities for practicing new behaviors during each group session. It is good to encourage members to think of ways in which they can continue such work between the sessions. They can carry out homework assignments and give a report in the next week's session on how well they succeeded with trying new ways of behaving in various situations. In this way the transfer of learning is maximized.

During the final stage of a group we emphasize the value of such actual practice (both in group situations and in outside life) as a way of solidifying and consolidating one's learning. We rely heavily on role-playing situations and rehearsals for anticipated interactions, teaching participants specific skills that will help them make their desired behavioral changes. We encourage them to take action and try out new behavioral patterns with selected others outside the group, both while the group is going on and after termination.

During the final few sessions we typically focus participants on preparing themselves to deal with those they live and work with. We ask members to look at themselves and the ways in which they want to continue changing, rather than considering how they can change others. If Carol would like her husband to show more interest in the family and be more accepting of her changes, we encourage her to tell her husband about *her* changes and about herself. We caution her about the dangers of demanding that her husband be different. In rehearsals and role-playing situations we typically ask members to state briefly the essence of what they want to say to the significant people in their life, so that they do not lose the message they most want to convey. For example, a man rehearses telling his father that he loves him and would like closer contact with him.

Feedback from others in the group is especially helpful as the members practice for the behavioral changes they expect to make in their everyday situations. If Carol appears apologetic, for example, members may comment on ways in which she might be more assertive. If in role playing she lectures her husband on all the ways he is deficient, people can share with her how they would be affected if they were her husband. This preparation for dealing with others outside the group is essential if members are to maximize the effects of what they've learned. They can benefit by practicing new interpersonal skills, by getting feedback, by discussing this feedback, and by modifying certain behaviors so that they are more likely to bring about the desired changes once they leave the group.

Giving and Receiving Feedback

Throughout the history of a group the members have been giving and receiving feedback, which has helped them assess the impact of their behavioral experiments on others. During the closing sessions, however, we like to emphasize a more focused type of feedback for each person. We generally begin by asking members for a brief report on how they've perceived themselves in the group, what the group has meant to them, what conflicts have become clearer, and what (if any) decisions they've made. Then the rest of the members give feedback concerning how they've perceived and felt about that person.

Here we want to point to a potential problem: too often people give only positive feedback at this time, particularly if they feel a closeness with the others and some misgivings about the termination of the group. Favorable comments may give a person a temporary lift, but we also like members to express doubts or concerns, in ways such as the following:

- My greatest fear for you is . . .
- My hope for you is . . .

- I hope that you will seriously consider . . .
- I see you blocking your strengths by . . .
- Some things I hope you will think about doing for yourself are . . .

We caution against global feedback that will be of little use to members in remembering how others saw them. Examples of feedback that is not too helpful are "I really like you." "I feel close to you." "You are a super person." "I will always remember you." In contrast, feedback that members can remember and can think about is most useful in making changes. Following are examples of this specific type of feedback:

- "I hope you remember that the reason you and I felt distant from each other is that we were scared of each other, yet we acknowledged this. What brought us closer is that we talked about our fears and our assumptions."
- "I like your ability to be direct and honest in giving feedback and at the same time to treat people with dignity."
- "Remember that people liked you much better when you stopped being sarcastic."
- "The times you gave advice, people tended to reject it. They responded more favorably to you when you shared your own struggles, rather than giving them solutions."
- "I hope you will remember how easy it was for me to respond to you when you stopped bombarding me with questions and instead started to make statements about yourself."
- "My fear for you is that you will forget that more often than not you are judging yourself more harshly than others."
- "Remember that when you started expressing your annoyances toward others in this group, you became much less hostile."
- "I hope that you remember that your isolation not only keeps others away from you but also keeps you lonely."
- "My hope for you is that when you criticize yourself and tell yourself that you are not enough, you will listen to the other voice that tells you that you are lovable."

The feedback at the end of a group needs to be constructive and to be stated in such a manner that the individual is not left hanging. It is inappropriate for members to unload now stored-up negative reactions, for the member being confronted does not have a fair opportunity to work through this feedback.

During this feedback session we emphasize that participants can make some specific contracts to explore further areas after the group ends. We suggest some type of group follow-up session at a later date, which gives the members added incentive to think about ways in which to keep some of their new decisions alive.

Ways of Carrying Learning Further

Assisting members to carry their learning into action is one of the most important functions of leaders. It is our practice to routinely discuss with participants various ways in which they can use what they've learned in the group in other situations. For many members a group is merely the beginning of personal change. At the end of a member's first group experience she might say: "One of the most valuable things I'm taking from this group is that I need to do more work on how I tend to invite people to walk all over me. Before this group I wasn't even aware of how passive I was. I let myself listen to what others in the group had to say about how I had affected them, and I really saw how I was backing away from any possible conflict. I intend to get some individual counseling, as well as join an assertion-training group, so that I can go further with what I've learned in here."

If a group has been successful, the ending stage is a *commencement;* members now have some new directions to follow in dealing with problems as they arise. Furthermore, members acquire some needed tools and resources for continuing the process of personal growth. For this reason, discussing available programs and making referrals is especially timely as a group is ending. In this way the end of a group leads to new beginnings.

The Use of a Contract

One useful way to assist members in continuing the new beginnings established during the group is to devote time during one of the final sessions to writing contracts. These contracts outline steps that the members agree to take to increase the chance of their successfully meeting their goals once the group ends. It is essential that the members *themselves* develop their own contract and that the plan be not so ambitious that they are setting themselves up for failure. If the participants choose to, they can read their contract aloud, so that others can give specific suggestions for carrying it out. It is also of value to ask members to select at least one person in the group to whom they can report on their progress toward their goals. This arrangement not only is useful for encouraging accountability but also teaches people the value of establishing a support system as a way to cope with possible setbacks and discouragement.

Guidelines for Applying Group Learning to Life

As we discussed in Chapter 4, certain behaviors and attitudes increase the chances that meaningful self-exploration will occur in a group. At this time we suggest that you refer to the section that deals with guidelines on getting the most from a group experience. As members are entering a group and during the early phase, we teach them how to actively involve themselves. This teaching continues throughout the life of the group. At the final phase we reinforce some teaching points to help members consolidate what they have learned and apply their learning to daily life. Toward the end of a group the participants are likely to be receptive to considering how they can extend what they have learned.

Realize That the Group Is a Means to an End.   Unfortunately, there are those who consider a group experience an end in itself. For them, the main payoffs are the social interaction within the group setting and the temporary excitement and emotional closeness they feel during the sessions. Although feeling close may be pleasant, the purpose of a group is to enable participants to make decisions about how they will change their outside life. Groups that are therapeutic encourage people to look at themselves, to decide whether they like what they see, and to make plans for change.

As a group approaches termination, it is your task to help members reflect on *what* they have learned, *how* they learned it, and *what* they intend do with their insights. Members are then in a position to decide what they are willing to do about what they have learned about themselves.

Example: Marnie came to the group as a frightened, tough, isolated, hurt, and skeptical person. To survive her hurts, she had learned to suppress her need for others, and she prided herself on her independence. During the course of the group she demonstrated great courage by letting others become important to her. She allowed herself to be needy and to trust people and, finally, made a decision to at least share the pain of her isolation and loneliness. The point is that after the group she acted on what she had learned—that some people can be trusted. She allowed herself to be loved by a few people outside of the group. She discovered that although she could still make it alone, life was more fulfilling if she allowed herself to care for others and others to care for her.

Realize That Change May Be Slow and Subtle.   People sometimes expect change to come about automatically, and once they do make changes, they may expect them to be permanent. This expectation can lead to discouragement when temporary setbacks occur. Ideally, members will bring these setbacks back to their group. This realization that the process of change is slow can make superb material for exploration in a group.

Example: In her group-therapy sessions Barbara decided that she would no longer allow herself to be controlled by her husband and children. She engaged in rehearsing and role playing, saw that she had become what she thought her husband expected, and eventually made a contract to change those behaviors that had resulted in her feeling powerless. Later she reported to her group that she had regressed—that she seemed to be even more susceptible to being controlled. She didn't fulfill her contract, and she began losing hope that she would really change. It would have been helpful if she had realized that setbacks are a part of the growth process, that entrenched habits cannot be changed quickly, and that she had, in fact, made many strides that she was not giving herself full credit for. Her expectations of overnight changes were unrealistic. More important than dramatic lifestyle changes are directional shifts in attitudes and behavior, for these subtle beginnings may be significant in the redecision and relearning processes.

Don't Expect One Group Alone to Renovate Your Life. Those who seek a therapeutic group sometimes cling to unrealistic expectations. They expect rapid, dramatic change. Members need to be reminded that a single therapeutic experience, as potent as it may be in itself as a catalyst for significant change, is not sufficient to sustain their decisions. People spend many years creating a unique personality, with its masks and defenses. It takes time to establish constructive alternatives. People do not easily relinquish familiar defenses, for even though the defenses may entail some pain, they do work. The change process is just that—a process, not a product. Unfortunately, many group members see the group experience as a convenient shortcut to becoming their ideal "finished product."

Example: Betty, a very busy university professor, joined a weeklong group and said at the initial session: "I really think I need to clean up some personal problems that are interfering with my research, writing, and teaching. So I've set aside this week to get myself in psychological shape." She seriously thought that in a week she could see what her problems were, work through them, and be able to resume her work without the annoying distractions of personal conflicts. The leaders of the group reminded Betty that personal growth can't be made to proceed according to a schedule. They told her they hoped her expectations would change so that she wouldn't wind up disappointed.

Decide What to Do with What You've Learned. At its best, a group will provide moments of truth during which clients can see who they are and how they present themselves to others. Ultimately, it is up to the members to do something with the glimpses of truth they gain.

Example: Linda became aware that she (not her husband) was primarily responsible for her misery and depression. Before her participation in the group she had blamed other people for her unhappiness. If only they would change, she thought, I would have what I want. In the group she came to accept that if she waited for others to make her feel worthwhile, she might indeed be condemned to a hopeless existence. By accepting that only she could change things, she opened up options for redecisions. Regardless of what she decided to do, she now knew that she was not helpless. The realization that we do have choices and that we're responsible for how we live and what we experience through our decisions may well be the most valuable outcome of participation in a group.

Think for Yourself. Many people seek therapy because they've lost the ability to find their own way and have become dependent on others to direct their life and take the responsibility for their decisions. When such people enter a group, they adopt a new standard (that of the group) as their own. Although they may shed some of their inhibitions, they are still not deciding on their own direction. They expect the group to decide for them, or they are sensitively attuned to being what the group expects them to be.

Example: Very soon after disclosing to the group her unhappiness with her marriage, Shirley decided to leave her husband. This decision was reached toward the end of her membership in a personal-growth group. Some participants had felt that because she had said she didn't love her husband anymore, for her own good she should file for divorce. Shirley might ultimately have reached this decision anyway, but she appeared to act in haste and somewhat under the influence of what other members felt.

Some Final Considerations

As our groups are coming to an end, we take the opportunity to remind participants of a few concerns:

▪ We again comment on the importance of keeping confidentiality, even after the group has ended. We caution that confidences are often divulged unintentionally by members enthusiastically wanting to share with others the details of their group experience. We provide examples of how they can talk about the group without breaking confidences. A suggestion we offer is that members can tell others *what* they learned but should be careful about describing the details of *how* they learned something. It is when members discuss the "how" of their experience that they are inclined to inappropriately refer to other members. Also, we encourage participants to talk about themselves and not about the problems of other participants.

▪ We have observed that even enthusiastic group members are not beyond forgetting and discounting what they have learned soon after the termination of their group. This is especially true if they leave a supportive group and go out into an environment that is not supportive or speaks disparagingly about the value of groups. For example, Dennis learned the value of being open and direct with people in the group. Later he tried this same approach with certain people at work, only to meet with resistance and hostility. Before the group ends, we ask members such as Dennis to imagine how they might discount the value of the lessons they have learned when they are faced with people who do not appreciate their changes. In the case of Dennis we might have said: "So talk out loud now about how honesty doesn't really work in everyday life. How might you convince yourself that the only place you can be direct and honest with people is in this group?" If people are able to foresee how they might minimize their hard-earned lessons, they are less likely to do so.

▪ Some type of rating scale can be devised to give the leader a good sense of how each member experienced and evaluated the group. Standardized instruments can also tap individual changes in attitudes and values. Such practical evaluation instruments can help the members make a personal assessment of the group and can also help the leader know what interventions were helpful and what aspects of the group were least helpful. A willingness to build evaluation into the structure of the group is bound to result in improving the design of future groups. In the following chapter we will talk about combining research and practice.

Evaluation of the Group Experience

After a group ends, we have at times sent out a questionnaire to the members. The responses tell us whether we succeeded in our therapeutic efforts. The following is a sample questionnaire:

1. What general effect, if any, has your group experience had on your life?
2. What were the highlights of the group experience for you? What were some of its most meaningful aspects?
3. What were some specific things that you became aware of about your lifestyle, attitudes, and relationships with others?
4. What are some changes you've made in your life that you can attribute at least partially to your group experience?
5. Which of the techniques used by the group leaders had the most impact on you?
6. What perceptions do you have of the group leaders and their styles?
7. What problems did you encounter on leaving the group and following up on your decisions to change?
8. Have the changes that occurred as a result of your group experiences lasted? If so, do you think the changes are permanent?
9. What questions have you asked yourself since the group? Were questions of yours left unanswered by the group?
10. Did the group experience have any negative effects on you?

11. What individual or group experiences have you been involved in since this particular experience?
12. What effects do you think your participation in the group had on the significant people in your life?
13. Have there been any crises in your life since the termination of the group? How did they turn out?
14. How might your life be different now had you not experienced the group? Do you feel that you would have made any significant changes in your behavior?
15. Have you become more aware since the end of the group of the part you played in the group process?
16. If a close friend were to ask you today to tell in a sentence or two what the group meant to you, how would you respond?
17. In retrospect, are you skeptical about the value of the group process or about the motivations of other people in the group?
18. Since the group have you encouraged others to become involved in a group or in some other kind of growth experience?
19. What is the potential of this form of group experience for helping people change in a positive direction? What are its limitations? its risks? How would you recommend it be used? Do the potential gains outweigh the risks?
20. What are some other questions you think we should ask in order to get a complete picture of the meaning the group had for you? Do you have anything else to say about yourself and your experience either during or since the group?

We have found it difficult to assess the process and outcomes of groups by empirical procedures such as statistical measures of change. Although we have made attempts at objective assessment through various inventories given both before and after a group, we have not been impressed with these methods. None of the measures proved adequate to detect subtle changes in attitudes, beliefs, feelings, and behavior. Therefore, we have continued to rely on subjective evaluation measures:

- We conduct individual follow-up interviews with members or keep in contact with members; letters and telephone conversations have been substituted when person-to-person interviews were not feasible.
- We hold one or more postgroup meetings, which will be described in a later section.
- We ask members to complete brief questionnaires, such as the one above, to assess what they found most and least valuable in their group experience.
- We ask or require (depending on the type of group) that members keep process notes in a journal. On the basis of their journal notes, which are private, they write several reaction papers describing their subjective experience in the group as well as what they are doing

outside the group. These reaction papers are given to us both during the life of the group and after the group has terminated.

We have found that asking the members to write about their group experience has been very useful in evaluating our groups. And members have continued to report to us that they found the writing they did both during and after the group extremely valuable to them in consolidating what they learned. By writing, members are able to focus on relevant trends and the key things they are discovering about themselves. Through the use of journals, they have a chance to privately clarify what they are experiencing and to rehearse what they want to say to significant people. Their writing also gives them a chance to recall turning points in the group for them, helps them evaluate the impact of the group in retrospect, and gives them a basis for putting this experience into meaningful perspective.

Co-Leader Issues as the Group Ends

It is critical that co-leaders agree on termination. They need to be in tune with each other about not bringing up new material that can't be dealt with adequately before the end of the group. At times, certain members save up some topics until the very end, almost hoping that there will be no time to explore them. It could be tempting to one of the co-leaders to initiate new work with such a member; the other co-leader may be ready to bring the group to an end.

There are some other specific areas that you and your co-leader can talk about during the final stage to ensure that you are working together:

- Is either of you concerned about any members? Are there any things you might want to say to certain members?
- Are there perceptions and reactions either of you has about the group that would be useful to share with the members before the final session?
- Are both of you able to deal with your own feelings of separation and ending? If not, you may collude with the members by avoiding talking about feelings pertaining to the termination of the group.
- Have both of you given thought to how you can best help members review what they've learned from the group and translate this learning to everyday situations?
- Do you have some plan to help the members evaluate the group experience before the end of the group or at a follow-up session?

Once the group ends, we encourage co-leaders to meet to discuss their experience in leading with each other and to put the entire history of the group in perspective. What follows are some ideas that you might want to explore with your co-leader as a way to integrate your experiences and learning:

- Discuss the balance of responsibility between the co-leaders. Did one co-leader assume primary responsibility for directing while the other followed? Did one leader overshadow the other?
- Was one co-leader overly supportive and the other overly confrontational?
- How did your styles of leadership blend, and what effect did this have on the group?
- Did you agree on basic matters such as evaluation of the group's direction and what was needed to keep the group progressing?
- You can each talk about what you liked and did not like about leading with each other. You can benefit by a frank discussion of what each of you learned from the other personally and professionally, including weaknesses and strengths, skills, and styles of leading.
- It would be helpful to evaluate each other in addition to evaluating yourselves. Comparing your self-evaluation as a leader with your co-leader's evaluation of you can be of great value. What is especially useful is to be aware of certain areas needing further work; in this way each of you can grow in your capacity to lead effectively.
- You both can learn much from reviewing the turning points in the group. How did the group begin? How did it end? What happened in the group to account for its success or failure? This type of global assessment helps in understanding the group process, which can be essential information in leading future groups.

Final Stage: Summary

Stage Characteristics

During the final phase of a group the following characteristics are typically evident:

- There may be some sadness and anxiety over the reality of separation.
- Members are likely to pull back and participate in less intense ways, in anticipation of the ending of the group.
- Members are deciding what courses of action they are likely to take.
- There may be some fears of separation as well as fears about being able to carry over into daily life some of what was experienced in the group.
- Members may express their fears, hopes, and concerns for one another.
- Group sessions may be devoted partly to preparing members to meet significant others in everyday life. Role playing and behavioral rehearsal for relating more effectively to others are common.
- Members may be involved in evaluation of the group experience.
- There may be some talk about follow-up meetings or some plan for accountability so that members will be encouraged to carry out their plans for change.

Member Functions and Possible Problems

The major task facing members during the final stage of a group is consolidating their learning and transferring it to their outside environment. This is the time for them to review and put into some cognitive framework the meaning of the group experience. Some tasks for members at this time are:

- dealing with their feelings about separation and termination
- preparing for generalizing their learning to everyday life
- offering feedback that will give others a better picture of how they are perceived
- completing any unfinished business, either issues they have brought into the group or issues that pertain to people in the group
- evaluating the impact of the group
- making decisions and plans concerning what changes they want to make and how they will go about making them

Some possible problems that can occur at this time are:

- Members may avoid reviewing their experience and fail to put it into some cognitive framework, thus limiting the generalization of their learning.
- Due to separation anxiety, members may distance themselves.
- Members may consider the group an end in itself and not use it as a way of continuing to grow.

Leader Functions

The group leader's central goals in the consolidation phase are to provide a structure that allows participants to clarify the meaning of their experiences in the group and to assist members in generalizing their learning from the group to everyday life. Group leader tasks at this period include:

- assisting members in dealing with any feelings they might have about termination
- providing members an opportunity to express and deal with any unfinished business within the group
- reinforcing changes that members have made and ensuring that members have information about resources to enable them to make further progress
- assisting members in determining how they will apply specific skills in a variety of situations in daily life
- working with members to develop specific contracts and homework assignments as practical ways of making changes
- assisting participants to develop a conceptual framework that will help them understand, integrate, consolidate, and remember what they have learned in the group

- providing opportunities for members to give one another constructive feedback
- reemphasizing the importance of maintaining confidentiality after the group is over
- administering some type of end-of-group assessment instrument to evaluate the nature of individual changes and to evaluate the strengths and weaknesses of the group

Follow-Up

Postgroup Sessions

A follow-up group session three to six months after the termination of a group can be an invaluable accountability measure. Because the members know that they will come together to evaluate their progress toward their stated goals, they are likely to be motivated to take steps to make changes. Participants can develop contracts at the final sessions that involve action between the termination and the follow-up session. Members often use one another as a support system. If they experience difficulties in following through on their commitments after the group, they can discuss these difficulties. It is a matter not so much of relying on one another for advice as of using the resources of the group for support.

At follow-up sessions the participants can share difficulties they have encountered since leaving the group, talk about the specific steps they have taken to keep themselves open for change, and remember some of the most positive experiences during the group itself. Follow-ups also give members a chance to express and possibly work through any afterthoughts or feelings connected with the group experience. The members report on whether and how they are using their expanded self-awareness in their relationships in the outside world. A member may have met with resistance or hostility from other people, and the group can reinforce the member's new style of behavior at a time when his or her will to change may be weakening.

We ask members at the follow-up session whether they are continuing to reach out for what they want. Are they taking more risks? What results are they getting from their new behavior? People frequently report: "The outside world isn't like this group. I've been honest with some people out there, and they don't know how to take me!" At this point we usually remind them again that people do need to be selective about whom to be completely honest with, because many people will resist directness and openness or will not desire intimacy. The follow-up can thus help the members become more realistic about their expectations.

A follow-up session offers us one more opportunity to remind people that they are responsible for what they become and that they must take risks in order to grow. We have found that some members make decisions at the follow-up session to seek further ways of challenging themselves. Some may decide to enter individual or group therapy, some will take a drama class, some will make the choice to return to college, some will get motivated to start a self-directed program to change certain behavior patterns, and so forth. Thus, the follow-up session provides a timely opportunity to discuss other avenues for continued personal growth.

If you administered any pretests to assess beliefs, values, attitudes, and levels of personal adjustment, the postgroup meeting is an ideal time to administer some of these same instruments for comparison purposes. We support the practice of developing an assessment instrument that can be given before members join a group (or at the initial session), again at one of the final sessions, and finally at some time after termination. If you meet with the members on an individual basis to review how well they have accomplished their personal goals, these assessment devices can be of value in discussing specific changes in attitudes and behaviors.

Of course, follow-up group sessions are not always practical or possible, for many reasons. Alternatives can be developed, such as sending a brief questionnaire to assess members' perceptions about the group and its impact on their life. Members can also be contacted for individual follow-up sessions.

Individual Follow-Up Interviews

If group follow-up sessions are impractical, an alternative is one-to-one sessions with as many members as would like such a meeting. Though ideally it is a good practice to meet with each member, even if the session lasts only 15 minutes, we realize the practical problems in arranging these sessions. If you are working in private practice, in a school setting, or in an institution and if you see the members on a fairly regular basis, then such follow-up interviews may be realistic. In other cases, the members may never be seen again.

The individual screening interview at the pregroup stage is partly devoted to ascertaining why people would like to join a group, helping them identify some personal goals, and discussing their expectations. The postgroup interview can be used to determine the degree to which members have accomplished their stated goals and met their expectations. Participants can also discuss what the group meant to them in retrospect. In addition, this one-to-one interview provides an ideal opportunity to discuss referral resources, should they be indicated. In our opinion this practice is one of the best ways for a leader to evaluate the effectiveness of a group.

The individual follow-up sessions can be very informal, or they can be structured with a common set of questions that the leader asks of each member. Of course, members should be given latitude to say whatever they want and not merely answer questions. The questionnaire to evaluate a group experience that we presented earlier can apply to individual follow-up meetings as well. You can adapt your questions to the population of your group. The data from these individual sessions, especially if they are combined with a follow-up group session, give you valuable information to decide how future groups could be improved.

In open groups it is not feasible to arrange for group follow-up sessions, because the membership changes over a period of time. However, it is an excellent practice to schedule an individual follow-up session about a month after a member terminates. This gives both the member and the leader an opportunity to review significant turning points in the group as well as the ways in which the group experience has influenced the member's behavior.

Postgroup Stage: Summary

Member Functions and Possible Problems

After their group is terminated, the members' main functions are applying in-group learning to an action program in their daily life, evaluating the group, and attending some type of follow-up session (if practical). Some key tasks of the postgroup stage for members include:

- finding ways of reinforcing themselves without the support of the group
- keeping some record of their changes, including progress and problems, so that they can determine the long-term effects of their group experience
- finding ways of continuing with new behaviors through some kind of self-directed program for change
- attending an individual session, if it is scheduled, to discuss how well their goals were met, or attending a follow-up group session to share with fellow members what they have done with their group experience after termination

Some possible problems that can occur at this time are:

- If members have difficulty applying what they learned in the group to everyday situations, they might become discouraged and discount the value of the group.
- Members may have problems in continuing with new behaviors without the supportive environment of the group.
- Members may forget that change demands time, effort, work, and practice, and thus they may not use what they've learned.

Leader Functions

Leaders have the following tasks after a group ends:

- offering private consultations if any member should need this service, at least on a limited basis to discuss a member's reactions to the group experience

- if applicable, providing for a follow-up group session or follow-up individual interviews, to assess the impact of the group
- finding out about specific referral resources for members who want or need further consultation
- encouraging members to find some avenues of continued support and challenge so that the ending of the group can mark the beginning of a search for self-understanding
- assisting members to develop contracts that will enable them to make use of support systems among the group members and outside the group
- if applicable, meeting with the co-leader to assess the overall effectiveness of the group
- administering some type of postgroup assessment to determine the long-range impact of the group

Exercises

Here are a few exercises appropriate to the final stage of a group. Again, most of the exercises we suggest are suitable both for a classroom and for a counseling group.

1. **Discounting Exercise.** After a group the participants may find ways of discounting that experience, or old patterns may erupt and block the establishment of new behavior. When she left her group, Jane felt close to many people and decided that it was worth it to risk getting close. She tried this at work, was rebuffed, and began telling herself that what she had experienced in the group was not real. In this exercise you are asked to imagine all the things you might say to yourself to sabotage your plans for change. The idea is to openly acknowledge tendencies you have that will interfere with your establishing new behavior.

2. **Feedback Exercises.** A student sits in the center of the circle, and the members express their hopes and fears for the person. Or the class details which traits, attitudes, or behaviors will interfere with, and which will increase, the person's effectiveness as a group leader.

3. **Group-Termination Exercise.** Students take turns pretending that they are leaders and that the class is a group about to terminate. The idea is for students to consider how to prepare members for leaving a group.

4. **Termination-Interview Exercise.** A person in the class volunteers to become a group leader and to conduct an interview with a group member (also a volunteer) as though they had just completed a group experience together. For about ten minutes the group leader interviews the client regarding the nature of his or her group experience. After the exercise the client reacts to the interview.

5. Future-Projection Exercise. During the last session, members can be asked to imagine that it is one year (or five years or ten years) in the future, and the group is meeting in reunion. What would they most hope to be able to say to the group about their life, the changes they have made, and the influence the group had on them? What fears might they have concerning this reunion?

6. Remembering Exercise. It is helpful to simply share memories and turning points during the group's history. Members could be given the task of recalling, in free-association style, events and happenings that most stand out for them.

7. Working on Specific Contracts. During the final sessions members might formulate contracts that state specific actions they are willing to take to enhance the changes they have begun. These contracts can be written down and then read to the group. Others can give each member feedback and alternative ways of completing the contract.

8. Reviewing the Class Experience. A useful exercise is to form small groups and discuss what you have learned about yourself up to this point that you think would either contribute to or detract from your effectiveness as a group leader. How willing have you been to take risks in this class? What have you learned about how groups best function (or what gets in the way of an effective group) through your experience in the class?

CHAPTER 8

Group Process and Practice in Perspective

FOCUS QUESTIONS

1. Assume that a member of your group, Joan, says "I'm afraid people in here will think I'm foolish." How might you intervene, depending on the relationship that you have established with her? Can you think of ways in which your intervention might be determined by the stage of the group's development?

2. What are your attitudes about combining research and practice in group work? Can you think of practical ways to apply research articles that you have read? How important is it for you to keep abreast of research that has implications for the practice of group work?

3. How confident are you in your present ability to conduct groups that are characterized by a culturally diverse membership? What specific knowledge and skills do you see yourself most needing to acquire to enhance your effectiveness in working with clients who are culturally different from you?

4. In what ways might you modify the techniques you use to suit the specific needs of clients from diverse backgrounds? How can you determine the level of effectiveness of the techniques that you employ in a culturally diverse group?

5. Now that you have read this far in the textbook, spend some time reviewing the ASGW's *Ethical Guidelines for Group Counselors*, found at the end of this chapter. Have you noticed any changes in your thinking about these ethical guidelines since you first read them? At this time, what ethical issues in group work do you think are most pressing? What practical steps can you take to incorporate these guidelines into the practice of your work with groups?

Introduction

This relatively brief chapter is designed to put some of the key concepts of the group process in perspective, especially as they pertain to clinical practice. The chapters to follow will continue this emphasis, for in Part Three the focus is on groups for clients of various ages. These chapters will take some of the group-process issues that we have discussed in the preceding chapters and apply them to a variety of groups that you may someday lead.

This chapter begins with an example of a fear that many members have and illustrates how we might use different interventions, depending on the stage of the group's development. This illustration is meant to serve as a review of the specific focus at each phase in the evolution of a group. We also discuss combining research and practice in group work, trends in group work, and developing a multicultural perspective as a group worker. And we provide a summary list of some of the key points that we hope you'll remember from Parts One and Two.

Working with a Member's Fear: An Overview of the Group's Development

As one way of putting the process of a group in perspective, we will describe our work with a particular member's fear at four stages of the group's development. For the sake of the discussion, assume that Joan, a member of an ongoing group, says "I'm afraid people in here will think I'm foolish." Members often express a range of similar apprehensions, fearing that others will see them as stupid, egocentric, weird, evil, crazy, and the like. The techniques that we describe in working with Joan's particular fear of looking foolish can easily be applied to these other fears. The way we work with her differs according to the depth of the relationship that we have established with her.

Interventions at the Initial Stage

During the initial phase our goal is to provide encouragement for Joan to say more about her fear of being seen as foolish and to talk about how this fear is affecting what she is doing in the group. We facilitate a deeper exploration of her concern in any of the following ways:

- We encourage other members to talk about any fears they have, especially their concerns over how others perceive them. If Susan also says that she fears others' reactions, we can ask her to talk directly to Joan about her fears. (Here we are teaching member-to-member interaction.)
- After the exchange between Susan and Joan we ask "Do any of the rest of you have similar feelings?" (Our aim is to involve others in this interaction by stating ways in which they identify with Susan and Joan.)
- Members who have fears that they would like to explore are invited to form a small inner group. We leave the structure open-ended, so that they can talk about whatever fears they are experiencing. (In a nonthreatening way we link Joan's work with that of others, and both trust and cohesion are being established.)

Interventions at the Transition Stage

If during the transition stage Joan makes the statement "I'm afraid people in here will think I'm foolish," we are likely to encourage her to identify ways in which she has already inhibited herself because of her fear. She can be asked to say *how* she experiences her particular fear in this group. Such an intervention demands more of her than our interventions at the initial stage. We ask her questions such as "When you have that fear, whom in this room are you the most aware of?" "What are your fears about?" "How have your fears stopped you in this group?"

"What are some of the things you've been thinking and feeling but haven't expressed?" "What do you fear would happen if people perceived you as being foolish?" We also suggest to Joan that she speak to the people whom she feels most foolish around and tell them what she imagines they are thinking and feeling about her. In this way we get her to ac- knowledge her possible projections and to learn how to check out her assumptions. We are also gathering data that can be useful for explora- tion later in the group.

We can bring group members into this interaction by inviting them to give their reactions to what Joan has just said. The interchange be- tween her and other members can lead to further exploration. She has probably created some distance between herself and others in the group by avoiding them out of fear of their negative reactions. By talking about her reactions to others, she is taking responsibility for the distance she has partially created. She can work out a new stance with those whom she has been avoiding.

The work that we have just described could be done during any stage. What makes this scenario characteristic of the transition stage is the fact that members are beginning to express reactions and perceptions that they have been aware of but have kept to themselves.

Interventions at the Working Stage

If Joan discloses her fear during the working stage, we look for ways to involve the entire group in her work. Members may acknowledge how they feel put off by her, how they feel judged by her, or how they harbor angry feelings toward her. By expressing feelings that they have kept to themselves, they are moving out of the transition stage and into the work- ing stage. They acknowledge reactions and perceptions, clear up pro- jections and misunderstandings, and work through conflict. The group can get stuck in the transition stage if people do not go further and ex- press reactions that have undermined their level of trust. What moves the group into the working stage is the members' commitment to work through an impasse.

We can use other techniques to help Joan attain a deeper level of self- exploration. One is to ask her to identify people in her life with whom she has felt foolish, allowing her to connect her past struggles to her present ones. We may then ask her to tell some members how she has felt toward significant people in her life. She may even let others in the group "become" these significant figures and may say things to them that she has kept to herself. Of course, doing this may well serve as a catalyst for getting others to talk about their unfinished business with important figures in their life.

Other strategies we might use:

- Joan can be invited to simply talk more about what it is like for her to be in this group with these fears: "How have your fears been affecting you in here? What have you wanted to say or do that you were afraid to say or do? If you didn't have the fear of looking foolish, how might you be different in this group?"

- Joan can role-play with a member who reminds her of her mother, who often cautioned her about making a fool of herself.
- Joan can write an uncensored letter to her mother, which she does not mail.
- By using role reversal, Joan can "become" her mother and then go around to each person in the room, telling them how they are foolish.
- She can monitor her own behavior between group sessions, taking special note of those situations in daily life in which she stops herself because of her fear of looking foolish.
- Using cognitive procedures, Joan can pay more attention to her self-talk and eventually learn to give herself new messages. Instead of accepting self-defeating messages, she can begin to say constructive things to herself. She can change her negative beliefs and expectancies to positive ones.
- She can make decisions to try new behavior during the group, giving herself full permission to be foolish.
- Both in the group and in daily life, Joan can make a contract to forge ahead with what she wants to say or do, in spite of fears she may have about being seen as foolish.

Interventions at the Final Stage

As can be seen, our interventions in working with Joan's fear are geared to the level of trust that has been established in the group, the quality of our relationship with her, and the stage of the group's development. In the later stage of a group we are inclined to emphasize the importance of her reviewing what she has learned, how she acquired these insights, and how she can continue to translate her insights into behavioral changes outside of the group. We hope that she has learned the value of checking out her assumptions with others before deciding that they are true. We challenge her to continue acting in new ways, even if this means putting herself in places where she runs the risk of looking foolish. By now she may have developed the personal strength to challenge her fears rather than allowing herself to be controlled by them.

Combining Research and Practice in Group Work

Research can provide another perspective on the practice of group work. Consumers and funders are increasingly demanding that practitioners demonstrate the value of their therapeutic strategies. Although researchers know that group treatments can be effective, there is still scant knowledge about why groups work and what makes them effective. It is no longer necessary for researchers and practitioners to operate in separate and distinct camps, for each can contribute to a richer knowledge of what makes groups productive. This section briefly reviews some of the obstacles to the advancement of research on group work, some reasons that practitioners give for not conducting research on groups, some practical ways to evaluate the process and outcomes of groups, and some suggestions for improving research with groups.

There is a gap between research and practice in group counseling, and closing it involves overcoming some major obstacles. Practitioners often view researchers as a "strange breed," preoccupied with trivial issues. They are likely to dismiss research without weighing its potential contributions. Counseling practitioners (as opposed to counselor educators, consultants, and administrators) are least likely to regularly read research articles or use published research findings in their work with groups (Robison & Ward, 1990). Furthermore, empirical findings are seldom reported in a way that encourages clinicians to translate research into practice (Dies, 1983b).

As Stockton has observed (see Bednar et al., 1987), the lack of collaboration between researchers and practitioners continues to be a key problem in group work. According to Stockton, each faction often lacks an appreciation for the contributions the other can make. Researchers often do not really understand what can be learned from clinical experience, and practitioners often perceive research as being irrelevant to clinical practice. Only a small percentage of group practitioners use research findings in any consistent manner or engage in research of their own. If this knowledge gap is to be bridged, practitioners and researchers need to develop an increased mutual respect for what each can offer, and they must learn to work cooperatively, accepting the dual role of practitioner/researcher (Morran & Stockton, 1985; see Stockton, in Bednar et al., 1987).

In a survey of research activities and attitudes among ASGW members, Robison and Ward (1990) found that few respondents had conducted research with groups at the time they completed the survey. Research activities, both current and past, were reported most frequently by counselor educators, consultants, and administrators and were reported least by practicing counselors and counseling students. Insufficient time, funds, and employer support were most frequently reported as reasons for not having conducted research. Other reasons included ethical considerations or policies prohibiting research with agency clients, lack of interest, unavailability of research facilities, lack of training in research methods, and lack of past success in presenting and publishing findings.

In an article on perspectives on research in group work, seven professionals in the field comment on overcoming obstacles to the future development of research (Bednar et al., 1987). The authors mention a number of common conceptual, methodological, and attitudinal impediments. They conclude that reducing these obstacles will necessitate a commitment among researchers and other professionals to improve conceptualizations of variables studied in relation to groups, to use research designs and methods that can assess the subtle nature of interactions among the leader and members, to improve reporting of the characteristics of treatment and control groups that are studied, and to focus on the applications of research findings. The authors call for more meaningful collaboration among researchers and group practitioners.

Several writers have identified some of these conceptual, methodological, and attitudinal difficulties inherent in conducting research on groups (Bednar & Kaul, 1978; Dies, 1983a; Kaul & Bednar, 1986; Stockton & Morran, 1982). A survey of over 40 years of research shows an abundance of evidence that group approaches are associated with clients' improvement in a variety of settings and situations (Bednar & Kaul, 1978, 1979; Bednar & Lawlis, 1971; Kaul & Bednar, 1978, 1986). When it comes to understanding the conditions that appear to foster this improvement, however, little is really known at this time. Researchers have very limited knowledge about basic concerns such as (1) how group processes mediate change in participants; (2) how members influence group processes; and (3) what dimensions of psychological functioning are most amenable to change in small groups. Quite simply, although researchers do know that group treatments can be effective, they have little clear knowledge of the underlying principles that mediate improvement. Moreover, current research efforts are addressing questions that have been answered before.

Because of their attitudes toward research, many group workers are not willing to devote time to devising evaluative instruments as a part of their clinical practice. It is possible, however, to make systematic observation and assessment basic parts of the practice of group work. Instead of thinking exclusively in terms of rigorous empirical research, practitioners can begin to consider alternatives to traditional scientific methods. One such alternative is evaluative research, which is aimed at gathering and assessing data that can be of value in making decisions about programs and in improving the quality of professional service (Dies, 1983a). In group work, pure research should not be seen as the only type of inquiry that has value. Practitioners and researchers can choose to do good field research instead (Morran & Stockton, 1985).

In writing about the best of all possible research worlds, Yalom (1983) envisions a project in which the members would be randomly and strategically assigned to various types of therapy groups and to a control group. Outcomes would be objectively determined, and correlations would be measured between the outcome and the nature of the group-therapy experience. Yalom adds that no such project has been or ever will be done, because the methodological problems are so overwhelming. He concludes that it is best to settle for studies that are less than perfect.

Whether leaders actually conduct research with their groups may be less important than their willingness to keep themselves informed about the practical applications of research. One survey asked practitioners how journal articles reporting research on groups could be made more useful to them in their own work (Robison & Ward, 1990). The suggestions for improving published research were as follows: (1) publish more articles on research that attempts to replicate earlier studies, (2) increase the specificity of research reports, (3) give more information about the experimental and control treatments used, (4) describe more fully the rationale for studies, (5) emphasize the relevance of research findings to group practice, (6) publish more high-quality studies using actual groups in school and agency settings, (7) increase the number of literature reviews of research, (8) define dependent and independent variables more specifically, and (9) place more emphasis on behavioral and attitudinal variables in published research.

Trends in Group Work

If we had to limit ourselves to singling out three significant trends in group practice during the last decade, we would identify these directions: an increase in short-term structured groups for special populations, a heightened awareness of the implications of living and practicing in a pluralistic society characterized by a range of cultures, and an increased realization by practitioners of the importance of dealing with ethical and legal issues.

Structured Groups for Specialized Populations

When we give workshops around the United States, we are struck by the range of structured groups dealing with specific problems. Such groups are limited only by a leader's interest, enthusiasm, and creativity. They tend to be of relatively short duration and to have an educational and a therapeutic focus. Perhaps one reason for this trend is the increased pressure that mental-health practitioners feel to be accountable. Consumers and insurance companies are demanding more evidence that a counselor's methods are, indeed, working. Many practitioners appear to be less interested in loosely structured or unfocused groups that merely promise self-actualization and growth experiences. In Chapter 1 we gave examples of the wide array of structured groups. In Part Three we will describe a number of short-term groups for specific populations, including children of divorce, children of alcoholics, people with AIDS, unwed teenage fathers, adolescents on drug rehabilitation, victims of incest, and dieters. If you are interested in reading further, see Shaffer and Galinsky (1989), on theme-centered groups and self-help groups; Lakin (1985), on self-help groups and a variety of helping groups; and Yalom (1983), on short-term, structured inpatient groups.

Multicultural Awareness in Group Practice

In addition to recognizing and respecting cultural differences, practitioners are highlighting the unique strengths of various cultures. Most graduate programs now require a course in cultural and ethnic diversity, and students receive specialized training in multicultural counseling both in their course work and as a part of their supervised fieldwork and internship.

Effective delivery of group-counseling services must take into account the impact of the client's culture. Culture is, quite simply, the values and behavior shared by a group of people. It does not refer just to an ethnic or racial heritage but can also be determined by age, sex, lifestyle, or socioeconomic status. Cultural diversity is a fact of life in our contemporary world. As a group practitioner, you cannot afford to ignore the issue, for culture will influence both the clients' behavior and yours, with or without your awareness. As an integral part of your training program, you need to develop an increased awareness of your cultural values and personal assumptions so that you can work sensitively with clients' many social differences.

Writers in the field often assert that many counseling approaches are failing to meet the complex needs of various ethnic and minority clients because of narrow, stereotyped perceptions of those needs. Asian Americans, Blacks, Hispanics, Native Americans, and members of other minority groups terminate counseling significantly earlier than do Anglo clients. This dropout rate is often caused by barriers such as language difficulties and culture-bound values that hinder the formation of a good counseling relationship (Mokuau, 1987; Pedersen, 1988; D. W. Sue, 1990). Regardless of your ethnic, cultural, and racial background, if you hope to build bridges of understanding between yourself and clients who are different from you, you will have to guard against rigid and stereotyped generalizations about social or cultural groups. In short, you will need to acquire a multicultural perspective in your practice.

Pedersen (1990) views multiculturalism as the "fourth force" in the counseling field, along with the psychodynamic, behavioral, and humanistic perspectives. He believes it to be the most important new idea to shape the profession in 20 years. Some of the assumptions that Pedersen (1988, 1989, 1990) makes about multiculturalism have a significant impact on techniques in group work:

- Culture is best defined broadly rather than narrowly, so that demographic variables (age, gender, and residence); status variables (social, educational, and economic); and affiliations (formal and informal) are considered as potentially salient cultural features.
- The multicultural perspective is relevant to all aspects of counseling practice, rather than being limited to exotic populations and special-interest groups.

- Multiculturalism needs to be understood as a continuous theme in all fields of counseling rather than as an attempt to develop a new and separate field of study.
- Multiculturalism can be the basis for people to disagree without one person being "right" and the other being "wrong."

If you intend to be involved in group work with culturally diverse populations, as most populations are, it will be essential to modify your concepts and techniques to meet the unique needs of the members (Mokuau, 1985). It is clear that no one "right" technique can be utilized across the board with all clients, irrespective of their cultural background. D. W. Sue (1990) contends that there is a lack of conceptual frameworks that might integrate cultural and sociopolitical factors in explaining why certain counseling styles would be more appropriate for certain populations. A review of the literature on cross-cultural counseling reveals that the rationale for culture-specific approaches lies in three major domains: (1) differences in communications styles, (2) sociopolitical facets of nonverbal communication, and (3) counseling as a communication style (D. W. Sue, 1990; D. W. Sue & D. Sue, 1990).

If you respect the members in your group, you will demonstrate a willingness to learn from them. You will be aware of hesitation on a client's part and will not be too quick to misinterpret it. Instead, you can attempt to enter the world of the client. It is not necessary for you to have the same experiences as your clients; what is more important is that you attempt to be open to a similar set of feelings and struggles. Your willingness to put yourself in situations where you can learn about different cultures will be most useful. If you model a genuine respect for the differences among clients in your groups, all of the group members will benefit from this cultural diversity.

In closing, we would like to point out certain advantages and limitations of using group formats with culturally diverse client populations. On the plus side, members can gain much from the power and strength of collective group feedback. They can be supportive of one another in patterns that are familiar. As members see their peers challenging themselves and making desired changes in their lives, it gives them hope that change is possible for them (Chu & Sue, 1984). But there are also some cautions to note. Some individuals may be reluctant to readily disclose personal material or to share family conflicts. They may see it as shameful even to have personal problems and all the more shameful to talk about them in front of strangers. People from some cultures usually rely on members of the extended family for help rather than seeking professional assistance. Another caution pertains to using confrontive interventions. Challenging client resistance too quickly and too directly can often be counterproductive with certain cultural groups. These clients may perceive the directness associated with confrontation as a personal criticism and as a personal attack (Ho, 1984; D. W. Sue & D. Sue,

1990). If they feel insulted, the chances are that they will also feel rejected or angry, and such feelings may cement their resistance to becoming involved in the group.

You need to find ways to reach clients who may want help but do not know where to find it or are reluctant to seek professional help. Try to accept the difficulties that clients experience in talking to you about themselves in personal ways, so that the foundation of a therapeutic relationship can be formed.

We have merely introduced this significant trend toward multicultural practice. We recommend the following as sources for educating yourself about these issues: Alonso and Rutan (1988); Atkinson, Morten, and Sue (1989); Christensen (1989); Chu and Sue (1984); Ho (1984); Lee, Juan, and Hom (1984); Mokuau (1985, 1987); Pedersen (1988, 1989, 1990); Pedersen, Draguns, Lonner, and Trimble (1989); D. W. Sue (1990); D. W. Sue and D. Sue (1990); and S. Sue (1988).

Ethical Awareness in Group Practice

The third trend involves practitioners' increased awareness of the ethical, professional, and legal issues relevant to group work. Several textbooks have chapters or sections that address these issues: (Bennett, Bryant, VandenBos, & Greenwood, 1990; G. Corey, M. Corey, & Callanan, 1988; Hopkins & Anderson, 1990; Rosenbaum, 1982; Van Hoose & Kottler, 1985). Malpractice awards to clients who were treated unprofessionally and irresponsibly have increased the anxiety level of many mental-health professionals. When groups reached their zenith in the 1960s and the 1970s, there were some excesses in the name of "experimentation." Practitioners who became aware of ethically questionable practices are now attempting to improve the reputation of groups by designing ethical and legal safeguards.

Because we devoted Chapter 2 to a detailed discussion of ethical issues facing group practitioners, we will not discuss this trend any further at this point, except to point out the role of the Association for Specialists in Group Work in promoting standards for both the training of group practitioners (ASGW, 1990) and in formulating guidelines for ethical practice (ASGW, 1989). At the end of this chapter are the association's ethical guidelines, to which you can refer as you review the preceding chapters and as you read the remainder of this book. You may want to insert a tab at the beginning of the guidelines so that you can have easy reference to them.

Points to Remember: Summary

Following is a list of 20 basic concepts and guidelines that we hope you will remember:

1. It is important to have a theoretical rationale that will help you make sense of what occurs in a group. Because each established group theory stresses a particular dimension of the group process, we encourage a selective borrowing of concepts from each of them. What is important is that you devote time to conceptualizing the group process.

2. Although we have described various group techniques, we believe that personality and character are the most important variables in the making of effective group leaders. Techniques cannot compensate for the shortcomings of leaders who lack self-knowledge, who are not willing to do what they ask group members to do, or who are poorly trained. Character traits of effective leaders, in our view, include courage, willingness to model, presence, caring, a belief in the group process, openness, nondefensiveness, personal power, endurance, a sense of humor, imagination, and self-awareness. We ask you to think about your personal characteristics and to try to decide which will be assets and which liabilities to you as a group leader.

3. In addition to having certain personal characteristics, effective group leaders are knowledgeable about group dynamics and have leadership skills. We suggest that you make frequent use of the inventories we have presented as a means of thinking about personal areas you might need to improve and competencies you might need to develop.

4. You will be faced with the need to take a stand on a number of basic issues, including how much responsibility for what goes on in the group belongs to the members and how much to you as the leader, how much and what type of structuring is optimal for a group, what kind of self-disclosure is optimal, what role and function you will assume, and how you will integrate both support and confrontation into group practice.

5. Ethical codes have been established by the various professional organizations, and those who belong to such organizations are bound by them. Thus, ethical guidelines governing group practice are not something you decide alone or in a vacuum. You should familiarize yourself with these established codes of ethics and with the laws that may affect group practice. The latter are particularly important if you are working with children or adolescents.

6. A solid academic background is desirable, but also important is an internship experience in which you can get supervised experience in leading and co-leading groups. Ongoing training groups and personal-growth groups are useful adjuncts to your academic program and your practical experience. Personal psychotherapy (both individual and group) is also valuable for you personally and for your development as a practitioner.

7. In developing a proposal for a group, include the selection procedures you plan to use, the composition you plan for the group, and details such as where and when you will hold the group. We recommend

an individual screening session for all applicants and a pregroup session. The initial stage of a group is crucial, for the level of trust is being established. During the first few meetings, issues such as who will wield the power in the group and whether the members will focus on themselves or others are being decided.

8. Group approaches to therapy have some distinct advantages over individual approaches, but they also have limitations. It is a mistake to think that groups are for everyone, and in designing a group be able to state clearly why a group is the treatment approach of choice. Such a written rationale should include descriptions of the goals of the group, the means that will be used to accomplish these goals, the role of the members, your function and role, and the means that will be used to assess the outcomes.

9. Psychological risks are associated with participation in a group. It is your responsibility to help the members identify and explore their readiness to deal with these potential risks. It is also your job to develop means of minimizing the risks.

10. A therapeutic group is a means to an end. Participants can use the group to learn more about themselves, to explore their conflicts, to learn new social skills, to get feedback on the impact they have on others, and to try out new behaviors. The group becomes a microcosm of society, in which members can learn more effective ways of living with others. Depending on the type of group, there are some clear advantages to constituting a group that is diverse with respect to age, gender, cultural background, race, and philosophical perspectives.

11. Members should clarify their goals at the beginning of a group. Developing contracts will help them do so, and doing homework assignments in between sessions will help them attain these goals.

12. It is a helpful practice to develop guidelines for behavior in groups and teach them to the members. Some of the behaviors you might stress are keeping the group's activities confidential, respecting the differences that characterize the members, taking responsibility for oneself, working hard in the group, listening, and expressing one's thoughts and feelings.

13. Remember that resistance does not have to be the enemy of group cohesion. In fact, if resistance is recognized and dealt with directly, the resistive behaviors provide the very material for group work. Learn to welcome resistance, rather than to fight it. It does serve a function, and at times resistive behavior makes perfectly good sense. Rather than labeling members, describe the behavior you see and your reaction as well. If you observe defensive behaviors that are bound to emerge in the course of a group, you are likely to learn about the ways in which members struggle with problems in their outside lives.

14. Pay attention to the diversity that exists within your group, and use this diversity to accentuate the members' work. Help members recognize the ways in which their cultural background is influencing their values and behavior, and highlight cultural themes as they surface during a session.

15. Throughout the life of a group, continue teaching members how to assess their individual progress so that they have a basis for determining the degree to which they are accomplishing their goals. Also, encourage the members to evaluate the group as a whole and how its time is being used.

16. Pay attention to how the sessions are opened and closed. Strive to make connections between the sessions. Toward the end of each session, try to get all of the members to at least briefly state what they have learned from the meeting.

17. Be aware of your reactions in the group. You can use them very effectively in enhancing the group process. Remember that they are your most useful therapeutic instrument as a group leader. Be willing to share your reactions to what is occurring within the here and now of the group sessions.

18. Take some time to think about your therapeutic style and its impact on the process and outcomes of your group. Be able to describe its key features in clear terms.

19. Some of the factors that operate in groups to produce positive changes in the participants are self-disclosure; hope; commitment to change; willingness to risk; the caring, acceptance, and empathy that the members offer one another; the intimacy that develops; respect for differences in world views; the freedom to experiment; feedback; catharsis; the learning of interpersonal skills; laughter; and cohesiveness.

20. Members need to be prepared for the termination of their group experience. If they are to get the most from a group, they must focus on how they can apply what they've learned in the group to their life. If you want to determine the impact of a group you've led, we strongly suggest that you plan a follow-up session. This meeting will give members the chance to share the experiences they've had since the termination of their group.

Ethical Guidelines for Group Counselors

ASGW 1989 Revision

Association for Specialists in Group Work

PREAMBLE

One characteristic of any professional group is the possession of a body of knowledge, skills, and voluntarily, self-professed standards for ethical practice. A Code of Ethics consists of those standards that have been formally and publicly acknowledged by the members of a profession to serve as the guidelines for professional conduct, discharge of duties, and the resolution of moral dilemmas. By this document, the Association for Specialists in Group Work (ASGW) has identified the standards of conduct appropriate for ethical behavior among its members.

The Association for Specialists in Group Work recognizes the basic commitment of its members to the Ethical Standards of its parent organization, the American Association for Counseling and Development (AACD) and nothing in this document shall be construed to supplant that code. These standards are intended to complement the AACD standards in the area of group work by clarifying the nature of ethical responsibility of the counselor in the group setting and by stimulating a greater concern for competent group leadership.

The group counselor is expected to be a professional agent and to take the processes of ethical responsibility seriously. ASGW views "ethical process" as being integral to group work and views group counselors as "ethical agents." Group counselors, by their very nature in being responsible and responsive to their group members, necessarily embrace a certain potential for ethical vulnerability. It is incumbent upon group counselors to give considerable attention to the intent and context of their actions because the attempts of counselors to influence human behavior through group work always have ethical implications.

The following ethical guidelines have been developed to encourage ethical behavior of group counselors. These guidelines are written for students and practitioners, and are meant to stimulate reflection, self-examination, and discussion of issues and practices. They address the group counselor's responsibility for providing information about group work to clients and the group counselor's responsibility for providing group counseling services to clients. A final section discusses the group counselor's responsibility for safeguarding ethical practice and procedures for reporting unethical behavior. Group counselors are expected to make known these standards to group members.

ETHICAL GUIDELINES

1. *Orientation and Providing Information:* Group counselors adequately prepare prospective or new group members by providing as much information about the existing or proposed group as necessary.
   - Minimally, information related to each of the following areas should be provided.
     a. Entrance procedures, time parameters of the group experience, group participation expectations, methods of payment (where appropriate), and termination procedures are explained by the group counselor as appropriate to the level of maturity of group members and the nature and purpose(s) of the group.
     b. Group counselors have available for distribution, a professional disclosure statement that includes information on the group counselor's qualifications and group services that can be provided, particularly as related to the nature and purpose(s) of the specific group.

From *ASGW Ethical Guidelines for Group Counselors*, Volume 15, Number 2, May 1990, 119–126. © American Association for Counseling and Development. Reprinted with permission. These guidelines were approved by the Association for Specialists in Group Work (ASGW) Executive Board, June 1, 1989.

c. Group counselors communicate the role expectations, rights, and responsibilities of group members and group counselor(s).

d. The group goals are stated as concisely as possible by the group counselor including "whose" goal it is (the group counselor's, the institution's, the parent's, the law's, society's, etc.) and the role of group members in influencing or determining the group's goal(s).

e. Group counselors explore with group members the risks of potential life changes that may occur because of the group experience and help members explore their readiness to face these possibilities.

f. Group members are informed by the group counselor of unusual or experimental procedures that might be expected in their group experience.

g. Group counselors explain, as realistically as possible, what services can and cannot be provided within the particular group structure offered.

h. Group counselors emphasize the need to promote full psychological functioning and presence among group members. They inquire from prospective group members whether they are using any kind of drug or medication that may affect functioning in the group. They do not permit any use of alcohol and/or illegal drugs during group sessions and they discourage the use of alcohol and/or drugs (legal or illegal) prior to group meetings which may affect the physical or emotional presence of the member or other group members.

i. Group counselors inquire from prospective group members whether they have ever been a client in counseling or psychotherapy. If a prospective group member is already in a counseling relationship with another professional person, the group counselor advises the prospective group member to notify the other professional of their participation in the group.

j. Group counselors clearly inform group members about the policies pertaining to the group counselor's willingness to consult with them between group sessions.

k. In establishing fees for group counseling services, group counselors consider the financial status and the locality of prospective group members. Group members are not charged fees for group sessions where the group counselor is not present and the policy of charging for sessions missed by a group member is clearly communicated. Fees for participating as a group member are contracted between group counselor and group member for a specified period of time. Group counselors do not increase fees for group counseling services until the existing contracted fee structure has expired. In the event that the established fee structure is inappropriate for a prospective member, group counselors assist in finding comparable services of acceptable cost.

2. *Screening of Members:* The group counselor screens prospective group members (when appropriate to their theoretical orientation). Insofar as possible, the counselor selects group members whose needs and goals are compatible with the goals of the group, who will not impede the group process, and whose well-being will not be jeopardized by the group experience. An orientation to the group (i.e., ASGW Ethical Guideline #1), is included during the screening process.

- Screening may be accomplished in one or more ways, such as the following:
  a. Individual interview,
  b. Group interview of prospective group members,
  c. Interview as part of a team staffing, and,
  d. Completion of a written questionnaire by prospective group members.

3. *Confidentiality:* Group counselors protect members by defining clearly what confidentiality means, why it is important, and the difficulties involved in enforcement.

a. Group counselors take steps to protect members by defining confidentiality and the limits of confidentiality (i.e., when a group member's condition indicates that there is clear and imminent danger to the member, others, or physical property, the group counselor takes reasonable personal action and/or informs responsible authorities).

b. Group counselors stress the importance of confidentiality and set a norm of confidentiality regarding all group participants' disclosures. The importance of maintaining confidentiality is emphasized before the group begins and at various times in the group. The fact that confidentiality cannot be guaranteed is clearly stated.

c. Members are made aware of the difficulties involved in enforcing and ensuring confidentiality in a group setting. The counselor provides examples of how confidentiality can non-maliciously be broken to increase members' awareness, and help to lessen the likelihood that this breach of confidence will occur. Group counselors inform group members about the potential consequences of intentionally breaching confidentiality.

d. Group counselors can only ensure confidentiality on their part and not on the part of the members.

e. Group counselors video or audio tape a group session only with the prior consent, and the members' knowledge of how the tape will be used.

f. When working with minors, the group counselor specifies the limits of confidentiality.

g. Participants in a mandatory group are made aware of any reporting procedures required of the group counselor.

h. Group counselors store or dispose of group member records (written, audio, video, etc.) in ways that maintain confidentiality.

i. Instructors of group counseling courses maintain the anonymity of group members whenever discussing group counseling cases.

4. *Voluntary/Involuntary Participation:* Group counselors inform members whether participation is voluntary or involuntary.

a. Group counselors take steps to ensure informed consent procedures in both voluntary and involuntary groups.

b. When working with minors in a group, counselors are expected to follow the procedures specified by the institution in which they are practicing.

c. Within voluntary groups, every attempt is made to enlist the cooperation of the members and their continuance in the group on a voluntary basis.

d. Group counselors do not certify that group treatment has been received by members who merely attend sessions, but did not meet the defined group expectations. Group members are informed about the consequences for failing to participate in a group.

5. *Leaving a Group:* Provisions are made to assist a group member to terminate in an effective way.

a. Procedures to be followed for a group member who chooses to exit a group prematurely are discussed by the counselor with all group members either before the group begins, during a pre-screening interview, or during the initial group session.

b. In the case of legally mandated group counseling, group counselors inform members of the possible consequences for premature self-termination.

c. Ideally, both the group counselor and the member can work cooperatively to determine the degree to which a group experience is productive or counterproductive for that individual.

d. Members ultimately have a right to discontinue membership in the group, at a designated time, if the predetermined trial period proves to be unsatisfactory.

e. Members have the right to exit a group, but it is important that they be made aware of the importance of informing the counselor and the group members prior to deciding to leave. The counselor discusses the possible risks of leaving the group prematurely with a member who is considering this option.

f. Before leaving a group, the group counselor encourages members (if appropriate) to discuss their reasons for wanting to discontinue membership in the group. Counselors intervene if other members use undue pressure to force a member to remain in the group.

6. *Coercion and Pressure:* Group counselors protect member rights against physical threats, intimidation, coercion, and undue peer pressure insofar as is reasonably possible.

  a. It is essential to differentiate between "therapeutic pressure" that is part of any group and "undue pressure," which is not therapeutic.

  b. The purpose of a group is to help participants find their own answer, not to pressure them into doing what the group thinks is appropriate.

  c. Counselors exert care not to coerce participants to change in directions which they clearly state they do not choose.

  d. Counselors have a responsibility to intervene when others use undue pressure or attempt to persuade members against their will.

  e. Counselors intervene when any member attempts to act out aggression in a physical way that might harm another member or themselves.

  f. Counselors intervene when a member is verbally abusive or inappropriately confrontive to another member.

7. *Imposing Counselor Values:* Group counselors develop an awareness of their own values and needs and the potential impact they have on the interventions likely to be made.

  a. Although group counselors take care to avoid imposing their values on members, it is appropriate that they expose their own beliefs, decisions, needs, and values, when concealing them would create problems for the members.

  b. There are values implicit in any group, and these are made clear to potential members before they join the group. (Examples of certain values include: expressing feelings, being direct and honest, sharing personal material with others, learning how to trust, improving interpersonal communication, and deciding for oneself.)

  c. Personal and professional needs of group counselors are not met at the members' expense.

  d. Group counselors avoid using the group for their own therapy.

  e. Group counselors are aware of their own values and assumptions and how these apply in a multicultural context.

  f. Group counselors take steps to increase their awareness of ways that their personal reactions to members might inhibit the group process and they monitor their countertransference. Through an awareness of the impact of stereotyping and discrimination (i.e., biases based on age, disability, ethnicity, gender, race, religion, or sexual preference), group counselors guard the individual rights and personal dignity of all group members.

8. *Equitable Treatment:* Group counselors make every reasonable effort to treat each member individually and equally.

  a. Group counselors recognize and respect differences (e.g., cultural, racial, religious, lifestyle, age, disability, gender) among group members.

  b. Group counselors maintain an awareness of their behavior toward individual group members and are alert to the potential detrimental effects of favoritism or partiality toward any particular group member to the exclusion or detriment of any other member(s). It is likely that group counselors will favor some members over others, yet all group members deserve to be treated equally.

  c. Group counselors ensure equitable use of group time for each member by inviting silent members to become involved, acknowledging nonverbal attempts to communicate, and discouraging rambling and monopolizing of time by members.

  d. If a large group is planned, counselors consider enlisting another qualified professional to serve as a co-leader for the group sessions.

9. *Dual Relationships:* Group counselors avoid dual relationships with group members that might impair their objectivity and professional judgment, as well as those which are likely to compromise a group member's ability to participate fully in the group.

  a. Group counselors do not misuse their professional role and power as group leader to advance personal or social contacts with members throughout the duration of the group.

b. Group counselors do not use their professional relationship with group members to further their own interest either during the group or after the termination of the group.

c. Sexual intimacies between group counselors and members are unethical.

d. Group counselors do not barter (exchange) professional services with group members for services.

e. Group counselors do not admit their own family members, relatives, employees, or personal friends as members to their groups.

f. Group counselors discuss with group members the potential detrimental effects of group members engaging in intimate inter-member relationships outside of the group.

g. Students who participate in a group as a partial course requirement for a group course are not evaluated for an academic grade based upon their degree of participation as a member in a group. Instructors of group counseling courses take steps to minimize the possible negative impact on students when they participate in a group course by separating course grades from participation in the group and by allowing students to decide what issues to explore and when to stop.

h. It is inappropriate to solicit members from a class (or institutional affiliation) for one's private counseling or therapeutic groups.

10. *Use of Techniques:* Group counselors do not attempt any technique unless trained in its use or under supervision by a counselor familiar with the intervention.

a. Group counselors are able to articulate a theoretical orientation that guides their practice, and they are able to provide a rationale for their interventions.

b. Depending upon the type of an intervention, group counselors have training commensurate with the potential impact of a technique.

c. Group counselors are aware of the necessity to modify their techniques to fit the unique needs of various cultural and ethnic groups.

d. Group counselors assist members in translating in-group learnings to daily life.

11. *Goal Development:* Group counselors make every effort to assist members in developing their personal goals.

a. Group counselors use their skills to assist members in making their goals specific so that others present in the group will understand the nature of the goals.

b. Throughout the course of a group, group counselors assist members in assessing the degree to which personal goals are being met, and assist in revising any goals when it is appropriate.

c. Group counselors help members clarify the degree to which the goals can be met within the context of a particular group.

12. *Consultation:* Group counselors develop and explain policies about between-session consultation to group members.

a. Group counselors take care to make certain that members do not use between-session consultations to avoid dealing with issues pertaining to the group that would be dealt with best in the group.

b. Group counselors urge members to bring the issues discussed during between-session consultations into the group if they pertain to the group.

c. Group counselors seek out consultation and/or supervision regarding ethical concerns or when encountering difficulties which interfere with their effective functioning as group leaders.

d. Group counselors seek appropriate professional assistance for their own personal problems or conflicts that are likely to impair their professional judgment and work performance.

e. Group counselors discuss their group cases only for professional consultation and educational purposes.

f. Group counselors inform members about policies regarding whether consultation will be held confidential.

13. *Termination from the Group:* Depending upon the purpose of participation in the group, counselors promote termination of

members from the group in the most efficient period of time.

a. Group counselors maintain a constant awareness of the progress made by each group member and periodically invite the group members to explore and reevaluate their experiences in the group. It is the responsibility of group counselors to help promote the independence of members from the group in a timely manner.

14. *Evaluation and Follow-up:* Group counselors make every attempt to engage in ongoing assessment and to design follow-up procedures for their groups.

a. Group counselors recognize the importance of ongoing assessment of a group, and they assist members in evaluating their own progress.

b. Group counselors conduct evaluation of the total group experience at the final meeting (or before termination), as well as ongoing evaluation.

c. Group counselors monitor their own behavior and become aware of what they are modeling in the group.

d. Follow-up procedures might take the form of personal contact, telephone contact, or written contact.

e. Follow-up meetings might be with individuals, or groups, or both to determine the degree to which: (i) members have reached their goals, (ii) the group had a positive or negative effect on the participants, (iii) members could profit from some type of referral, and (iv) as information for possible modification of future groups. If there is no follow-up meeting, provisions are made available for individual follow-up meetings to any member who needs or requests such a contact.

15. *Referrals:* If the needs of a particular member cannot be met within the type of group being offered, the group counselor suggests other appropriate professional referrals.

a. Group counselors are knowledgeable of local community resources for assisting group members regarding professional referrals.

b. Group counselors help members seek further professional assistance, if needed.

16. *Professional Development:* Group counselors recognize that professional growth is a continuous, ongoing, developmental process throughout their career.

a. Group counselors maintain and upgrade their knowledge and skill competencies through educational activities, clinical experiences, and participation in professional development activities.

b. Group counselors keep abreast of research findings and new developments as applied to groups.

SAFEGUARDING ETHICAL PRACTICE AND PROCEDURES FOR REPORTING UNETHICAL BEHAVIOR

The preceding remarks have been advanced as guidelines which are generally representative of ethical and professional group practice. They have not been proposed as rigidly defined prescriptions. However, practitioners who are thought to be grossly unresponsive to the ethical concerns addressed in this document may be subject to a review of their practices by the AACD Ethics Committee and ASGW peers.

▪ For consultation and/or questions regarding these ASGW Ethical Guidelines or group ethical dilemmas, you may contact the Chairperson of the ASGW Ethics Committee. The name, address, and telephone number of the current ASGW Ethics Committee Chairperson may be acquired by telephoning the AACD office in Alexandria Virginia at (703) 823-9800.

▪ If a group counselor's behavior is suspected as being unethical, the following procedures are to be followed:

a. Collect more information and investigate further to confirm the unethical practice as determined by the ASGW Ethical Guidelines.

b. Confront the individual with the apparent violation of ethical guidelines for the purposes of protecting the safety of any clients and to help the group counselor correct any inappropriate behaviors. If satisfactory resolution is not reached through this contact then:

c. A complaint should be made in writing, including the specific facts and dates of the alleged violation and all relevant supporting data. The complaint should be included in an envelope marked "CONFIDENTIAL" to ensure confidentiality for both the accuser(s) and the alleged violator(s) and forwarded to all of the following sources:

1. The name and address of the Chairperson of the state Counselor Licensure Board for the respective state, if in existence.
2. The Ethics Committee
   c/o The President
   American Association for Counseling and Development
   5999 Stevenson Avenue
   Alexandria, Virginia 22304
3. The name and address of all private credentialing agencies that the alleged violator maintains credentials or holds professional membership. Some of these include the following:

   National Board for Certified Counselors, Inc.
   5999 Stevenson Avenue
   Alexandria, Virginia 22304

   National Council for Credentialing of Career Counselors
   c/o NBCC
   5999 Stevenson Avenue
   Alexandria, Virginia 22304

   National Academy for Certified Clinical Mental Health Counselors
   5999 Stevenson Avenue
   Alexandria, Virginia 22304

   Commission on Rehabilitation Counselor Certification
   162 North State Street, Suite 317
   Chicago, Illinois 60601

   American Association for Marriage and Family Therapy
   1717 K Street, N.W., Suite 407
   Washington, D.C. 20006

   American Psychological Association
   1200 Seventeenth Street, N.W.
   Washington, D.C. 20036

   American Group Psychotherapy Association, Inc.
   25 East 21st Street, 6th Floor
   New York, New York 10010

REFERENCES AND SUGGESTED READINGS FOR PARTS ONE AND TWO

Alonso, A., & Rutan, J. S. (1988). The experience of shame and the restoration of self-respect in group psychotherapy. *International Journal of Group Psychotherapy, 38*(1), 3–14.

American Association for Counseling and Development. (1988). *Ethical standards.* Alexandria, VA: Author.

American Association for Marriage and Family Therapy. (1988). *AAMFT code of ethical principles for marriage and family therapists.* Washington, DC: Author.

American Group Psychotherapy Association. (1978). *Guidelines for the training of group psychotherapists.* New York: Author.

American Mental Health Counselors Association. (1980). *Code of ethics for certified clinical mental health counselors.* Alexandria, VA: Author.

American Psychological Association. (1973). Guidelines for psychologists conducting growth groups. *American Psychologist, 28*(10), 933.

American Psychological Association. (1989). *Ethical principles of psychologists.* Washington, DC: Author.

Association for Specialists in Group Work. (1980). *Ethical guidelines for group leaders.* Alexandria, VA: Author.

*Association for Specialists in Group Work. (1989). *Ethical guidelines for group counselors.* Alexandria, VA: Author.

*Association for Specialists in Group Work. (1990). *Professional standards for the training of group workers* [Working document]. Alexandria, VA: Author.

Atkinson, D. R., Morten, G., & Sue, D. W. (1989). *Counseling American minorities (3rd ed.).* Dubuque, IA: William C. Brown.

Aubrey, M., & Dougher, M. J. (1990). Ethical issues in outpatient group therapy with sex offenders. *Journal for Specialists in Group Work, 15*(2), 75–82.

Barnette, E. L. (1989). Effects of a growth group on counseling students' self-actualization. *Journal for Specialists in Group Work, 14*(4), 202–210.

Bass, S., & Dole, A. (1977). Ethical leader practices in sensitivity training for prospective professional psychologists. *Journal Supplement Abstract Series, 7*(2), 47–66.

*Books and articles marked with an asterisk are recommended for further study.

Bednar, R. L., Corey, G., Evans, N. J., Gazda, G. M., Pistole, M. C., Stockton, R., & Robison, F. F. (1987). Overcoming obstacles to the future development of research on group work. *Journal for Specialists in Group Work, 12*(3), 98–111.

Bednar, R. L., & Kaul, T. J. (1978). Experiential group research: Current perspectives. In S. L. Garfield & A. E. Bergin (Eds.), *Handbook for psychotherapy and behavior change: An empirical analysis* (2nd ed.) (pp. 769–815). New York: Wiley.

Bednar, R. L., & Kaul, T. J. (1979). Experiential group research: What never happened. *Journal of Applied Behavioral Science, 11,* 311–319.

Bednar, R. L., Langenbahn, D. M., & Trotzer, J. P. (1979). Structure and ambiguity: Conceptual and applied misconceptions. *Journal for Specialists in Group Work, 4*(4), 170–176.

Bednar, R. L., & Lawlis, F. (1971). Empirical research in group psychotherapy. In A. E. Bergin & S. L. Garfield (Eds.), *Handbook for psychotherapy and behavior change* (pp. 812–838). New York: Wiley.

Bednar, R. L., Melnick, J., & Kaul, T. J. (1974). Risk, responsibility, and structure: A conceptual framework for initiating group counseling and psychotherapy. *Journal of Counseling Psychology, 21,* 31–37.

Bennett, B. E., Bryant, B. K., VandenBos, G. R., & Greenwood, A. (1990). *Professional liability and risk management.* Washington, DC: American Psychological Association.

Bloch, S., Browning, S., & McGrath, G. (1983). Humour in group psychotherapy. *British Journal of Medical psychology, 56,* 89–97.

Borgers, S. B., & Tyndall, L. W. (1982). Setting expectations for groups. *Journal for Specialists in Group Work, 7*(2), 109–111.

Burlingame, G. M., & Fuhriman, A. (1990). Time-limited group therapy. *The Counseling Psychologist, 18*(1), 93–118.

Caple, R. B., & Cox, P. L. (1989). Relationships among group structure, member expectations, attraction to group, and satisfaction with the group experience. *Journal for Specialists in Group Work, 14*(1), 16–24.

Carroll, M., & Wiggins, J. (1990). *Elements of group counseling: Back to the basics.* Denver: Love.

Childers, J. H., Jr., & Couch, R. D. (1989). Myths about group counseling: Identifying and challenging misconceptions. *Journal for Specialists in Group Work, 14*(2), 105–111.

Christensen, C. P. (1989). Cross-cultural awareness development: A conceptual model. *Counselor Education and Supervision, 28*(4), 270–289.

Chu, J., & Sue, S. (1984). Asian/Pacific-Americans and group practice. In L. E. Davis (Ed.), *Ethnicity in social group work practice* (pp. 23–35). New York: Haworth Press.

Clark, A. J. (1989). Questions in group counseling. *Journal for Specialists in Group Work, 14*(2), 121–124.

Cohn, B. R. (1988). Keeping the group alive: Dealing with resistance in a long-term group of psychotic patients. *International Journal of Group Psychotherapy, 38*(3), 319–336.

Cole, S. A. (1983). Self-help groups. In H. I. Kaplan & B. J. Sadock (Eds.), *Comprehensive group psychotherapy* (2nd ed.) (pp. 144–150). Baltimore: Williams & Wilkins.

Colson, D. B., & Horowitz, L. (1983). Research in group psychotherapy. In H. I. Kaplan & B. J. Sadock (Eds.), *Comprehensive group psychotherapy* (2nd ed.) (pp. 304–311). Baltimore: Williams & Wilkins.

Conyne, R. K., Harvill, R. L., Morganett, R. S., Morran, D. K., & Hulse-Killacky, D. (1990). Effective group leadership: Continuing the search for greater clarity and understanding. *Journal for Specialists in Group Work, 15*(1), 30–36.

Corey, G. (1981). Description of a practicum course in group leadership. *Journal for Specialists in Group Work, 6*(2), 100–108.

Corey, G. (1982). Practical strategies for planning therapy groups. In P. Keller & L. Ritt (Eds.), *Innovations in clinical practice: A sourcebook* (Vol. 1). Sarasota, FL: Professional Resource Exchange.

Corey, G. (1983). Group counseling. In J. A. Brown & R. H. Pate (Eds.), *Being a counselor: Directions and challenges* (pp. 95–123). Pacific Grove, CA: Brooks/Cole.

Corey, G. (1984). Ethical issues in group therapy. In P. Keller & L. Ritt (Eds.), *Innovations in clinical practice: A sourcebook* (Vol. 3). Sarasota, FL: Professional Resource Exchange.

*Corey, G. (1990). *Theory and practice of group counseling* (3rd ed.) and *Manual*. Pacific Grove, CA: Brooks/Cole.

Corey, G. (1991a). *Case approach to counseling and psychotherapy* (3rd ed.). Pacific Grove, CA: Brooks/Cole.

Corey, G. (1991b). *Theory and practice of counseling and psychotherapy* (4th ed.) and *Manual*. Pacific Grove, CA: Brooks/Cole.

Corey, G., & Corey, M. (1990). *I never knew I had a choice* (4th ed.). Pacific Grove, CA: Brooks/Cole.

Corey, G., Corey, M., & Callanan, P. (1981). In-service training for group leaders in a prison hospital: Problems and prospects. *Journal for Specialists in Group Work, 6*(3), 130–135.

Corey, G., Corey, M., & Callanan, P. (1982). *A casebook of ethical guidelines for group leaders*. Pacific Grove, CA: Brooks/Cole.

*Corey, G., Corey, M., & Callanan, P. (1988). *Issues and ethics in the helping professions* (3rd ed.). Pacific Grove, CA: Brooks/Cole.

Corey, G., Corey, M., & Callanan, P. (1990). Role of group leader's values in group counseling. *Journal for Specialists in Group Work, 15*(2), 68–74.

Corey, G., Corey, M., Callanan, P., & Russell, J. M. (1980). A residential workshop for personal growth. *Journal for Specialists in Group Work, 5*(4), 205–215.

Corey, G., Corey, M., Callanan, P., & Russell, J. M. (1982). Ethical considerations in using group techniques. *Journal for Specialists in Group Work, 7*(3), 140–148.

*Corey, G., Corey, M., Callanan, P., & Russell, J. M. (1992). *Group techniques* (3rd ed.). Pacific Grove, CA: Brooks/Cole.

Corey, M., & Corey, G. (1986). Experiential/didactic training and supervision workshop for group leaders. *Journal of Counseling and Human Service Professions, 1*(1), 18–26.

Corey, M., & Corey, G. (1989). *Becoming a helper*. Pacific Grove, CA: Brooks/Cole.

Couch, R. D., & Childers, J. H. (1987). Leadership strategies for instilling and maintaining hope in group counseling. *Journal for Specialists in Group Work, 12*(4), 138–143.

DeLucia, J. L., Bowman, V. E., & Bowman, R. L. (1989). The use of parallel process in supervision and group counseling to facilitate counselor and client growth. *Journal for Specialists in Group Work, 14*(4), 232–238.

Diedrich, R. C., & Dye, H. A. (Eds.). (1972). *Group procedures: Purposes, processes, and outcomes.* Boston: Houghton Mifflin.

Dies, R. R. (1980). Current practice in the training of group psychotherapists. *International Journal of Group Psychotherapy, 30*(2), 169–185.

*Dies, R. R. (1983a). Bridging the gap between research and practice in group psychotherapy. In R. R. Dies & R. MacKenzie (Eds.), *Advances in group psychotherapy: Integrating research and practice* (American Group Psychotherapy Association Monograph Series) (pp. 1–26). New York: International Universities Press.

*Dies, R. R. (1983b). Clinical implications of research on leadership in short-term group psychotherapy. In R. R. Dies & R. MacKenzie (Eds.), *Advances in group psychotherapy: Integrating research and practice* (American Group Psychotherapy Association Monograph Series) (pp. 27–28). New York: International Universities Press.

*Dies, R. R. (1985). Research foundations for the future of group work. *Journal for Specialists in Group Work, 19*(2), 68–73.

*Dies, R. R., & MacKenzie, R. (Eds.). (1983). *Advances in group psychotherapy: Integrating research and practice.* (American Group Psychotherapy Association Monograph Series). New York: International Universities Press.

Drum, D. J. (1990). Group therapy review. *The Counseling Psychologist, 18*(1), 131–138.

Duncan, J. A., & Gumaer, J. (Eds.). (1980). *Developmental groups for children.* Springfield, IL: Charles C Thomas.

Elbirlik, K. (1983). The mourning process in group therapy. *International Journal of Group Psychotherapy, 33*(2), 215–228.

Ettin, M. F. (1989). "Come on, Jack, tell us about yourself": The growth spurt of group psychotherapy. *International Journal of Group Psychotherapy, 39*(1), 35–57.

Evans, N. J., & Jarvis, P. A. (1980). Group cohesion: A review and reevaluation. *Small Group Behavior, 11,* 359–370.

Fischer, L., & Sorenson, G. P. (1985). *School law for counselors, psychologists, and social workers.* New York: Longman.

Forester-Miller, H. (1989). Dr. Irvin Yalom discusses group psychotherapy. *Journal for Specialists in Group Work, 14*(4), 196–201.

Forester-Miller, H. (Ed.) (1990). Ethical and legal issues in group work [Special issue]. *Journal for Specialists in Group Work, 15*(2). Alexandria, VA: American Association for Counseling and Development.

Forester-Miller, H., & Duncan, J. A. (1990). The ethics of dual relationships in the training of group counselors. *Journal for Specialists in Group Work, 15*(2), 88–93.

Friedman, W. H. (1989). *Practical group therapy: A guide for clinicians.* San Francisco: Jossey-Bass.

*Fuhriman, A., & Burlingame, G. M. (1990). Consistency of matter: A comparative analysis of individual and group process variables. *The Counseling Psychologist, 18*(1), 6–63.

*Gazda, G. M. (1989). *Group counseling: A developmental approach* (4th ed.). Boston: Allyn & Bacon.

Glasser, W. (1985). *Control theory: A new explanation of how we control our lives.* New York: Harper & Row (Perennial Paperback).

Gumaer, J., & Martin, D. (1990). Group ethics: A multimodal model for training knowledge and skill competencies. *Journal for Specialists in Group Work,* *15*(2), 94–103.

Gumaer, J., & Scott, L. (1985). Training group leaders in ethical decision making. *Journal for Specialists in Group Work,* *10*(4), 198–204.

Hall, R. P., Kassees, J. M., Hoffman, C., & Frew, J. E. (1986). Treatment for survivors of incest. *Journal for Specialists in Group Work,* *11*(2), 85–92.

Hill, C. E. (1990). Is individual therapy process really different from group therapy process? The jury is still out. *The Counseling Psychologist,* *18*(1), 126–130.

Ho, M. K. (1984). Social group work with Asian/Pacific Americans. In L. E. Davis (Ed.), *Ethnicity in social group work practice* (pp. 49–61). New York: Haworth Press.

Holiman, M., & Engle, D. (1989). Guidelines for training in advanced Gestalt therapy skills. *Journal for Specialists in Group Work,* *14*(2), 75–83.

Hopkins, B. R., & Anderson, B. W. (1990). *The counselor and the law* (3rd ed.). Alexandria, VA: American Association for Counseling and Development.

Huhn, R. P., Zimpfer, D. G., Waltman, D. E., & Williamson, S. K. (1985). A survey of programs of professional preparation for group counseling. *Journal for Specialists in Group Work,* *10*(3), 124–133.

Hummel, D. L., Talbutt, L. C., & Alexander, M. D. (1985). *Law and ethics in counseling.* New York: Van Nostrand Reinhold.

Jacobs, E. E., Harvill, R. L., & Masson, R. L. (1988). *Group counseling: Strategies and skills.* Pacific Grove, CA: Brooks/Cole.

Jacobs, M. K., & Goodman, G. (1989). Psychology and self-help groups: Predictions on a partnership. *American Psychologist,* *44*(3), 536–545.

Johnson, D. W. (1990). *Reaching out: Interpersonal effectiveness and self-actualization* (4th ed.). Engelwood Cliffs, NJ: Prentice-Hall.

Johnson, D. W., & Johnson, F. P. (1991). *Joining together: Group theory and group skills* (4th ed.). Englewood Cliffs, NJ: Prentice-Hall.

Jourard, S. M. (1968). *Disclosing man to himself.* New York: Van Nostrand Reinhold.

Jourard, S. M. (1971a). *Self-disclosure: An experimental analysis of the transparent self.* New York: Wiley.

Jourard, S. M. (1971b). *The transparent self* (rev. ed.). New York: Van Nostrand Reinhold.

Kaplan, H. I., & Sadock, B. J. (Eds.). (1983). *Comprehensive group psychotherapy* (2nd ed.). Baltimore: Williams & Wilkins.

Kaul, T. J., & Bednar, R. L. (1978). Conceptualizing group research: A preliminary analysis. *Small Group Behavior, 9,* 173–191.

*Kaul, T. J., & Bednar, R. L. (1986). Experiential group research: Results, questions, and suggestions. In S. L. Garfield & A. E. Bergin (Eds.), *Handbook for psychotherapy and behavior change* (3rd ed.) (pp. 671–714). New York: Wiley.

Kees, N. L., & Jacobs, E. (1990). Conducting more effective groups: How to select and process group exercises. *Journals for Specialists in Group Work,* *15*(1), 21–29.

Kottler, J. A. (1983). *Pragmatic group leadership.* Pacific Grove, CA: Brooks/Cole.

*Kottler, J. A. (1991). *The compleat therapist.* San Francisco: Jossey-Bass.

*Kottler, J. A., & Blau, D. S. (1989). *The imperfect therapist: Learning from failure in therapeutic practice.* San Francisco: Jossey-Bass.

Kramer, S. A. (1990). *Positive endings in psychotherapy: Bringing meaningful closure to therapeutic relationships.* San Francisco: Jossey-Bass.

Kriner, L., & Waldron, B. (1988). Group counseling: A treatment modality for batterers. *Journal for Specialists in Group Work, 13*(3), 110–116.

Lakin, M. (1985). *The helping group: Therapeutic principles and issues.* Reading, MA: Addison-Wesley.

Lakin, M., Oppenheimer, B., & Bremer, J. (1982). A note on old and young in helping groups. *Psychotherapy: Theory, Research, and Practice, 19*(4), 444–452.

Lanning, W., & Carey, J. (1987). Systematic termination in counseling. *Counselor Education and Supervision, 27*(2), 168–173.

Lazarus, A. A. (1989). *The practice of multimodal therapy.* Baltimore: John Hopkins University Press.

LeCluyse, E. E. (1983). Pretherapy preparation for group members. *Journal for Specialists in Group Work, 9*(4), 170–174.

Lee, P. C., Juan, G., & Hom, A. B. (1984). Group work practice with Asian clients: A sociocultural approach. In L. E. Davis (Ed.), *Ethnicity in social group work practice* (pp. 37–47). New York: Haworth Press.

Levine, B. (1979). *Group psychotherapy: Practice and development.* Englewood Cliffs, NJ: Prentice-Hall.

Libo, L. (1977). *Is there a life after group?* New York: Anchor Books.

Lieberman, M. A., Borman, L. D., & Associates. (1979). *Self-help groups for coping with crisis.* San Francisco: Jossey-Bass.

*Lieberman, M., Yalom, I., & Miles, M. (1973). *Encounter groups: First facts.* New York: Basic Books.

*Lloyd, A. P. (1990). Dual relationships in group activities: A counselor education/accreditation dilemma. *Journal for Specialists in Group Work, 15*(2), 83–87.

Long, K., Pendleton, L., & Winter, B. (1988). Effects of therapist termination on group process. *International Journal of Group Psychotherapy, 38*(2), 211–222.

Luft, J. (1984). *Group processes: An introduction to group dynamics* (3rd ed.). Palo Alto, CA: Mayfield.

McWhirter, J. J., & Liebman, P. C. (1988). A description of anger-control therapy groups to help Vietnam veterans with posttraumatic stress disorder. *Journal for Specialists in Group Work, 13*(1), 9–16.

Meadow, D. (1981). The preparatory interview: A client-focused approach with children of Holocaust survivors. *Social Work with Groups, 4,* 135–144.

*Meadow, D. (1988). Preparation of individuals for participation in a treatment group: Development and empirical testing of a model. *International Journal of Group Psychotherapy, 38*(3), 367–385.

Miller, M. J. (1986). On the perfectionistic thoughts of beginning group leaders. *Journal for Specialists in Group Work, 11*(1), 53–56.

Mokuau, N. (1985). Counseling Pacific Islander–Americans. In P. Pedersen (Ed.), *Handbook of cross cultural counseling and therapy* (pp. 147–155). Westport, CT: Greenwood Press.

Mokuau, N. (1987). Social workers' perceptions of counseling effectiveness for Asian-American clients. *Journal of the National Association of Social Workers, 32*(4), 331–335.

*Morganett, R. S. (1990). *Skills for living: Group counseling activities for young adolescents.* Champaign, IL: Research Press.

Morran, D. K. (1982). Leader and member self-disclosing behavior in counseling groups. *Journal for Specialists in Group Work, 7*(4), 218–223.

*Morran, D. K., Robison, F. F., & Stockton, R. (1985). Feedback exchange in counseling groups: An analysis of message content and receiver acceptance as a function of leader versus member delivery, session, and valance. *Journal of Counseling Psychology, 32,* 57–67.

Morran, D. K., & Stockton, R. (1980). Effect of self-concept on group member reception of positive and negative feedback. *Journal of Counseling Psychology, 27,* 260–267.

*Morran, D. K., & Stockton, R. (1985). Perspectives on group research programs. *Journal for Specialists in Group Work, 10*(4), 186–191.

Muller, E. J., & Scott, T. B. (1984). A comparison of film and written presentations used for pregroup training experiences. *Journal for Specialists in Group Work, 9*(3), 122–126.

Napier, R. W., & Gershenfeld, M. K. (1989). *Groups: Theory and experience* (4th ed.). Boston: Houghton Mifflin.

National Association of Social Workers (1979). *Code of ethics.* Washington, DC: Author.

National Association of Social Workers (1981). *Standards for the private practice of clinical social work.* Washington, DC: Author.

National Board for Certified Counselors (1987). *Code of ethics.* Alexandria, VA: Author.

National Federation of Societies for Clinical Social Work (1985). *Code of ethics.* Silver Spring, MD: Author.

Nishio, K., & Bilmes, M. (1987). Psychotherapy with Southeast Asian–American clients. *Professional Psychology: Research and Practice, 18*(4), 342–346.

Ohlsen, M. M., Horne, A. M., & Lawe, C. F. (1988). *Group counseling* (3rd ed.). New York: Holt, Rinehart & Winston.

Ormont, L. R. (1988). The leader's role in resolving resistances to intimacy in the group setting. *International Journal of Group Psychotherapy, 38*(1), 29–46.

Paradise, L. V., & Kirby, P. C. (1990). Some perspectives on the legal liability of group counseling in private practice. *Journal for Specialists in Group Work, 15*(2), 114–118.

Patterson, C. H. (1989). Values in counseling and psychotherapy. *Counseling and Values, 33*(3), 164–176.

*Pedersen, P. (1988). *A handbook for developing multicultural awareness.* Alexandria, VA: American Association for Counseling and Development.

Pedersen, P. (1989). Developing multicultural ethical guidelines for psychology. *International Journal of Psychology, 24,* 643–652.

Pedersen, P. (1990). The multicultural perspective as a fourth force in counseling. *Journal of Mental Health Counselors, 12*(1), 93–94.

*Pedersen, P., Draguns, J., Lonner, W., & Trimble, J. (Eds.). (1989). *Counseling across cultures* (3rd ed.). Honolulu: University Press of Hawaii.

*Pierce, K. A., & Baldwin, C. (1990). Participation versus privacy in the training of group counselors. *Journal for Specialists in Group Work, 15*(3), 149–158.

Pinney, E. L., (1983). Ethical and legal issues in group psychotherapy. In H. I Kaplan & B. J. Sadock (Eds.), *Comprehensive group psychotherapy* (2nd ed.) (pp. 301–304). Baltimore: Williams & Wilkins.

*Piper, W. E., & Perrault, E. L. (1989). Pretherapy preparation for group members. *International Journal of Group Psychotherapy, 39*(1), 17–34.

Pope, K. S., Tabachnick, B. G., & Keith-Spiegel, P. (1987). Ethics of practice: The beliefs and behaviors of psychologists as therapists. *American Psychologist, 42*(11), 993–1006.

Priddy, J. M. (1987). Outcome research on self-help groups: A humanistic perspective. *Journal for Specialists in Group Work, 12*(1), 2–9.

Remley, T. P., Jr. (1991). *Preparing for court appearances* [Monograph]. Alexandria, VA: American Association for Counseling and Development.

Richards, R. L., Burlingame, G. M., & Fuhriman, A. (1990). Theme-oriented group therapy. *The Counseling Psychologist, 18*(1), 80–92.

Riordan, R. J., & Beggs, M. S. (1988). Some critical differences between self-help and therapy groups. *Journal for Specialists in Group Work, 13*(1), 24–29.

Robison, F. F., Morran, D. K., & Hulse-Killacky, D. (1989). Single-subject research designs for group counselors studying their own groups. *Journal for Specialists in Group Work, 14*(2), 93–97.

Robison, F. F., & Ward, D. (1990). Research activities and attitudes among ASGW members. *Journal for Specialists in Group Work, 19*(4), 215–224.

Rogers, C. (1987). The underlying theory: Drawn from experiences with individuals and groups. *Counseling and Values, 32*, 38–45.

Rogers, C. R. (1970). *Carl Rogers on encounter groups.* New York: Harper & Row.

Rose, S. D. (1989). *Working with adults in groups.* San Francisco, CA: Jossey-Bass.

Rosenbaum, M. (1982). Ethical problems of group psychotherapy. In M. Rosenbaum (Ed.), *Ethics and values in psychotherapy: A guidebook* (pp. 237–257). New York: Free Press.

Rosenbaum, M. (1983). Co-therapy. In H. I. Kaplan & B. J. Sadock (Eds.), *Comprehensive group psychotherapy* (2nd ed.) (pp. 167–173). Baltimore: Williams & Wilkins.

*Rothke, S. (1986). The role of interpersonal feedback in group psychotherapy. *International Journal of Group Psychotherapy, 36*(2), 225–240.

Rutan, J. S., Alonso, A., & Groves, J. E. (1988). Understanding defenses in group psychotherapy. *International Journal of Group Psychotherapy, 38*(4), 459–472.

Sadock, B. J. (1983). Preparation, selection of patients, and organization of the group. In H. I. Kaplan & B. J. Sadock (Eds.), *Comprehensive group psychotherapy* (2nd ed.) (pp. 23–32). Baltimore: Williams & Wilkins.

Saidla, D. D. (1990). Cognitive development and group stages. *Journal for Specialists in Group Work, 15*(1), 15–20.

Schutz, B. M. (1982). *Legal liability in psychotherapy.* San Francisco: Jossey-Bass.

*Shaffer, J., & Galinsky, M.D. (1989). *Models of group therapy* (2nd ed.). Englewood Cliffs, NJ: Prentice-Hall.

Shuttleworth-Jordan, A. B., Saayman, G. S., & Faber, P. A. (1988). A systematized method for dream analysis in a group setting. *International Journal of Group Psychotherapy, 38*(4), 473–490.

*Sklare, G., Keener, R., & Mas, C. (1990). Preparing members for "here-and-now" group counseling. *Journal for Specialists in Group Work, 15*(3), 141–148.

Stockton, R. (1978). Reviews and bibliographies of experiential small group research: Survey and perspective. *Small Group Behavior, 9*, 435–448.

Stockton, R. (1980). The education of group leaders: A review of the literature with suggestions for the future. *Journal for Specialists in Group Work, 5*(2), 55–62.

Stockton, R., & Barr, J. (1977, February). *The experiential small group: An examination of process and outcome variables.* Paper presented at the Henry Lester Smith Conference and Educational Research, Bloomington, IN.

Stockton, R., Barr, J., & Klein, R. (1981). Identifying the group dropout: A review of the literature. *Journal for Specialists in Group Work, 6*, 75–82.

Stockton, R., & Hulse, D. (1981). Developing cohesion in small groups: Theory and research. *Journal for Specialists in Group Work, 6*(4), 188–194.

Stockton, R., & Hulse, D. (1983). The use of research teams to enhance competence in counseling research. *Counselor Education and Supervision, 22*(4), 303–310.

Stockton, R., & Morran, D. K. (1980). The use of verbal feedback in counseling groups: Toward an effective system. *Journal for Specialists in Group Work, 5*, 10–14.

Stockton, R., & Morran, D. K. (1981). Feedback exchange in personal growth groups: Receiver acceptance as a function of valence, session, and order of delivery. *Journal of Counseling Psychology, 28*, 490–497.

Stockton, R., & Morran, D. K. (1982). Review and perspective of critical dimensions in therapeutic small group research. In G. M. Gazda (Ed.), *Basic approaches to group psychotherapy and group counseling* (3rd ed.) (pp. 37–85). Springfield, IL: Charles C Thomas.

Stokes, J. P. (1983). Toward an understanding of cohesion in personal change groups. *International Journal of Group Psychotherapy, 33*(4), 449–468.

Sue, D. W. (1990). Culture-specific strategies in counseling: A conceptual framework. *Professional Psychology: Research and Practice, 21*(6), 424–433.

*Sue, D. W., & Sue, D. (1990). *Counseling the culturally different: Theory and practice* (2nd ed.). New York: Wiley.

Sue, S. (1988). Psychotherapeutic services for ethnic minorities: Two decades of research findings. *American Psychologist, 43*(4), 301–308.

Unger, R. (1989). Selection and composition criteria in group psychotherapy. *Journal for Specialists in Group Work, 14*(3), 151–157.

Van Hoose, W., & Kottler, J. (1985). *Ethical and legal issues in counseling and psychotherapy* (2nd ed.). San Francisco: Jossey-Bass.

Vinogradov, S., & Yalom, I. (1989). *Concise guide to group psychotherapy.* Washington, DC: American Psychiatric Association.

Weigel, R. G., & Corazzini, J. G. (1978). Small group research: Suggestions for solving common methodological and design problems. *Small Group Behavior, 9*, 193–220.

Weinberg, R. B. (1990). Serving large numbers of adolescent victim-survivors: Group interventions following trauma at school. *Professional Psychology: Research and Practice, 21*(4), 271–278.

Wenz, K., & McWhirter, J. J. (1990). Enhancing the group experience: Creative writing exercises. *Journal for Specialists in Group Work, 15*(1), 37–42.

*Williams, G. T. (1990). Ethical dilemmas in teaching a group leadership course. *Journal for Specialists in Group Work, 15*(2), 104–113.

Woodward, B., & McGrath, M. (1988). Charisma in group therapy with recovering substance abusers. *International Journal of Group Psychotherapy, 38*(2), 223–236.

*Woody, R. H. (1988). *Protecting your mental health practice: How to minimize legal and financial risk.* San Francisco: Jossey-Bass.

*Woody, R. H. (1989). *Business success in mental health practice.* San Francisco: Jossey-Bass.

Woody, R. H., & Associates (1984). *The law and the practice of human services.* San Francisco: Jossey-Bass.

Woolsey, L. K. (1986). Research and practice in counseling: A conflict of values. *Counselor Education and Supervision, 26*(2), 84–94.

*Yalom, I. D. (1980). *Existential psychotherapy.* New York: Basic Books.

*Yalom, I. D. (1983). *Inpatient group psychotherapy.* New York: Basic Books.

*Yalom, I. D. (1985). *The theory and practice of group psychotherapy* (3rd ed.). New York: Basic Books.

Yalom, I. D., Houts, P. S., Newell, G., & Rand, K. E. (1967). Preparation of patients for group therapy. *Archives of General Psychiatry, 17,* 416–427.

Zaslav, M. R. (1988). A model of group therapist development. *International Journal of Group Psychotherapy, 38*(4), 511–520.

Zimpfer, D. G. (1976). Professional issues. In D. G. Zimpfer (Ed.), *Group work in the helping professions: A bibliography.* Washington, DC: Association for Specialists in Group Work.

Zimpfer, D. G. (1981). Follow-up studies of growth group outcomes: A review. *Journal for Specialists in Group Work, 6*(4), 195–210.

*Zimpfer, D. G. (1984a). *Group work in the helping professions: A bibliography.* Muncie, IN: Accelerated Development.

*Zimpfer, D. G. (1984b). Pattern and trends in group work. *Journal for Specialists in Group Work, 9*(4), 204–208.

Zimpfer, D. G. (1985a). Demystifying and clarifying small-group work. *Journal for Specialists in Group Work, 10*(3), 175–181.

Zimpfer, D. G. (1985b). Texts used most widely in preparation for group counseling. *Journal for Specialists in Group Work, 10*(1), 51–56.

Zimpfer, D. G. (1989). Groups for persons who have cancer. *Journal for Specialists in Group Work, 14*(2), 98–104.

Zimpfer, D. G. (1990a). Groups for divorce/separation: A review. *Journal for Specialists in Group Work, 15*(1), 51–60.

Zimpfer, D. G. (1990b). Group work for bulimia: A review of outcomes. *Journal for Specialists in Group Work, 15*(4), 239–251.

Zimpfer, D. G., & Carr, J. J. (1989). Groups for midlife career change: A review. *Journal for Specialists in Group Work, 14*(4), 243–250.

Zimpfer, D. G., Waldman, D. E., Williamson, S. K., & Huhn, R. P. (1985). Professional training standards in group counseling—Idealistic or realistic? *Journal for Specialists in Group Work, 10*(3), 134–143.

GROUP PRACTICE:
Some Specific Groups

In Part Two our focus was on describing the group process at the various stages of a group's history. In Part Three we describe how to apply these concepts and practices to groups geared to the particular needs of clients at various ages. We also discuss the special responsibilities of group leaders who work with children, adolescents, adults, and the elderly. As usual, we have drawn on our own experiences and those of our colleagues. We describe how we set up these specialized groups and share with you approaches that we hope will be useful to you as you design your own groups.

Students in counseling and related programs must often complete an internship involving work with a variety of people: children or adolescents, the elderly, clients with substance-abuse problems, hospital patients, and outpatients in a community agency. On your job as a mental-health worker, you may be asked to set up and lead a variety of groups. If you work with children, you may have a group of children of divorce, a group of acting-out children, or a group of terminally ill children. For adolescents, you may be asked to organize a group program for alcohol and drug rehabilitation, a growth group to meet normal developmental needs, or a group for young people who are the victims of some tragedy. For adults, there are groups for single parents, for middle-aged people doing career planning, and for the physically handicapped. With the elderly population, you may find yourself leading a preretirement group or a theme-oriented personal-growth group. The types of groups available for each of the four age levels are as many as there are special problems and needs. Of course, not all of them can be described in this book, but a sample of programs can give you ideas to apply in creating a group that especially appeals to you. Our intention, then, is to stimulate you to think creatively about how to design groups to effectively meet the needs of diverse clients. Suggestions of where to go for further leads are provided at the end of each chapter, as are suggested readings.

You will notice that Chapters 9 and 12, which describe groups for children and for the elderly, are partly written from the personal perspective and experience of one of the authors (Marianne Schneider Corey). The tone and the writing style are deliberately more personal than some of the other sections in Part Three, in which we describe a variety of groups. Although these two chapters emphasize a personal approach of working with children in groups and organizing groups for the elderly, we think that the ideas presented can be adapted to your own groups with these populations. We encourage you to adapt these practices in ways that are suitable to your personal style and are appropriate to your settings and to the populations with which you work.

CHAPTER 9

Groups for Children

Introduction

This chapter begins with a discussion of Marianne Corey's group-counseling program for children in an elementary school. We will also describe a children's group that was led by a colleague who works in a community agency and two groups for children from divorced families that were led by school counselors. The general group format set forth in this chapter can be applied to various other settings, such as private practice and public and private clinics. You can also use many of the ideas in this chapter in groups dealing with a variety of special needs, including those of abused children, children of alcoholic families, and children with learning and behavioral disorders.

This chapter alone will not provide you with enough information to conduct your own groups with children. We hope, however, that it will stimulate you to do further reading, attend specialized workshops, and arrange for supervised field experience.

A School Counseling Program*

The school program that I set up was federally funded. Although my work was rewarding and proved to be an excellent learning experience, I suffered some frustration at first because the funding was always in jeopardy and could have been cut on short notice. I expended much energy worrying about the future of the project, a drain that affected my work with the children, although I wasn't aware of it at the time. Counselors who work with children, both in schools and in community agencies, are often faced with this uncertainty.

Another initial source of frustration was the fact that I had been given few instructions. I knew only that I would be working with schoolchildren, ranging in age from 6 to 11, who had been designated as a "problem" by their teacher or the principal. It was up to me to design a program that would improve the children's behavior in class. Ten to fifteen children would make up my caseload, and I was to see each child at least once a week for about an hour, for a total of 24 visits.

To be referred to me, the children would have to be acting out their emotional disturbance in some way, such as through aggressive behavior. Passive and withdrawn children, who were as much in need of counseling as those who were expressing their anger, were not likely to be included in this program. Those children who showed one or more of the following behaviors or attributes were considered candidates for referral:

- excessive fighting
- inability to get along with peers

*This section is written from the perspective of Marianne Corey.

- frequent hurting of other children
- violation of school rules
- poor attitude toward school
- stealing from the school or from peers
- violent or angry outbursts
- neglect of appearance
- hunger symptoms or frequent failure to bring lunch to school
- chronic tiredness
- lack of supervision at home
- excessive truancy

My job was dealing with the problems underlying the child's behavior, thereby alleviating the child's school difficulties and preventing more serious ones from developing.

The Initial Phase

Contact with School Personnel. Being fully aware that counselors are often mistrusted in schools, I set out to earn the trust of the teachers and administrators. First, I met with them to determine what they hoped the project would accomplish. I told them that I wanted to work closely with them, providing feedback about the children, making specific recommendations, and getting their suggestions. I let them know that I intended to work with the children individually and in groups and to involve the parents in the treatment process, too. I explained that I would have the children play with clay and puppets, tell stories, and role-play, all activities that allow self-expression.

Accordingly, I developed a program in which I was in continuous contact with the children's teachers, principal, and parents. The teachers and the principal were very cooperative about meeting with me. I also spoke frequently with the school psychologist, the school nurse, and the school secretaries about particular children, gathering as much information as I could. This information turned out to be most helpful.

The Setting. The setting for my work with the children was not ideal. The school was short on space (a new school was being built), and I was continually looking for a place to meet with the children. When the weather allowed, we often met on the school lawn, because I needed a place where they could explore, touch, talk loudly, shout if they were angry, or give vent to any other emotions they were experiencing. If I took them off campus or did anything special with them, I first obtained written permission from the parents and the school authorities, preferring to be extremely cautious in my dealings with this public institution. Although I never had an ideal place to work, this did not keep me from working effectively with the children, as we often improvised together.

Because the same private office was not available to me on a regular basis, I had to pick up the children from their classrooms, something that concerned me. How would the children react to being singled out? Would my special attention to them amid their peers affect them negatively? Fortunately, I found the contrary to be true. The children responded very positively to my coming to pick them up and were always ready to come with me, even during recess time. Frequently, some of their classmates would ask whether they could come see me, too.

Initial Contact with the Parents. After meeting with the school staff, who identified which children I would be working with, I contacted the parents of each child. The parents knew before I visited them about my intended involvement with their child, because I had asked the principal and the child's teacher to contact them. During my initial contact I explained that their child had been referred to me by the teacher, who had become concerned about the student's behavior in class. This interview gave the parents a chance to get to know me and to ask questions, and it gave me the chance to get the parents' permission to work with their child. At this time I gathered information regarding any difficulties the parents were having with the child and collected the data I needed in order to complete numerous forms. If parents became anxious over my probing or over the fact that *their* child had been singled out for counseling, I explained to them that because teachers have to deal with so many children, they can't always provide all the attention a child needs. It would be my job, I said, to provide this extra attention.

Although the school's policy stipulated obtaining parental permission for children to become participants in a group, this is not a required policy in all school districts. State laws regarding parental permission to counsel minors also vary. As a general rule, I think it is best to get the parents' permission and to work with them as allies, rather than risking their disapproval by counseling their children without their knowledge and consent. There are exceptions, however. When counselors are not legally required to secure the consent of parents and when notifying them could be detrimental to the minor client, the welfare of these children should always take priority.

I had previously counseled only people who had requested my services. It was a new experience to be confronted by the suspicions of parents who had been informed that their child needed my services. But for the most part parents were willing to cooperate and gave their consent. In response to my question about any difficulties they might be experiencing with their child at home, which I asked in order to get clues to the child's behavior in school, the parents were guarded at first. They became much more open with time and frequent contacts. My aim was not to communicate in any way that they were "bad" parents, as this would certainly have aroused their defensiveness. Their children were experiencing difficulties, and I wanted to solicit their help in assisting the students to work through these problems. By going into the child's home, I was able to get much more information relating to the problems the child was exhibiting that would otherwise have been difficult, if not impossible, to obtain.

I told the parents that their children would be discussing with me problems related to school, home, and peers. I explained that I wished to keep as confidential as possible what the child and I would be exploring in our sessions. Therefore, I explained, I would let them know in a general way how I was proceeding with the child but would not reveal any of the specifics, unless I was required to do so by law. The parents were agreeable. I also told them that I hoped to see them alone sometimes and together with their children at other times. It was often difficult to schedule further contacts with parents, though, because every one of them was employed. I was unable to see some parents again after my initial contact. However, I was able to make at least some additional contact with most parents, and I spoke with others on the telephone.

Initial Contact with the Children. Before participating in this project, I had worked only with adults and adolescents who were able to express themselves articulately. During my initial individual contact with children, I relied very heavily on my verbal skills, expecting that they would be verbal with me in turn. But talking with the children proved difficult. They were reluctant to initiate a conversation, being accustomed only to answering questions. The children needed some structure and some guidelines for expressing themselves and an acknowledgment that it was difficult for them. Catalysts such as naming five things they liked and didn't like about school were helpful.

I introduced myself to them, saying that I was a special type of teacher called a counselor. I explained that their teacher was concerned about their behavior in class and that they would be talking with me several times a week—individually, as a group, and in their homes. I told them that we would be discussing problems they had in school, at home, or with fellow pupils and that we would talk about feelings.

I let the children know that I would be talking about them with their parents and teachers and that I would tell them when I made such contacts. Although I said I did consider much of what we would talk about in the group to be confidential, I told them I would discuss with their parents and teachers anything that would be important in helping them work through any of their difficulties. I felt strongly that it was just as important for a 6-year-old to know that what he or she told me would be treated with confidentiality as it would be for a 60-year-old. Children's rights are too often violated, and their need for privacy is too often ignored. At this time I also let them know that they were not to talk to others about what fellow group members revealed. This was one of the rules we discussed again in the group sessions. I told them that they could talk about matters that concerned them, including their fears and their hurts. Additionally, I let them know that I could not keep everything confidential, especially if it concerned their safety. In language that they could understand, I explained the purpose of confidentiality and its limitations. They were also informed that they would not be allowed to hurt other children, either physically or verbally, or to destroy any property. Other rules were established, and I made the children aware of their responsibility. In order to be part of the group, they had to agree to follow these rules.

There turned out to be little problem with maintaining confidentiality. When others in the children's classes asked them what they did in their sessions, I heard them say that they played games and talked about feelings.

Evolution of the Group

Working with the Children in a Group. My goal was not to do intensive psychotherapy, for this would have been unrealistic given my limited time. I did hope to pinpoint some of the children's maladaptive behaviors, teach them more effective ways of interacting with others, and provide a climate in which they would feel free to express a range of feelings. It seemed important to teach them how to express emotions without hurting themselves or others. I wanted to convey to the youngsters that feelings such as anger did not get them into trouble; it is certain ways of acting on these feelings that can lead to problems. In an effort to teach them ways of safely expressing the full gambit of their feelings, I involved them in a variety of activities, including role playing, play therapy, acting out social situations, painting, finishing stories that I began, putting on puppet shows, playing music, and dancing.

The groups that were easiest to work with and most productive were composed of three to five children of the same age and same sex. In larger groups I found myself (1) unable to relate intensely to individuals, (2) slipping into the role of disciplinarian to counteract the increased distractions, (3) feeling frustrated at the number of children competing for my attention, and (4) not having enough time left over to pay attention to underlying dynamics. In addition, children between the ages of 6 and 11 tend to become impatient if they have to wait very long for their turn to speak.

I took care to combine withdrawn children with more outgoing ones, but I also felt that it was important for the children to be with others who were experiencing similar conflicts. For example, I put in the same group two boys who felt much anger, hurt, grief, and frustration over their parents' divorces and subsequent remarriages. They slowly learned how to express their feelings about not having much contact with the parent they didn't live with. At first, the boys could only express their feelings symbolically, through play; later, they learned to put words to their emotions and to talk about their feelings.

As I had planned, I provided some time for each child during which he or she could have my attention alone. I noticed that in the group all the children became less jealous of one another about me and trusted me more once I had begun to provide this individual time. Alone, the children were more cooperative, less competitive, and more affectionate than in the group. They felt less need to show off. Having an adult spend time with them individually gave them a sense of importance. With the teacher's consent I also visited the children who were in my group frequently in their classrooms and on the playground, sometimes just observing and sometimes making a brief contact through touch or words.

Our scheduled group and individual sessions took place twice a week and lasted from half an hour to an hour. It would have been a mistake for me to insist that sessions always last a certain length of time, because the children's patience varied from session to session. When they wanted to leave a group session, I would say in a friendly manner that they were free to leave, but I wished they would stay until the session was over. They usually elected to stay. Most of the time the children enjoyed the sessions. I learned by trial and error that it was a good practice to let them know in advance that a session was coming to an end and then to be firm about having them leave and not give in to their demands that the group continue.

My groups were open, in that new members could join. The children already in the group handled this situation very well. They knew the newcomer from school and didn't meet the child with any negative reactions or resistance, contrary to what I have experienced with adults.

At first, I was eager to get to work on a child's specific problem as it was perceived by teachers, parents, and others. I found, however, that I needed to go beyond the specific problem area, because the children did not perceive themselves as having a problem. For me to talk to a girl about what was going on when she had violent outbursts and suddenly struck out was futile. Instead, I learned to let the children lead the way and listened to what they had to say, directly or through various symbolic means. Playing with puppets turned out to be an excellent means of revealing a variety of emotions and dramatizing situations that produce conflict. I made puppets available to the first- and second-grade children but found that even the fourth- and fifth-grade students were able to use them to vent their pent-up emotions.

The groups offered the children the opportunity to act out situations that aroused conflicting feelings. Sometimes I would suggest a problem situation, and at other times the children would select a problem to act out. The children would take the role of teacher, friend, principal, parent, brother, sister, or whoever else was involved. In this way they were able to release their emotions without hurting others.

At times I had to remind myself to be patient and to allow the children to take their time in expressing themselves. Several sessions might pass before a child would speak freely. I sat close to the children during the sessions, often maintaining physical contact, which seemed to have a calming effect by itself. I listened to them attentively, often reflecting for them what they were saying but, more importantly, communicating to them, usually nonverbally, that I was with them, what they were saying was important, and that I cared about what they had to say. I insisted that other members in the group listen and reassured all of them that each would have a time to speak. This is a very difficult concept to get across, especially to a 6- to 7-year-old, who is still very self-centered and learning to share.

Sometimes, after a session that I thought had been unproductive, I was surprised to hear a teacher comment on a child's changed behavior. After one such session a boy who had previously been very destructive and disobedient became cooperative and able to relate to this peers. Pounding a lump of clay, which I had interpreted as nonproductive, turned out to have been very important for him. It had relieved much of his anger and so reduced his need to strike out at others.

In retrospect, I can see that I trusted my intuition to a great extent, yet intuition alone is not enough to ensure effective work with children. It is important to have a good understanding of different theories of personality, including psychosexual and psychosocial development, and to be familiar with various counseling schools. In order to understand the underlying causes of the child's problem behavior, as I have said, I included the parents in the treatment process as much as possible.

At times I questioned whether my work with the children was doing any good. Changes in their behavior were slow in coming and sometimes temporary. Some children gave the appearance of improving one week, yet the next week their behavior would again be very negative. My firm belief that a child can change if afforded the opportunity to change was challenged again and again.

However, most children made definite changes, as observed by the teacher, the principal, the parents, and me. Truants began to come to school more regularly. A boy who was in the habit of stealing and giving his loot to other children so they would like him learned that his behavior was one of the reasons that others disliked him in the first place, and he began to get their attention through more positive actions. A girl who had been conditioned not to trust learned to make friends and to reach out first, doing what at one time she had most feared.

These changes, though encouraging, needed to be reinforced at home. Although most parents welcomed many of their child's new behaviors, some found the new behavior threatening. For instance, one girl caused her mother some anxiety by beginning to ask probing questions about her absent father. I encouraged this mother—and other parents facing similar problems—to try to listen to the child nondefensively.

It was disconcerting to know that some of the children frequently faced difficult circumstances at home, and yet I realized that I did not have control over that domain. Rather than allowing myself to get too discouraged over the fact that I could not change their situation at home, I had to remind myself that I could provide them with a positive experience at school that would have a constructive impact on them. As counselors we need to remind ourselves to focus on what we can do and not become overwhelmed by all that we cannot do.

Termination of the Group. When I began to work with the children, I told them that the sessions would go on for only a limited time during the school year. Several sessions before termination, I reminded them that the group and individual sessions would be ending soon, and we discussed the imminent termination of our meetings. I had seen some of the children over a period of eight months, and we had formed strong attachments. It was as difficult for me to leave them as it was for them to see me leave, and we shared this sadness openly.

Although I had been affectionate with the children during our time together, I hadn't deceived them by becoming a substitute mother or by establishing myself as a permanent fixture who would totally satisfy all their needs. I was aware of establishing appropriate boundaries in carrying out the primary purpose of the group experience. By being realistic about the limits of my job from the beginning, I was able to prevent termination from being a catastrophic experience for the children.

Teacher Evaluation of the Counseling Program. Like the parents, the teachers provided me with ongoing information regarding the children's progress. I was able to use this information in deciding how long to see a particular child or what problem area to focus on. In addition, the teachers prepared written evaluations for my program director, and they shared these evaluations with me. The following are some of their comments:

- "These children have emotional and educational problems, and the individual care given each of them has helped them understand better their limitations and assets."
- "Both children were very explosive and lashed out at other children without provocation. The counselor's attitude and positive outlook helped to calm them, and they now are getting along well in the classroom and with their peers."
- "A student with a high absentee record, who seldom communicated with others, began to change after her involvement in the counseling program. She began to initiate conversation, and she no longer preferred sitting alone; rather, she began to want to be with others. She even began to smile."
- "They are fighting less and are better able to talk things out. The special attention these boys received helped make their second year of school a more successful experience than it would otherwise have been."
- "I believe they have developed a stronger sense of identity—a foundation for self-love—and have developed some positive ways of resolving problems."

- "The counseling program has helped me understand the children and has created a valuable link between the school and the home."

Why the Group Format Was Effective. My clients, aged 6 to 11, were at a stage of growth in which they were leaving parents and home part of the day, expanding their relationships to include other adults, exploring and testing out-of-home environments, and developing peer relationships. Since most of my referrals were children who had deficiencies in relating to others, the group was an excellent means for them to learn and practice relational skills.

In addition, using the group format allowed me to spend more time with each child than would have been possible had I used only individual sessions. However, since individual sessions are valuable for their own reasons, I preferred having both types of contact with each child. The groups also allowed me to experience the child as the teacher did, thus giving me another perspective to assess interactions with peers. I could witness interactions firsthand, and I could give immediate feedback. This process maximized the chances that learning would take place. By its very nature, the group encouraged the children to discuss problems they had in common. After directly expressing emotions that had been bottled up, the children had less need to express these feelings indirectly by withdrawing, fighting, or getting sick.

Special Problems Requiring Out-of-Group Attention

Children have a multitude of developmental problems, and there are many avenues of help for these problems. In working effectively with children, counselors must be willing to involve as many resources and people as possible. There is much room for creativity in developing a variety of programs to meet the diverse needs of children. It is important to let the parents know about these programs and resources so that they, too, are involved in the helping process.

Academic Problems. The children who were referred to me, almost without exception, were identified as having learning problems. Often these learning disabilities were a reflection of their emotional conflicts. Because I was unable to provide the necessary tutorial assistance, I contacted a nearby university and recruited five graduate students to tutor the children for credit in their child-psychology course. In addition to providing tutorial services, they gave the children additional positive individual attention. This tutoring proved very successful for both the children and the university students, and the program was continued after I left.

Nutrition, Hygiene, and Health Care. Several of my children repeatedly came to school hungry, tired, sloppily dressed, and emanating strong body odors. These children had poor self-images and were victims of teasing by their peers. To deal with these problems, I taught personal hygiene, secured some nicer clothes, and made arrangements for certain children to receive free lunches at school. (The school had a free-lunch program, but many parents had neglected to enroll their children in it.) Besides teaching the children personal grooming, I was able to convince some parents of the importance of hygiene in improving the child's self-image. Often a change in a child's outward appearance had a significant positive effect on his or her behavior at school. When I detected health problems, I referred the child to the school nurse. When I suspected neglect or abuse, I took the appropriate action. Counselors who work with minors need to be aware of the reporting laws for suspected abuse in their state as well as their work setting. They must know the specific steps to be taken in making the required reports. It is always helpful to communicate with Child Protective Services to obtain information on assessing and reporting suspected child abuse.

Lack of Supervision, Attention, and Affection in the Home. Because both parents of every child I worked with were employed full time, they had little time for involvement with their children. (This was true not only of the children in my caseload. It also applied to the vast majority of the children at that school, which suggests that, in itself, the full-time employment of the parents was not responsible for the children's psychological problems.) Some of these children, as young as 6 years old, spent several hours a day at home alone. In working with the parents of my clients, I became aware that positive contact with the children was almost nonexistent. When the parents did come home, they were tired and burdened with household chores. Many of the parents deceived themselves by saying that the quality, not the quantity, of the time spent with their children was important. In most cases I found that the quality was as poor as the quantity was small. Occasionally I discovered that if I discussed this matter with the parents in a nonaccusatory way, they would accept the fact that they were contributing to their child's school difficulties and realize that their responsibility for their child's healthy development called for them to change. One parent who had many children began to spend a few minutes a day alone with each child. Another parent started regular family sessions during which each family member could discuss his or her concerns about home and school.

Problems Associated with Single-Parent Homes. During the last two decades the number of single-parent households has more than doubled, with the majority of them being maintained by women (Wright, Coley, & Corey, 1989). Many of these single-parent families have problems with money, stress, and even the disapproval of society. Of course, a critical problem is the impact on childhood socialization of nontraditional sex roles or of the absence of either the male or female role. Many single parents of both genders complain about the psychological toll that this role has taken on their lives and the lives of their children (Wright et al., 1989).

In line with trends mentioned above, I found that the children from single-parent homes with whom I worked manifested a wide array of problems. In the group sessions I became aware that much of the children's hurt and anger related to the breakup of their home. I allowed the students to vent these feelings of sadness and anger. I discovered that many parents were unaware of their child's conflict, and I encouraged these parents to listen to their children and allow them to openly express their emotions without fear of the parent's becoming defensive. The children were much more likely to resolve their conflicts if the parent permitted them to talk about the divorce. (Later in this chapter we will describe in some detail two groups designed for this special population.)

Working outside the Group

Working with Families. I've already stressed that I contacted the parents as often as I could in order to involve them in their child's counseling. On several occasions I was able to arrange for family sessions, not only discussing the child's problems but also inquiring into the child's behavior within the context of the family. I felt enthusiastic about working with entire families, yet it was hard to arrange such sessions, for reasons of time and scheduling. I found that stopping by a child's home just to visit or to show movies and pictures of the child that I had taken during a trip to the mountains or at a swimming party was just as valuable as "work" sessions. It seemed especially meaningful to show the movies of the children to the families, because this made the children feel special and proud. These visits increased the parents' trust in what I was doing and their willingness to cooperate with me.

Working with Teachers. I was working with an exceptionally enthusiastic and caring teaching staff. We combined our efforts to come up with ways of improving the children's overall school experience. Our enthusiasm was infectious, and we were able to learn much from one another. The teachers instituted classroom procedures that were extensions and continuations of the work I was doing. For instance, a teacher might give a few moments of individual positive attention when he or she saw that the child was about to ask for attention in a negative way. In addition to meeting with the teachers, I also made frequent contacts with the principal, the school nurse, the school secretaries, the school psychologist, and the school librarian to solicit additional information about the children and feedback about what I was doing.

Tapping Outside Resources. Because a counselor works with the total child, he or she needs to know what services, agencies, associations, companies, and individuals can be contacted for help when counseling is not enough. Many children are undernourished, underclothed, and in need of medical assistance, recreational opportunities, or supervision after school. Counseling is more likely to have an effect if the child's basic needs are being met. I found that I had to become actively involved as a kind of social worker to provide for many of the children's physical needs. I learned to rely on myself to do much of the legwork required to obtain food, clothing, money, or special services for the children and their families. Some families resisted turning to outside agencies because of pride or fear that strings would be attached or simply out of ignorance about where to go for help. When a family did want help with emotional, economic, or medical problems, I referred it to one of the appropriate agencies. I did this rather than dealing with problems I wasn't qualified to handle or taking on additional counseling loads that I might not have had time to follow through on. However, I often made the contacts with the agencies and did the paperwork they required. More often than not, counselors do not have the time to make the contacts I've described. But they can sometimes be creative in finding ways to delegate these tasks to others.

Probably the most important (and most often overlooked) method of obtaining services for children and their families is asking. Private companies, concerned citizens, and the school staff are all potential resources, both for material goods and for suggestions about where else to go for help. I can't stress enough that the total needs of the child must be considered if his or her emotional needs are to be met.

Children's Groups in Community Agencies

One of our colleagues, Randy Alle-Corliss, who has worked as a clinical social worker in several community mental-health agencies, has designed groups for children with much the same basic structure and format as the one just described. What follows are some of the highlights of his way of organizing and leading these groups.

Randy originally got the idea to organize groups for children as a result of working with parents who came to his agency complaining about the behavioral problems of their children. When he began his first group, he sought out other therapists on the staff as referral resources, giving them information that would help them determine what kind of children might benefit from his group. Conversely, the themes of his groups are often determined by the needs of the referral sources. He also typically obtains additional information by consulting with teachers, parents, and therapists who have any involvement with the children to be placed in the group.

In much the same manner as described earlier, Randy screens and orients the children, as well as educating parents about the nature of the group. He meets with each child alone to build rapport, he sees the parents without the child, and then he sees the parents and the child together to get a sense of the family situation. Selecting the group membership is extremely important. He purposely screens to balance the qualities in the group—for example, mixing acting-out children with passive/withdrawn children. He also believes that balancing the group by gender is important. The age of the children is another important factor. The age range among the members should not be too wide, or else it is difficult to provide for a commonality of developmental issues and concerns of the children.

Randy prefers to work with a female co-leader. This structure provides adult modeling and allows for parental-transference issues to be explored in the sessions. His groups are limited to nine months, with some changing membership. They meet once a week for an hour. During the first 20 minutes the co-leaders talk with the children. The next 20 minutes is devoted to various play activities. The children draw pictures, use sand trays, and engage in both structured and spontaneous play. The leaders are involved in the play, either by observing or by actually participating in the activities. The final 20 minutes is set aside to discuss what happened during the play session, which often serves as a catalyst for brief role playing. Common topics and themes that are explored in these sessions are family conflicts; school problems; peer relationships; abandonment, loss, and death; dealing with frustration, aggression, and anger; and dealing with reactions to others in the group.

A few of the main goals of this group are learning that feelings are acceptable; learning how to express feelings constructively; identifying with others and feeling less alone with one's problems; learning to change those attitudes, beliefs, feelings, and behaviors that they have the power to change; and accepting the things one can't change, such as the reality of parents' divorce.

Randy reports outcomes similar to those mentioned earlier, including improved peer relations and social skills, a cohesion within the group, an increased ability to express feelings appropriately, and a decrease of target behaviors such as aggression or withdrawal.

Randy and his co-leader deal with the eventual termination of the group by alerting the children four weeks in advance. Children thus prepared are given opportunities to express their feelings about separation, loss, and death. The co-leaders use many of the techniques described in Chapter 7, including reviewing the highlights of the group's history and doing a lot of reminiscing. The leaders help the children remember what they have talked about and help reinforce the gains they have made during the group. Many times there is food and a party at the final session as a way of celebrating the end of a meaningful experience.

If you would like further information from Randy Alle-Corliss about this group for children, contact him at his place of work: Kaiser Permanente, Montclair Mental Health, 5330 San Bernardino Road, Montclair, CA 91763; telephone: (714) 399-3729.

A Group for Children of Divorce: I

It is not uncommon for many children in any elementary school to come from divorced homes. These pupils face a number of personal and social problems, which include being lonely, feeling responsible for the divorce, experiencing divided loyalties, not knowing how to deal with parental conflicts, and facing the loss of family stability. Schools and community agencies are addressing the needs of these children by offering groups structured around these themes. This section and the one to follow describe two counseling groups designed for children from divorced families. First, Karen Kram Laudenslager, an elementary school counselor, tells about her groups in the Allentown School District in Pennsylvania. Then we give an account of groups designed by Marilyn Chandler, an elementary school counselor in North Carolina.

Preliminary Considerations in Forming the Group*

Before actually getting a group going, a great deal of careful preliminary work needs to be done. This preparation includes conducting a needs survey, announcing the group to children and teachers, obtaining parental permission, orienting the children to the rules for participating in a group, and presenting my goals in a clear way to the children, parents, teachers, and administrators. If adequate attention is not given to these preliminary details, the group may never materialize.

Beginning with a Survey of Children's Needs. It is very helpful to assess the needs of children before deciding on a program. I do this by making an initial classroom visit to discuss with both the teachers and the children how small-group counseling can be beneficial. I explain the topical focus of these groups, or as I later refer to them, "clubs." These topics include divorce, stepfamilies, death, stress, and friendship. I run these groups from kindergarten through the fifth grade. The family club is geared for grades two through five. I explain that a specific day and time have been scheduled for club meetings at each grade level and that all clubs run for 30 minutes once a week for six sessions.

The needs survey is then handed out, and I ask all students to think about the issues and react truthfully. I explain that these surveys are private and will be read only by the classroom teacher and myself. The selection of students is based on comments by both students and teachers. I clearly state that not all students will be able to participate.

This survey allows students to have a direct role in determining areas of concern that they are open to and willing to deal with. At the end of the survey, space is provided for students to write in detail about specific feelings or situations they would like me to know about.

---

*The material to follow is written from the perspective of Karen Kram Laudenslager.

Obtaining Parental Permission. A letter, which is reproduced here, is sent home with every child who has agreed to participate in the group. This letter outlines the issues and topics to be discussed and requests parental permission. It also encourages parental support and involvement as well as opening up lines for communication.

Sample Parental-Consent Letter

Dear Parents,

During my time as guidance counselor at _____ Elementary School, I have found that many children have questions and concerns about family situations.

Research has shown that it is helpful for children to share their concerns and feelings with others in a small group. Through this interaction with others who have similar feelings, the child learns to accept and deal with family situations in a positive way.

During the next few months, I will be meeting with children who have experienced a family separation, divorce, remarriage, or loss of a loved one. Some of the topics we will be discussing are feelings, divorce and separation, skills for coping with problems, and building identity and self-esteem.

The groups will be made up of approximately six students from your child's school and will meet for six weeks.

If you have any questions about the group or would like to speak to me about your child, please call me at _____.

Please return the permission form below by _____ to let me know if your child will be participating in the program.

Sincerely,

Karen Laudenslager

....

I acknowledge and support my son's/daughter's participation in the above program and hereby give my written consent.

Parent's signature	Date

Group Rules. All students voluntarily agree to be a member of the club. I encourage children who are shy or slightly reluctant to give it a try. Anyone who wishes to discontinue the group is free to do so, but to date I have never had a student drop out.

Children always have the right to remain silent. I reinforce the importance of listening and learning from one another. Some students feel more comfortable knowing that they will never be forced to share or discuss any issue that they feel is private. The other rules include these: everyone is listened to, no laughing or making fun of what anyone says is allowed, honesty is required, and confidentiality is respected.

The students, with my guidance, make up the rules during the first session. They usually come up with all of the above on their own. If the group does not identify some critical norms, I will add them to our list of rules. I explain the reasons for the rules, which increases the chances that the children will abide by them.

What Children Need to Know. Following is a list of what I have found through my research, reading, and direct contact with children to be important messages for them to hear. I continually discuss, explain, and reinforce these statements throughout the six-week sessions:

- You are all right.
- You are special.
- You will get through this difficult time.
- You have people who care about you.
- It [the divorce or separation] is not your fault.
- You are not to blame.
- It is not your divorce, and no one is divorcing you. Mom and Dad are divorcing each other.
- You did not cause the problems between your parents, and you can't fix them.

What I Hope to Accomplish. I have a number of objectives in these groups, some of which are listed below:

- to give support when needed
- to let children know they are not alone
- to teach coping skills
- to reinforce students' need to talk about and deal with feelings
- to help them deal with emotional and behavioral concerns so they can reach their potential
- to offer resources to students and parents such as bibliotherapy and outside private counseling when needed
- to help children open lines of communication with other students, teachers, and parents

Highlights of the Group Sessions

The focus of these clubs is developmental rather than therapeutic. The groups are designed to provide support, teach coping skills, and help children of changing families explore ways in which to express and deal with their feelings. When more involved counseling is needed, the parents are always contacted, and an outside referral is made.

Sessions of 30 minutes each, once a week for six weeks, work well for me, for many reasons. This schedule allows more time to run more groups and see more children. With so many students experiencing family changes, I try to help as many as possible. This time structure interferes only minimally with classroom learning. I try to be sensitive to the reactions of both students and teachers to interrupting the learning process. Too much time out of class for extended periods can cause additional stress, and we are all concerned with supporting and enhancing the learning process, not disrupting it.

The Initial Meeting. The first session is clearly structured by focusing on a discussion of the purpose of the club, on my role as a group facilitator, and on helping the children identify why they are in the group. We play a "name game," in which the children introduce themselves by selecting an adjective describing them that starts with the first letter of their first name (such as Wonderful Wanda or Nice Nick). The only guideline is that the adjective must be a positive one. We define *family*, and each child introduces himself or herself by answering the question "Who am I, and who lives at my house?" I encourage them to describe how it is for them to be in their family. At this session the ground rules are established and written on chart paper for use as a reminder at all subsequent sessions. My goal for this first meeting is to help the children find out that they are not alone in their situation. If time allows, I encourage them to see similarities and differences in their family situations. I may ask "Who would like to share how your family is the same as or different from others in this group?"

The Next Four Sessions. I have found that my groups differ somewhat. Depending on the themes that are brought out at the initial session, I use selected exercises as a focus for interaction. The middle four sessions are structured in accordance with the needs of those who are in the group. Below are a few of the activities that are often a part of these sessions:

▪ We play the "feeling game." Students brainstorm feelings, and we write them down. The children then select three feelings that describe how they feel about their family situation, and we discuss them.

▪ The children identify three wishes they have for their family. One overwhelming wish that generally emerges is that their mother and father will get back together. They also wish to spend more time with the noncustodial parent. These children often express how difficult it is for them to be placed in the middle of a struggle, and they wish for peace. They would like this harmony at any cost, and they are willing to do anything to bring it about.

▪ The children decide "what I want each of my parents to know." (Stepparents and stepbrothers and stepsisters may also be included, if appropriate.) I often find that the children are hesitant to reveal some differences they might have with their new stepmother or stepfather. They frequently want their parents to understand their feelings about being in a new family. Sometimes children feel forced to make an adjustment before they are ready, and they often have uncomfortable feelings that have not been discussed.

▪ We discuss what children can control and what they cannot. For example, they can control their own behavior. We also talk about ways in which they *can* also control certain feelings. However, they cannot control the decisions that their parents make about the divorce or current living situation. I also talk with the children about the fact that this is not *their* divorce. In other words, Mom and Dad are divorcing each other, not the children. What I hope to get across to the group members is that they did not cause the divorce and cannot "fix" the situation. Thus, much of our time is devoted to exploring and brainstorming alternatives for changing *themselves* in their situations at home.

- We read and discuss the following books, depending on relevance and interest:

> Brown, L. K., & Brown, M. (1986). *Dinosaurs Divorce: A Guide for Changing Families*. Boston: Little, Brown.
> Stenson, J. S. (1979). *Now I Have a Step Parent and It's Kind of Confusing*. New York: Avon.
> Sinberg, J. (1978). *Divorce Is a Grown-Up Problem*. New York: Avon.
> Ives, S. B., Fassler, D., & Lash, M. (1985). *The Divorce Workbook: A Guide for Kids and Families*. Burlington, VT: Waterfront Books.

The Last Session. As is true of the initial session, the final meeting is fairly structured, this time around the tasks of termination. The children typically discuss feelings about the club ending and identify what they have learned from these sessions. There is also some time for a special celebration with cupcake treats. Each student receives a recognition certificate, which says: *The Counselor Said I Am Special!*

The Role of Teachers and Parents in the Group Program

Any counselor who works in an elementary school can testify to the importance of getting feedback and support from teachers and parents. I have found that it is critical to involve parents, teachers, and administrators in these group programs, so that they become allies of the children and the counselor. Their support of the program goes a long way toward ensuring its success; their resistance can thwart its progress.

Comments from Teachers. Teachers' feedback is critical, because they see the student daily and can monitor changes in behavior. I make an effort to talk with each classroom teacher as often as possible, yet time often works against me. I hope to develop a teacher checklist and rating scale to document and facilitate this interaction. I have found that most teachers are concerned about the emotional and behavioral blocks that interfere with learning. They can tell counselors about pupils' self-esteem, self-confidence, interaction with their peers, and homework completion. They can also share comments and reactions that students make in class, both orally and in their written work. All of this information helps me monitor the students' emotional and social progress.

Parental Support. I always send the letter seeking parental permission home with the student and encourage each child to discuss the group with both parents. However, I realize that this does not always happen. I have considered requesting both signatures in the hope of opening lines of communication to both parents, although I have never actually tried this practice. My concern is not to cause more stress for the child, and I attempt to be sensitive to each individual family situation. Yet I am convinced of the value of involving both parents.

Outcomes, Follow-Up, and a Personal Perspective

Student Perceptions. Students report feeling more comfortable with themselves and with their family situations when they belong to the club and realize that they are not alone. They need to identify with other children who are experiencing similar concerns and feelings. Together, group members can begin to understand the stages that everyone goes through and can learn skills to help themselves feel better. They help one another, through the group process, let go of what they cannot control and take responsibility for what they can control.

Teachers' and Administrators' Perceptions. Teachers report that students in the groups can often concentrate better in class. Johanna Price, a second-grade teacher, said that "as teachers strive to adjust the learning environment to meet each child's needs, they may find that the many demands of the school day allow little opportunity to offer the child the kind of individual attention and interaction that is provided during the club sessions." Julie Zager, a fourth-grade teacher, commented: "The days are full, and classes are large. Teachers provide personal attention, but it is not always possible to give as much encouragement and support to an individual student as might be needed. Small-group clubs led by a caring and sensitive counselor can provide feedback to help the teacher raise self-esteem, which in turn can increase student achievement." According to Dennis Blankowitsch, a school principal, "The school family now becomes the most consistent, predictable support for children adjusting to changing families."

Parents' Perceptions. Parents report that their children enjoy the club meetings and often talk about what was discussed. They see their children gaining a better understanding of divorce and learning how others adjust. I find that parents are often in so much pain and conflict themselves during the separation or divorce that they are relieved and happy that someone else is there supporting their child.

Follow-Up. My follow-up consists of asking teachers about the students' progress and checking in with the children themselves by making classroom visits, by seeing them individually, and by encouraging self-referrals. I also try to hold club "reunions" the following year to see how things have been going.

Personal Sources of Frustrations. The biggest frustration for me is ending the clubs. The children always resist terminating and bargain or plead to continue with more sessions. I find it extremely difficult to end when I know how much these children need to talk and learn. Some of the children's problems that I am unable to solve directly and that add to my level of frustration are:

- infrequent visitations with a parent as a result of the parent's emotional problems
- dislocations because a child is "interfering" with a parent's new relationship
- frequent court testimony in a sexual-abuse case
- conflicts over being asked by parents to choose sides
- parents' extramarital affairs
- alcohol and drug abuse
- spousal abuse
- physical or emotional abuse
- custody battles
- financial concerns

Another source of frustration is time. There never seems to be enough time to see all the students who need help. Nor is there enough time to meet with all of the parents to discuss the progress of each child. I do, however, refer families for outside counseling if during the club sessions I see a need for more in-depth therapy.

For more information about the groups described above, write to Karen Kram Laudenslager, Ritter Elementary School, Plymouth and East Washington Streets, Allentown, PA 18102; school telephone (215) 820-2128.

A Group for Children of Divorce: II

This section describes a counseling group designed for children from divorced families. Marilyn Chandler, an elementary school counselor in North Carolina, compiled many of these ideas from reading and attending workshops pertaining to counseling children.

Overview of the Group

Marilyn reports that she limits her divorce groups to fifth- and sixth-grade children. She finds that divorce groups with younger students are less successful, because these children lack the maturity to generalize from the group experience to daily life. Most of her counseling with children below the fifth-grade level on divorce or stepfamily issues is done on an individual basis.

With her divorce group Marilyn begins by establishing the ground rules of confidentiality. She also stresses to the children that they have been chosen to participate in this group on the basis of their progress with her in their individual counseling sessions.

She reports that as the sessions progress, the children share more of their feelings and are surprisingly supportive of one another. She makes sure that the students are aware that they can pursue some highly personal issues with her privately. If a child makes what she feels is an inappropriate self-disclosure, she may take the initiative by saying "Maybe this is something you and I might want to talk more about together."

Before the group starts, parental-permission slips are sent home. Below is a sample copy of this letter to parents.

Parental-Permission Form

Dear Parent,

We are planning to offer a series of small group-counseling sessions for fifth- and sixth-grade students who are interested in working with other students on the topic of divorce. The time will give the students an opportunity to share feelings, concerns, and coping skills with others whose families are also separated. With the help of a supportive group, we hope, the children will learn to accept their own family's situation in a positive way and will be better prepared to handle other life crises.

The six weekly sessions will last approximately 30 to 40 minutes. The group leader, Marilyn Chandler, is the school counselor.

Parent permission is requested for a student to participate in the group. The classroom teachers have been consulted on scheduling, and students will not be penalized for missing class time.

If you have any questions, please call the school. Your support is greatly appreciated.

Sincerely,

Guidance Counselor

....

I give my child _____ permission to participate in the group-counseling series.

_____   _____
Parent's signature   Date

A Format for Divorce-Group Counseling

Following is Marilyn Chandler's six-session program for helping elementary students from divorced families.*

GOALS

1. to help students talk about and come to understand their feelings about their parents' divorce

---

*Adapted from *Group Counseling for Children of Divorce*, by Janice Hammond, 1981. Ann Arbor, MI: Cranbrook. (Order from Cranbrook Publishing Company, 2815 Cranbrook, Ann Arbor, MI 48104.)

2. to help children understand that they are not alone in their feelings and experiences
3. to give students an opportunity to learn coping skills and to share successful coping strategies with others in the group
4. to help children gain a more realistic view of the divorce and move toward acceptance of themselves and their families

SESSION CONTENT

Session 1: "Getting to Know You"
a. *Group introductions.* Have students form pairs, interviewing each other to learn five new things about the other. Have students introduce their partner to the group.
b. *Discussion of group goals and plans.* Explain goals and activities, answer questions, and ask students to share what they hope to get from participating in the group.
c. *Group guidelines.* List the guidelines on newsprint, and keep for future reference.

Session 2: Filmstrip and Discussion
a. *Film or filmstrip.* Suggested titles: *Breakup* (Inside/Out)—16mm or video cassette; *Coping with Your Parents' Divorce* (Learning Tree)—sound filmstrip; *Understanding Changes in the Family* (Guidance Associates)—sound filmstrip.
b. *Discussion.* Ask for students' reactions. Discuss characters' feelings, using questions in the manual if available. Summarize.

Session 3: "Things I Wish My Parents Knew"
a. *Values voting* [from Simon, Howe, & Kirschenbaum, 1972]. Have students vote on statements and myths regarding divorce and step-families.
b. *Brainstorming.* List on newsprint the "things I wish my parents knew" about the effects of divorce on children. Discuss.
c. *Role playing.* Have students act out and discuss common problem situations, such as where the child goes for holidays, parents' criticism of each other, or meeting a parent's new "friend." This role playing may be structured by writing situations on cards for the students to draw or asking the students to suggest situations. Discuss the feelings shown, and ask students to tell about times when they have felt that way.

Session 4: Bibliotherapy
a. *Booklist.* Compile a list of divorce-related books appropriate for the students' ages. Show them whatever books you have access to, let them peruse them, and allow them to check them out from you if possible.
b. *Reading aloud.* For younger students, read "Zachary's Divorce," from *Free to Be You and Me* [Sitea, 1984]. Have older students read orally from *My Dad Lives in a Downtown Hotel* [Mann, 1973] or *It's Not the*

End of the World [Blume, 1972]. (If the books are available, it would be ideal to give them out the week before and assign the reading in advance.)

c. *Discussion.* Discuss characters' feelings and behaviors. Some common themes are children's feelings of responsibility for their parents' divorce, anger and aggressive behaviors, wishing the parents would get back together, and embarrassment about the new family situation. Encourage personal discussion, and elicit suggestions for dealing with these problems.

Session 5: Empathic Assertion
a. *"You're Not Bad If You Get Angry."* Read pages 48–58 from *The Boys and Girls Book About Divorce* [Gardner, 1970] on anger.
b. *Assertive response.* Practice expressing feelings and needs while showing some understanding of others' feelings. (See page 32 of Hammond [1981] for good handout and discussion questions.)

Session 6: "The Uh-Oh Game"
a. *The Uh-Oh Game.* Available from the Friends Next Door, Inc., 10907 Oakwood Street, Silver Spring, MD 20901. Encourages children to discuss common problem situations, gives them a chance to share their feelings. A fun concluding activity.
b. *Summary.* List on newsprint the lessons that have been learned. Evaluate by asking students what they liked most, what was most helpful, and so one.
c. *Strength bombardment.* Close on a positive note. Ask students to write one positive statement about each group member on separate stick-on labels. Have them use the labels to make a poster for each member.

Outcomes of the Group

According to Marilyn, her divorce groups help her develop bonds with her counselees. When she works with children individually, she often makes a remark such as "Remember when this came up in the group?" She finds that children are able to take issues they worked on in group sessions and apply them to one-on-one counseling situations. For her, group counseling is a useful adjunct to individual counseling.

The children involved in these groups develop bonds that they can take beyond the group experience. Many strong friendships develop from the group and last the rest of the year. The children express mutual concern and an interest in helping one another.

Parental response has been positive. An increasing number of parents see the school counselor as an important helper in stepfamily or divorce situations.

Guidelines for Group Work with Children and Adolescents

This section consists of some practical guidelines for counselors who are considering setting up groups for minors. These guidelines apply to groups for adolescents, which we consider in the next chapter, as well as to children's groups.

Developing a Sound Proposal

In designing your proposal, make sure that you describe your goals and purposes clearly. Avoid arousing suspicion with global language or loaded words such as *sensitivity group* or *group therapy*. Develop a clearly stated rationale for your proposed group. State your aims, the procedures to be used, the evaluation devices that you will use, and the reasons that a group approach has particular merit. Too many potential groups fail to materialize because the leader has impulsively decided to lead a group but has put little serious thought into planning an effective design. Refer to Chapter 3 for more information on developing a group proposal.

The support of administrators is essential, and if your design for a group is well organized, you will probably receive support and constructive suggestions from them. It may be necessary to make certain compromises in your proposal, so keep an open mind. Remember that the school principal or the agency head—not you—will probably be the target of criticism if your counseling group is ineffectively run or compromises the integrity of the institution. The administrator will be the one who, if you've overlooked the need to get parental permission, fields the calls from parents who want to know what right the school has to probe into the personal lives of their children. One practitioner reported that she had encountered resistance from her school principal when she suggested a "divorce group" for children. She formally proposed a "loss group," which satisfied the principal but confused the children. They reported to the office saying "We're the *lost* group; we're here to get found."

Legal Considerations

Be aware of your state's laws regarding children. Know the rules and regulations as they specifically apply to your agency or institution, as well as its ethical principles. For example, don't tell the children that you can keep everything they discuss confidential and then be put in the position of having to disclose information about them to your agency or school administrator. Be clear about what you can and cannot promise in the way of privacy. Be aware of your legal responsibility to report abuse or suspected abuse of minors. In this situation, confidentiality *must* be broken, because the law requires you to take action by notifying the appropriate authorities. For other ethical considerations in setting up groups for minors, review the discussion of such standards in Chapter 2.

For some groups, written parental permission may be a legal requirement. It is usually a good idea to secure the written consent of the parents or guardians of any person under 18 who wishes to participate in group counseling.

Practical Considerations

The size and duration of a group depend on the age level of the members. As a rule of thumb, the younger the children, the smaller the group and the shorter the duration of the sessions. Take into account the fact that the attention span of a child aged 4 to 6 is quite different from that of a child who is 10 to 12. Another consideration in forming a group is the severity of the children's problems. For example, a group of hyperactive 12-year-olds might have to be as small as a group of preschoolers. You must also consider your own attention span and tolerance for dealing with children who will test your limits. Resist getting impatient at each session, thus becoming more of a disciplinarian than a counselor.

The Setting. Consider the meeting place in terms of its effectiveness for the work you want to do with your young clients. Will they be able to roam around freely and not have to be continually asked to talk softly so as not to disturb others in an adjacent room? Will the site for group meetings provide privacy and freedom from interruptions? Is there anything in the room that could easily be damaged by the children or that is obviously unsafe for them?

Communication of Your Expectations. Be able to tell the children or adolescents in a simple way about the purpose of your group, what you expect of them, and what they can expect from you. Make sure that they understand the basic, nonnegotiable ground rules and, as much as is realistic, attempt to involve them in the establishment and reinforcement of the rules that will govern their group. In setting certain rules, it is essential to follow through with firmness (without an autocratic tone and style). For example, you may have the policy of not allowing members who have left a session to return. Be careful not to give in to their demands for a "second chance." Young people will quickly learn that you mean what you say. They may not always like what you do at the time, but your chances for earning their respect are increased.

Preparation. Prepare adequately for each session. In fact, you may need to structure sessions even more carefully than you would for some adult groups. However, be flexible enough to adjust your format and topics for a given session in order to respond to spontaneous situations. Avoid insisting on "covering your agenda" no matter what; be creative but not careless.

Involvement of Parents. As with the young people, explain to their parents your expectations and purposes in such a way that they can understand and not become suspicious. You reduce the chances of encountering resistant and defensive parents by approaching them with an attitude of "How can you help me in my work with your child, and how can we work as a team for a common purpose?" Rather than communicating to them in subtle ways that they are incompetent and that you are the expert who can remedy the situation, be sincerely interested in their reactions to your program. You might spend an evening presenting your program in a group meeting of parents, or you might send them a letter briefly describing your groups. This letter can be sent with the parental-consent form.

Tactics in the Group

Use Judgment. Consider the purposes and goals of your group in deciding how much to encourage self-disclosure, especially in matters relating to family life. It is difficult to say what is the right degree of disclosure. The counselor needs to be careful because children may not keep confidentiality and may talk to other children about disclosures made in the group. It is more difficult to maintain confidentiality in a school setting than in private practice, where the children may have no contact outside of the group. Should you encourage an open discussion of personal matters? For example, in a group in an elementary school, you may not want to let a child go into detail about a parental fight. An important intervention is directing this child to express how he or she was affected by the incident. In any case, the focus of disclosure should be the child, not the parent.

Don't Take Sides. Avoid siding with children or adolescents against their parents or a particular institution. They may like and admire you for your patience and understanding and complain about missing these traits in parents or teachers. Deal with this complaint realistically, keeping in mind that you are spending an hour each week with them as opposed to living with them every day. Try to get the young people to understand the other side, through role playing, for example.

Use Appropriate Exercises and Techniques. If you use interaction exercises, you can explain their purpose in a general way without diminishing their impact. Realize, too, that young people should be granted the right not to participate in some activities. Although their unwillingness to take part often stems from a lack of understanding, children or adolescents will sometimes be resistant because they see such exercises as inappropriate. For example, it may be appropriate to ask 6-year-olds of the opposite sex to hold hands, but you are likely to meet with resistance if you ask 12-year-olds to do the same.

Listen and Be Open.   Learn to listen to young people; let them say what they need to say in their own words. Let them lead the way, and follow their clues. Listen to their words, and also pay attention to the possible meanings of their behavior. For example, if a child is acting out, is she telling you "Please stop me, because I can't stop myself"? If a child is continually screaming, he might be saying "Notice me! Nobody else does." Remaining open to what children are trying to tell you about themselves is difficult if you cling to preconceived labels and diagnoses. The children you work with are often categorized and labeled. Be careful not to limit their ability to change by responding to them in terms of rigid categories.

Prepare for Termination.   Children are quick to form attachments with adults who display a concerned and caring attitude toward them. Well before your group ends—for example, 3 sessions before the end of a 12-session group—you must let the children know that the termination point is not far off. This notice allows the children to express their sadness, and it allows you to share your sadness with them. Avoid promising them that you will keep in contact with them, if that is not possible. If you don't deal with these issues, they may see you as running out on them and consider you as one more adult they cannot trust. (At this point it is a good idea to review the guidelines for the final stage of a group, described in Chapter 7.)

Know Your Limitations.   Be realistic, and realize that you cannot work effectively with every child or provide all the needed services. It is essential that you know the boundaries of your competence. You should also make it a practice to know referral resources and be willing to make use of these resources when it is in the child's best interest.

Personal and Professional Qualifications

Some of the *personal* characteristics that we see as important in working with children are patience, caring, playfulness, a good sense of humor, the ability to tune in to and remember one's own childhood and adolescent experiences, firmness without punitiveness, flexibility, the ability to express anger without sarcasm, great concern for and interest in children, and the other characteristics of group leaders that were described in Chapter 1.

Four of the *professional* qualifications that we believe are especially important for those leading groups with children are:

1. a thorough understanding of the developmental tasks and stages of the particular age group
2. a good understanding of counseling skills, especially as they pertain to group work
3. supervised training in working with minors in groups before leading a group alone
4. knowledge of the literature and significant research pertaining to counseling children and adolescents

In addition to the above qualifications, other specific competencies and skills are essential to effectively lead groups of children or adolescents. For a listing, refer to Chapter 2 and review the *Professional Standards for Training of Group Workers* of the Association for Specialists in Group Work.

A Concluding Thought

It is easy to overextend yourself in working with children and adolescents whose problems are pressing and severe. You may find yourself working with youngsters who are abused and neglected and find it difficult to separate yourself from their life situations. If you are consistently preoccupied with their problems, you may discover that this stress is affecting your life and your relationships negatively. It is a personal matter for counselors to discover how much they are capable of giving, as well as how much and what they need to do to replenish themselves in order to stay excited and creative in their work.

Where to Go from Here

A most useful resource, containing a wide variety of books for children and adolescents, is *Paperbacks for Educators: School Counselor Edition, K–12, Catalog*. This yearly catalog can be obtained by contacting Paperbacks for Educators, 426 West Front Street, Washington, MO 63090; telephone: (800) 227-2591. It consists of an annotated list of books dealing with topics such as abuse and neglect, addictions, at-risk students, birth order, career/life planning, conflict resolution, discipline, divorce and stepfamilies, family problems, group activities, group counseling, health and wellness, learning problems, loss, parenting, peer pressure, self-esteem, sexuality, single parenting, social skills, stress and relaxation, suicide, time management, and values.

Another excellent resource is *Paperbacks for Educators: Bibliotherapy for Children and Teens, Catalog*, also published by Paperbacks for Educators. This catalog contains annotations of books on a variety of subjects, including adoption, assertiveness, children's problems, divorce and stepfamilies, fears, friendships, school problems, sibling relationships, social behavior, study skills, and weight problems.

Two useful books for those who counsel children in groups are *Windows to Our Children: A Gestalt Approach to Children and Adolescents* (Oaklander, 1978) and *Developmental Groups for Children* (Duncan & Gumaer, 1980). *Windows* is a how-to book that describes Oaklander's work with children in a very sensitive and straightforward manner and points out cautions and pitfalls to the counselor. Duncan and Gumaer's collection has several excellent articles, including pieces on peer-facilitated groups, assertion training in groups, parent groups, rational-emotive groups for children, growth-centered group procedures, group techniques for staff development, and an overview of developmental groups for children.

Other books that contain chapters of specific interest to those conducting groups with children are:

- *Working with Children and Adolescents in Groups* (Rose & Edleson, 1987). This excellent book presents a specific guide for the multimethod approach to treating children in groups. The book gives many examples covering children from kindergarten through adolescence. Separate chapters deal with topics for each stage of a group, including preparation and orientation, assessing children's problems, setting goals, methods of changing behavior, stress-coping techniques, use of games and activities, influencing group structure and resolving group problems, homework assignments and behavioral practice, and strategies for the transfer and maintenance of learning.

- *Counseling Children* (Thompson & Rudolph, 1988). Chapters that may be of particular interest are Chapter 13, which deals with group counseling; Chapter 14, dealing with special needs and concerns of children; Chapter 16, on legal and ethical considerations; and Chapters 17 and 18, on interventions for a variety of problem behaviors.

- *Counseling and Therapy for Children* (Gumaer, 1984). This book contains several chapters on counseling children in groups. Other chapters deal with family therapy, play therapy, art therapy, music therapy, bibliotherapy, behavioral counseling, and relaxation and guided fantasy.

- *Group Counseling: A Developmental Approach* (Gazda, 1989). This book deals largely with structured groups aimed at teaching various skills in living. It discusses group procedures for children in preschool and the lower grades.

- *Group Counseling* (Ohlsen, Horne, & Lawe, 1988). There are chapters on the emotionally debilitated client, the other-controlled client, and the reluctant client. See particularly Chapter 12, on group counseling with children.

References and Suggested Readings

Alberti, R. E., & Emmons, M. L. (1987). *Your perfect right* (5th ed.). San Luis Obispo, CA: Impact.

Axline, V. M. (1976). *Dibs: In search of self.* New York: Ballantine.

Blume, J. (1972). *It's not the end of the world.* New York: Bantam Books.

Brown, L. K., & Brown, M. (1986). *Dinosaurs divorce: A guide for changing families.* Boston: Little, Brown.

Burt, M. S., & Burt, R. B. (1983). *What's special about our stepfamily? A participation book for children.* Garden City, NY: Doubleday (Dolphin).

Davis, D. (1985). *Something is wrong at my house: A book about parents fighting.* Seattle: Parenting Press.

Dinkmeyer, D., & McKay, G. D. (1982). *The parent's handbook: STEP—Systematic training for effective parenting.* Circle Pines, MN: American Guidance Service.

Dinkmeyer, D. C., & Muro, J. J. (1979). *Group counseling: Theory and practice* (2nd ed.). Itasca, IL: F. E. Peacock.

*Duncan, J. A., & Gumaer, J. (Eds.). (1980). *Developmental groups for children.* Springfield, IL: Charles C Thomas.

Ely, D. F., & Associates (1988). *California laws relating to minors.* Gardena, CA: Harcourt Brace Jovanovich.

Forward, S., & Buck, C. (1988). *Betrayal of innocence: Incest and its devastation.* New York: Penguin Books.

Gardner, R. A. (1970). *The boys and girls book about divorce.* New York: Bantam Books.

Gardner, R. A. (1978). *The boys and girls book about one-parent families.* New York: Putnam.

*Gazda, G. M. (1989). *Group counseling: A developmental approach* (4th ed.). Boston: Allyn & Bacon.

Gumaer, J. (1984). *Counseling and therapy for children.* New York: Free Press.

*Hammond, J. (1981). *Group counseling for children of divorce.* Ann Arbor, MI: Cranbrook.

Ives, S. B., Fassler, D., & Lash, M. (1985). *The divorce workbook: A guide for kids and families.* Burlingon, VT: Waterfront Books.

Kennedy, J. F. (1989). The heterogeneous group for chronically physically ill and physically healthy but emotionally disturbed children and adolescents. *International Journal of Group Psychotherapy, 39*(1), 105–125.

Lederman, J. (1973). *Anger and the rocking chair: Gestalt awareness with children.* New York: Viking Press.

LeShan, E. (1976). *Learning to say goodbye when a parent dies.* New York: Macmillan.

Mann, P. (1973). *My dad lives in a downtown hotel.* New York: Doubleday.

McElmurry, M. A. (1981). *Feelings: Understanding our feelings of sadness, happiness, love and loneliness.* Carthage, IL: Good Apple.

*Morganett, R. S. (1990). *Skills for living: Group counseling activities for young adolescents.* Champaign, IL: Research Press.

*Oaklander, V. (1978). *Windows to our children: A Gestalt approach to children and adolescents.* Moab, UT: Real People Press.

*Books and articles marked with an asterisk are recommended for further reading.

Ohlsen, M. M., Horne, A. M., & Lawe, C. F. (1988). *Group counseling* (3rd ed.). New York: Holt, Rinehart & Winston.

Rofes, E. E. (Ed.). (1982). *The kids' book of divorce: By, for and about kids.* New York: Random House (Vintage Books).

Rose, S. D., & Edleson, J. L. (1987). *Working with children and adolescents in groups: A multimethod approach.* San Francisco: Jossey-Bass.

*Schaefer, C. (Ed.). (1979). *Therapeutic use of child's play.* New York: Aronson.

*Scheidlinger, S. (1984). Short-term group psychotherapy for children: An overview. *International Journal of Group Psychotherapy, 34*(4), 573–585.

*Simon, S., Howe, L., & Kirschenbaum, H. (1972). *Values clarification: A handbook of practical strategies for teachers and students.* New York: Hart.

Sinberg, J. (1978). *Divorce is a grown-up problem: A book about divorce for young children and their parents.* New York: Avon.

Sitea, L. (1984). Zachary's divorce. In Thomas, M. (Ed.), *Free to be you and me.* New York: McGraw-Hill.

Sour, S. R. (1981). *Seven steps to successful stepparenting.* Sewickley, PA: SRS Associates.

Stenson, J. S. (1979). *Now I have a stepparent and it's kind of confusing.* New York: Avon.

Thoft, J. S. (1977). Developing assertiveness in children. In R. E. Alberti (Ed.), *Assertiveness: Innovations, applications, issues* (pp. 195–203). San Luis Obispo, CA: Impact.

*Thompson, C. L., & Rudolph, L. B. (1988). *Counseling children* (2nd ed.). Pacific Grove, CA: Brooks/Cole.

Wilkinson, G. S., & Bleck, R. T. (1977). Children's divorce groups. *Elementary School Guidance and Counseling, 11,* 204–213.

Wright, J., Coley, S., & Corey, G. (1989). Challenges facing human services education today. *Journal of Counseling and Human Service Professions, 3*(2), 3–11.

*Zimbardo, P. G. (1978). *Shyness.* New York: Jove Press.

*Zimpfer, D. G. (1984). *Group work in the helping professions: A bibliography* (2nd ed.) Muncie, IN: Accelerated Development.

CHAPTER 10

Groups for Adolescents

Introduction: Special Needs and Problems of Adolescents

A detailed description of the unique needs and problems of adolescents is beyond the scope of this book. For group leaders who work with adolescents, good courses in the psychology of adolescence are essential. Reading and reflecting on one's own adolescent experiences and perhaps reliving some of these experiences are also valuable means of preparing oneself to counsel adolescents. Those who wish to review the field of the psychology of adolescence can refer to the suggested readings at the end of this chapter.

The adolescent period is a time of searching for an identity and developing a system of values that will influence the course of one's life. One of the most important needs of this period is to experience successes that will lead to a sense of self-confidence and self-respect. Adolescents need to recognize and accept the wide range of their feelings, and they need to learn how to communicate with significant others in such a way that they can make their wants, feelings, thoughts, and beliefs known.

The adolescent years can be extremely lonely ones; it is not unusual for adolescents to feel that they are alone in their conflicts and self-doubt. It is a period of life when people feel a desperate need for universal approval yet must learn to distinguish between living for others' approval and earning their own. During these years the dependence/independence struggle becomes central. While part of the teenager yearns for independence from parents, another part longs for security. Adolescents must cope with decisions, such as vocational and educational choices, that will influence their future. In order to make these choices wisely, they must have information both about their abilities and interests and about such realities as job opportunities and college entrance requirements.

Sexual conflicts are also a part of this period; adolescents not only need to establish a meaningful guide for their sexual behavior but also must wrestle with the problem of their sex-role identification. Teenagers may have real difficulty clarifying what it means to be a man or a woman and what kind of man or woman they want to become.

Adolescents are pressured to succeed; they are expected to perform, frequently up to others' standards. They need to be trusted and given the freedom to make some significant decisions, and they need the faith and support of caring adults. But they also need guidelines and limits.

Adolescence is a time for continually testing limits, for this period is characterized by an urge to break away from control or dependent ties that restrict freedom. Although adolescents are often frightened of the freedom they do experience, they tend to mask their fears with rebellion and cover up their dependency needs by exaggerating their newly felt autonomy. They are often moody, negativistic, and rebellious. The rebellion of adolescents can be understood as an attempt to determine the course of their own life and to assert that they are who and what they want to be, rather than what others expect of them.

A central part of the adolescent experience is peer-group pressure, a potent force that pulls at the person to conform to the standards of friends. Because of adolescents' exaggerated need for approval, there is a danger that they will sell themselves out and increasingly look to others to tell them who and what they should be. The need for acceptance by one's peer group is often stronger than the need for self-respect. This can lead to a range of behaviors that cause problems for adolescents such as dependence on drugs or alcohol in order to feel anything or to escape from painful feelings.

Adolescents tend to be more aware of what the world does to them than of what they do to the world. Thus, they can be highly critical and fault finding. At times they may want to drop out of society, yet at other times they may idealistically strive to reform society. Adolescents confront dilemmas similar to those faced by the elderly in our society: finding meaning in life and wrestling with feelings of uselessness. Older people are often forced to retire before they feel ready to do so, and the young have not yet completed their education or acquired the skills essential for many lines of work. Thus, adolescents are continually preparing for the future, which is often marked by uncertainty.

In sum, for most people adolescence is a difficult period, characterized by paradoxes: they strive for closeness, yet they also fear intimacy and often avoid it; they rebel against control, yet they want direction and structure; although they push and test limits imposed on them, they see some limits as a sign of caring; they are not given complete autonomy, yet they are often expected to act as though they were mature adults; they are typically highly self-centered, self-conscious, and preoccupied with their own world, yet they are expected to cope with societal demands and go outside of themselves by expanding their horizons; they are asked to face and accept reality, and at the same time they are tempted by many avenues of escape; and they are exhorted to think of the future, yet they have strong urges to live for the moment and to enjoy life. With all these polarities it is easy to understand that adolescence is typically a turbulent and fast-moving time, one that can accentuate loneliness and isolation. Group experiences can be very useful in helping teenagers deal with these feelings of isolation and make constructive choices for a satisfying life.

This brief sketch of some of the main currents of adolescent life should make obvious the need for developmental counseling. And group counseling is especially suitable for adolescents, because it provides a place in which they can identify and experience their conflicting feelings, discover that they're not unique in their struggles, openly question their values and modify those they find wanting, learn to communicate with peers and adults, learn from the modeling provided by the leader, and learn how to accept what others offer and to give of themselves in return. Adolescents often need to learn to label and verbalize their feelings. Groups provide a place in which they can safely experiment with reality and test their limits. A unique value of group counseling is that it lets adolescents be instrumental in one another's growth; group members help one another in the struggle for self-understanding. Most important, a group gives adolescents a chance to express themselves and to be heard and to interact with their peers.

Sample Proposal for an Adolescent Group

We have worked with adolescents in groups using a developmental model, with a focus on the normal life concerns they face. The following proposal for a group could be modified to fit many special-interest adolescent groups and some children's groups as well. It could be adapted to various settings such as mental-health clinics, community centers, public schools, residential facilities, and family-service agencies.

Rationale

Adolescence is a time of paradox, in that conflicts often lead to considerable anxiety and feelings of separateness. Adolescents can benefit from having a place to openly explore a range of their developmental concerns at this juncture in life. Young people need to learn how to cope with increasing freedom and the responsibilities that accompany it. A group can provide the opportunity to share common problems and to find ways of making responsible choices.

Type of Group

This will be a personal-growth and self-exploration group for clients between the ages of 15 and 18. The group is not designed to treat personality and behavioral problems. Instead, it is aimed at prevention. This time-limited group will consist of ten members and the two co-leaders. The group will meet for two hours each week, from 7 to 9 P.M., for 15 weeks, and there will be one all-day session around the fifth week. Membership is voluntary. A prerequisite for joining this group is attendance at an individual screening and orientation meeting. Once all the members have been selected, there will be a preliminary session designed to get acquainted with one another and to prepare the participants for a productive group experience. After this pregroup meeting those members who decide to participate in the group will be asked to make a commitment to remain for its duration.

Goals and Objectives

The group will be a place for self-exploration and for sharing of ideas and feelings. Participants will be invited to examine their values, behaviors, and relationships with others and to look at the direction of their life to determine what changes they want to make. It is the members' responsibility to decide for themselves the nature and extent of these changes. The members will decide when to share personal issues and how much to share. Participants are expected to be active in the sessions, at least to the degree of sharing their reactions to the here-and-now events within the group.

Although each member will be assisted in developing specific, concrete, and personal goals early in the group, the following are some general goals that will provide direction:

- to grow in self-acceptance and self-respect
- to become tolerant of others, to respect others' differences, and to develop a genuine caring for others
- to become sensitive to the needs of others
- to clarify values and examine one's philosophy of life
- to learn how to live with struggles and how to make one's own decisions and accept the consequences of these choices
- to explore conflicts and look for one's own answers
- to develop sufficient trust within the group to allow for an honest sharing of attitudes and feelings
- to learn ways of applying what is learned in the group to everyday situations

Basic Information

The proposal gives the names, qualifications, and experience of the co-leaders. It provides pertinent information concerning the fees (if any), dates, and how to sign up for a screening interview.

Basic Ground Rules

The group will operate under these rules:

- Members are expected to attend all the sessions and to participate by disclosing themselves and giving feedback to others.
- Members are asked to make a commitment to remain in the group for its entire 15-week life span.

- Members must maintain the confidential nature of others' disclosures.
- It is the participants' responsibility to decide on specific personal goals. This choice will be made within the first few sessions by developing a contract that clearly states what members want to change and how they will go about it.
- Members will not come to group meetings under the influence of drugs or alcohol.
- Smoking is not allowed during the sessions.
- Members must have the written consent of their parents to participate in the group.

Topics for Possible Group Exploration

The initial session is typically devoted to teaching the participants how to get the maximum benefit from a group experience, orienting them to the ground rules, and working toward the establishment of trust. Subsequent sessions can be designed jointly by the members and the leaders. Collectively, they can decide on certain common themes and personal issues to provide some structuring to the group. Some examples of theme-oriented sessions are the following:

- dealing with alcohol and drug abuse
- learning how to cope with feelings (of depression, guilt, anxiety, anger, rejection, hostility, loneliness)
- discussing the differences between being alone and being lonely
- exploring conflicts related to school
- discussing careers and post–high school plans
- discussing love, sex, and intimacy
- defining sex roles
- exploring the quality and meaning of one's life
- exploring identity issues ("Who am I?")
- considering the struggle for autonomy
- discussing conflicts with parents; learning how to live with and appreciate them

Other topics of concern to group participants can be developed as the sessions progress.

Evaluation Methods

A follow-up meeting will be arranged about six weeks after the group ends to assess the impact that the group has had on clients. The meeting can provide reinforcement to members, especially to those who have had setbacks since the termination of the group. Referrals will be made to other sources to help members continue building on the gains they made in the group.

Organizing the Group Experience for Adolescents

Once the proposal for a group for adolescents has been designed, the next major task is dealing with all the preliminary details involved in forming a group. We suggest that you refer to the discussion of procedures for forming groups in Chapter 3 and also review the guidelines for group work with children and adolescents in Chapter 9.

Much of the tedious work of getting a group into operation begins well before the initial meeting. In her very useful manual, *Skills for Living: Group Counseling Activities for Young Adolescents,* Morganett (1990) describes the following ten steps in forming and conducting a structured counseling group for young people:

1. **Conduct a needs assessment.** This process will help you focus your efforts on critical group services that are needed by specific clients in a particular setting. The assessment can be one of the instruments used as part of the accountability process. (Morganett provides a sample assessment in an appendix of her book.)
2. **Develop a written proposal.** As can be seen by the sample proposal described above, this proposal consists of a general description and rationale, objectives, logistics, procedures, and evaluation methods.
3. **Advertise the group.** As a way of letting potential participants know about a group, educate referral sources such as administrators, teachers, and counselors.
4. **Obtain informed consent from the parents or guardians.** Informed consent involves giving specific information about a group so that both the participant and the parent or guardian can make an intelligent decision about whether to participate. (Morganett also provides a sample parent/guardian consent form.)
5. **Conduct pregroup interviews.** In addition to giving a general orientation to the group experience, the purposes of this interview are to ask for the student's commitment and to obtain information that will be useful in making decisions about whom to admit.
6. **Select the group members.** Selections will be largely determined by the purpose of the group. It is the leader's responsibility to choose members who have a good chance of having a positive experience and to screen out those applicants who may not be appropriate for a particular group.
7. **Administer a pretest.** The practice of giving pretests and posttests can provide a framework for assessing the degree to which an individual or the group as a whole has benefited from the experience. (Morganett provides examples of pretests and posttests.)
8. **Conduct the group sessions.** The length of the group can be determined by the group's topic or theme. In most school settings, 8 to 12 sessions are optimum. Morganett provides detailed descriptions of ways to organize group agendas around the following themes:

- dealing with a divorce
- meeting, making, and keeping friends
- learning to communicate assertively
- developing self-esteem
- learning stress-management skills
- learning anger-management skills
- surviving and succeeding in school
- coping with grief and loss

9. **Administer a posttest.** After the termination of a group (or at the final group session), it is a good practice to administer the pretest as a posttest instrument.

10. **Conduct a postgroup follow-up and evaluation.** One to two months after the final group session, schedule a follow-up meeting. This will allow members to share their accomplishments and relate the impact that the group has had on them. This is a good time to offer encouragement and provide referrals for further growth experiences. The follow-up meeting is also an excellent source for evaluating the outcomes of a group.

Description of an Adolescent Group

In this section we discuss ways of motivating the adolescent to become an active group participant and guidelines for conducting the sessions and keeping the meetings moving in a meaningful direction. We address dealing with resistance, facilitating action, using role playing, sustaining the interest of the group, and involving as many members as possible.

We use as an example our experiences as co-leaders of a weekly counseling group for adolescents. Our group consisted of students from a local high school. This was an experimental 15-week program, offered free to the school district and to the participating members. The members were expected to attend all the sessions, which were on Wednesday evenings from 7 to 9 for one semester. In addition to these 15 meetings we held one all-day ten-hour marathon. The group consisted of ten members, all of whom were there by choice. Most of the participants were functioning relatively well, so the focus of the group was developmental and preventive rather than remedial. In many respects the group became a personal-growth group. Members were encouraged to initiate discussions of matters important to them at that time in their life.

During the initial sessions we talked to the members about the need to specify group goals as well as individual ones. We devoted the beginning sessions to encouraging the participants to formulate their personal goals as concretely as possible. Contracts were useful in this respect. Some of the personal goals that members set were "to feel less self-conscious and more comfortable around members of the opposite sex," "to decide what to do after high school," "to learn to like myself better and to feel more self-confident," "to learn how to get along with my parents," "to learn ways of expressing anger without getting into trouble," "to feel less lonely and different," "to learn how to communicate what I really feel," "to learn how to be a part of a group and to be accepted by others," and "to figure out what my values really are." Most adolescents are struggling with these concerns, although they may state them in different words. One of our functions was to help members translate their goals into behaviors that they could practice inside and outside of the group.

Establishing Trust and Dealing with Resistance

At a point early in an adolescent group's history we might say something like: "We hope you will come to feel free enough to say in the group what you think and feel, without censoring or rehearsing. It is especially important that you talk about any fears you are having about being in this group. What do you imagine it would be like for you to talk about personal struggles with the people in this room? We hope this will become a place where you can reveal personal concerns and find, with the help of others, a way of recognizing, understanding, and perhaps resolving certain problems. Our aim is to create a climate in which you can feel that what you say is important and that you're respected for who you are. The value of the sessions depends on your level of commitment. If you merely show up and listen, you are likely to leave disappointed. We'd like you to think about what you want from each session. These sessions are aimed at exploring any topics that you bring to the group. There may be times when you will be uncomfortable in here, and we encourage you to take the risk of talking about your discomfort. You are likely to discover that the atmosphere in this group differs from many other social settings. It is our expectation that you will be honest with yourself and with others in this group."

As a part of the discussion in an initial session, we also make sure to cover issues such as confidentiality, group norms, ground rules, ways to get involved in the group, how to give and receive feedback, and suggestions for applications outside of the group. (For other topics that we typically explore during the early phase of a group as a way of generating trust, refer to the discussion in Chapter 4 on the initial stage.)

Remember that many of the freedoms a group offers typically do not exist for adolescents in their daily life. Their teachers may not be interested in their personal views or concerns, the atmosphere of their school may be one of oppression and control, and their parents may not hear what they say or appreciate them as young adults. We've found that adolescents will test us to determine whether we mean what we've told them about the group. How we respond to their testing tells the members how much they can trust us as group leaders. If we accept their testing in a nonjudgmental and nondefensive way and resist giving lectures about how they should be, we progress a long way toward gaining their acceptance. We've found that adolescents are quick to detect phoniness (as well as sincerity) and that practicing what we preach is the surest way to earn their respect and to generate an atmosphere of trust in the group.

Working with Involuntary and Resistant Adolescents

Although the group we have described consisted of voluntary members, many groups are composed of court-referred or school-referred clients. In working with adolescents who are reluctant to participate, we have found some of the following interventions helpful, and we suggest that you consider how these ideas could be applied to some groups you may lead or co-lead.

First of all, much of the resistance of adolescents to participating in a group can be effectively explored by meeting first with them individually. At this meeting you can find out about their reservations, give them specific information about the group, and in a nondefensive way explore their negative attitudes and provide them an opportunity to express their reactions to being "forced" into the group. You can also point out to them that they *did* make a choice to come to the group. They could have refused and then taken the consequences of not complying with the directive. During the individual pregroup meeting it is helpful to explore any of the adolescent's past experiences with therapy. You can do a lot to demystify the process by providing accurate information about the goals of a group, your role as a group leader, and other considerations that we discussed in Chapters 2 and 3.

Another way to work with uncooperative adolescents is to go *with* resistance, rather than fighting *against* it, and to attempt to work out alternatives to a group. One example of such an option is to continue seeing these adolescents individually for a number of sessions to establish a relationship with them before putting them in a group. You might also invite them to join the group for three sessions and to make a sincere effort to participate. Then if they are still reluctant, allow them to leave. The rationale for this strategy is that these adolescents will have some basis for a decision after they have been to a few group sessions. Even though they were directed to "get counseling," this is one way to provide some increased element of choice. Because forced therapy would only entrench negative attitudes, the leader may genuinely be able to help them find another solution.

Another alternative is to invite a skeptical adolescent to attend the group for a session or so without any pressure to participate. It is important to let the other members know that this person is an observer, there to determine if he or she wants to continue. They are less likely to resent the nonparticipant, and they can let this person know whether they themselves have overcome resistance to being in the group.

Adolescents who attend a session involuntarily often show their resistance through sarcasm and silence. It is important to respond not with defensiveness but with honesty, firmness, and caring confrontations. Assume that Darren says "I don't want to be here!" Examples of unhelpful responses are: "Look, I don't want to be here either." "Well, if you don't like being here, leave." "I don't care what you want. You're here, and I expect you to participate." "Life is tough. We don't always get what we want." Obviously, these leader responses are very defensive and do not invite an exploration of resistance; nor do they encourage the will to participate. What follows are some other interactions between Darren and the leader.

> **Leader** (in a nondefensive tone): How come you don't want to be here?
> **Darren:** They sent me, and I don't need this group.
> **Leader:** I know it's difficult doing something that you don't want to do. I don't like it when people tell me what to do either. So tell me a bit more what it's like for you to be here.

Rather than responding too quickly in a defensive manner, the leader asks for more information in order to understand Darren's resistance. Instead of getting into a debate over whether he needs the group, the leader accepts his immediate feelings and makes them the focus of discussion. There are many appropriate responses to his reluctance, a few of which are:

- "How about if you come to the group twice to see what this is about and then decide if you want to continue?"
- "A lot of the members in the group felt the same way you do. Maybe they could tell you what it was like for them."
- "Do you know anything about counseling? Have you ever participated in a group before?"
- "Why do you think you were sent here?"
- "I understand that you don't want to be here. Are there consequences if you choose not to attend?"

It is essential to follow the adolescent's lead and go with the resistance, instead of fighting it or taking it personally. If you were a leader who was the recipient of this resistance, you might feel personally rejected. But it is essential not to get bogged down in feeling useless and unappreciated. You cannot afford the luxury of feeling vulnerable to rejection. Taking as a personal affront all the abrasiveness and defensiveness that some adolescents display is a quick route to burnout.

We are not suggesting that you give resistant adolescents permission to verbally abuse you. It is possible to stand up for yourself in a direct and nondefensive way. If an involuntary client taunts you with "You're a phony, and you're only in it for the money," it is not helpful to lash out and then proceed to defend your altruistic bent and your dedication to helping others. Doing this can easily lead to becoming entangled in countertransference. An alternative response could be: "I don't like being called a phony by you. We've just met, and you don't have enough information about me to make that judgment. I'd like to have a chance with you before you dismiss me." This is an example of speaking for oneself and keeping the lines of communication open.

One of our colleagues, Paul Jacobson, works with imprisoned young gang members who are ordered into counseling by the court. Paul has conducted a variety of groups for this involuntary population, including emancipation groups, groups for youthful sex offenders, drug-education groups, groups for teenage fathers, groups for those who chronically fail to conform to the rules of the residential facility, and groups for both perpetrators and victims of abuse. After he read about our high school group, he commented about how foreign our experience sounded compared with his experience with his adolescent population. He finds that his clients lack both insight and sophistication in expressing their thoughts and feelings. Another striking contrast is that their motivation for self-exploration is very low. His involuntary clients typically approach counseling with skepticism, doubt, and hostility. They do not believe that what occurs in a group can be applied to themselves and their life situation. In working with this difficult population, Paul has formulated some useful suggestions:

- Modify your expectations. Understand the client's world, which may be foreign to your life experience.
- Learn to accept subtle behavioral changes.
- Don't be blocked or put off by the client's abrasive language, especially if the client is cooperating behaviorally.
- Be aware of setting limits and establishing boundaries that may differ from individual to individual.
- Earn trust by being honest and direct in your reactions to clients personally.
- Find ways of supporting the expression of clients' feelings without necessarily approving of destructive actions.
- Be aware of your own motivations for choosing to work with a difficult population.
- Realize that the rewards may not be dramatic and that you may not often have the satisfaction of knowing that you have made a difference in a person's life.

In working with highly resistant adolescents, Paul continually reevaluates his goals and reflects on the issues mentioned above. He knows that it is essential to pay attention to the impact that his work has on him personally and to take preventive measures against the ever-present threat of burnout.

The Influence of the Leader's Personality

Our experience with adolescents continues to teach us how great an influence the personality of the group leader has on the evolution of the group. We find that adolescents respond well to a willingness to share oneself with the group, a caring attitude, enthusiasm and vitality, openness, and directness. Counselors are likely to learn that the respect they expect because of their title or position may not be forthcoming. Instead of relying on professional accomplishments or techniques, effective counselors know the value of using themselves as a therapeutic instrument.

Adolescents learn from watching the behavior that you model, but your behavior doesn't have to be perfect in order for them to benefit. In fact, adolescents will generally relate well to you if you appropriately reveal your personal experiences or concerns. If you genuinely respect and enjoy adolescents, you will typically be rewarded with a reciprocal respect.

Adolescents will also be aware if you have never fully experienced your adolescence or if you have some major unfinished business from those years that gets in your way as a leader. For example, an adult who has never faced or resolved certain adolescent fears related to sexuality or lovability may find these fears resurfacing as he or she leads an adolescent group. For this reason, it is crucial that those who lead adolescent groups be willing and courageous enough to explore, and perhaps relive, much of their own adolescent experience so that it will not interfere with their work with adolescents or so that they won't become enmeshed in countertransference.

In addition, adolescents may be psychologically threatening to adults, for they are full of energy, are often free from major responsibilities, have the capacity to have fun and experience joy, and are able to feel intensely. Leaders may feel that they have lost some of these lively qualities. They may be faced for the first time with the facts of their aging and their loss of the capacity to savor life. Such leaders can prevent the growth of resentment by first accepting the fact of their aging and then looking for new meaning and excitement in their life.

We think it is wise to avoid trying to become "one of the gang." Because you want to win their approval, for instance, you might imitate the slang and manner of speaking of adolescents. Young people will be quick to detect your insincerity if you use expressions to impress them and to give the appearance of being "with it." Because of trying too hard to become accepted, you may have difficulty gaining the adolescents' trust and respect. You would do well to remember that you hold a different position from theirs and that they usually expect you to act differently. If you are powerful but don't use your power to control and stifle members, the chances are that they will treat you with respect.

Finally, our experience with adolescents has taught us that we have the most influence on them when we are attempting to be in our life what we are encouraging them to become. This does not mean that in order to be effective we must be ideal people whom the members can imitate. Rather, it means that we are most effective when the members feel that we practice what we preach.

Keeping the Sessions Moving

In our weekly adolescent group a valuable skill was keeping the sessions going, which we accomplished mainly by helping the members speak for themselves in concrete terms. This was not an easy task, primarily because it was a challenge to get the participants to focus on themselves in the here and now. Especially in a beginning adolescent group, members have a tendency to tell stories endlessly, going into every detail yet going nowhere. When we listen to a member who is losing our attention because of wordiness, we may say something like: "I'd like to understand you, but I'm getting lost with all the details. Why is your story important at this moment in this group?" It is sometimes useful to say to a member after a long-winded story "If I allowed you only one sentence to express what you have just said, what would it be?" A detailed story that bores others could be simply stated as "I sometimes resent my girlfriend for the way she treats me!" Our task is to teach members to express themselves in personal and concrete ways and to steer them away from telling irrelevant stories.

Using Personal Statements. We have asked members to try to say how they were affected by a situation rather than how other people acted toward them. For instance, Carol began by talking about how she felt misunderstood by her mother. She started to tell stories about her mother, blaming her for her unhappiness, and focused on her mother's feelings. One of us remarked: "You seem to be talking more about your mother right now than about yourself. Why not tell us how you're affected by your mother's behavior?"

Another dynamic that commonly keeps a group from reaching a productive level is one member bombarding another with questions instead of making a personal statement. When such questioning occurs, it is appropriate for the group leader to make a comment such as "Marco, instead of questioning Charlene, tell her what it was that provoked you to ask the question." Unless the questioning is stopped in this way, the intensity of Charlene's emotional experience may soon be dissipated. The leader can try to prevent this from happening by stressing that it is far better for members to say how they are affected by someone's emotional experience and in what ways they're identifying with the person than to distract the member with questions.

Teaching members how to share themselves through statements rather than questioning is more effective when it's done in a timely, appropriate, and sensitive manner as certain behaviors or interactions are occurring in the session. If members experience the intimidation of being bombarded by questions, they are receptive to learning alternative behaviors.

Structuring Sessions. We favor active intervention and structuring for adolescent groups, particularly during the initial stage. Some structuring can provide the direction needed to keep the sessions moving. It might involve specifying a theme or topic for the group to deal with. Such topics should be related to the interests and needs of the adolescents and not merely be issues the leader feels are important, such as "How can you improve your study habits?" "What can be done to reduce the absentee rate in classrooms?" "How can you learn to respect your teachers?" The group may well have little interest in these topics, and the sessions are bound to bog down.

In our adolescent group we developed themes with the participants during the sessions. We didn't say "Since this is your group, what do you want to talk about?" Instead, we structured by limiting the choices somewhat, saying: "In working with groups like this, we have found that certain themes are of concern to most young people. A few of these are 'What do I want from my life, and what is stopping me from getting it?' 'Can I be who I am and be sincerely accepted by my parents?' 'How can I better understand my feelings of loneliness?' 'How am I like other people?' 'How can I deal with others more effectively?' These are only a few of the topics that we might consider. Every group moves in its own direction. What, in particular, would each of you like to see us focus on in this group?"

A general agenda for the next session can be decided on at the end of each meeting. Flexibility should be built into the structuring, though, for members will often spontaneously bring up pressing problems that are not related to the scheduled theme, and this deviation from the plan can be very fruitful. A theme, like an interaction exercise, is only a means to the end of involving the members in meaningful group work. It is important that topics or techniques not become ends in themselves. Our adolescent group once planned, at the end of a session, to deal with a certain theme the next week. However, a classmate of the group members committed suicide the night before the next session, and the group was preoccupied with him. The session was devoted to exploring the effect that this tragedy was having on each group member, and the topic of death was explored in a very personal way.

Action-Oriented Techniques of Role Playing

In our adolescent groups we usually rely heavily on action-oriented methods, especially role playing. We find that role playing is an excellent way to keep the interest level high, to involve a lot of the members, and to give a here-and-now flavor to the work being done. Role playing fosters creative problem solving, encourages spontaneity, usually intensifies feelings, and gets people to identify with others. By role playing, participants can learn how to express themselves more effectively. They can test reality and practice new behavior.

If members are well prepared for action-oriented techniques, then Gestalt and psychodramatic methods can bring vitality to the sessions. For instance, if Scott is complaining about how his girlfriend, Dawn, treats him, he can be asked to imagine that she is sitting in an empty chair and to tell her how he feels. If appropriate, another member can "sit in" for Dawn and carry on a dialogue with Scott. Scott might "become Dawn" and tell everyone in the group what she thinks of Scott; this could be useful in helping him stand in her shoes. Through such action-oriented techniques, more feelings are elicited, and boring stories are minimized. Members also get a chance to say out loud things that they have kept inside. Through role reversal, they can gain empathy for others in their life.

We've found that it helps members become comfortable with role playing more quickly if we participate at first. For instance, if a girl has been describing how she views her parents and how frustrated she feels when she tries to talk with them, we might take the part of her mother and father. That will allow her to deal directly, albeit symbolically, with her parents and feel her frustration intensely. We can then stop the action and ask her: "What are you experiencing now? What would you most like to do now? If you could reach us, make us really hear you, what would you most want to say?" The role playing may be brief. When it's over, the person should discuss the experience and plan how to handle this situation when it arises in the future.

Adolescents are often self-conscious about getting involved in role playing. It is useful to provide a general orientation to the techniques you employ, which could be done at a pregroup session. Both the timing and manner of introducing techniques are directly related to whether adolescents are likely to cooperate. When an adoelscent says he or she would feel silly in role playing, you might respond with "I know it seems silly and a bit awkward, but how about trying it anyway and seeing what you might learn about yourself?" Or you could say "I know it seems silly, but who says we always have to be serious?" Generally, if we approach role playing in this light and gentle way, the resistance dissipates, and before the participant knows it, he or she is playing a role with gusto. We check frequently to see whether a person wants to explore a particular problem and is willing to use role playing to do so. One of us might say: "You seem to be unclear about how your mother really affects you and how you should deal with her. Are you willing to try something?"

There are many variations of role-playing techniques. To illustrate, we'll use the example of Sally, who discloses that she feels she can never please her father and that this hurts her. She says that she and her father are not close and that she would like to change that. She is afraid of her father, for she sees him as critical of her, and she feels that unless she is perfect, she cannot win his approval. Several role-playing situations are possible:

- Sally can play her father, to provide a picture of how she perceives him. We can ask her to give Sally a long lecture and tell her all the things that she must become before she is worthwhile in his eyes. Speaking as her father, Sally might say something like: "I know you have a lot more ability than you show. Why didn't you get all "A"s?

Yes, I'm proud of you for getting five "A"s, but I must confess I'm let down by that one "B." If you really put your mind to it, I know you could do better." We would encourage her to stay in her father's role for a time and say things that she imagines he is thinking but not expressing.

- A group member who identifies with Sally can play her while Sally continues playing her father. From the dialogue that ensues, Sally can get an idea of how her father feels with her. A group member with a similar conflict can benefit from involvement in the situation.
- A member who feels that he or she can identify with the father can play that role. If nobody in the group jumps at this opportunity, the leader can take the parent role. This situation allows Sally to intensify her feelings and to demonstrate how she deals with her father. As the role playing continues, she may achieve insight into herself that will help her make some changes.
- Sally can play both herself and her father. She can be directed to say (as her father) what she wishes he would say to her. This is a future projection, and it taps the person's hopes.
- Sally can present a soliloquy, talking aloud as her father, saying what she imagines her father might say about her. She can also use the soliloquy approach when she is in her own role, after she finishes an exchange with her father. She can express many of the thoughts and feelings she generally keeps locked within herself when she talks with her father.
- Several other group members can sit in for Sally and show how they would deal with her father. This may suggest to her options she hadn't thought of.
- Other members who role-played Sally's father can provide helpful feedback to her by telling her what they felt as they were listening to her. She may be less defensive in hearing from her peers about how they were put off by her abrasive style than if an adult provided this feedback.

Because it is important for members to process these dramas, the leader should ask them to think about the implications of what they observed in themselves in the role-playing situations. At this time feedback from other members and interpretations from the leader can enable the members to see with more clarity their own part in their conflicts with others and what they can do to make life better for themselves. (If you are interested in a more in-depth discussion of role-playing techniques in groups, refer to Chapter 8 ("Psychodrama") and Chapter 11 ("Gestalt Therapy") in G. Corey (1990).

Getting Group Members to Participate and Initiate

During the sessions we look for many ways of bringing uninvolved group members into the interactions. After Sally's role playing, for example, we might encourage other members to tell what they experienced as she was working with her father. We might ask: "Can any of you give Sally feedback? What did you see her doing? Did she spark any feelings in you?" Adolescents are usually most eager to become personally involved when other members touch vulnerable spots in them. As we've mentioned, one real advantage of group counseling is that the members can be of service to their peers by giving their perceptions, revealing similar problems, suggesting alternatives, supporting them in times of despair, reflecting what they hear them saying, and confronting their inconsistencies.

Therefore, we try to involve as many members as possible in the group process. In addition, we try to shape the group so that we will be less and less required to give direction. One of the signs of an effective group is that members gradually assume an increasing share of the leadership functions. For instance, if a group that usually functions effectively begins to stray aimlessly, a member will probably point this out. If a group member gets bogged down in storytelling and intellectualizing, we expect members to react. In short, one of our aims is to teach adolescents to monitor themselves in their group and become less dependent on us for direction.

The Use of Peer Counselors

Peer counselors can be used both in the classroom in human-relations courses and as a part of the outreach program of the school's counseling and guidance program. Given proper training and supervision, peers can often be as effective in reaching fellow students as counselors or teachers.

An important consideration in using peer counselors is teaching them the boundaries of their competence. There is a strong possibility that peer counselors will become deeply involved in others' lives. They can play a supportive role, they can challenge fellow students to evaluate their behavior honestly, and they can share their own life experiences and learning with others. But they are not qualified to render psychotherapy. Thus, it is critical that peer counselors learn how to function as liaisons so that students who need professional assistance can get it.

For instance, a counselor we know commented that her groups explored the issue of adolescent suicide. Many of her counselees experience depression and alienation, and some are suicide-prone. A number use drugs and alcohol heavily, to the point that this abuse has interfered with their life. It is essential for peer counselors to know the agencies to which to refer students who need further professional assistance. A valuable skill is being able to present information to young people in such a manner that they are likely to accept a referral in those situations that call for it.

Finally, in working with adolescents in personal areas, it is important for both counselors and their peer counselors to learn how to set personal limits so that they do not become burned out. For example, adolescents can easily become dependent on an adult or a peer counselor whom they respect and have affection for. Counselors who make it a practice to say "Here is my phone number, and don't hesitate to call whenever you'd like" are likely to find themselves swamped by demands and not able to live up to what they promised. To remain effective in working with young people, the counselor must recognize personal limitations and take care to ensure that resentment does not build up over constantly being asked to help others in crisis situations.

Involving Parents

Parent-Consultation Groups

Leaders of adolescent groups are potentially valuable as consultants both to parents and to teachers. It is essential to demonstrate sensitivity toward parents who may feel defensive over being perceived as inadequate mothers or fathers. They may feel anxious about the group but could experience relief in learning that other parents share their feelings and difficulties.

Most parents care about their children. Yet most go through a period when they would like to "divorce" their adolescent, for the possibility of any real communication seems remote. Like their adolescent children, parents need some assistance. They need more than general information about parent/adolescent relationships or methods of control. They need to talk about their feelings of inadequacy, guilt, resentment, and rejection. Many feel deeply unappreciated and believe that no matter how sincerely they try to improve relations at home, things won't get better. A consultation group can give parents a chance to express some of their frustration and ambivalence. A good group leader can sensitize parents to the dynamics of adolescence and widen their perspectives, and they can raise questions and bring up problems that they would like to discuss with other parents and the leader.

Programs can also be designed for those willing to invest time and energy in becoming better parents. Many group leaders offer parent-effectiveness-training groups. Such groups can be held at the local high school or at one of the parent's homes one evening a week. Parents in such groups are encouraged to read books and discuss them in the group. (See the suggested readings at the end of this chapter.) Role playing gives parents a chance to examine their relationships with their children and experiment with new, more effective behaviors

Groups of Parents and Adolescents

Groups of adolescents and their parents, or multiple-family groups, are usually conducted in psychiatric hospitals, residential treatment centers, or community clinics. They are primarily adjuncts to other methods of treatment in which the adolescent is usually the identified patient. One of our colleagues, Paul Jacobson, who is a licensed marriage and family therapist, has had experience in leading multiple-family groups in several agencies. He has found this format exciting because of its possibilities for creatively combining family therapy with more traditional group work. In his groups he has had from as few as two families (with four parents and four children) to as many as five different families (with a total of about 15 individuals). His groups typically meet weekly for 90 minutes. The groups are open, in that the membership changes periodically. What follows are some of Paul's observations about the values of combined parent/adolescent groups.

Theoretically, such a group can be thought of in three ways: as composed of discrete family units; as two subgroups, one of adolescents and another of parents; or as a group of individuals. All are occurring simultaneously and are developing throughout the various stages of the group. The facilitator needs to be aware of these different subgroups and the impact of them on the unfolding of the group interactions. For example, members of the adolescent subgroup may have contact with one another outside of the group (such as in a hospital or residential facility) and may consequently be more familiar, comfortable, and less guarded with one another than the parent subgroup, which may meet only infrequently. A minimal level of trust needs to be developed within the parental subgroup, whereas some basis for trust may already exist with the adolescents.

This process of differential rates of building trust is probably also reflected within each family. Parents are usually more reticent in discussing their own difficulties than they are in talking about the problems of their children. By initially focusing on parent/child difficulties, the leader can largely bypass parental resistance and defensiveness. Eventually, many parents become more willing to accept some of the responsibility for the problems between their child and themselves. Because the parents are not the focus of treatment, however, the main goal is improving skills in communication, problem solving, and parenting.

This type of group also enhances the treatment of adolescent populations that are not usually amenable to traditional counseling. The majority of adolescent problems involve parent/child conflicts, inappropriate conduct, or other behavioral difficulties. These adolescents frequently do not feel the need for relief through counseling, and they tend to resist this process. If skillfully conducted, these groups can lead to a family discussion of issues that are usually avoided. Furthermore, groups can be instrumental in modifying underlying tensions, attitudes, and motivations for acting-out behaviors.

Many adolescents present an entirely different demeanor to others than they do to their parents. This tendency can be used in a group for therapeutic gain. For example:

- If parents tolerate extreme rudeness from their daughter but observe her being polite to other adults in the group, they may then alter their own expectations.
- If parents view their son at home in highly negative ways, they could be looking for data to support their negativity. But if they observe their child being helpful or supportive within the group, they may alter their perceptions.
- If an adolescent girl can communicate in an adult manner with other parents in the group, she can generalize this skill to avoid the explosive temper she displays with her own parents.
- If an adolescent boy uses passive/avoidance silence, his parents can view how others may respond to this style and develop new options for relating to him.

Another advantage of combining families is that the leader can teach parenting skills. Unlike the traditional lecture approach to parent education, which usually falls on deaf ears, the group format can provide lessons in how to deal more effectively with problems by discussing them with others. At these times, the parents are more receptive to assistance and can be guided toward practicing new skills within the group and then trying them at home. In traditional parent education, the focus is often on learning techniques that may not take the underlying problems into full consideration. A group process that involves all parties, in contrast, can bring about significant learning that changes styles of interaction.

It takes considerable skill and sensitivity to keep group meetings that involve parents and adolescents from degenerating into gripe sessions. The leader needs to focus on both parents and teenagers learning how to listen with understanding. The group can be kept small, especially if the leader has not led such a group before. Before facilitating multiple-family groups, it is necessary to gain some education, training, and supervision in family therapy. Groups of parents and adolescents have the potential for improving relationships at home, especially if contracts are formed that include both parents' and adolescents' taking specific steps toward agreed-on changes.

If you have an interest in discussing Jacobson's work with multiple-family groups, you can write him: Paul Jacobson, P. O. Box 2352, Idyllwild, CA 92349; telephone: (714) 659-4484.

Groups for Children of Alcoholics

Who Are Children of Alcoholics?

Counselors in many schools are offering groups for young people who have grown up in an alcoholic family. Many high school students are themselves struggling with substance-abuse problems or are in a program following alcohol or drug rehabilitation. Groups can be therapeutic for this population.

Children raised in alcoholic families enter adolescence with strategies for survival that worked to some degree in their childhood years. But at this time in their lives, these coping strategies may be costly in terms of their psychological health and well-being. Over the years they have refined certain behaviors, such as being superresponsible, adjusting, or placating as well as not talking, not trusting, and not feeling. When they grow up, most adult children of alcoholics (sometimes referred to as "ACAs") continue to struggle with problems related to trust, dependency, control, identification, and expression of feelings.

In her research and therapeutic work, Black (1987) has found that these adults often act out the same three roles they played as children. First is the role of *being superresponsible*. Children who miss out on their childhood by having to mature early often take on household and parenting responsibilities for other siblings. When structure and consistency are not provided, these children provide it for themselves. They rely completely on themselves, for they have learned many times over that they cannot count on their parents. Second is the role of the *adjuster*, who makes an early decision that "because I can't do anything about the family situation, I'll adjust to it." As children, adjusters become detached; as adults, they have no sense of self, they are not autonomous, and they typically feel that they have few choices. Third is the role of the *placater*, who has become skilled at listening and providing empathy. Placaters have a difficult time in dealing with their own feelings. For example, if they cry, they tend to cry alone.

It is best not to treat people according to any label, including labels such as "ACAs" or "codependents," as well as "responsible ones," "adjusters," or "placaters." Instead of thinking of rigid categories that box people in, it is better to consider certain general patterns of learned behavior. These roles evolve from childhood and follow one into adulthood. As children, for example, placaters busy themselves by taking care of others; as adults, they often become professional helpers, carrying the pain of others. Yet if they don't attend to their own needs and feelings, they eventually burn out. They have a difficult time in asking for what they need for themselves, and in their personal relationships they tend to seek out others who are takers.

In *It Will Never Happen to Me!* Black (1987) vividly portrays the life histories of adult children of alcoholics. We have adapted much of the material in this section from her book. She discusses three central familial injunctions that she detects over and over in her work with these clients: "Don't talk," "Don't trust," and "Don't feel."

In the "Don't talk" message, children are conditioned not to discuss real issues in the family but to ignore these problems in the hope that the hurt will go away. They learn not to rock the boat. The key dynamic is denial of the family secret of alcoholism. Of course, this injunction is challenged by the very nature of the group format. It can be therapeutic for these young people simply to share the secret that they have been burdened with for so long. Because the entire group is composed of people who are struggling with the same pain of denial and not talking, the group atmosphere can represent a significant turning point.

In the case of the "Don't trust" message, adult children of alcoholics learn always to be on guard, to rely on themselves, and not to trust others with their feelings. In alcoholic homes children learn that their parents are not consistently available and cannot be relied on for safety. Unfortunately, they carry this pattern of not trusting into their adulthood. Again, the group affords opportunities for taking the risk of trusting both peers and an adult leader. They can potentially learn that their family's lack of trustworthiness does not necessarily imply that the rest of the world is not to be trusted.

In the "Don't feel" message, children develop a denial system to numb their feelings. To bring stability and consistency to their lives, they acquire coping mechanisms. They learn not to share what they feel, because they are convinced that their feelings will not be validated within their family. Gradually, they build walls for protecting themselves from a feared world. They learn to deny and discount their feelings, they hide their pain, and they do not express what is inside of them. This process of denial is interfering with their emotional and social lives as adolescents, and the pattern will most likely continue into adulthood unless there is a therapeutic intervention. A group can encourage these young people to at least begin talking about the fortress they have built around themselves. The group also provides them with a place to share their pain of isolation instead of continuing to hide it. Through the support and encouragement within the group, they learn that they *can* feel and that they are not alone.

A High School Group for Children of Alcoholics

The following section describes a counseling group designed for high school students living with a family member who has a problem with alcohol or other drugs. Deborah Lambert is a coordinator of a student assistance program at North Allegheny Senior High School in Pennsylvania. She works with Nancy Ceraso English, an education specialist with expertise in chemical dependency, to provide weekly support to students from dysfunctional families.

Practical Considerations

The groups are limited to ten students and are offered to students aged 16 to 18. This curriculum has also been used with students of 14 to 16 at North Allegheny Intermediate School. The length of the weekly sessions is one class period, typically 40 minutes. Two facilitators work together to provide a blend of academic and mental-health expertise. The co-leaders explain that the groups do not offer counseling per se but that therapeutic gains can occur. They also emphasize the importance of going to Al-Anon, Al-Ateen, Alcoholics Anonymous (AA), Narcotics Anonymous (NA), or other community groups that will provide the students with additional tools and opportunities to practice sharing. The ground rules for confidentiality are presented and clarified. No one is permitted to share any information outside of the group. The only exceptions pertain to suspected child abuse or suicidal ideation.

Letters are sent home letting the parents know what the school is offering. There is typically a lot of secrecy associated with addicted families, and the co-leaders do not want to perpetuate the cycle of concealment. Before letters are sent, one of the counselors sits down with students who have been recruited to join and clarifies the group's purpose. Students see a copy of the letter so they know that the co-leaders are encouraging open communication. The letter would not be sent home if a student were anxious about the outcome.

Group Goals

The aims of the group are to:

- learn how chemical dependency affects *all* family members
- learn alternatives to chemical use
- talk about our feelings and how they can help or hurt us
- meet with others who have had similar experiences
- have a safe place where confidential matters can be shared
- learn about codependent behaviors
- learn about the addiction process
- learn about community resources

Following is a typical format for meeting these goals in the group:

SESSION 1: GROUP INTRODUCTION

- Members introduce themselves and participate in the establishing of group rules—for example, everyone is expected to participate, students are expected to make up missed class work and assignments, it is good to speak for oneself, members should strive to be honest about their thoughts and feelings, and confidentiality is observed.
- Members explore the purpose of the group.
- Members identify the problem of addiction in their life.

SESSION 2: THE IMPACT OF ADDICTION ON THE FAMILY

- Members share how a family member's addiction has affected their life.
- On an easel board, the members list all possible consequences when a family member is addicted.

SESSION 3: INTRODUCING ADDICTION

- The co-facilitators discuss the progressive disease of addiction.
- Members draw a picture of a time when they were sick.
- After members share their pictures, the co-leaders introduce more facts about the disease of addiction as it parallels or differs from their pictures.

SESSION 4: "MY FEELINGS ABOUT ADDICTION"

- Members share their feelings as they relate to a family member's addiction.
- Members think up as many "feeling words" as they can, and the co-leader puts these words on the easel board.
- Members are asked the question "What does it feel like when someone in the family is addicted?"

SESSION 5: THE ADDICTED PARENT

- Members talk about the behaviors that accompany addiction.
- Members draw a picture of the worst thing that has happened because of a family member's addiction.

SESSION 6: THE ADDICTED PARENT (CONTINUED)

- Members view a film or television show depicting an alcoholic parent.
- At various points in the film or video it is turned off to allow for discussing the reality of the situation.
- Time is allotted for open dialogue and sharing of the members' situations.

SESSION 7: THE RECOVERING PARENT

- The co-facilitators explain the process of recovery and the dynamics of relapse.
- Members complete a handout and discuss the internal and external factors contributing to a relapse of their loved ones into addiction.

SESSION 8: CODEPENDENCY

- Members are sensitized to the nonaddictive parent's predicament.
- The group lists behaviors typically associated with codependency.
- Members make a collage representing their own codependent tendencies.

SESSION 9: ROLES

- The co-facilitators discuss the roles that generally characterize children of alcoholics.

- Members fill out a handout on how they've assumed these roles at different stages in their life.

SESSION 10: COPING AND HOPING

- Members select a card from a special deck, the "Problems Pack," and either talk about or role-play how they would feel and what they would do in each problem situation. Examples are as follows:
  a. It is very late, and your parent is not home from the bar.
  b. You need help with your homework, but your parent tells you "Sorry, I have to go to an AA meeting."
  c. You are in a car with a drunken driver.
- Each member receives an updated listing of community resources and a schedule of the various support-group meetings.
- Students are encouraged to go alone, with a friend, or with the group to an Al-Ateen or Al-Anon meeting.

SESSION 11: SELF-AFFIRMATIONS

- Students learn to avoid negative self-talk and to make statements about themselves that increase their self-esteem.
- In small groups, each member shares one or two self-criticisms and changes them into affirmations.

SESSION 12: GOOD THOUGHTS, GOOD FEELINGS, AND GOOD-BYES

- The members talk about what the group has meant.
- One member sits in the center and receives positive feedback on his or her contributions.
- Each student gets an index card for listing phone numbers from the group.
- Students are asked to fill out a two-page questionnaire on the group process. This activity is optional.

Outcomes of the Group

Written and verbal responses from members consistently reflect positive feelings, attitudes, and experiences. The four areas of praise highlighted in all the evaluations are peer support; validation of thoughts, feelings, and experiences; exchange of practical and timely suggestions; and the opportunity to experience trust and intimacy. Some recommendations for changes include longer and more frequent sessions and additional specialty groups, such as ones dealing with divorce, family violence, and sexual abuse.

Parents of participating members have given their support. The teachers of participating members have routinely provided updates on the members' academic progress. Teachers have tended to be positive in backing the group. Administrators have offered continuing support, which has promoted effective outcomes.

Rewards and Frustrations

Some of the rewards for the co-leaders are:

- participating in and witnessing students' personal growth
- sharing in the relief that accompanies personal disclosures
- observing members gain insight into their codependent behaviors and their attempts to correct them
- helping members establish and maintain contact with one another
- fostering and restoring playfulness in members

  Some of the frustrations the co-leaders have experienced are:

- facing members' hesitancy to seek out community supports such as Al-Ateen and Al-Anon
- seeing the consequences of family dysfunction continue after members leave the group

Aftercare: A Group for Students following Drug Rehabilitation

In addition to the groups just described, Deborah Lambert and Nancy Ceraso English offer a support group for students who are coming out of drug rehabilitation. If you would like to contact them to discuss these groups, write them at North Allegheny High School, 10375 Perry Highway, Wexford, PA 15090; telephone: (412) 934-7260. Or contact English at 6932 Bishop Street, Pittsburgh, PA 15206-1128.

Group Overview

Because drug rehabilitation is a lifelong process, the school offers a continuing support group. The leaders meet with the students weekly and design rules and review the goals of the group. They try to obtain releases of information from the treatment facility so they can complement the student's already prescribed aftercare plan.

Counselors, teachers, students, and administrators all refer high school students to the group. The leaders also advertise in the school newspaper so everyone is aware that support groups are available to students. (See Chapter 3 for a description of the procedures used to identify and recruit group members.) They strongly urge students to continue with their AA, NA, therapy, or other aftercare groups.

The goals of the group are for the members to:

- learn about chemical dependency, relapse, and recovery
- focus on school-related issues
- talk about successes and problems associated with recovery
- practice sharing in a safe place
- learn about healthy alternatives to chemicals

- communicate with other students and community groups
- enjoy fellowship with others having similar experiences

A Format for Aftercare

The groups are run for one period a week for the entire school year. Lambert and English have provided a sample of the sessions.

SESSION 1: GROUP INTRODUCTION

- Members introduce themselves and brainstorm to create a list of appropriate group rules and guidelines.
- The co-facilitators describe the purpose of the group.

SESSION 2: THEIR OWN ADDICTION

- Students review the rules and the issue of confidentiality.
- Members provide a chronology of their abuse of drugs.
- Students share with the group some of their background of addiction.

SESSION 3: SAFEGUARDS FOR SPECIAL EVENTS

- The co-leaders discuss issues and hazards associated with holidays and school-sponsored events such as dances, football games, and proms.
- Students compile a list of "relapse signals."

SESSION 5: REVIEW OF RECOVERY

- Students review their academic behavior and their attendance at AA or NA.
- Students discuss their worries and fears.

SESSION 10: RELAPSE

- Discussion focuses on a student's admission of a relapse. The group talks about relapse signals, which are typically ignored.
- Each student has the opportunity to say something positive and supportive.

SSESSION 30: FINAL GROUP

- The final session lasts all day. A young recovering addict from a nearby college can provide a lead. The group can meet at a nearby park for a picnic.
- Students have the chance to ask questions and share their own experiences.
- The lead speaker also talks about ways to protect sobriety during the summer vacation.
- Members have the chance to say their good-byes to one another.

Suggestions for Designing Aftercare Groups

Based on their experiences in designing and co-leading these aftercare groups, Lambert and English offer some pointers that may help others in setting up similar groups:

- Have a designated room and time. The time is best rotated at mid-semester or within each grading period, as opposed to more frequently.
- Have an established curriculum. Make it flexible to accommodate crises and special concerns of members.
- Prepare members for upcoming school functions and holidays that threaten sobriety.
- Have members give brief weekly updates on their sobriety, their attendance at AA or NA, and their aftercare agency in the community. Reinforce the effectiveness of AA, NA, and community aftercare groups.

Crisis-Oriented Groups for Adolescents

Adolescents are frequently left without the resources to cope with a short-term crisis in their school or community, such as a student's suicide or an automobile accident in which students are killed. Many school districts have set up crisis-intervention services, but the demand is likely to outstrip the limited supply of these resources. Weinberg (1990) describes small groups for meeting the needs of large numbers of high school students who are affected by a tragedy.

The group leader has been trained in crisis-intervention methods and is capable of identifying a student whose condition warrants outside referral. The groups consist of 4 to 12 students, and the session generally lasts about an hour. The small-group format allows the leaders to identify students who display acute reactions to a tragedy or those who may be at greater risk for more serious long-term effects. The ideal crisis-intervention group contains students who know one another, for this allows for a greater degree of interaction.

After the leader explains the purpose of the group, the students introduce themselves and describe where they were when they found out about the incident and how they reacted to it. Although the members are supported in their full expression of feelings, the leader typically attempts to have each person say something before the focus is given to a tearful student. The assumption is that the members will feel more included if all of them have had a chance to at least briefly say something. The students are encouraged to express their fears and sadness in these sessions. The leaders comment on the powerful source of support that exists within the group and encourages mutual aid. Because the leader will be present for only a short time in the group and because the members will be able to see one another after the sessions, attempts are made to promote this sense of mutual support.

These groups frequently focus on examining whether guilt may be compounding any of the students' problems. In cases of tragedies, people sometimes have regrets over what they have said or done or have failed to do. After the opportunity for expressing sadness, fear, and guilt, the focus of the discussion is on encouraging healthy coping behavior and acquiring various problem-solving strategies. For example, one student described the internal struggle that he had experienced after the death of a friend. Although he was very sad, he was embarrassed to express this feeling openly, because his socialization had led him to believe that men are not supposed to cry.

Toward the ending of the group the leader makes sure to address the benefits of physical exercise, finding some creative means of self-expression, and establishing a support system. If time allows, members are introduced to deep breathing and progressive muscle relaxation as modes of coping with anxiety. The students are cautioned that the sadness they experienced will probably return at times but is likely to diminish over time, especially if they are able to fully express their feelings. They are told that individual counseling is available if they feel the need for it. They are encouraged to practice the coping methods they have learned in the group, and it is also suggested that they create a support group among themselves.

One of the purposes of these small groups is to identify students who might be at risk for more serious disturbance because of their exposure to a tragic situation. The leaders are limited in the treatment they can offer. However, they make appropriate referrals for more careful evaluation or treatment as needed. Six indicators have been observed in crisis groups that have frequently led to referrals: (1) the absence of emotional reactions in a student who was close to the victim; (2) an inability to bring emotion under control; (3) excessive self-blame or anger that is directed toward oneself; (4) allusions to suicidal thoughts or intentions; (5) evidence of bizarre behavior or thought disturbance; and (6) preoccupation with personal, family, or relationship problems. Group leaders are cautioned to use their clinical judgment and intuition in determining whether a student is at high risk.

A Group for Unwed Teenage Fathers

Wayne Huey, a former counselor at Gordon High School in Decatur, Georgia, designed a group called MALE (Maximizing a Life Experience). It included eight students, aged 14 to 18, who were already fathers or expectant fathers. He created this group after one of his school-board members commented on his school's counseling program for pregnant girls and wondered what help was available for the teenage fathers. After reviewing the literature, Huey concluded that counseling programs for unwed teenage fathers were practically nonexistent, especially in the schools. The remainder of this section describes the steps taken in setting up and evaluating this creative program.

Initial Steps

The pregnant girls in the school were contacted, but it was found that none of them was pregnant by a student at the high school. Huey then contacted counselors, teachers, administrators, and coaches, and eight names of boys were eventually secured. The program was outlined to each of them, and they were asked if they wanted to make a commitment to participate in the group. Parental consent was required to join. All eight identified youths got parental consent, all made the commitment, and all completed the nine-session group.

Goals and Objectives

The MALE group had the general goal of offering assistance in a nonjudgmental way. The initial plan focused on three Rs: rights, responsibilities, and resources. The specific objectives were for the participants (1) to learn more about themselves and their feelings in relation to their situation, (2) to understand their legal and emotional rights and responsibilities, (3) to identify and explore present and future options, (4) to learn to make sound decisions, (5) to realize what resources were available to them, (6) to accept that pregnancy is not an accident, and (7) to obtain information about contraception.

Structure of the Group Sessions

The nine sessions were held for an hour each week. They were held during the school day on a rotating schedule, so that no class was missed more than once or twice. The members were to make up all missed assignments. The nine sessions were structured as follows:

Session 1. An overview of the program was explained, as were general group goals and ground rules. Members got to know one another and developed their own personal goals.

Session 2. The group viewed and discussed the film *Teenage Father.*

Session 3. The group viewed and discussed the filmstrip *His Baby, Too: Problems of Teenage Pregnancy* (available from Sunburst Communications, 39 Washington Avenue, Room KT7, Pleasantville, NY 10570). The members also prepared questions on legal issues.

Session 4. The group explored legal issues, with a focus on the rights and responsibilities of unwed teenage fathers in Georgia. A guest speaker from the Legal Aid Society was heard.

Session 5. The reproductive system and contraception were discussed. A guest speaker from Planned Parenthood appeared.

Session 6. There was a field trip to Planned Parenthood, which included a tour of the facility and an overview of services provided for both girls and boys. There was also a presentation on sexually transmitted diseases.

Session 7. A session on problem solving and decision making was held, including models and practice activities.

Session 8. Problem-solving and decision-making models were used with actual personal situations.

Session 9. At the final session members summarized what they had learned about their rights and responsibilities, and there was a discussion of school resources. The members completed a written evaluation and discussed the effectiveness of the program.

Outcomes of the Program

Results. According to Huey, the program was a tremendous success. The overall group rating was 9.5 on a scale of 10 when the members were asked if the group had been helpful to them. The young men wanted the group to last longer, and they considered it very helpful. They had shared their feelings of anger, guilt, frustration, confusion, and fear. They explored concerns about their situation and the impact it might have on their future and the future of their baby.

Follow-Up. At one- and two-year follow-ups, none of this first group had fathered a second child, and all were progressing toward their career goals as they had imagined that they might be without a child. Three were in college or technical school, two were in the military, two were working full time, and one was still in high school. None of them had married the mother of his child; in fact, only two were still dating her a year later. All of them were contributing something toward the support of their child, and those who were close enough to visit were seeing the baby on a regular basis.

Summary

This group is another example of a specific program designed to meet the needs of a particular population. Such a group can be replicated in a community agency. The steps taken to set up this program and the general structure of the sessions can suggest a model for other specialized short-term groups for adolescents. This group illustrates the possibilities involved in combining an *educational* program (one designed to impart certain information) with a *therapeutic* program (one geared to helping members explore their feelings, attitudes, and values and make decisions). If you are interested in more detailed information on this type of group, write Wayne Huey at Lakeside High School, 3801 Briarcliff Rd., N.E., Atlanta, GA 30345; telephone: (404) 634-4412.

A Systemwide Program for Counseling Young People in Groups

This chapter has thus far described the formation of specific counseling groups for adolescents in schools and agencies. Now we consider organizing a group-counseling project on a larger scale for adolescents in senior and junior high school and for children in the elementary grades. The project to be described demonstrates that it is possible to set up a program, including training and supervision of professional group counselors, on a systemwide scale.

Background of the Program

Project Group Work was initiated in Bettendorf, Iowa, to train group counselors working with elementary and secondary students. The focus of the original training was on school social workers, psychologists, and teachers serving behaviorally disordered youths. Since the project's inception in 1984, the training has been expanded to include elementary and secondary counselors who provide service to "at-risk" students. At-risk students include those who are depressed, suicidal, homeless, or abused and those who have experienced significant losses in their lives. In reaction to the crisis element involved in working with these students, the project has incorporated crisis-management training.

This project is noteworthy in that it:

- emphasizes group counseling with special-education and at-risk regular-education students in the elementary through secondary grades
- provides supervised training in group work in a school setting
- emphasizes the importance of therapeutic relationships between group leaders and students
- uses a discussion approach in identifying problematic issues and devising solutions
- establishes a peer support system
- uses classroom teachers as co-leaders
- blends concepts from a variety of group-counseling theories
- incorporates crisis-management techniques as a part of group-counseling training

The groups are viewed as therapeutic discussion groups. Their purpose is to provide a safe environment in which students feel comfortable discussing issues that are interfering with their educational functioning. The groups, with a range of 6 to 12 students, meet for a minimum of one class period a week.

Topics or issues discussed in the group include academic difficulties, adolescent/adult relationship problems, feelings associated with having a disability, value conflicts, family problems, and child abuse. The students are often poorly motivated or exhibit behavioral difficulties in school because of their personal stress. For them the group becomes a place for expressing feelings, learning to care for oneself and others, and gaining insight into healthy ways of coping.

Basic Elements of the Group Experience

Phil Piechowski and Tom Ciha, directors of Project Group Work, report that the following elements have been found to be essential in conducting school counseling groups:

- **Fostering hope.** The at-risk student generally feels a sense of hopelessness. Participants in the group must be helped to see that positive change is possible.
- **Developing a sense of belonging.** At-risk students perceive themselves as alienated from the "mainstream" of school activities. Participation in the group promotes a feeling of togetherness and fosters a desire to be included in desirable social roles.
- **Focus on the here and now.** Although an understanding and discussion of the student's past history is helpful, the student is encouraged to identify goals for the present and future.
- **Reinforcement system.** A system for reinforcing appropriate social skills is often necessary in the initial stage of the group.
- **Changing an image.** Many at-risk students have either poor self-esteem or an inflated ego. Students participating in the group are encouraged to explore their feelings of self-worth and to evaluate their feelings against objective information about their accomplishments.
- **Teacher participation.** The involvement of a student's teacher as a co-leader with the counselor, social worker, or psychologist is important. The teacher adds significantly to the group because he or she is involved with the student daily and can lend support throughout the week. The teacher's capacity for understanding and accepting these students is increased because he or she becomes aware of some of the students' personal struggles through the group sessions.

Training Group Leaders

Since the project's inception in 1984, hundreds of counselors, teachers, school social workers, and psychologists have received intensive training in crisis management and group counseling. The training has included developing practitioners' skills in crisis intervention, group leadership, and using group dynamics to establish a cooperative learning experience. No single theoretical model is promoted; these practitioners have been exposed to a variety of counseling theories. The group training involves the establishment of a peer support system and supervision by a knowledgeable group leader. Groups are observed, and practitioners videotape sessions for review of their leadership skills.

The practitioners meet regularly for peer support and consultation. On attaining the desired degree of proficiency, each group leader assists in the training of additional professionals.

Conclusions

Project Group Work has been well received by counselors, teachers, social workers, psychologists, and students. Schools have not only started counseling groups for students with special needs and at-risk regular-education students but have also developed crisis-intervention plans to respond to a variety of situations. Many schools are better prepared, because of the training received through Project Group Work, to respond effectively to suicidal crises, the sudden death of a student or faculty member, and other severely stressful events experienced by adolescents.

Project Group Work practitioners have found that students who are offered the opportunity to discuss personal concerns begin to view the school as a more caring institution. This project has demonstrated that students' behavior and school work improve when they perceive the school as supportive.

For additional information about Project Group Work, write Phil Piechowski, Supervisor, School Social Work Services, Mississippi Bend Area Education Agency, 729 21st Street, Bettendorf, IA 52722; telephone: (319) 359-1371.

Where to Go from Here

A very useful resource guide is *Skills for Living: Group Counseling for Young Adolescents* (Morganett, 1990). This is a practical group leader's manual that presents guidelines for conducting skill-building counseling activities for young adolescents. The book presents ways of getting groups for adolescents off the ground. The chapters are organized around developmental concerns of adolescents such as dealing with a divorce in the family, making and keeping friends, learning communication skills, developing self-esteem, learning stress-management skills, acquiring skills for managing anger, surviving and succeeding in school, and coping with grief and loss. Morganett has pretests and posttests for each of the topics listed above. She also has a variety of sample forms (a needs assessment, a parental-consent form, and letters to students, faculty members, and parents). This manual will provide many ideas for those who want to set up a group for adolescents.

Another useful resource for group work with adolescents is *Working with Children and Adolescents in Groups* (Rose & Edleson, 1987). This excellent book presents a specific guide for the multimethod approach to treating adolescents in groups. Many examples cover children in all age groups, but most of the illustrations are drawn from the preadolescent and early-adolescent periods. Separate chapters deal with topics for each stage of a group, including preparation and orientation, assessing members' problems, setting goals, methods of changing behavior, techniques for coping with stress, influencing group structure and resolving group problems, homework assignments and behavioral practice, and strategies for the transfer and maintenance of learning.

Psychotherapy with Adolescent Girls (Lamb, 1978) has ideas that group workers with adolescents might find both stimulating and challenging. Although the author mostly describes individual therapy, many of the concepts can be used in group work.

The following group-counseling texts contain a chapter on groups for adolescents: *Group Counseling: A Developmental Approach* (Gazda, 1989); and *Group Counseling* (Ohlsen, Horne, & Lawe, 1988).

Elements of Group Counseling: Back to the Basics (Carroll & Wiggins, 1990) is a practical book that gives specific strategies and intervention techniques. It has a chapter on working with young people and is a useful resource for peer support groups, single-parent groups, child-abuser groups, and school groups.

A few other resources you might want to consult in setting up groups for adolescents include *It Will Never Happen to Me!* (Black, 1987), for a description of children of alcoholics; *I Never Knew I Had a Choice* (G. Corey & M. Corey, 1990), for a theme-oriented approach that can be applied to groups; *Group Techniques* (G. Corey, M. Corey, Callanan, & Russell, 1992), for examples of ways to develop action-oriented techniques; *Developmental Groups for Children* (Duncan & Gumaer, 1980), for a discussion of peer-facilitated groups, assertion-training groups, parent groups, and growth-centered groups.

Readers who are interested in using concepts and techniques drawn from a variety of models can find concise overviews in *Theory and Practice of Group Counseling* (G. Corey, 1990). The following theoretical approaches to group counseling are described: psychoanalytic, Adlerian, psychodrama and role playing, existential, person-centered, Gestalt, transactional analysis, behavioral, rational-emotive, and reality.

Two most useful resources that contain a wide variety of books for children and adolescents are *Paperbacks for Educators: School Counselor Edition, K–12, Catalog* and *Paperbacks for Educators: Bibliotherapy for Children and Teens, Catalog* (see the corresponding section in Chapter 9 for details).

A series of four books, all by Jeanne Warren Lindsay, can be used in conjunction with group work: (1) *Teens Look at Marriage: Rainbows, Roles and Reality* (1983); (2) *Teenage Marriage: Coping with Reality* (1984); (3) *Teens Parenting: The Challenge of Babies and Toddlers* (1981); and

(4) *Pregnant Too Soon: Adoption Is an Option* (1980). This series is published by Morning Glory Press, 6595 San Haroldo Way, Buena Park, CA 90620.

For an extensive bibliography of group procedures for adolescents, refer to *Group Work in the Helping Professions: A Bibliography* (Zimpfer, 1984, section 6.16, pp. 270–274). This source also contains a wide range of references on group procedures directed at behavior problems, substance abuse, unwed pregnancy, battering, child abuse, acting out, antisocial behavior, social withdrawal, dating inhibition, and groups in correctional settings (section 16.4, pp. 240–262).

References and Suggested Readings*

*Black, C. (1987). *It will never happen to me!* New York: Ballantine.
*Bloomfield, H. H., with Felder, L. (1983). *Making peace with your parents.* New York: Ballantine.
Bolles, R. N. (1990). *What color is your parachute?* Berkeley, CA: Ten Speed Press.
Bolton, F. G., Jr. (1980). *The pregnant adolescent: Problems of premature parenthood.* Newbury Park, CA: Sage Publications.
Brooks-Gunn, J., & Furstenberg, F. F. (1989). Adolescent sexual behavior. *American Psychologist, 44*(2), 249–257.
Burgess-Kohn, J. (1979). *Straight talk about love and sex for teenagers.* Boston: Beacon.
Carroll, M., & Wiggins, J. (1990). *Elements of group counseling: Back to the basics.* Denver: Love.
Corder, B. F., & Cornwall, T. (1984). Techniques for increasing effectiveness of co-therapy functioning in adolescent psychotherapy groups. *International Journal of Group Psychotherapy, 34*(4), 643–654.
Corey, G. (1990). *Theory and practice of group counseling* (3rd ed.). Pacific Grove, CA: Brooks/Cole.
*Corey, G., & Corey, M. (1990). *I never knew I had a choice* (4th ed.). Pacific Grove, CA: Brooks/Cole.
Corey, G., Corey, M., Callanan, P., & Russell, J. M. (1992). *Group techniques* (2nd ed.). Pacific Grove, CA: Brooks/Cole.
*Duncan, J. A., & Gumaer, J. (Eds.). (1980). *Developmental groups for children.* Springfield, IL: Charles C Thomas.
Elkind, D. (1984). *All grown up and no place to go: Teenagers in crisis.* Reading, MA: Addison-Wesley.
Ely, D. F., & Associates (1988). *California laws relating to minors.* Gardena, CA: Harcourt Brace Jovanovich.
*Erikson, E. (1968). *Identity: Youth and crisis.* New York: Norton.
Frankl, V. E. (1963). *Man's search for meaning* (rev. ed.). Boston: Beacon.
Furstenberg, F. F., Brooks-Gunn, J., & Chase-Lansdale, L. (1989). Teenaged pregnancy and childbearing. *American Psychologist, 44*(2), 313–320.

*Books and articles marked with an asterisk are recommended for further reading.

Gazda, G. M. (1989). *Group counseling: A developmental approach* (4th ed.). Boston: Allyn & Bacon.

Ginott, H. (1973). *Between parent and teenager.* New York: Avon.

Gordon, T. (1970). *P.E.T., Parent effectiveness training: The tested new way to raise responsible children.* New York: New American Library.

Grant, D. (1988). Support group for youth with AIDS virus. *International Journal of Group Psychotherapy, 38*(2), 237–252.

Hesse, H. (1951). *Siddhartha.* New York: New Directions.

Hesse, H. (1965). *Demian.* New York: Harper & Row.

James, M., & Jongeward, D. (1971). *Born to win: Transactional analysis with Gestalt experiments.* Reading, MA: Addison-Wesley.

Kennedy, J. F. (1989). The heterogeneous group for chronically physically ill and physically healthy but emotionally disturbed children and adolescents. *International Journal of Group Psychotherapy, 39*(1), 105–125.

Kraft, I. A. (1983). Child and adolescent group psychotherapy. In H. I. Kaplan & B. J. Sadock (Eds.). *Comprehensive group psychotherapy* (2nd ed.) (pp. 223–234). Baltimore: Williams & Wilkins.

*Lamb, D. (1978). *Psychotherapy with adolescent girls.* San Francisco: Jossey-Bass.

Leaman, D. R. (1983). Group counseling to improve communication skills of adolescents. *Journal for Specialists in Group Work, 8*(3), 144–150.

*Morganett, R. S. (1990). *Skills for living: Group counseling activities for young adolescents.* Champaign, IL: Research Press.

Newcomb, M. D., & Bentler, P. M. (1989). Substance use and abuse among children and teenagers. *American Psychologist, 44*(2), 242–248.

*Oaklander, V. (1978). *Windows to our children: A Gestalt approach to children and adolescents.* Moab, UT: Real People Press.

Ohlsen, M. M., Horne, A. M., & Lawe, C. F. (1988). *Group counseling* (3rd ed.). New York: Holt, Rinehart & Winston.

*Osborne, W. L. (1990). Ben Cohn: Group counseling and the acting-out underachieving adolescent. *Journal for Specialists in Group Work, 15*(1), 2–9.

Powers, S. I., Hauser, S. T., & Kilner, L. A. (1989). Adolescent mental health. *American Psychologist, 44*(2), 200–208.

Robertson, D., & Mathews, B. (1989). Preventing adolescent suicide with group counseling. *Journal for Specialists in Group Work, 14*(1), 34–39.

*Rose, S. D., & Edleson, J. L. (1987). *Working with children and adolescents in groups: A multimethod approach.* San Francisco: Jossey-Bass.

Russell, E. E. H. (1984). *Sexual exploitation: Rape, child sexual abuse, and workplace harassment.* Newbury Park, CA: Sage Publications.

*Weinberg, R. B. (1990). Serving large numbers of adolescent victim–survivors: Group interventions following trauma at school. *Professional Psychology: Research and Practice, 21*(4), 271–278.

Zelnik, M., Kantner, J. R., & Ford, K. (1981). *Sex and pregnancy in adolescence.* Newbury Park, CA: Sage Publications.

*Zimbardo, P. G. (1978). *Shyness.* New York: Jove Press.

*Zimpfer, D. G. (1984). *Group work in the helping professions: A bibliography* (2nd ed.). Muncie, IN: Accelerated Development.

CHAPTER 11

Groups for Adults

Introduction
Theme-Oriented Groups
Groups for College Students
  Common topics in college groups ▪ A cautionary note
Groups for Weight Control
  Review of selected literature on weight-control groups
  A group program for repeat dieters
Groups for Substance Abusers
  Rationale ▪ Requirements for member participation
  Group techniques ▪ Implications
The AIDS Crisis as a Challenge for Group Workers
  Dealing with your resistance ▪ Exploring the stigma of AIDS
  How groups can help ▪ An educational focus in AIDS groups
One Counselor's Story: Starting an AIDS Support Group
  How the group began ▪ Help and support
  Format ▪ Group issues ▪ Personal concerns ▪ Looking ahead
A Transition Group in a Community Agency
  Structure and policies ▪ Topics ▪ Stages of group development
  Implications
A Women's Support Group for Victims of Incest
  Purpose and rationale ▪ Setting up the group
  Structure of the group ▪ Implications
A Long-Term Therapy Group for Incest Survivors
  Basic information on incest ▪ Rationale for long-term group therapy
  Selection of group members ▪ Group process ▪ Leadership
An Adult Group for Personal Growth
  Nature of the group ▪ Personal perspectives of the co-leaders
  Responses by group members
(continued)

351

Introduction

This chapter describes a variety of special-interest groups for adults, with emphasis on these areas: themes and topics as useful catalysts for group interaction, the structuring of adult groups, special considerations in designing and conducting groups for adults, characteristics that leaders need to work with various special-interest groups, and the rationale for group approaches. We try to be as practical as possible, so that you will be able to incorporate our suggestions in your practice.

   This chapter begins with some observations on a theme-oriented approach to adult groups. We describe several special-interest groups for college students, which can be formed in public and private agencies as well as in college counseling centers. Also described are groups for weight control, groups for substance abusers, AIDS support groups, a transition group in a community agency, a women's support group for victims of incest, a long-term therapy group for incest survivors, a short-term weekly personal-growth group for adults, and our weeklong residential workshops in life choices.

Theme-Oriented Groups

Theme-oriented groups have many advantages for adults. If topics reflect the life issues of the participants, they can be powerful catalysts. It is good to consider several factors if you decide to structure your groups around topics.

   It helps to think about the common developmental life concerns characteristic of the group membership. If the group you are leading is made up largely of adults in their early 20s, they are likely to be involved in choosing a career, choosing a lifestyle, revising their life plan, seeking meaning in life, and wrestling with unresolved dependence/independence issues. If your group is composed of people making the transition from their late 20s to their early 30s, you can expect such concerns as changes in their values and beliefs, parent/child issues, job difficulties, and depression over not having met goals they've set for themselves.

   For groups made up of middle-aged participants, leaders can structure the group around such themes as coping with the pressure of time, adjusting to children's growing up and leaving home, marital crises, changing roles of men and women, coping with aging, the death of one's parents, divorce and separation, stagnation in work, changing one's occupation or career, finding meaning in life apart from rearing a family, creatively coping with stress, and facing loneliness.

Who decides on the themes for a group? This depends on many factors, including your leadership style and the level of sophistication of your group. Topics do not have to be imposed on members in an insensitive way. You and the members can cooperatively develop themes that will provide direction for the sessions. You need to consider the readiness of members to fully explore these themes. Death, loneliness and isolation, anger, depression, and other potentially intense topics can trigger the opening of feelings that have been repressed for many years, and both the leader and the members must be able to handle the emotional intensity that is likely to be generated. If members select the themes, rather than being pushed into exploring a given topic, there is a greater chance that they will be able to face them.

Groups for College Students

A common complaint we hear from students is that it is easy to feel isolated on a university campus. Students feel that whereas much attention is paid to their intellectual development, relatively little attention is paid to their personal development. From our work in the counseling centers of universities, we have come to realize that many students seek counseling services not only because of serious problems but also because they want to develop aspects of their personality in addition to their thinking abilities. These students are hungry for personal nourishment, and they actively seek group experiences in which they can be nourished and can grow by nourishing others. In a weekly group with fellow students (and a group leader) they can formulate goals, explore areas of themselves that they've kept hidden from themselves and that are causing them difficulties in interpersonal relating, and identify the internal blocks that have been impeding their full use of their capacities. By dealing with their personal problems, students are able to free themselves of certain emotional blocks to learning. Many who clarify their values and make decisions about what they want from life become far better students, approaching their studies with a sense of enthusiasm and commitment.

When we speak about college students, we are not restricting ourselves to those in their late teens or early 20s. The groups that we've led and co-led on university campuses draw a cross-section of students in their 20s and 30s as well as many middle-aged people. There are, for instance, women who are returning to college after their sons and daughters leave home and many middle-aged men and women preparing for major changes in their career and life. We have found a diversity of special needs on the college campus that can be met partly through a group experience.

Common Topics in College Groups

Some themes seem to arise often in our college counseling groups. These common themes, which provide the content of the group encounters, include the desire to be genuine, interpersonal difficulties, psychosomatic illnesses, the denial of problems, sexual conflicts, dealing with hostility, feelings of rejection, the desire for acceptance and approval, wanting to love and be loved, relationships with parents, uneasiness about one's body, trusting oneself and others, feelings of loneliness, emptiness, and alienation, value confusion, the search for meaning in life, dependency problems, identity confusion, problems associated with drugs and alcohol, the impact of the AIDS crisis, religious conflicts, vocational indecision, learning how to use leisure and how to balance work and leisure, anxiety, and lack of self-confidence.

It is possible to structure a personal-growth group, either in a community agency or in a college counseling center, around topics appropriate for the clientele. As an example of structuring a group along thematic lines, we offer the following topics, which we have used both in personal-growth groups and in self-exploration courses in college:

- **Identity.** Who are you? What is important in your world now? What main factors have influenced your life? What kind of person do you wish to become? How do you perceive the world?
- **Independence.** To what degree have you gained psychological independence from your parents?
- **Reviewing your childhood and adolescence.** In what ways are your earlier life experiences affecting your present situation? What are some examples of unfinished business from the past that is interfering with your effective functioning?
- **Work and leisure.** Are you able to balance work and leisure to your satisfaction? In what ways do work and leisure provide meaning in your life?
- **Your physical self.** How well are you taking care of your body? How do you express yourself through your body? What effect does stress have on you physically and psychologically? How do you cope with stress?
- **Sex roles.** What are the implications for you of the changing concepts of masculinity and femininity? How can you resolve your conflicts about your role?
- **Love.** How capable are you of loving? What barriers in your life prevent love? What is it like for you to experience love?
- **Sex.** What are your views about sexuality? What are your main concerns regarding your own sexuality?

- **Intimate relationships.** What are the dynamics within and between two individuals that determine the success or failure of a relationship? How satisfied are you with the quality of your intimate relationships? What are some barriers to developing and maintaining intimate relationships?
- **Loneliness.** How do you cope with your loneliness? Do you distinguish between being alone and loneliness?
- **Death.** What are your views of death and dying? Do they affect the way you live? How do you grieve over a loss? Are you dead in psychological ways?
- **Search for meaning and values.** What are the values that give your life meaning, and where did you get them? What role does spirituality play in your life?
- **Evaluation of the group experience.** What has this group meant to you? What have you learned about your own attitudes, values, beliefs, and behavior? To what extent have you carried this learning into your outside life? What areas do you need to continue working on in your life?

As another example of the variety of structured groups, consider the following programs that are frequently offered at college counseling centers: both therapy and support groups for adult children of alcoholics, anxiety-management groups, family-issues groups, groups for older students, groups for those with relationship concerns, self-esteem groups, groups for survivors of childhood sexual abuse, and personal-identity groups. These groups are typically short term, lasting from four weeks to one semester, and they are aimed at meeting a variety of special needs by combining a therapeutic focus with an educational one. The scope of the topics for structured groups is really limited only by the need of the population and the creativity of the counselor.

A Cautionary Note

Although there are clear advantages to topical or structured groups, caution is in order. It is possible for leaders to develop a special-interest group as a way of working on their own unresolved issues. For example, a male leader who is stuck with resentment toward women may form a men's group and use it as a forum for his own catharsis. We are not implying that leaders should be completely free of their own problems before they lead a group. However, we do see it as a misuse of groups if leaders use session time to grind an ax over some personal issue. Leaders who are unaware of their motivations are not facilitating participants' growth. This problem can be avoided with careful supervision during the leader's training period as well as continual self-examination and in-service training for those who lead groups.

Groups for Weight Control

In this society there are great cultural pressures to have a thin body. Although weight control and body image are concerns regardless of gender, women especially feel pressured to have an "ideal body," because there is a strong social bias against "overweight" women. Women tend to internalize societal messages to be unrealistically thin, and if they are not, there are psychological and social prices to pay. Many overweight women experience chronic depression and low self-esteem (McNamara, 1989a).

Review of Selected Literature on Weight-Control Groups

University counseling centers are increasingly offering groups for people with eating disorders. These groups are often designed for women who are bulimic or anorexic or are compulsive eaters. There is a growing recognition that individuals with eating disorders can benefit from group psychotherapy (Brisman & Siegel, 1985; Hendren, Atkins, Sumner, & Barber, 1987; Roth & Ross, 1988).

Roth and Ross (1988) designed long-term groups using cognitive-interpersonal therapy for people with eating disorders. They contend that most people with eating disorders also suffer from systematic distortions of their personal and social worlds. These clients usually have a number of self-defeating beliefs about weight, eating patterns, body image, sense of autonomy, and self-esteem. Some of the beliefs they commonly hold are:

- "I am fat and ugly."
- "Thinness gives me self-worth."
- "I can restrictively diet without any side effects to my health."
- "I am not able to control my life."
- "I am a worthless person."

Their personal relationships are often dissatisfying because of these assumptions about themselves. They also tend to hold distorted interpersonal beliefs that lead them to feel misunderstood by others. Some of these beliefs are:

- "People are basically untrustworthy."
- "People expect me to be perfect."
- "If people get to know me, they'll find me uninteresting."
- "It is essential that I always please others."
- "It is wrong for me to express my anger directly toward others."

In the long-term cognitive groups that Roth and Ross describe, clients with eating disorders have a forum to address the relationship between dysfunctional cognitions, maladaptive social skills, faulty relationships with others, and eating behaviors. In these groups the focus is on cognitive restructuring and learning a range of social skills. The self-defeating beliefs and behaviors that members manifest can be explored and corrected within the group.

In their article, Hendren, Atkins, Sumner, and Barber (1987) describe their experience in treating about 200 people with eating disorders in five open groups combining inpatients and outpatients. Although their groups seemed promising for individuals suffering from bulimia and anorexia nervosa, they emphasized the need for more rigorous and extensive long-term follow-up studies as a prerequisite for making definitive conclusions about the lasting benefits of group therapy for such patients.

Brisman and Siegel (1985) recognized the limitations of therapy groups that meet weekly for people with bulimia. They developed a three-phase, multidimensional group program that was aimed at increasing the cohesion of the group, which was thought to accelerate the therapy process. The program they describe began with an intensive weekend workshop, at which the members developed contracts in which they pledged to change their behavior. There was a follow-up session at which the members were able to deal with problems they had encountered in fulfilling their contracts. They also reported their successes, and these were reinforced. In the final phase, the members met without their therapists to offer support to one another, to reevaluate their contracts, and to share their feelings about the progress of their treatment. In general, the authors found that modified group therapy was a viable treatment, which might be considered before resorting to psychiatric approaches.

Zimpfer (1990b) reviewed studies on the outcomes of groups for the treatment of bulimia. He concluded that group work was a preferred treatment for this population. He found a noticeable increase in the number of follow-up studies of group treatment. All of the follow-ups except one revealed effectiveness in maintaining overall reduction in binge/purge behavior. Also, all but one showed effectiveness in maintaining psychological improvement. In every study reviewed, there was a reduction or elimination of binge/purge behavior, depression was reduced, and body image was improved.

McNamara (1989a) did a study of group counseling for overweight and depressed college women comparing behavioral and cognitive-behavioral group programs aimed at weight control. She found that both of these approaches were effective in producing weight reductions as well as alleviating depression, easing the fear of negative evaluations, and reducing social avoidance and distress. She concluded that the addition of the cognitive-restructuring component did not improve the efficacy of the behavioral weight-control program.

A Group Program for Repeat Dieters

McNamara (1989b) conducted a structured group program for women who were repeat dieters and who were potentially at risk of developing more serious eating disorders. These groups were composed of eight to ten college women who met for eight weeks for 90-minute sessions. This group is an example of programs that can be organized both for teaching purposes and for supporting the participants in their attempt to change their eating patterns.

This program consisted of structured group meetings designed to accomplish two main goals: (1) to replace dieting with healthier eating patterns and a regular exercise program and (2) to improve self-esteem and body image by encouraging self-acceptance and the resistance of unrealistic societal expectations for thinness. The leaders recruited group members by making announcements in large introductory psychology classes. Some screening was done, and potential participants were informed about the purpose of the group. They were assisted in deciding whether they were motivated to meet the goals of the program. Individual members developed their own personal goals, which was an integral part of the ongoing group process. Those who joined the groups expressed their frustration with their prior attempts at dieting and their desire to feel better about their bodies.

The eight sessions included some brief lectures, structured exercises, cognitive-restructuring strategies, opportunities for sharing reactions and behavior, and assigning of homework and discussing of this homework at following meetings. The first three sessions of this group program focused heavily on eating behavior, although the structure was designed to gradually facilitate deeper levels of self-disclosure and self-exploration. Beginning with the fourth meeting, the topics tended to shift away from food and eating habits to internal factors that contribute to negative body image and excessive preoccupation with food and weight. Following are some of the issues and tasks for each of the eight sessions.

Session 1: Introduction. After the members get acquainted with one another, the leaders emphasize the importance of confidentiality and ask the members for their reasons for dieting. A brief lecture focuses on the risks associated with repeat dieting and the vicious circle of dieting. The goals of the group are clarified, and members are invited to discuss their reactions about replacing their dieting behavior with healthier habits. For homework, the members are asked to keep a food diary that consists of recording their food intake and their feelings both before and after eating.

Session 2: Changing Eating Behavior. This session focuses on eating behavior, weight, and calories. Emphasis is given to setting a realistic goal for a target weight. Members are then helped in determining how many calories they can consume to maintain their weight goal. They are asked to begin a regular exercise program, which they choose, for at least 30 minutes, three times a week. They are also asked to stop dieting and to start establishing a healthy eating style.

Session 3: Changing Thought Patterns. This session opens with a report on how each person did with her homework assignment for the previous week. The leaders encourage participating and providing encouragement and support. They also look for common themes, especially the feelings, struggles, and accomplishments that the women share. By this time, there is a growing cohesion within the group because of these common experiences. This allows for the introduction of goal-oriented, problem-solving strategies. Members are introduced to the circular relationship that exists between thoughts, feelings, and behaviors. They are shown how dysfunctional thinking tends to lead to dysfunctional eating behavior. The leaders ask the members to share with others their thoughts and feelings about the experiences, both before and after eating, that they have recorded in their diaries. The leaders comment on common themes that the participants raise and encourage further group interaction. Participants are also taught how to identify negative thoughts and how to replace them with constructive coping responses. The members are asked to work on one new coping response during the week and to record their efforts in their food diaries.

Session 4: Perfectionism, Depression, and Self-Esteem. At this time in the group's development, the members are unified by the common goal of adopting healthy eating habits. Because of the trust and cohesion that have generally been established by this meeting, the participants are ready to reveal more personal aspects of themselves. The members have some opportunity to discuss the new coping techniques they have tried during the previous week. The topic of perfectionism is then introduced with an exercise, and a brief lecture deals with the relationship between perfectionism, depression, and self-esteem. Members learn that women who have eating and body-image problems tend to be perfectionistic and to experience depression when they do not live up to their unrealistically high ideals. The women learn how to challenge the underlying assumptions of this perfectionism and how to replace their "shoulds" and "oughts" with more realistic goals. They also learn how to nourish themselves without food. The homework assignment consists of taking home a small, attractive box that the group leaders distribute and taking out nourishing activities or thoughts when they feel down and are tempted to use food as their defense.

Session 5: Anger and Assertiveness. The topics of this session follow from the previous discussion of how perfectionism leads to depression. Anger and assertiveness are introduced by asking women in the group to look at situations in which they might be reluctant to assert themselves. Members are asked "What price do you pay for being non-assertive?" They generally recognize the relationship between their feelings of frustration and anger and their eating patterns. Because anger is considered unfeminine in this society, many women report that they seek food as an outlet for their feelings of anger or resentment. The co-leaders explore with the members the difficulties they encounter in being assertive, especially at times when they feel angry. The members are encouraged to challenge one another's self-defeating thoughts and behaviors and to support self-enhancing behaviors.

Session 6: Societal Standards of Thinness and Beauty. An exercise introduces the members to a discussion of how society places unrealistic pressures on women to be thin. Members are asked to list the qualities of the "perfect woman." These characteristics are then discussed, and the leaders encourage group interaction on the topic of the cultural pressures to be "superwomen." The group explores the messages in magazine advertisements that have been brought in by the leaders. For homework the members are asked to have a man they know identify a woman he finds attractive. They are instructed to ask him what he finds attractive about her and to listen for qualities other than weight that he mentions. The purpose of this exercise is to challenge the belief that women must be superthin in order to be considered attractive. Members are also asked to bring in a magazine photo of a woman whose body looks like theirs and one whose body they wish they had.

Session 7: Improving Body Image. This session opens with a mirror exercise that introduces the topic of body image. Members form triads and are given a full-length mirror. They are instructed to take turns standing in front of the mirror. Starting at the top of her body and moving down, each woman comments only on what she likes about her body. After the exercise, participants talk about what they felt during the exercise, including what made them feel uncomfortable, what they felt good about, and how they felt in the triad. The leaders ask the members what they would be losing if they were to like their bodies. Later in this session the focus is on correcting distortions in body image. The women also discuss what the men they talked to during the previous week reported that they found sexy and attractive in women.

Session 8: Termination. At this time members are helped to consolidate the gains they have made in the group sessions with respect to acquiring healthy eating behaviors and improving their body image. They are reminded that this is the final meeting, and each person is asked to say in a few words what she considers to be most valuable about the group and what the most important thing is that she learned about herself. The members are encouraged to exchange feedback concerning positive changes they have observed in one another. Each person is asked to complete this sentence: "The one thing I want to continue to work on when I leave this group is . . . " Members are given referral resources for additional counseling if they feel the need for this service.

McNamara reports that the participants concluded that the group had been effective in reducing repeat dieting and improving body image. The results suggest that this kind of program is an efficient preventive strategy for women who may be at risk for developing more serious eating problems. This program is probably best presented as a short-term preventive group for people with eating problems, but it could be lengthened for clients with more serious eating disturbances. If these modifications were made, the sessions might focus on the dysfunctional family dynamics that frequently underlie eating disorders. Male and female co-leaders might work together in a more expanded version of this program to deal with the fears, anger, and likely transferences that the participants might have toward the male leader.

This group program was based on the work of Weiss, Katzman, and Wolchik (1985) with bulimic individuals. McNamara revised their work to meet the needs of repeat dieters and others at risk for an eating disorder. If you are interested in further information about this group program, refer to the articles describing group approaches to weight control (McNamara, 1989a, 1989b). You can also contact Kathleen McNamara, Psychology Department, Colorado State University, Fort Collins, CO 80523; telephone: (303) 491-6061.

Groups for Substance Abusers

A large number of people drink, use drugs, or having eating patterns that cause them severe problems in daily living. One therapeutic approach to dealing with the impact of substance abuse on individuals and society is group counseling. Some years back we gave a professional-development workshop on group counseling for the European branch of the American Association for Counseling and Development in Germany. Many of the participants specialized in drug and alcohol counseling for military personnel, and most of them were conducting substance-abuse groups. They seemed eager to learn therapeutic strategies for dealing with the resistance that is often associated with involuntary groups.

Groups such as these, and other groups designed for people who have problems controlling the use of alcohol, drugs, and food, appear to be gaining popularity in public and private mental-health agencies. Because you may eventually lead this type of special group, we briefly present the rationale for group treatment, requirements for member participation, group techniques, and a summary of common elements of most group programs for substance abusers.

Rationale

As a rule, substance abusers feel socially isolated and lack interpersonal skills. Further, they are dependent and manipulative and use defenses such as denying, blaming, and rationalizing as ways to avoid accepting personal responsibility for their problems. Some of the specific values of group treatment for substance abusers have been identified by Fuhrmann and Washington (1984a, 1984b) and Altman and Plunkett (1984):

- Groups provide a safe setting for members to break through their sense of isolation.
- Groups can teach such clients that others share their problem and that they have the capacity to learn more appropriate social skills.
- The protected setting offers members both the support and the confrontation they need for resocialization and for problem solving.
- The group can encourage clients to let go of some of their defenses.
- Especially through feedback from peers, members can begin to see themselves as others do and can learn how they affect others.
- The group can help the abuser confront difficult issues and learn to cope more effectively with the stresses of daily life.
- Clients can explore a range of mutual issues besides those related directly to substance abuse, such as problems in their personal relationships at home and at work.

Requirements for Member Participation

Although specific groups designed for substance abusers will have particular criteria for inclusion, the following are some general requirements for outpatients: (1) for a drug and alcohol population, abstinence is necessary if they are to function effectively in a group; (2) clients should show some degree of motivation to change; (3) they need some capacity to look at themselves and to interact with others; and (4) it is helpful if they have some social-support system outside of the group. Clients with psychoses are excluded. Another criteria for admission is the client's being involved full time in structured activities such as work, school, or home-care responsibilities. Although most programs prefer voluntary clients, some will accept involuntary members as long as they meet the other criteria for inclusion.

Group Techniques

In their review of the programs on group work for substance abusers, Fuhrmann and Washington (1984a) conclude that a factor common to most of these groups is an eclectic orientation of the leader. Such groups draw on affective, cognitive, and behavioral techniques, and all of these approaches appear to work at various times for various clients. The needs of the clientele determine the appropriateness of particular intervention strategies. The leaders typically employ a high degree of structuring during the early phase of a group, with less direction and more emphasis on an interactive style during the later stages. For clients in crisis, more directive cognitive-behavioral techniques are generally utilized. Many of these groups use a female/male co-leader team. There is an emphasis on here-and-now interaction and action-oriented techniques, which focus not only on the problem of substance abuse but also on all the needs and concerns of the participants. These groups frequently employ present-oriented techniques such as role playing, problem solving, coaching, modeling, interpretation, self-disclosure, feedback, confrontation, and imparting of information; creating a social-support network outside of the group; and the use of referrals and community resources (Fuhrmann & Washington, 1984a).

Implications

Groups are especially useful in the treatment of substance abusers because members can observe and participate in the treatment of others with similar problems. Doing so is therapeutic and reinforces newly acquired insights and behavioral skills. Being able to help others is a key therapeutic factor, for many of these individuals have long felt devalued and worthless and thus have not offered their views to others. The group process involves elements of psychotherapy, resocialization, and reeducation. These factors help clients in dealing with barriers to their growth and in completing unresolved developmental tasks (Altman & Plunkett, 1984). An increasing number of mental-health workers are being trained in the treatment of substance abuse. Now the challenges facing these practitioners are to learn as much about the prevention of drug abuse as they know about treatment and to design group approaches aimed at prevention. If you desire further information about groups for substance abuse, we recommend the following sources, besides the ones cited in this section: Lowinson (1983), Martin and Privette (1989), Vannicelli (1988), Vannicelli, Canning, and Griefen (1984), and Woodward and McGrath (1988).

The AIDS Crisis as a Challenge for Group Workers

Acquired immune deficiency syndrome (AIDS) has become one of the most critical health problems facing contemporary society. This fatal disease is complicated by a myriad of psychosocial problems on top of the physical complications (Spector & Conklin, 1987). AIDS already affects a wide population and will certainly become an increasing problem. It has been called an "equal opportunity disease" that strikes at diverse populations. As a counselor you will inevitably come in contact with people who have AIDS, with people who have tested positive and are carriers of the human immunodeficiency virus (HIV), or with people who are close to them. You simply cannot afford to be unaware of the many issues surrounding the AIDS epidemic. You will not be able to educate those with whom you come in contact unless you learn about the problem yourself. We encourage you to explore your own attitudes, values, and fears about working with AIDS patients, with HIV-positive clients, and with those who have been affected by the AIDS epidemic.

Dealing with Your Resistance

The AIDS crisis has created anxiety among many medical personnel and mental-health professionals. Never before have mental-health practitioners worried that they will be infected with a fatal disease that their clients are carrying. Thus, these counselors often resist close contact with those who have been infected.

As a counselor you may say "I don't know anything about this disease, and I'm not competent to deal with people who are affected by the problem." If you find yourself identifying with this statement and feeling somewhat overwhelmed, it is not necessary to remain this way. There is no reason to remain ignorant, because you can get the basic information you need about this disease. As a minimum step you can do some reading. You can also attend a workshop on AIDS or contact one or more of the many clinics that are being started all over the country as a resource for learning what you need to know.

In addition to this basic information about AIDS, it is imperative that you have skills in crisis intervention if you are considering facilitating a support group for AIDS patients or for those who have tested HIV-positive. People who come to you because they have discovered that they are carriers of the AIDS virus are typically highly anxious. Both those who have tested positive and those who have contracted AIDS are typically in need of immediate and short-term intervention to help them cope. They need to find a system to support them through the troubled times they will endure. Not only can you be of support by listening to them and helping them deal with their immediate feelings, but you can be instrumental in assisting them to find a broader network, such as an AIDS support group. Caring and supportive relationships are valuable for individuals who are facing stressful life events. The isolation that clients experience when they learn about an HIV-positive diagnosis often leads to a sense of helplessness, which can be eased by contact with others who are in the same situation (Grant, 1988).

Exploring the Stigma of AIDS

In some of your groups you may have clients who have manifested the more severe symptoms of AIDS. You will also see clients who have discovered that they have the virus within them and who live with the anxiety of wondering whether they will come down with this incurable disease. Most of them also struggle with the social stigma attached to AIDS. They live in fear not only of developing a life-threatening disease but also of being discovered and thus being rejected by society in general and by significant persons in their life. Along with the HIV epidemic has come an "epidemic of fear" that Bruhn (1989) describes in an article on counseling people with a fear of AIDS. He notes that AIDS has created fear and panic as it has spread to people of all ages, ethnicity, and social status. As a result of this epidemic of fear, people with AIDS have been denied admission to schools, apartments, churches, and places of employment, and they have been refused care by health professionals and hospitals. This array of fears, which usually results from ignorance about the disease and how it is transmitted, is prevalent throughout the country, regardless of one's level of education. This epidemic of fear directly contributes to the social stigma that is associated with people who have contracted the virus.

The stigma is attached to the fact that most, but certainly not all, of those in the United States who have contracted AIDS are either sexually active homosexual or bisexual men or present or past abusers of intravenous drugs. Among the mainstream population, there is still a general negative reaction toward people who are homosexual or bisexual. People who are highly intolerant of those who are different from them often engage in denial and seek a target for their resentments. Any educational program must be directed toward minimizing denial and homophobia. Typically, people who develop AIDS are afflicted with a double-edged stigma, because of their lifestyle and because of the disease, which is often viewed as the result of their homosexuality. This stigma is not reserved exclusively for the gay population. It is often transferred to individuals who have acquired the virus through blood transfusions or as the partner of an HIV carrier.

In addition to feeling different and stigmatized, those with AIDS typically have a great deal of anger. They often feel left alone and without support. This feeling is frequently grounded in reality. In some cases friends and family members actually "disown the outcast." This rejection of those who are infected only deepens their feelings of estrangement from those whose support they most need at this critical turning point. It is not surprising that they also feel isolated, for it is difficult for them to see any meaning in their plight. Consequently, they often allow themselves to become depressed, and they develop anger at having a life-threatening condition. They express this anger by asking: "What did I do to deserve this? Why me?" This anger is sometimes directed at God for letting this happen, and then they may feel guilty for having reacted this way. Anger is also directed toward others, especially those who are likely to have given them the virus and those who are abandoning them in this time of need.

Bruhn (1989) observes that diseases with stigmas tend to linger in the public mind and that appeals for compassion are frequently rebuffed with the attitude that "they got what they deserved." He makes an excellent point about the role of counselors: "As caretakers of persons in need of compassion and caring, counselors should not allow themselves to be turned off by the disease a person has but should be sensitive to the person who has the disease" (p. 457).

How Groups Can Help

A support group can provide a safe place for the participants to deal with the impact of this social stigma and vent their anger, enabling them to get a new perspective on dealing with this anger. People afflicted with AIDS often stigmatize themselves and perpetuate beliefs such as "I feel guilty and ashamed," "I feel that God is punishing me," "I am a horrible person, and therefore I deserve to suffer," and "I am to blame for getting this disease." Indeed, they often accept what they have heard from others that "you got what you deserved." In the supportive climate of a group, these people can openly talk about the burdens of carrying the stigma and can begin to challenge self-destructive beliefs. Instead of blaming themselves, they can begin to forgive themselves and decide how to make the most of the time they do have.

By sharing their fears, these participants can find some measure of hope. They can realize that they are not completely alone in facing an uncertain future. The fact that others are waging a common struggle brings about a high level of cohesiveness in this kind of support group. The participants have many physical, psychological, and spiritual challenges to meet, and a group can be of major help.

Bruhn offers the following guidelines for those who lead AIDS support groups:

- Determine the mental status of the client. Is the client HIV-positive? Has he or she been diagnosed with AIDS?
- Determine the nature of the client's fears, including whether they are real or imagined.
- Determine the client's current needs in all areas.
- Determine realistic goals. It is useful to explore hopes, expectations, and wishes regarding family, spouse, and work.
- Determine both short-term and long-term counseling needs and strategies for meeting these needs.

Applying these guidelines can help group leaders create an atmosphere of acceptance and concern in which clients can voice their most pressing concerns and learn as much as possible about what is known about the disease.

The issues that are typically talked about in a support group for young AIDS victims include feelings of helplessness, social stigmatization, guilt, shame, isolation, anger, and anxiety and concerns related to clients' identity and intimacy with a partner (Grant, 1988). For instance, when clients initially learn that they are infected with the virus, they frequently feel powerless to change their situation. The social stigma associated with the disease is an added burden on gay youths who often already feel isolated by the lack of a supportive social network. Clients also experience anxiety over their prognosis. Most youths are making decisions about furthering their education and establishing their careers; a positive HIV diagnosis tends to cast doubt and uncertainty on these plans. One of the developmental tasks youths face is developing intimacy with a partner; infected youths worry about the rejection they expect if they were to tell a potential partner about their condition. The supportive climate of the group provides these youths with the means for coping more realistically and effectively with their situation.

An Educational Focus in AIDS Groups

It is disconcerting to consider that accurate knowledge about AIDS may not lead people to change their sexual behavior. In a study of college students' knowledge of AIDS and behaviors, Gray and Saracino (1989) found that knowledge alone did not appear to translate into behavioral change. These researchers emphasize the professional, ethical, and moral obligation of counselors in taking an active stance to combat AIDS. Some of the procedures that they suggest are:

- Provide young adults with explicit sexual terms for discussing sexual behavior and values.
- Use role-playing approaches and sexual decision-making strategies as a way to bridge the gap between what young people know cognitively and what they do behaviorally. Help sexually active clients develop and use specific and personal "safer sex" strategies.
- Discuss sexual behavior from an integrated and personal perspective. Include topics such as personal values, relationship status, religious influence, and decision-making skills.

The supportive environment of a group provides an ideal means of reinforcing and maintaining behavior change. This kind of group can be aimed at helping young people translate what they know into specific actions. But there must be a plan to include information in a meaningful way. In AIDS support groups it is important that there be an educational component as well as a therapeutic focus. People in these groups, as well as their friends and family members, often labor under a host of myths and misconceptions about AIDS. As a responsible practitioner, you must dispel the misconceptions surrounding AIDS and help people acquire realistic knowledge and attitudes. For example, a major misconception is that AIDS affects only the gay population and that if you are not gay, you have no need to worry about being infected. In fact, heterosexuals have become infected through blood transfusions and through sexual contact with members of the opposite sex who themselves are carriers of the virus. The truth of the matter is that the AIDS epidemic does affect many of us, either directly or indirectly.

Education of various target groups is the key in preventing sharp rises in the number of AIDS victims. In order to be able to educate members of your groups, you will need to have current information. This certainly includes an awareness of the values, mores, and cultural background of the various clients you serve. In attempting to change the habits of racial, cultural, and religious groups, you are likely to run up against considerable resistance unless you are able to "speak their language." Furthermore, in educating the general public, it is important to realize that victims of AIDS and those who are HIV-positive can easily become the scapegoat of people's projections of their unconscious fears and hatred.

In his support groups for youths with the AIDS virus, Grant (1988) focuses on education as well as offering support to members at each session. These sessions begin with crisis intervention aimed at encouraging those clients who feel upset and isolated to talk about their feelings. Using a flexible approach, Grant gauges the reactions of the members to determine when it is appropriate to move into teaching. These topics of discussion include the use of condoms, sexual bargaining, and learning to set limits. Some time is devoted during the sessions to providing information on a wide range of subjects such as nutrition, stress management, strategies for making behavioral changes, and methods of modifying substance abuse. Grant reports that the group encourages individuals to practice safer sex to avoid infecting others and to make the necessary lifestyle changes that could increase the chances of maintaining their physical and emotional health.

Spector and Conklin (1987) organized a therapy group for AIDS patients around the principles of supportive psychotherapy. They reported that the terminal patients in their group typically experienced feelings of isolation, both psychological and physical. These clients felt alone in their existential dilemma, especially when those close to them and caretakers distanced themselves from them as they approached death. The primary therapeutic goal of their group was to restore some measure of lost support and compassionate contact that could come about through the cohesive group. Spector and Conklin reaffirmed their belief in group psychotherapy as providing a valuable support system for people with AIDS. They list the following suggestions for group therapists who are interested in conducting a group for people with AIDS:

- In selecting members, it is good to group individuals at similar stages of the disease. The co-therapists found that mixing patients whose disease was far advanced with those in a relatively early stage led to intolerable fears in the latter.
- It is essential that the group leaders be as knowledgeable as possible in all aspects of the disease, as the members often bring the information they receive from the media, relatives, and friends to the group sessions for clarification.
- Group therapists need to regularly monitor the mental status of each patient to detect any psychological changes.
- The co-leaders must be comfortable discussing sexuality, drug use, and sexual techniques aimed at safer practices.

- It is useful for the therapists to be prepared to offer clear, up-to-date information concerning resources such as social services, long-term care facilities, and local support groups.

In summary, in reviewing some support groups for people with AIDS, it seems clear that they offer valuable therapeutic and educational functions. Members in these groups can learn the truth about the facts surrounding their disease, and they can acquire a range of cognitive and behavioral strategies for enhancing their quality of life. The acceptance and caring within the group can foster an increased sense of hope and can facilitate the development of their inner resources to create a meaningful existence.

One Counselor's Story: Starting an AIDS Support Group

Steven Lanzet is an assistant professor of counselor education at the College of Idaho, practices as a Licensed Professional Counselor at the Boise Counseling Center, and is the support services coordinator of the Idaho AIDS Foundation, which is the organization that sponsored the support group described below. He is a doctoral candidate at Seattle University and is now in the process of writing his dissertation on the burnout experiences of leaders of AIDS service organizations.

How the Group Began*

In 1987, after a doctor told me that I was suffering from an illness that could be associated with ARC (AIDS-related complex), I decided to take an HIV test. I had grave fears that I was going to test positive and wouldn't have long to live. If indeed I was going to die, I needed to make some plans. This crisis proved to be the catalyst for clarifying my values and making decisions about changing my life.

Later, I received word that I had tested negative. I experienced a great deal of emotional turmoil while waiting for the results, and I suspected that others went through a similar experience. Being a group counselor and believing in the power of the group process, I decided to begin a support group for people who were dealing with AIDS. Although most people said that they thought the group was a good idea, they felt it was highly unlikely that anyone would come to the group, because I work in a very conservative community. There was a chance that victims would not attend for fear of discovery. It did not take long for me to realize that there were two epidemics, one called AIDS, and the other called AFRAIDS.

*The material to follow is written from the perspective of Steven Lanzet.

I met a nurse epidemiologist at the local health department who was administering the HIV tests, Linda Poulsen, and discovered that many people were testing positive. Linda also had the idea that a support group would be helpful. Together we sat down and planned our ideal group. We decided that whether or not people showed up, we would sit there every time for at least an hour each session. We were very surprised to find out in our first group that eight people showed up for what turned out to be a powerful session. Most of these people had many things in common, best captured by the statement "I felt as if I was the only one who was going through this."

Help and Support

As we started to reach out, we realized that, unfortunately for us (in 1987 in Boise, Idaho), there wasn't a lot of support from the medical community. In designing the group, however, I found Linda, who was able to answer the questions of group participants about the physiological aspects of AIDS. The health department is often a good place to look for help and a co-leader when you decide to start a group. These people have direct knowledge and experience in dealing with the virus. In addition to the department, our major source of support is the Idaho AIDS Foundation. To find out what help is available in your community, call the National AIDS Hotline at (800) 342-AIDS.

One of our first tasks was to find a suitable location. Even though churches are abundant in our community and available for this kind of purpose, many gay people aren't welcomed in some of the mainline denominations. We also ruled out the use of the health department, because it was the place where many poeple had found that they were HIV-positive, and we thought they would have negative associations to it. We wanted a space that was comfortable, relaxed, and as noninstitutional as possible. Eventually, we decided to use the YMCA. It was very flexible and had a reputation of being open to new ideas.

Another source of support was the local gay community. The Gay Community Center put us in touch with the various gay organizations, and we were able to put out the word that we were starting the group. After a few months, we sent a flier to health-care providers, psychologists, counselors, and social workers about the services we could offer. I found out quickly that if we showed some flexibility, many people in the community were willing to work with us and to share their knowledge. We invited guest speakers to every other group session.

Format

From the outset, I decided that it would be best to use trained group leaders rather than to rely on volunteers. Professionals expressed interest in working with people with AIDS, and I provided ongoing coordination.

The format for these groups was the result of trial and error. When we began, we decided on an open support group to include a variety of people with AIDS, people who had tested HIV-positive, friends, family, parents, and those who were worried about being infected. In addition, health professionals and volunteers could attend.

I was concerned that we would get people who were in such advanced stages of the disease that it would be very difficult for me or the other clients to relate to them. But we found real benefit in having dying people, because the participants who were relatively healthy saw that it could happen to them and also were provided with a mode of strength. The members could begin to anticipate how to build a support system to solve problems that others were discussing. I have come to believe that a heterogeneous group including people dealing with all stages of the disease is advisable. Some people, however, felt uncomfortable with having participants in the group who were at stages considerably different from theirs. In a large community it is possible to create groups that are more homogeneous. The categories of people could be:

- family and friends
- those who have not tested HIV-positive but who are worried about being carriers of the virus
- newly diagnosed patients
- those who are HIV-positive without symptoms
- those who are HIV-positive with symptoms
- people with full-blown AIDS
- those with terminal-stage AIDS

When I talk to people elsewhere who organize separate groups, I find they have a difficult time knowing when to transfer someone out of one group and into another. These groups build up a genuine cohesiveness and are very resistant to making a switch. I quickly found out that we were better off with a heterogeneous approach. I recommend that you assess your situation and decide on what works best for you and your group members.

At our first and second meetings we asked people to brainstorm with us about what topics would be most interesting and relevant to deal with in the group. We did this exercise a number of times in different groups and combined the needs-assessment lists. They became the foundation for the guest speakers we asked to our groups. Some of the topics that came up were:

- the grief and loss process
- assertiveness training (dealing with doctors and other professionals)
- family issues
- spirituality
- medication and other health-care concerns
- nutrition and exercise

- learning about how to be sexually safer
- coping with homophobia and other forms of discrimination
- living wills and other legal issues
- coping with depression and other mental-health concerns

Based on our experience with several groups, we have developed a structure that serves the purposes of the group well. We typically begin a group session with a quick go-around. The importance of confidentiality is emphasized at the beginning of each session. If the members care to, they talk about what has brought them to the meeting that night. Often they go into their history, how they came to be HIV-positive, and what their experience has been before and after that time. As early as possible in each group meeting, the group leaders help members to identify common concerns and link the work of members. Before people come to these groups, their overwhelming feeling is that "I am all alone with this issue." It is difficult to maintain this defense when they see other people dealing with similar concerns.

Later in the session, we invite questions and comments from the participants. We try to keep this section short unless somebody asks a question that seems to be a theme for the whole group, in which case we will discuss it at length. We also bring in outside resources to lead the group on a particular question raised by the members. These guests have been well received, and this practice also introduces members to the resources available in the community.

At each meeting we encourage members to bring up personal concerns that they want to explore. Below are a few typical concerns:

- "I told my mother about my health."
- "My lover left me."
- "I have this purple blotch on my skin, and I don't know what to do."
- "I've been in jail since I last saw you."
- "I'm feeling good [I'm feeling bad]."

The role of the co-leaders at this time is to help people express themselves and to encourage people to speak to one another in the group rather than through the leaders. People are allowed to respond to what others say, but we ask them to be nonjudgmental, to use "I" language, and to speak directly to the other person.

The group ends with some sort of ritual. One of our early rituals was standing in a circle and giving a mutual shoulder rub. I assumed that many of the participants in our group had stopped getting touched after they were diagnosed and that if they came to the group, they could be guaranteed a little bit of nonsexual body contact such as a couple of hugs. We encourage people to give and get hugs if they so desire. At some groups, participants have asked if people would be willing to share names and phone numbers so that they could develop a network outside of the group.

Group Issues

Over the years that I have been running the groups, I have found a number of issues resurfacing, one of which is confidentiality. We continually need to redefine confidentiality, answer any questions about it, discuss it fully, and get everybody to agree to abide by this practice. At times, we spent as much as half of a meeting discussing confidentiality.

When an individual has knowingly broken confidentiality, the members tell the person that he or she is no longer welcome at the group. The group has been consistent with this norm. I stress that no one can confirm an individual's HIV status except that person. Nevertheless, group members remain afraid of disclosure and have had serious consequences when their status was disclosed.

Dealing in the group with people who are ill is a matter that must be addressed. Our members have depressed immune systems, and we ask those who are contagious not to come to the group that evening. We have had people come to the group when they were very ill yet noncontagious. Certain other members have had a variety of reactions, which need to be dealt with in an open fashion.

When a new member enters the group, we encourage the returning members to share more about their stories before asking the new client to participate. In telling their stories, returning members often relate what their life was like before they were HIV-positive, what it was like to test positive, and what their subsequent experience has been. They also tend to talk about what the group has meant to them. By the time we come around to the new individuals, it is much easier for them to express themselves. We then say, "You probably have some questions that you would like answered, and this would be a good time to do it." A typical question is: "I'm feeling very depressed, too. Tell me about that and what you have done about it." Or: "I haven't told my parents, and you said you haven't told your parents. I'm curious who has told their parents." This practice helps the new member get involved with the group and feel connected.

There is a lot of humor in our groups. At first, people who are new to the group are somewhat put off by the laughing, but eventually most of them learn the value of humor in putting concerns into perspective. The leaders must remember to accentuate the feelings that go along with the laughter and to look for the pain as well as the humor.

Dealing with grief and loss is a recurring theme. We are constantly reminding people about the grief cycle. Probably the most common reaction we get in the group is members experiencing an emotion and feeling as if they're going crazy or out of control. It is essential to teach people to identify where in the grief cycle they are so that when their anger erupts, they see it as a natural and necessary process. Almost always there is someone else in the group who has experienced the same kind of feeling and can speak to this issue.

When a member of the group either becomes very ill or dies, it is essential to explore the feelings evoked in other members. We spend some time at the meeting following the member's death in remembering him or her and talking about things that we liked about that person. Of course, along with this process comes dealing with the members' feelings about dying and grief. Usually there is talk about the funeral, which sometimes leads to a discussion about what others hope their memorial service will be like. We encourage this kind of talk, because it helps to reveal some of the members' own issues and helps them cope with the fear of dying.

Personal Concerns

As a result of leading these groups, I have learned to cope with anger at me. The first time someone in the group got mad at me, I didn't know how to respond. It took me awhile to figure out that anger was sometimes directed at me because the clients felt more comfortable with me than with other people. One of the doctors in our area who deals with AIDS patients told me that he had many patients who were angry with him. As we talked, I began to realize the pattern. A great deal of anger is associated with AIDS, but people have few places where it can be directed. The client knows that I'm a safe and nonrejecting target. I try to help the client redirect some of the anger and find ways to work through it.

Perhaps the greatest anxiety I experience is the feeling that the time I have to work in the AIDS area is limited. I realize that no matter how hard I try to fight it, there is always a sense of burnout tapping at my shoulder. I have learned that support for the group leaders is imperative. The toll of running a group like this many times and losing people in the group has been high. The best way to deal with our personal reactions is for us as leaders to meet outside of the sessions to talk about our feelings. I have been leading AIDS support groups for four years. This has been possible because I have taken periodic breaks from facilitating groups and have reduced the frequency of the groups that I do. The support groups that I have developed with other counselors who don't deal primarily with AIDS continue to be a key way to prevent burnout.

Looking Ahead

Our plans for the future include doing a statewide needs assessment, providing more training and supervision for group leaders, maintaining a follow-up system, and expanding the number of groups to include more members of minority groups and rural residents. I urge any trained group facilitator to learn more about AIDS to help meet urgent community needs and to consider starting or helping with an AIDS support group. It is both very demanding and very rewarding.

If I can answer any questions or be of assistance, please feel free to contact me: Steven I. Lanzet, The College of Idaho—Graduate Studies, 2112 Cleveland Boulevard, Caldwell, ID 83605; or Steven I. Lanzet, Idaho AIDS Foundation, P. O. Box 421, Boise, ID 83701. Or you may call me at one of the following phone numbers: The College of Idaho, (208) 459-5211; Idaho AIDS Foundation, (208) 345-2277; and Boise Counseling Center, (208) 345-1259.

A Transition Group in a Community Agency

Our friend and colleague Randy Alle-Corliss, the clinical social worker in a community mental-health center whose children's group we described in Chapter 9, also created and co-leads adult groups in the agency to help clients make the transition from a hospital or partial hospital program to independent living in the community. The primary goal of the transition group is to teach the members basic coping skills needed to reengage in the world.

Structure and Policies

The transition group, consisting of eight members, meets once a week for 90 minutes. Even though these groups are open, in that membership can change, they typically develop cohesion, and significant learning occurs. Being an open group does not mean that the group is loosely structured, without any ground rules. There is a core of regular members who make cohesion possible. Clients are expected to make at least a six-week commitment. They also agree to be on time for all sessions, to give 24 hours' notice if they need to cancel a group session, and not to miss two sessions in a row. The members sign a contract, which is also signed by the co-leaders, providing that failure to meet any of the above conditions means they will be terminated from the group. Any extenuating circumstances need to be discussed with the co-leaders. If members are dropped from the group and want to return, they must set up a private conference with both co-leaders. These policies tend to promote commitment and consistency.

Topics

Although each group develops a unique "personality," most of the transition groups deal with themes such as the following: socialization issues; communication skills; problem-solving skills; fears and struggles in independent living; individuation issues, such as learning to take care of oneself; family conflicts; topics related to work, such as getting a job or dealing with supervisors; relationships issues, including meeting people and making and maintaining friendships; fears of going out into the community; fears of being alone and learning to express and deal with loneliness and isolation; coping with loss and death; expressing and working through suicidal thoughts and feelings; and learning constructive ways of expressing and dealing with anger.

Topics such as these are generally dealt with through verbal techniques, although the co-leaders do employ role playing to make the sessions come to life. For instance, if a member is working on her fear of interviewing for a job, one of the co-leaders is likely to take on the role of an interviewer. In addition to identifying her specific fears about the interview situation, she also benefits from the feedback of others in the group, and she learns specific behavioral skills that she can practice to help her overcome her fears and increase her chances of succeeding in a real interview situation. The co-leaders make attempts to involve the other group members by inviting them to bring up their own related fears that they would like to explore.

Participants are also strongly encouraged to carry out behavioral homework assignments in between the sessions. They are expected to return with a report of what they thought, felt, and did in situations in which they applied newly acquired skills. By using the group as a laboratory for learning and practicing these social skills, the members do more than simply ventilate emotions and talk about problems. The emphasis is on dealing with interpersonal problems in the here and now in an action-oriented way.

Stages of Group Development

The transition group has all the characteristics of a closed group, but the stages are focused more on individual members than on the group as a whole. Some members are functioning at the initial stage, others may be transitional, and some have advanced into the working phase. New members are introduced into the group as old members terminate. The core members are usually at the same stage, and their work provides modeling for others and gives the group direction. As a member terminates, separation and loss issues emerge into the forefront and are explored.

Implications

Many agencies expect that groups will be open to new members, since there is a constant turnover of clientele in typical community clinics. Practitioners must learn how to adapt the group process to an open and changing structure. It is a mistake to cling to the defeating notion that such an arrangement is "secondary" in preference to a closed group, because there are some unique values of the open structure. In families, new babies are born, grow up, and eventually leave, all of which have an impact on the entire family system. In a like manner, the open group incorporates new members as others in the "family" leave, and everyone has opportunities to work through issues of separation and change within the group structure. If participants are prepared, such changes do not necessarily result in fragmentation or superficial group interaction. The group just described demonstrates that open groups can have identified goals and a clear structure and can result in many of the same member outcomes as a closed group.

If you are interested in obtaining a more detailed description of this transition group, the children's group described in Chapter 9, or the following women's support group, write Randy Alle-Corliss at Kaiser Permanente, Montclair Mental Health, 5330 San Bernardino Road, Montclair, CA 91763; telephone: (714) 399-3729.

A Women's Support Group for Victims of Incest

Another colleague, Lupe Alle-Corliss, a clinical social worker in a community agency, co-leads groups for women who have incest in their family background. She designed these support groups along the lines of a time-limited therapy group for women with a history of incest (Herman & Schatzow, 1984). The following description includes key features of both the group described by Herman and Schatzow and the one designed by Lupe and her co-leader, Myrna Samuels.

Sexual abuse of children by family members is increasingly coming to the attention of mental-health professionals. Approximately 10 percent of White, middle-class women in the United States indicate that they had a childhood sexual experience with an older male relative (Herman & Schatzow, 1984). A sexual encounter with a trusted family member not only typically results in a major psychological trauma itself but also frequently leads to emotional problems for the victim later in life. Some of the common problems include impaired self-esteem, negative identity formation, difficulty in intimate relationships, sexual dysfunction, and repeated victimization (Herman, 1981; Meiselman, 1978, 1990).

Purpose and Rationale

A group approach, or a combination of group and individual therapy, is generally considered to be the treatment of choice. The aim of the group is to provide a safe and therapeutic environment for women who were sexually abused during their childhood. Other objectives are to help women share their secret and recognize that they are not alone, understand the current impact of this experience, and begin to work through and resolve feelings associated with their trauma and to make changes. In a group situation women find a commonality and a basis for identification. The supportive environment within the group tends to encourage women to make contacts with others outside of the group. A new type of family can emerge, one that is different from the clients' original family, which may have been dysfunctional.

Setting Up the Group

Both Randy (whose group we described earlier) and Lupe have learned the value of recruiting potential members by publicizing their groups within their own agency. They do this through memos, announcements, and personal contact with colleagues. In considering members for the women's support group, they seek clients who display a readiness to deal openly with the trauma of incest. Typically, most of these women are already in individual therapy. If the women have a therapist other than the group leaders, a release form is asked for so that the co-leaders can consult and coordinate with the individual therapist.

As far as screening is concerned, both co-leaders meet individually with each potential member. Clients are asked about why they want such a group, and an attempt is made to determine how ready each individual is to talk in a group setting about the incest and its impact. Other questions sometimes asked during the screening include: "If there is any previous group experience, what was this like for you?" "Were you, or are you now, involved in individual therapy, and what was (is) this experience like?" "What are your personal goals for the group?" "What are your expectations, hopes, and fears about participating in the group?" Applicants are also encouraged to interview the co-leaders, asking questions about the group.

It is critical that members possess the ego strength to deal with the material that will be explored during the sessions. Members need to have enough interpersonal skills to deal with others in a group situation. People with suicidal and extremely self-destructive tendencies and people who do not have adequate contact with reality are screened out. Care is taken not to include family members or friends in the same group. Also excluded are those who are not ready or willing to talk openly about their experiences.

Herman and Schatzow (1984) use three criteria for inclusion in a group: (1) the clients must express generally positive feelings about participating in a group with others who have experienced incest; (2) the potential participants must not be in a crisis state—that is, must be functioning reasonably well in daily life; and (3) they must have an appropriate ongoing relationship with an individual therapist.

Structure of the Group

The group is closed and meets for 75 minutes for a 12-week period. This time limitation is designed to facilitate bonding and to produce a reasonable degree of pressure necessary to work through the members' resistances. Although each group has its own process, these groups generally go through the phases to be described.

Initial Phase. The initial stage involves getting to know one another and establishing ground rules. Aspects that are emphasized are the importance of regular attendance, being prompt, confidentiality, the limitations of time, and bringing any unresolved issues back to the group, rather than dealing with them outside of the group. A date for a post-group meeting, which is typically about three months after termination, is established at the first session. In the early phase of the group, members express empathy with one another over the difficulty of sharing the incest issue. The following guideline questions are provided to help them deal directly with the impact of incest on them: "How did the molestation happen? Who molested you? How old were you? How long did it go on? How did you deal with it? How did you feel toward the people who were in a position to protect you from the molestation, but failed to do so?"

Much of the initial phase is focused on identifying personal and specific goals in writing and then discussing them. This procedure allows all in the group to know of each person's goals and provides a direction for the sessions. Members generally feel much anxiety and apprehension at first. A member often feels that she is the only one with such a terrible burden, and she may feel that she would be an outcast if others knew about her secret. As the women realize that they have a common experience, they begin to open up and find the support that is available in the group. By sharing the incest experience, the women free themselves to look at how it continues to affect them. The focus of the sessions is not merely on reporting the details of the specific acts but also on exploring their feelings, beliefs, and perceptions about what happened.

As well as gaining insight into her own dynamics, a woman learns that she can be of help to others through her disclosures. Initially, a woman may show resistance by becoming the "helper" or "caretaker" of others in her group. Herman and Schatzow (1984) observed that the increased risk taking involved in discussing feelings and beliefs about the incest story led to an increase in the group's cohesiveness. They found that the discharging and sharing of intense emotions resulted in a bonding and mutual supportiveness that allowed for exploring common themes of secrecy, isolation, shame, helplessness, fear, hurt, and anger.

Middle Phase. During the middle stage there is a focus on accomplishing the individual members' goals. Connections are made between a woman's past behavior and her present behavior. In this way she begins to see patterns and to understand her own dynamics. For instance, a woman may have chosen men who dominated her, abused her, or in some way took advantage of her. She sees with greater clarity her own part in allowing this type of treatment to continue. A group is a good way to help such a woman become aware of and challenge her faulty belief system. For example, women may hold themselves responsible for initiating the molestation. Through the group process, these women can rid themselves of destructive self-blame and can learn to create functional self-statements. There are a number of therapeutic strategies that promote a change of feelings, attitudes, and behaviors. Examples include learning that they behaved normally in an abnormal situation; reading books in a personal way; keeping a diary or journal that inlcudes thoughts, feelings, and behaviors in certain situations; writing letters that are not sent; talking to other family members; and recording and sharing dreams.

Final Phase. Toward the end of the group the women are reminded of the upcoming termination. The co-leaders assist them in reviewing what has happened in the group as a whole as well as what they have learned individually and how they can continue to apply their insights and newly acquired behaviors to situations outside of the group. Role playing helps in this consolidation process. The co-leaders give a structured questionnaire to help the members pull together and assess their learning. The members evaluate their progress and determine future plans, including what work they still need to do. They write down and give feedback to one another, and they identify certain people in the group whom they are willing to contact should they feel a need for help and support. Although the women cognitively know that the group will soon be over, it is a common reaction for them to say that they do not want it to end. Members are asked how they want to celebrate the ending of the group, within limits. The follow-up meeting three months later reinforces what was learned and provides renewed support.

Implications

You might want to organize a group such as the one just described or another specific type of group for adults. We encourage you to follow your interests. Do additional reading in this area. Seek out a colleague with some experience with the population you will work with. And then design a group that will allow you to try out some therapeutically creative ideas. As we mentioned in Chapter 7, building follow-up procedures into your design gives you a basis for understanding the longer-term value of the group experience as well as improving your design for future groups. In the short-term groups reported on by Herman and Schatzow (1984), the results of a six-month follow-up survey of 28 women supported their assumption that this therapeutic approach had been particularly effective in resolving the issues of shame, secrecy, and stigmatizing associated with incest. The single most helpful factor was the contact with other women who had been incest victims. Should you be interested in learning more about designing groups for women with a history of incest, we strongly recommend reading the article by Herman and Schatzow as a beginning. Then follow up by reading books and articles on incest, some of which are among the suggested readings at the end of this chapter. Some especially useful resources include Butler (1978), Courtois and Leehan (1982), Finklehor (1984), Forward and Buck (1978), Geller, Devlin, and Flynn (1985), Goodwin (1982), Herman (1981), Justice and Justice (1979), Laidlaw, Malmo, and Associates (1990), Maltz (1991), Maltz and Holman (1987), Mandell and Damon (1989), McBride and Emerson (1989), Meiselman (1978, 1990), Rush (1980), Sprei and Goodwin (1983), and Steward, Farquhar, Dicharry, Glick, and Martin (1986).

If you would like to discuss this group with Lupe Alle-Corliss, you can contact her at Rancho Cucamonga Counseling Services, 9651 Business Center Drive, Rancho Cucamonga, CA 91730; telephone: (714) 945-4316.

A Long-Term Therapy Group for Incest Survivors

Another colleague, Sandi Burns, a psychotherapist in Billings, Montana, has been conducting long-term groups for incest "survivors" for over ten years. Her type of group offers an alternative to the preceding illustration of a short-term group.

Basic Information on Incest *

When incest occurs, there is a violation of one's most private self. However, the actual physical sexuality is but a small part of the dynamics that occur. First of all, children who are sexually abused by a family member feel betrayed and generally develop a mistrust of others who could potentially take advantage of them. Secondly, the sexual abuse is often just one of several dysfunctions within these families. There may also be physical abuse of children and spouse, substance abuse, or a multitude of other family problems. Thirdly, the perpetrators use many distortions to persuade children to participate in the sexual abuse or to allow them to continue taking advantage of them. Most victims, even by adulthood, have no idea of how this happened. They usually recall only the sexual contacts. Thus, they are unaware of how emotionally abusive this situation was, not just between themselves and the perpetrator but within the whole family.

Victims of sexual abuse tend to repeat the psychodynamic patterns in their adulthood. Many grow into adulthood with the same distortions they were taught, enter further abusive relationships, and may continue to be victimized. Because incest cannot continue unless the secret of it

*The material to follow is written from the perspective of Sandi Burns.

is kept, victims learn to keep many secrets. Also, most victims of incest stop their emotional development at about the age at which the incest begins. Thus, even though they may have sexual knowledge far beyond their chronological age, they have been conditioned to blunt their feelings about the abusive situations.

Rationale for Long-Term Group Therapy

Group therapy appears to be the treatment of choice for most victims of incest. Although some may also need individual treatment, they gain many benefits through a homogeneous group. First is identification with others. Incest victims often feel "different" and isolated. In group sessions with others who have had similar experiences, they often feel an immediate relief that they are not "alone." This commonality among members helps establish a therapeutic alliance. It becomes easier for victims to acknowledge their abuse in this situation than in talking to an individual therapist. This disclosure further helps break the cycle of "secret" that the victim may have lived with for many years. Also, a well-organized group provides safety for its members to explore emotions that they have repressed over the years and also offers a chance to explore their beliefs about their situation. With identification and support from others, they can begin to receive feedback that challenges the distorted beliefs they hold and the distorted childhood messages they received.

Victims of incest usually need a great amount of validation, support, and consistency to enable them to really delve into the issues of abuse. This process takes time. Eventually, real levels of trust begin to develop as well as some methods for learning discrimination. Time is also needed for more extensive working through of the trauma. If given enough permission, support, and leeway, clients gradually unfold all the incestuous dynamics spontaneously within the group situation. Incest victims begin to look more realistically at their own denial, minimization, and other defenses. They learn new ways of coping and have opportunities to try out new behaviors as other group members provide support and feedback.

The groups for adult victims that I have led are not limited by time. A six-month commitment is required for admission. The majority of clients attend for at least a year, with the average stay 18 months to two years. No new members are admitted until there is a termination.

Selection of Group Members

Assessment. Each member admitted to the group must be able to function in the world. People who are psychotic, extremely suicidal, or homicidal are not candidates for the group. In making an assessment, I look for factors such as ego strength, motivation, interpersonal skills, life circumstances, and current functioning.

It is my belief that people are ready at different times to look at issues in their lives. Consequently, the groups I run are always voluntary, and decisions are made with the client at intake whether the timing is appropriate for them. Because I do require at least a six-month commitment, the clients who are accepted into the group are usually quite motivated.

Intake Interview. All potential members are interviewed at least once before group participation. This interview is aimed at assessing their readiness for participating in a long-term group, level of motivation, current coping skills, and emotional stability. Also, the leader tells the client of the purposes of the group, its structure and functioning, and the ground rules. Although every new client is apprehensive in joining such a group, the anxiety is usually gone after the first meeting. For those who may appear to be acceptable in the assessment process but who feel undecided, several other individual sessions will be planned. Some may decide to continue some individual therapy with later consideration of group participation. Generally, a mutual decision is reached between the screening therapist and the client.

During the intake interview, the ground rules are explained and clarified:

- Confidentiality is very important to those who have experienced incest because of the past secrecy, the shame they feel, and the many issues of trust.
- It is important to stress that attendance at all sessions is important so that the group members can develop a safe environment that will allow disclosure of such emotional and personal issues.
- Members are asked to make a six-month commitment, which will allow an exploration in some depth of these traumatic issues.
- If people are chemically dependent, they are not admitted to the group. Such clients are encouraged to get involved in drug treatment, self-help, or both.
- Individuals who are in a crisis are not accepted, for they will probably need more individualized attention than the group could provide.
- Individuals who exhibit a high degree of denial by insisting that they have no current problems in coping with their past childhood trauma are not admitted to the group.
- Socialization with other members outside the group is not permitted. This practice has proved to be more harmful than helpful to the members.
- A requirement for termination is that members devote at least two sessions in working through the termination with all group members. This process also gives members good practice for other termination issues in their lives.

Group Process

Although the commonalities within this homogeneous group help build cohesion, at the same time, acceptance of individual differences is emphasized. Each person needs to be accepted at whatever level she is currently functioning, and she needs to work at her own pace. All members' experiences and reactions are accepted without condemnation. One of the benefits of these group experiences is an increased empathy for others.

Control and boundaries are key therapeutic issues in incest groups. As children being victimized, clients seldom felt as though they had any control. Now as adults, they need to be able to make choices and attempt to exert control. If a person is feeling frightened, needs time out, or wants to quit talking because her emotions are becoming too tense, this wish needs to be respected. Also, victims of incest often fear a "loss of control" over their emotions. In our groups, considerable work is done in teaching the women deep breathing, body awareness, and other methods of releasing pent-up emotions. This work is reinforced through guidelines and boundaries. Incestuous families have few boundaries to follow. The therapist must set these boundaries in the group—for example, by intervening in harmful interaction between members. Certain boundaries are emphasized throughout the duration of the group, such as not harming yourself or another person or destroying property. Clients are encouraged to express their emotions in a safe, constructive, and nonthreatening way.

Many victims of incest feel rather powerless and have low self-esteem. This issue is addressed near the beginning of the group and throughout as new clients enter. Members are taught that if they want time in the group to talk, need some attention from others, or want responses from others, they need to speak up and ask, breaking one of the patterns of incest victims.

Some members have adopted "caretaking" patterns and have consistently placed others' needs above their own. They have the task of learning how to take care of themselves. They must also learn to avoid rescuing others or taking away others' responsibilities. Skills of negotiation, feedback, and conflict resolution are modeled by the therapist and encouraged among members.

Leadership

To run a group for incest survivors, leaders need two essential forms of knowledge. First, the therapist should know about group process and dynamics. Second, the therapist needs a knowledge of incest, the dynamics of child sexual abuse, and incestuous family dynamics. The victims of incest have many "blind spots" in their present lives. They require a skilled and knowledgeable leader to help them discover and work through their distortions.

Throughout the group process, transference issues develop between members and the therapist. It is important to address these issues and attempt to work with them. Again, there may be difficulties with boundary issues that the therapist will have to firmly address. Incestuous families lack clear boundaries. Some are too rigid, and some are too loose or become enmeshed. The boundary issues and communications parallel their dysfunctional family patterns. The task is for them to identify their learned patterns of interactions and to address problems of self-definition and self-regulation.

The therapist's function is to be a process facilitator, educator, observer, parental role model, alter ego, and limit setter. Two qualities needed for leading these groups are firmness and warmth. The women in these groups need to experience gentleness, understanding, nurturing and reliability. However, the therapist also needs to be able to be firm in setting boundaries that these survivors have lacked. The group facilitator needs to create a safe environment for group members to explore relationships among themselves and with the therapist.

If you have an interest in further details of this kind of long-term group for incest victims, write to Sandi Burns, 1020 N. 27th Street, Suite 200, Billings, MT 59101; telephone: (406) 248-6333.

An Adult Group for Personal Growth

The following description of a personal-growth group is based on material provided by Julianne Christinson, a licensed marriage and family counselor, and Linda Gilbert, a psychologist, who have conducted this group both in their private practices and at the Center for Health Promotion at Loma Linda University in California.

Nature of the Group

The co-leaders meet individually with candidates for screening and orientation before placing clients in a group. They provide the written information described below, which they discuss with each person during the initial interview and again at the first meeting of the group. This is the gist of what potential clients are given:

Why a Group? Groups provide a dynamic and stimulating way to learn about yourself and your relationships. Often, we are dissatisfied and unaware of our own self-defeating behaviors. In the privileged environment of a group, others can be counted on for spontaneous and truthful reactions and feedback that can help you see yourself more clearly. The group allows you to discover how you relate to others, how others are affected by you, and how you make it easy or difficult for others to be close to you. Your strengths and growth areas will be highlighted as you challenge yourself to take risks in the group setting.

This group is open to both women and men, and it offers a constructive experience in understanding self and others. Personal concerns are appropriate for this group, including making major life transitions, breaking free of a codependent relationship, or developing a healthy, meaningful relationship. The group can assist you in learning more about how to start caring for yourself and how to stop controlling others. Below are some pertinent facts about this group:

- Enrollment is limited. Early sign-up improves your chance for participation.
- All groups are "closed" (meaning new members will not be added after the second session). This facilitates the formation of a trusting, committed environment.
- The group meets for 12 consecutive Wednesday evenings from 6 to 8 P.M. The fee is $20 per week. Your commitment to attending is essential.
- An individual appointment ($20 fee) is required before joining the group.

Type of Group. This is a self-exploration group for adults. During the initial session, the co-leaders give specific suggestions to assist the participants in getting the most from their group experience. During this initial meeting the focus is on getting acquainted, developing a climate of trust, discussing possible topics for group exploration, and learning how to function productively as a group member.

Goals and Objectives. The group is a place for interpersonal learning and personal growth. As a participant in a group, you are invited to examine your values, behaviors, and relationships with others. You are expected to take a serious and honest look at the quality of your life. You are the person who needs to decide what, how much, and when to share yourself. It is your responsibility to determine the nature and extent of changes you want to make. However, if you join this group, you are expected to become active and contributing members. Some specific goals are as follows:

- to develop sufficient trust in the group to allow for an honest sharing of feelings and attitudes, and to learn how to carry this trust into everyday life
- to grow in self-acceptance and self-respect
- to become tolerant of others and to respect others' differences
- to learn how to make decisions and accept the consequences
- to become less isolated by discovering that others in the group have similar problems
- to clarify values and to determine the congruence between behavior and these values
- to become sensitive to ways in which we affect other people and ways in which they affect us

- to learn specific ways of applying in everyday life what is learned in the group

Basic Group Rules. Five ground rules are established to help you attain your personal goals:

1. You are expected to be present at all the group meetings, because absence affects the entire group. If you are unable to attend a meeting because of an emergency, you will have to pay for the missed group as though you had attended.
2. You are expected to keep confidential what other members do and say within the group.
3. You are to decide on your own specific goals and on the issues you are willing to explore.
4. You must avoid sexual involvements with others in the group during its duration.
5. You are not to use physical violence in group sessions, nor are you to be verbally abusive to others in the group.

How Can You Get the Most from the Group?   Twelve weeks is not a great deal of time, but it is long enough for you to find out if you are serious about change. Behavior change involves hard work, and you need to commit yourself to practicing new behaviors that you learn in the group in everyday life situations.

(For more details on the specific guidelines the co-leaders teach the members for getting the most from their group, refer to the discussion in Chapter 4. The co-leaders draw many of their guidelines from that material.)

Personal Perspectives of the Co-Leaders

Julianne and Linda say that they find it challenging to co-lead these groups. Each of them gets a different perspective from the other, and their styles have a balancing effect on the group. One of the co-leaders tends to focus on work with individual members in the group context, and the other co-leader tends to look for ways to link members and to encourage interaction within the group.

Both Linda and Julianne find that working with various groups confirms their belief in the unique value of the group process as a catalyst for significant change. They report that as a group unfolds, they witness a willingness of the members to engage in hard work, and they see results in changed behavior. Most of the members give signs of some degree of success in applying what they are learning in the group sessions to their everyday life. The leaders report that the sessions are characterized by a balance between the problems that members bring to the group sessions and a focus on how these problems are manifested in the here-and-now interactions in the group. The leaders operate on the model of the group as a sample of the members' usual styles of interacting. Thus, they facilitate a process that helps members see connections between the problems they bring to the sessions and the problems that may be emerging within the group.

Responses by Group Members

The following comments were written by group members in response to the questions "What has this group meant to you? What is something you will take with you—something you have learned by participating in this group?"

- "Being in this group has meant tension and stress, but at least I got to try some things here before going into the real world. I think I'm more assertive at times now, and find I'm doing more things in the group than I do in the outside world to take care of myself."
- "The group has been a place to come where I didn't have to be an authority on anything but myself. . . . I found out where I stood with myself and the group as a whole. I, as a person, am different from the image of myself out there. Out there I am in many roles: manager, father, authority. This [in the group] is probably the real me."
- "The group for me provided a focus. It was a crystallization process for feelings I've had for a long time. The group gave me permission to deal with them more, and then I was able to move ahead with them. This has been a privileged environment. I saw myself carry this into other relationships."
- "*Challenge* is the word that comes to mind. I'm low on outside relationships. Being here is the most intense thing in my life at this point. My challenge has been staying *in* the group. I kept popping out, withdrawing. It was hard, I would get feedback and be mirrored. My self stood out in high relief. My friends are too nice to tell how I come across. I've found that what's on the inside doesn't match what's on the outside, and I want to bring the two together more."
- "I still stare through a glass darkly. For me it's been an opening, a chance. As far as closure goes, that's irrelevant, I still have too far to go. I'm seeing things and plan to do the next group."
- "It was hard for me. A majority of the time I found the group stressful. I was generally quiet, I don't relate to things very well. I have realized that there is a lot I need to do to get where I want to go."
- "I continue to benefit from the feedback that I get in my group. I'm in a rut, and others have suggested other options. It's so hard when you've been stuck to take that extra step. The feedback has been 'You're exactly where you want to be.' I can't seem to take steps. I can see what I do that might keep other people from being around me. That's hard. But, at least now I have an idea of where to go from here. I guess you could say being here has been a kick in the butt."

- "Group:
  A place to be bold, a place to be safe,
  A place to begin to be free;
  Here I have found a privileged space
  Where it's OK to be me."

If you would like further information about the design of these groups, contact either Julianne Christinson, 116 North Santa Fe, Hemet, CA 92343; telephone: (714) 872-4548, or Linda Gilbert, Loma Linda University, Center for Health Promotion, Loma Linda, CA 92350; telephone: (714) 824-4496.

A Residential Group for Adults

Description and Purpose

Along with some of our colleagues we have designed what we consider a unique course and experiential workshop in personal growth, one with combined educational and therapeutic aims. Since 1972 we have done these workshops through California State University at Fullerton's Continuing Education Program every summer. These weeklong residential workshops include 16 participants, ranging in age from 18 to 65, and four co-leaders. The groups are composed of people from various socioeconomic classes representing a wide range of occupations. With the experience of over 50 of these weeklong groups with around 875 people, we have found themes that appear to have universality for the participants.

The purpose of the workshop is to provide the tools for self-confrontation and self-help methods to make change possible. We hope that participants will leave the group with a greater awareness of how they typically initiate and respond in their world, how they avoid coming to grips with their full potential, and how they can take specific steps to challenge areas in their lives where they feel stuck.

Structure and Format

We follow the guidelines that we described in Chapter 3 relating to preliminary procedures, screening and selection, conducting individual interviews and a pregroup session, preparing the participants, asking them to do some reading and write personal papers, and teaching them ways of getting the most from the workshop. We place considerable emphasis on ways of translating what they experience in the workshop into practical changes in their everyday behavior.

We find that one of the exciting features of any type of adult group is the fact that a group of strangers can drop their social masks and become more intimate with one another, building a caring community that leads to taking action in their daily life. Once they decide to risk opening up to their inner experiencing, a wide range of feelings and thoughts emerges, and the basis is formed for pursuing some universal themes that unite the members.

A residential group is particularly valuable in this regard. The structure of the group provides for at least eight hours daily of leader-directed groups, in addition to many opportunities for informal interactions with other individuals and in small groups. The residential setting makes this a unique experience in living and learning within a community, something that is difficult to achieve in meetings that last for only a few hours once a week. Moreover, the structure allows participants to block out the distractions of daily living and focus for a week on what they want to change in their life.

The themes that are explored in a residential workshop are the same as those we have discussed at the outset of this chapter when we addressed theme-oriented groups. We don't expect the issues that are explored to be resolved during the week, but our intention is to give people an opportunity to view themselves in a new light. As a way for them to continue their growth pattern, we inform members of the resources for individual and group counseling that are available to them both on the university campus and in the community.

Exploring Inner Conflicts

A great deal of what members do in the residential workshop has to do with resolving inner conflicts. They also come to appreciate that what they previously viewed as conflicting aspects of themselves can be complementary. For example, members learn that love and hate, distance and closeness, toughness and tenderness, and pain and joy are not mutually exclusive. In fact, these aspects contribute to the range and depth of being human. The members find that much of their energy has been invested in the struggle between their conflicting inner selves. The following are a few of the conflicts that come to light during a workshop.

▪ **The struggle between knowing oneself and the fear of discovering only emptiness inside.** Members often fear that if they search within themselves, they will find that they are merely reflections of what everyone expects them to be, having introjected their parents' and others' standards. They also express their hope to learn more about themselves, yet they are fearful about what they might find out.

▪ **The struggle between being oneself and the fear of finding that one is like one's parents.** Some people are very upset by their awareness that they have turned out to be just like their parents. They may want to reject all of the qualities they have in common with their parents, including the positive ones. In the group they make clearer choices about what aspects of their parents they want to keep and what characteristics they want to modify.

- **The struggle between the desire for security and the desire to break new ground.** A young woman in one of our workshops found herself bored with her life—with herself, her husband, and her children. She described how one part of her was saying: "Accept what you have. Settle for security. Don't rock the boat. After all, things could be a lot worse. Don't make waves, or you might lose what you have now—and then what?" But the part of her that wanted more than security was saying: "Is this all I'm worth? Don't I deserve more? I'm bored and growing stale. If I accept that now, what will my life be like five years from now? I'll challenge myself and take the risk of revealing to my husband what I'm thinking and feeling. I'll demand more, even if I might wind up without security."

- **The struggle between being self-sufficient and depending on others.** A woman in one of our workshops had been on her own for a long time. She had not suffered from this; her life was arranged in such a way that she experienced success in her personal endeavors. Yet she had never fully allowed others into her world. During the workshop she realized that she feared being hurt by others. She began to see how she distanced herself from others and suppressed her need for them. In short, she began to let herself experience the conflict between her need for others and her desire to be self-sufficient.

- **The struggle between protecting oneself and making oneself vulnerable.** Some people who come to a workshop have developed a hard exterior shell or wall, behind which they hide. These people may have acquired their tough exterior in response to a great number of disappointments and hurts. In the workshop they may let themselves feel their gentleness and compassion and may consider anew whether their suit of armor is necessary. As a result of their learning in the group, they often get better at distinguishing between those situations where it is appropriate to be guarded and those times when it is safe to become open and vulnerable.

- **The struggle between self-respect and self-criticism.** This struggle is exemplified by the group member who was very much overweight and who seemed to make running himself into the ground a way of life. His obesity prevented him from liking or respecting himself, and it also made him unattractive to others. It was as though he was wearing a sign telling people that he was worth little. His dependency and his self-deprecation were a drain on others. He learned that there were some sides of himself that he could begin to appreciate. He decided to take certain steps that would earn him not only the respect of others but also his self-respect.

- **The struggle between wanting revenge and the desire to forgive.** In every group we hear the angry cries of those who feel that they were abandoned by their parents. Our cushions are torn, and our battacas are ripped at the seams! The desire to hurt the father or mother who was not there when needed is expressed in most groups. After a catharsis, clients often find that there is room in themselves for forgiveness instead of being stuck with blaming. They may want to express love to their parents, rather than to wait indefinitely for the parents to make the first move.

The Final Stage

During the closing days of the workshop our primary goal is to help the members integrate and consolidate what they've learned. We pay particular attention to the points we developed in Chapter 7. We systematically apply procedures designed to assist members in consolidating their workshop experiences. Other key tasks include dealing with termination issues, arranging for follow-up procedures, and taking care of evaluation measures.

The closing phase of the group is designed to bridge for the participants the gap between the world they've experienced for a week and the world they will soon reenter. The workshop is not meant to be an end in itself but, rather, a means by which people can come to a better understanding of their internal world in order to reshape their external world. The aim of the workshop is to help the participants see the richness of their capacities, the ways in which they prevent themselves from realizing their potentials, the ineffective ways in which they relate to others, and the advantages of recognizing and utilizing the power they have as individuals.

As we mentioned in Chapter 7, follow-up procedures are of great value, which is the reason we schedule a group session three months after the weeklong residential group has come to an end. In this way, the members have an added incentive to keep their commitments, and a note of accountability is added to the workshop. As leaders, we find these follow-up sessions useful in evaluating the outcomes of the workshop experience. Most of these follow-up meetings involve reporting on both the successes and the setbacks members have experienced. This session allows for reinforcing the gains that they have made and encouraging them to refine their action plans to contribute to their changes. We also emphasize the importance of creating and maintaining a supportive network within the group itself so that their efforts can be sustained during difficult times.

Concluding Comments

Our preferred format for working with adults is a residential one that provides for intensity and the time to work in a sustained way. However, the outcomes and directional changes that appear to result from successful group participation seem strikingly similar among all types of adult groups. We've found that the participants take an honest look at the quality of their life, make certain decisions after their experience in the group, and take active steps to carry out their plans. We have observed in working with various special-interest groups (including, but not limited to, residential workshops) that participants often achieve such outcomes as:

- an increased desire to get more from their relationships with significant people
- a tendency to be more direct and honest in relating with selected others
- a greater willingness to take risks and to live with uncertainty
- an understanding of how and why they are keeping themselves from getting what they say they want from life
- an understanding of ways in which they often sabotage their own growth
- a recognition that they are to a large degree the product of their choices and that if they don't like the direction of their life, they have the power to do something to change it

After many years of doing these residential workshops in our home, we still find that they are a highlight of our professional activities. This experience allows us to see clients at their best as they dare to be different by becoming the people they were meant to become. It is a privilege to be able to be a part of a caring community in which people are willing to reach out to others by sharing their common human experiences. As this community takes its unique shape, we are all able to see that even though we have our differences, we are engaged in a universal set of personal struggles. Not only have we gained in a professional sense, but we continue to benefit personally from this special experience, for we are also challenged to review the direction of our own lives. For a more detailed discussion of the typical themes we explore during the week, see G. Corey, M. Corey, Callanan, and Russell (1992). Also, for a discussion of the making of a community much like the one we describe, see Peck (1987).

Where to Go from Here

Because groups for adults are so varied, it is difficult to list one or two books as a place to begin. The readings suggested below do not all pertain to group work, but ideas for leading various adult groups can be found in these resources. Depending on your interests, you may find the following books particularly helpful in getting ideas for your groups.

If you want to do further reading on topics that can be explored in groups, see I Never Knew I Had a Choice (G. Corey & M. Corey, 1990), which deals with existential concerns that people bring to groups. The book contains many exercises and activities that leaders can use for their groups. Each chapter is followed by numerous annotated readings appropriate for developing themes and topics for adult groups.

A very useful book that provides a step-by-step approach for group work is *Working with Adults in Groups* (Rose, 1989). Written from a cognitive-behavioral perspective, this book describes the multimethod approach to working with adults. There are detailed discussions of guidelines for starting and conducting groups, using cognitive-behavioral intervention strategies in small groups, and using techniques to help members carry their learning beyond the sessions.

Two other books with a cognitive-behavioral slant can easily be used as the basis for structuring themes in adult groups: *Feeling Good: The New Mood Therapy* (Burns, 1981) and *Control Theory* (Glasser, 1985).

Group leaders who work with adults can find an excellent discussion of both the theory and practice of therapy groups in the works of Irvin Yalom. His classic work is *The Theory and Practice of Group Psychotherapy* (1985). In his *Existential Psychotherapy* (1980) is an outstanding discussion of ways in which the themes of death, freedom, isolation, and meaninglessness can be integrated into clinical practice and group work. *Inpatient Group Psychotherapy* (1983) is a highly readable source for group practitioners who work with both higher- and lower-level inpatient groups. He integrates techniques with relevant research findings.

A key resource for an extensive bibliography of interest to practitioners with adult groups is *Group Work in the Helping Professions* (Zimpfer, 1984). Of special use are the references dealing with group procedures for parents, relatives, families, couples, and spouses; separation and divorce groups; parent education; enrichment; marriage encounter; and premarital counseling in groups (section 6.10, pp. 200–224). This work also is an excellent source of articles pertaining to women's groups (section 6.20, pp. 303–315) and men's groups (section 6.21, pp. 315–320).

If you want to read further about the ways of creating your own techniques in working with various adult groups, we recommend *Group Techniques* (G. Corey, M. Corey, Callanan, & Russell, 1992), which describes our approach to techniques for all the stages of group development. Most of the techniques that we describe in this book have grown out of our 18 years of co-leading the summer weeklong residential workshops we describe in this chapter. Also, *The Different Drum: Community Making and Peace* (Peck, 1987) deals with the true meaning of community, the genesis of community, and the stages of community-making—all of which seem to apply to our weeklong residential workshops in many important respects.

References and Suggested Readings*

Alberti, R. E., & Emmons, M. L. (1986a). *Your perfect right: A guide to assertive behavior* (5th ed.). San Luis Obispo, CA: Impact.

---

*Books and articles marked with an asterisk are recommended for further reading.

Alberti, R. E., & Emmons, M. L. (1986b). *Your perfect right: A manual for assertiveness trainers.* San Luis Obispo, CA: Impact.

Altman, L. S., & Plunkett, J. J. (1984). Group treatment of adult substance abusers. *Journal for Specialists in Group Work, 9*(1), 26–31.

Barrows, P. A., & Halgin, R. P. (1988). Current issues in psychotherapy with gay men: Impact of the AIDS phenomenon. *Professional Psychology: Research and Practice, 19*(4), 395–402.

Basow, S. A. (1986). *Gender stereotypes: Traditions and alternatives* (2nd ed.). Pacific Grove, CA: Brooks/Cole.

*Brisman, J., & Siegel, M. (1985). The bulimia workshop: A unique integration of group treatment approaches. *International Journal of Group Psychotherapy, 35*(4), 585–601.

*Bruhn, J. G. (1989). Counseling persons with a fear of AIDS. *Journal of Counseling and Development, 67,* 455–457.

Bumagin, S., & Smith, J. M. (1985). Beyond support: Group psychotherapy with low-income mothers. *International Journal of Group Psychotherapy, 35*(2), 279–294.

Burns, D. D. (1981). *Feeling good: The new mood therapy.* New York: New American Library (Signet).

*Butler, S. (1978). *Conspiracy of silence: The trauma of incest.* New York: Bantam Books.

*Carroll, M., & Wiggins, J. (1990). *Elements of group counseling: Back to the basics.* Denver: Love.

*Castronovo, N. R. (1990). Acquired immune deficiency syndrome education on the college campus: The mandate and the challenge. *Journal of Counseling and Development, 66,* 578–580.

Cole, S. A. (1983). Self-help groups. In H. I. Kaplan & B. J. Sadock (Eds.), *Comprehensive group psychotherapy* (2nd ed.) (pp. 144–150). Baltimore: Williams & Wilkins.

Corey, G. (1990). *Theory and practice of group counseling* (3rd ed.). Pacific Grove, CA: Brooks/Cole.

*Corey, G. & Corey, M. (1990). *I never knew I had a choice* (4th ed.). Pacific Grove, CA: Brooks/Cole.

Corey, G., Corey, M., Callanan, P., & Russell, J. M. (1980). A residential workshop for personal growth. *Journal for Specialists in Group Work, 5*(4), 205–215.

*Corey, G., Corey, M., Callanan, P., & Russell, J. M. (1992). *Group techniques* (2nd ed.). Pacific Grove, CA: Brooks/Cole.

*Courtois, C., & Leehan, J. (1982). Group treatment for grown-up abused children. *Personnel and Guidance Journal, 60*(9), 564–566.

Cox, A. A. (1984). A description of behavioral group treatment for depression. *Journal for Specialists in Group Work, 9*(2), 85–92.

Dougherty, P. (1990). A personal perspective on working with men in groups. In D. Moore & F. Leafgren (Eds.), *Problem solving strategies and interventions for men in conflict* (pp. 169–182). Alexandria, VA: American Association for Counseling and Development.

Elsenrath, D. E. (1990). Counseling suicidal men. In D. Moore & F. Leafgren (Eds.), *Problem solving strategies and interventions for men in conflict* (pp. 213–233). Alexandria, VA: American Association for Counseling and Development.

*Finklehor, D. (1984). *Child sexual abuse: New theory and research.* New York: Free Press.

*Forward, S., & Buck, C. S. (1978). *Betrayal of innocence: Incest and its devastation.* Los Angeles: J. P. Tarcher.

Fuhrmann, B. S., & Washington, C. S. (1984a). Substance abuse and group work: Tentative conclusions. *Journal for Specialists in Group Work, 9*(1), 62–63.

Fuhrmann, B. S., & Washington, C. S. (1984b). Substance abuse: An overview. *Journal for Specialists in Group Work, 9*(1), 2–6.

*Geller, M., Devlin, M., & Flynn, T. (1985). Confrontation of denial in a fathers' incest group. *International Journal of Group Psychotherapy, 35*(4), 545–567.

*Glasser, W. (1985). *Control theory.* New York: Harper & Row.

*Goodwin, J. (1982). *Sexual abuse: Incest victims and their families.* Boston: John Wright.

*Grant, D. (1988). Support groups for youth with AIDS virus. *International Journal of Group Psychotherapy, 38*(2), 237–251.

*Gray, L. A., & Saracino, M. (1989). AIDS on campus: A preliminary study of college students' knowledge and behaviors. *Journal of Counseling and Development, 68,* 199–202.

*Grusznski, R., & Bankovics, G. (1990). Treating men who batter: A group approach. In D. Moore & F. Leafgren (Eds.), *Problem solving strategies and interventions for men in conflict* (pp. 201–212). Alexandria, VA: American Association for Counseling and Development.

Hawes, E. C. (1985). Personal growth groups for women: An Adlerian approach. *Journal for Specialists in Group Work, 10*(1), 19–27.

*Hendren, R. L., Atkins, D. M., Sumner, C. R., & Barber, J. K. (1987). Model for the group treatment of eating disorders. *International Journal of Group Psychotherapy, 37*(4), 589–602.

*Herman, J. (1981). *Father–daughter incest.* Cambridge, MA: Harvard University Press.

*Herman, J., & Schatzow, E. (1984). Time-limited group therapy for women with a history of incest. *International Journal of Group Psychotherapy, 34*(4), 605–616.

*Justice, B., & Justice, R. (1979). *The broken taboo: Sex in the family.* New York: Human Science Press.

Kimmel, M. S. (Ed.) (1987). *Changing men: New directions in research on men and masculinity.* Newbury Park, CA: Sage Publications.

*Laidlaw, T. A., Malmo, C., & Associates. (1990). *Healing voices: Feminist approaches to therapy with women.* San Francisco: Jossey-Bass.

Lieberman, M. A., Borman, L. D., & Associates (Eds.). (1982). *Self-help groups for coping with crisis.* San Francisco: Jossey-Bass.

Lott, B. (1987). *Women's lives: Themes and variations in gender learning.* Pacific Grove, CA: Brooks/Cole.

Lowinson, J. H. (1983). Group psychotherapy with substance abusers and alcoholics. In H. I. Kaplan & B. J. Sadock (Eds.), *Comprehensive group psychotherapy* (2nd ed.) (pp. 256–262). Baltimore: Williams & Wilkins.

*Maltz, W. (1991). *The sexual healing journey: A guide for women and men survivors of sexual abuse.* New York: Harper Collins.

*Maltz, W., & Holman, B. (1987). *Incest and sexuality: A guide to understanding and healing.* Lexington, MA: D. C. Heath (Lexington Books).

*Mandell, J. G., & Damon, L. (1989). *Group treatment for sexually abused children.* New York: Guilford Press.

*Martin, S., & Privette, G. (1989). Process model of grief therapy in an alcohol treatment program. *Journal for Specialists in Group Work, 14*(1), 46–52.

*McBride, M. C., & Emerson, S. (1989). Group work with women who were molested as children. *Journal for Specialists in Group Work, 14*(1), 25–33.

*McNamara, K. (1989a). Group counseling for overweight and depressed college women: A comparative evaluation. *Journal for Specialists in Group Work, 14*(4), 211–218.

*McNamara, K. (1989b). A structured group program for repeat dieters. *Journal for Specialists in Group Work, 14*(3), 141–150.

*Meiselman, K. (1978). *Incest: A psychological study of cause and effects with treatment recommendations.* San Francisco: Jossey-Bass.

*Meiselman, K. (1990). *Resolving the trauma of incest: Reintegration therapy with survivors.* San Francisco: Jossey-Bass.

*Moore, D. (1990). Helping men become more emotionally expressive: A ten-week program. In D. Moore & F. Leafgren (Eds.), *Problem solving strategies and interventions for men in conflict* (pp. 183–200). Alexandria, VA: American Association for Counseling and Development.

*Moore, D., & Leafgren, F. (Eds.) (1990). *Problem solving strategies and interventions for men in conflict.* Alexandria, VA: American Association for Counseling and Development.

*Peck, M. S. (1987). *The different drum: Community making and peace.* New York: Simon & Schuster (Touchstone).

*Rose, S. D. (1989). *Working with adults in groups: Integrating cognitive-behavioral and small group strategies.* San Francisco: Jossey-Bass.

Roth, D. M., & Ross, D. R. (1988). Long-term cognitive-interpersonal group therapy for eating disorders. *International Journal of Group Psychotherapy, 38*(4), 491–510.

*Rush, F. (1980). *The best kept secret: Sexual abuse of children.* Englewood Cliffs, NJ: Prentice-Hall.

Sadock, V. A. (1983). Group psychotherapy with rape victims and battered women. In H. I. Kaplan & B. J. Sadock (Eds.), *Comprehensive group psychotherapy* (2nd ed.) (pp. 282–285). Baltimore: Williams & Wilkins.

*Spector, I. C., & Conklin, R. (1987). AIDS group psychotherapy. *International Journal of Group Psychotherapy, 37*(3), 433–439.

*Sprei, J., & Goodwin, R. (1983). Group treatment of sexual assault survivors. *Journal for Specialists in Group Work, 8*(1), 39–46.

*Steward, M., Farquhar, L., Dicharry, D., Glick, D., & Martin, P. (1986). Group therapy: A treatment of choice for young victims of child abuse. *International Journal of Group Psychotherapy, 36*(2), 262–277.

Vannicelli, M. (1988). Group therapy aftercare for alcoholic patients. *International Journal of Group Psychotherapy, 38*(3), 337–354.

Vannicelli, M., Canning, D., & Griefen, M. (1984). Group therapy with alcoholics: A group case study. *International Journal of Group Psychotherapy, 34*(1), 127–148.

Watson, D. L., & Tharp, R. G. (1989). *Self-directed behavior: Self-modification for personal adjustment* (5th ed.). Pacific Grove, CA: Brooks/Cole.

Weiss, L., Katzman, M., & Wolchik, S. (1985). *Treating bulimia: A psychoeducational approach.* Elmsford, NY: Pergamon Press.

*Woodward, B., & McGrath, M. (1988). Charisma in group therapy with recovering substance abusers. *International Journal of Group Psychotherapy, 38*(2), 223–236.

*Yalom, I. (1980). *Existential psychotherapy.* New York: Basic Books.

*Yalom, I. (1983). *Inpatient group psychotherapy.* New York: Basic Books.

*Yalom, I. (1985). *The theory and practice of group psychotherapy* (3rd ed.). New York: Basic Books.

*Zimbardo, P. G. (1978). *Shyness.* New York: Jove Press.

*Zimpfer, D. G. (1984). *Group work in the helping professions: A bibliography* (2nd ed.). Muncie, IN: Accelerated Development.

Zimpfer, D. G. (1990a). Groups for divorce/separation: A review. *Journal for Specialists in Group Work, 15*(1), 51–60.

Zimpfer, D. G. (1990b). Group work for bulimia: A review of outcomes. *Journal for Specialists in Group Work, 15*(4), 239–251.

CHAPTER 12

Groups for the Elderly

Introduction: Some Personal Observations*

My interest in working as a counselor with the elderly stems partly from my German upbringing. When I was growing up, old people were always present. In Germany, old and young live together. More often than not, children grow up in households that include their grandparents. Today, there appears to be an increase in the construction of homes exclusively for the elderly, but the practice of living with one's children still prevails among old people, because Germans continue to believe that the elderly should be taken care of by family members rather than by strangers.

Our children, Heidi and Cindy, frequently spend their summers with their grandparents in Germany. They experience old and young people living together harmoniously—and sometimes not so harmoniously. These regular interactions of people of all ages, I believe, prevent the development of stereotypes and negative attitudes toward the elderly. During a trip to China my family and I visited a home for the aged. I noted with interest that the home was referred to as "the respected home for the elderly." Only older people who have no relatives to take care of them live in these homes. Throughout my stay in China I observed that older people were highly respected and generally lived with younger relations.

My long contact with elderly people has left me with fewer fears about aging than most Americans seem to have. I have noticed that many Americans are threatened by the aging process, perhaps because they fear their own deterioration. This is truly sad, for I take pleasure in looking at an old person's face, in which I see a treasure of character, beauty, and wisdom. I remember hearing rumors as a child that in the United States old people were considered useless and were locked up. Since I have been in the United States, I've learned that the facts are not so horrible as I had imagined; however, I do detect many differences between the United States and Germany in the treatment of and attitudes toward the aged.

Until recently it was considered unusual for a young person to be seriously interested in a career working with the aged. People, even old people, asked me "Why does a young person like you want to work with old people?" I hear such comments less frequently now, and the number of young people working in the field of geriatrics is increasing with the passing years. Americans are beginning to perceive old people as vital members of society and to treat them with more respect.

A liking for old people does not alone make a good counselor. This unique population requires special skills and knowledge. To further my understanding of this age group, I attended the summer institution that is part of the geriatrics program at the University of Southern California. I continue to attend workshops and have listened to many lectures, read extensively, and visited numerous homes for the elderly in several countries. Although I have not recently been involved in leading groups

*This chapter is written from the perspective of Marianne Corey.

for the elderly, I have continued my involvement with them through individual counseling, by giving lectures (both to the elderly and to other age groups), by personal contacts with older people, and as a consultant for group leaders in training who work with the aged.

Much of this chapter is based on a description of my group work with the elderly in institutions. At the time I was leading the groups that I describe, it was not easy for me to pursue my interest, for there were few places that offered group work with the elderly. Today it is not so difficult to find an agency that offers such groups. Nevertheless, counselors may encounter many obstacles in organizing such groups. Some of the barriers are due to the unique characteristics of this population, but other obstacles are found within the system or the institutions themselves—for example, lack of interest in therapeutic work for the elderly, lack of administrative support for group work, and lack of cooperation from staff workers. Another obstacle is the difficulty in reaching the elderly as a target population. Because of many restraining factors, group leaders may find themselves losing their enthusiasm and motivation for setting up such groups. I want to encourage you to persist in this very important area of group work.

Unique Characteristics of the Elderly

Leaders who are forming their first groups for the elderly will find some definite differences from their work with other age groups. They need to be aware of the particular life issues faced by older people. Although not exhaustive, the following is a list of observations I have made over the years as a result of my personal and professional contact with the elderly:

- Themes that are more prevalent with the elderly than with other age groups include loneliness and social isolation; loss; poverty; feelings of rejection; the struggle to find meaning in life; dependency; feelings of uselessness, hopelessness, and despair; fears of death and dying; grief over others' deaths; sadness over physical and mental deterioration; and regrets over past events.
- Some older people are more difficult to reach, for they may not be so likely to come to a counselor's office. They may be more resistant and skeptical about the effectiveness of counseling than are other populations, and it may take more time to establish trust. It is very important to carefully consider the titles you use in describing your services for the elderly, because older people are more sensitive to feeling stigmatized when they seek out a mental-health professional.
- The attention span of the elderly is often short because of physical or psychological difficulties. Consequently, the pace of the group needs to be slower.

- Old people are often taking medications that interfere with their ability to be fully present.
- With some who are in advanced stages of senility, reality orientation becomes a problem. Sometimes they simply forget to come to sessions.
- Regular attendance at group sessions often becomes problematic for a variety of other reasons, such as physical ailments, transportation problems, interruptions in the schedules of institutions, and conflicting appointments with doctors and social workers.
- Older people often need support and encouragement more than they need confrontation. Therefore, group work is oriented less toward radical personality reconstruction and more toward making life in the present more meaningful and enjoyable. However, never to challenge or confront older people could be seen as patronizing and may be based on the distorted belief that they cannot change.
- The elderly have a great need to be listened to and understood. Respect is shown by accepting them through hearing their underlying messages and not treating them in a condescending way. The elderly often suffer from "conversation deprivation." To be encouraged to share and relate with others has therapeutic value in itself (Burnside, 1984b).

Special Types of Groups for the Elderly

Not all old people can be placed in the same type of group. Leaders must take into account the special needs of potential group members. Some groups that are commonly offered include those with an emphasis on reminiscing, physical fitness, body awareness, grief work, occupational therapy, reality orientation, music and art therapy, combined dance and movement, preretirement and postretirement issues, remotivation, preplacement (preparing people to move from an institutional to a community setting), organic brain syndrome, education, poetry, health-related issues, family therapy, and assertion training. This is certainly not a complete list, and leaders can invent ways to bring their particular talents into a group setting to promote interaction among elderly members. For example, in this chapter I describe a group composed of adolescents and the elderly. Leaders who have artistic hobbies can have members do something with their hands. In the process of creating products, the members often talk about themselves in spontaneous ways. Groups that entail the members' doing something specific can promote more interaction than groups that are limited to discussion.

I want to share an example of a group that naturally evolved from an exercise class at a senior citizens' center in our community. Jerry and I were invited by a 70-year-old man to attend the class, which was very physically challenging. The leader of this class, May, was also an elderly person who had several talents that she combined fruitfully and shared with her group. May not only directed activities designed for physical fitness but also provided a climate that fostered meaningful personal and social interactions. For example, she was very patient with members who interrupted the exercises by talking about problems that were preoccupying them that day. Sometimes they described the details of an enjoyable weekend, at times they listed numerous complaints ranging from home problems to world problems, and often they engaged in nonmalicious community gossip. If May had held to a rigid notion of what an exercise class should be, many of these spontaneous interchanges would not have evolved. Her talent and enthusiasm inspired both humor and seriousness of purpose. May had a special gift of gently pushing and confronting the members to exceed what they thought were their physical limits. Thus, people typically left feeling both physically rejuvenated and psychologically uplifted.

A Program for Institutionalized Elderly People

As I mentioned, I faced some obstacles in securing a group for the elderly. I was able to arrange to work with geriatric patients in a state mental institution—the only institution that provided counseling for a large number of old people. During a two-hour interview conducted by the program director and a staff member, I was questioned (at first with suspicion) concerning my motives for seeking this kind of experience. The staff member expressed her surprise about my request to work with the elderly, since, as she put it, "Nobody wants this assignment." However, the general tone of the interview was very positive; how my needs and the needs of the program could be integrated was given serious consideration.

New group leaders should be aware that they may not be accepted by the staff of an institution until they prove themselves, especially in facilities where group work has not been part of the treatment plan (Burnside, 1984b). Program directors or others with influence may do anything they can to undermine the newcomer's well-intentioned design for a group. Therefore, it is good to provide the personnel in charge of an agency with a detailed description of the goals and procedures of the group and to do anything you can to solicit trust in and cooperation with your plans.

My initial impression of the ward I was assigned to was that it was very unattractive. The atmosphere seemed depressingly lifeless. Many of the 44 male and female patients were either standing by themselves or sitting in front of a television set; most were staring blankly into space. I noticed very little contact among the ward members. They seemed quite isolated from one another, even though they shared a relatively small area. Eight to ten beds occupied a single room, so there was a complete lack of privacy. The old people were dressed in unattractive state-issued clothing that could have added nothing to their self-esteem. I was convinced that the surroundings were having a strong negative effect on the patients' ability to change. I felt that their environment contributed to their sense of hopelessness and isolation.

One staff member was setting a patient's hair; another was working with patients on art projects. However, most of the staff were in a centrally located glass-walled office from which they could view the activities of the patients on the ward.

I was readily accepted by the ward members; they seemed willing to talk to me if I approached them first. I was to work with a social worker assigned to the ward two days a week, and he and I decided to form two groups. One was to be a preplacement group for people who were ready to leave the institution and were waiting either to be placed in some type of home for the elderly or to return to their own home. The other group would be for patients suffering from organic brain syndrome (OBS), a condition associated with impaired cognitive abilities. People with OBS evidence severe impairments of memory, intellectual functioning, and judgment; they are disoriented and show little emotional response.

The Preplacement Group

As with other group populations, it is necessary to give careful consideration to the selection of members. A group is not likely to function well if severely disturbed and hallucinating members are mixed with clients who are psychologically intact. It is a good practice, however, to combine talkative and quiet people, depressed and ebullient types, excitable with calmer clients, suspicious with more trusting individuals, and people with different backgrounds. The size of the group is determined by the level of psychological and social functioning of the participants. A group of ten relatively well-functioning people is much easier to manage than even a smaller number of regressed clients.

The preplacement group that my co-leader and I formed consisted of three men and four women—a good balance of the sexes and a workable number for two leaders. Before the first meeting I contacted the members individually and gave them a basic orientation to the group. I told them the purpose of the group, what the activities might be, and where, when, and for how long the group would meet. I let each person know that membership was voluntary. When people seemed hesitant to attend, I suggested that they come to the initial session and then decide whether they wanted to continue.

Before the first session my co-leader and I decided on a few general goals for the group. Our primary goal would be to provide an atmosphere in which common concerns could be freely discussed and in which members could interact with one another. We wanted to provide an opportunity for members to voice complaints and to be included in a decision-making process. We strongly felt that these people could make changes and that the group process could stimulate them to do so.

The group met once a week for an hour in the visitors' room. Before each group session I contacted all the members, reminded them that the group would meet shortly, invited them to attend, and accompanied them to the group room. I learned that it was difficult for them to remember the time of the meetings, so individual assistance would be important in ensuring regular attendance. Those who were absent were either ill or involved in an activity that couldn't be rescheduled, such as physical therapy. The group was an open one; members would occasionally be discharged, and we encouraged newly admitted patients to join. This didn't seem to bother the members, and it didn't affect the cohesion of the group. As leaders, we also attempted to make entrance into the group as easy as possible. We always allowed some time for the new members to be introduced and to say anything they wanted to about being new to the group, and we asked current group members to welcome them.

The Initial Stage. During the initial sessions the members showed a tendency to direct all of their statements to the two leaders. In the hope that we could break the shell that isolated each person in a private and detached world, my co-leader and I immediately began to encourage the members to talk to one another, not to us. When members talked about a member, we asked them to speak directly to that member. When members discussed a particular problem or concern, we encouraged others to share similar difficulties.

In the beginning the members resisted talking about themselves, voicing complaints, or discussing what they expected after their release from the institution. Their usual comment reflected their hopelessness: "What good will it do? No one will listen to us anyway." Our task was to teach them to listen to one another.

The Importance of Listening and Acting. My co-leader and I felt that one way of teaching the old people to listen would be by modeling—by demonstrating that we were really listening to them. Thus, when our clients spoke of problems related to life on the ward, my co-leader and I became actively involved with them in solving some of these conflicts. For example, one member complained that one of the patients in his room shouted for much of the night. We were able to get the unhappy member placed in another room. When some members shared their fears about the board-and-care homes they were to be released to, we arranged to take them to several such homes so that they could make an informed choice of placement. One woman complained that her husband did not visit her enough and that, when he did take her home, he was uncaring and uninterested in her sexually. On several occasions my co-leader and I held private sessions with the couple.

Some men complained that there was nothing to do, so we arranged for them to get involved in planting a garden. Another group member shared the fact that she was an artist, so we asked her to lead some people in the group and on the ward in art projects. She reacted enthusiastically and succeeded in involving several other members. One member complained during several sessions that he felt trapped and that he did not belong in the hospital; the staff agreed with this assessment of the situation. He was waiting for something to happen, and with the passing of time he became increasingly depressed. After discussing his case with the director and the social worker, I encouraged this man to take steps to get himself released instead of depending on others to do it. He then obtained a pass that permitted him to leave the ward, and on several occasions he visited his conservator (the legal guardian appointed for him by the state) in an effort to make himself visible to the authorities. Too often patients like him, who are ready to be released, are lost in the paperwork required for hundreds of other cases. Despite our help, it took this man almost a year to get out of the institution.

All these stories illustrate the importance of a counselor's working with the immediate problems that old people face. Our philosophy was to encourage them to again become active, even in a small way, in making decisions about their life. There were two things that we learned *not* to do: (1) encourage a patient to participate in an activity that would be frustrating and thereby further erode an already poor self-image, and (2) make promises we couldn't keep.

Listening to Reminiscences. In addition to dealing with the day-to-day problems of the members, we spent much time listening as they reminisced about sadness and guilt they had experienced, their many losses, the places they had lived and visited, the mistakes they had made, and so on. By remembering and actively reconstructing their past, old people can hope to resolve the conflicts that are still affecting them and decide how to use the time left to them. In addition, they enjoy remembering happy times, when they were more productive and powerful than they are now. I believe that this life review is an important and healthy process and that old people need to experience it.

Most agencies that work with the elderly offer reminiscence and life-review groups. According to Lewis and Butler (1984), the life review is seen as a universal psychological process that is associated with increased awareness of one's finiteness. The myth of immortality gives way to an acceptance of one's death. The life review involves a progressive return to consciousness of earlier experiences, a resurgence of unresolved past conflicts, and the bringing up of memories that have been deeply buried in the unconscious. Although some older people are aware of a need to put their entire life into a meaningful perspective, others avoid this type of review as a protection against painful memories.

The Use of Exercises. My role as a leader of this group differed from the roles I had played in other types of group. I found that I was more directive, that I was much less confrontive and much more supportive, and that I spent a lot of time teaching the members how to express themselves and listen to others. My co-leader and I designed a variety of exercises to catalyze member interaction. The exercises often succeeded in getting meaningful discussions started, and sometimes they were just plain fun. We always began by showing how an exercise could be done. Some of the exercises we assigned the group were as follows:

- Go on an imaginary trip, and pick a couple of the other group members to accompany you. (Although you may have to deal with feelings of rejection expressed by those not chosen, this exercise is very helpful for people who are reluctant to reach out to one another and make friends.)
- If you could do anything you wanted, what would it be?
- Pick a new name for yourself, and talk about what that name means to you.
- Bring a favorite photograph, and share it with others in the group.
- Draw a picture of you and your family, and talk about your place in the family.
- Describe some of the memories that are important to you.
- Tell what your favorite holiday is and what you enjoy doing on that day.

Another exercise that helps the elderly focus and contributes to member interaction is the sentence-completion method for low-level clients (Yalom, 1983). Incomplete sentences can be structured around a variety of themes, such as:

- self-disclosure (One thing about me that people would be surprised to know is _____ .)
- separation (The hardest separation that I have ever had is _____ _____ .)
- anger (One thing that really irritates me is _____ _____ .)
- isolation (The time in my life when I felt most alone was _____ _____ .)
- ward events (The fight on the ward last night made me feel _____ _____ .)
- empathy (I feel touched by others when _____ _____ .)

- here-and-now interactions (The person whom I am most like in this room is _____ .)
- personal change (Something I want to change about myself is ____ _____ .)
- stress (I experience tension when _____ .)

Working with incomplete sentences can trigger intense emotions. Thus, the group leader needs to be skilled in dealing with these feelings.

We used exercises as simple means of getting group interaction going. One of our group sessions fell on the day before Thanksgiving. We asked the participants to remember a special Thanksgiving day from the past—to recall all of the people who were with them and everything that happened. The members received these instructions enthusiastically, and everyone participated. My co-leader and I pointed out to them that the fun and excitement they had experienced during past holidays was due partly to their interaction with people and could certainly be experienced again if they made a special effort this Thanksgiving to reach out to and make contact with one another. The Thanksgiving celebration did, in fact, go well for the group members. Several of them made a point of sitting together, and they reported at the next session the fun they had had.

These exercises, by encouraging the members to express themselves, led to their getting to know one another, which led in turn to a lessening of the "what's the use" feeling that was universal in the beginning.

Debunking Myths. My co-leader and I explored some myths and attitudes that prevail regarding the aged, in order to challenge the members' acceptance of these myths. The following are some of the beliefs we considered:

- Old people can't change, so it's a waste of time and effort to try to help them with counseling or therapy.
- All people who retire become depressed.
- It is disgraceful for an old person to remarry.
- Young people are never forgetful; old people always are.
- Forgetfulness is a sign of senility.
- Old people cannot contribute to society.
- There are many child molesters among the aged.
- Most young people want to neglect the elderly members of their family.
- Old people are always emotional and financial burdens, whether their children take them into their home or not.
- People should retire at 65.
- Old people are not creative.
- An elderly person will die soon after his or her mate dies.
- Becoming old always means having a host of serious physical problems.

- Old people do not understand the problems of younger people.
- Old people are no longer beautiful.
- Old people are dependent and need to be taken care of.
- Most old people are lonely.
- There is a high degree of alcoholism among the aged—higher than among younger people.
- Old people are no longer interested in sex.
- Old men are impotent.
- Old people are not afraid to die.

Outcomes. To work successfully with the elderly, one must take into account the basic limitations in their resources for change yet not adopt a fatalistic attitude that will only reinforce their sense of hopelessness. Had my co-leader and I expected to bring about dramatic personality changes, we would soon have been frustrated, because the changes that occurred were small and came slowly. Instead, we expected to have only a modest impact, and so the subtle changes that took place were enough to give us the incentive and energy to continue. The following are some of the outcomes we observed:

- Members realized that they were not alone in experiencing problems.
- The participants learned from one another's feedback.
- People in the group felt an acceptance of their feelings and realized that they had a right to express them.
- Members said that they liked coming to the meetings, and they told this to patients who weren't members.
- The group atmosphere became one of trust, caring, and friendliness.
- The members continued the socializing that had begun in the group outside group sessions.
- The members learned one another's names, which contributed to increased interaction on the ward.
- Participants engaged in activities that stimulated them rather than merely waiting for their release.
- The members began to talk more personally about their sorrows, losses, hopes, joys, memories, fears, regrets, and so on, saying that it felt good to be listened to and to talk.
- The enthusiasm of the members and the staff led to the formation of another group for ward members.
- The nurses reported seeing a change in the patients and expressed a desire to learn the skills needed to facilitate such groups.
- Staff members noticed positive changes, such as elevated spirits, in some of the members.
- Staff members became involved in thinking of appropriate activities for different members and helped the members carry them out.

My co-leader and I encountered some frustrating circumstances during the course of the group. For instance, the members occasionally seemed very lethargic. We later discovered that this occurred when the participants had received medication just before the group session. Still, it was difficult to discern whether a member's condition was due to the medication or to psychological factors. It was not uncommon to find a member functioning well one week and feeling good about herself and then to discover, the next week, that she had had a psychotic episode and was unable to respond to anyone. Another heartbreaking reality was the slowness with which patients who were ready for placement in outside agencies had their papers processed for release. People who had to remain in this institution after they no longer needed it could be seen to suffer, both physically and psychologically.

Some small changes that occurred in the group sessions were undone by the routine of ward life. On the one hand, some of the members resisted making their life on the ward more pleasant for fear of giving the impression that their stay would be a long one. It was as though they were saying "If I communicate that I like it here , you might not let me go." On the other hand, some members resigned themselves to institutional life and saw the ward as their home, expressing very directly that they did not want to leave. These people had developed such a fear of the outside world that they were willing to give up the chance it offered of a richer life.

Termination. I was to be co-leader of this group for only three months, and I prepared the members for my departure several weeks in advance. After I left, my co-leader continued the group by himself. On occasion I visited the group, and I was remembered and felt very welcome. One year later this group was still in existence, although the membership had changed.

The Group for Patients with Organic Brain Syndrome

Some of the patients on the ward were severely handicapped by organic brain syndrome, and my co-leader and I decided to form a group with these people that would provide them with some sensory stimulation. The group would have the same format as the preplacement group, but the activities would be somewhat different.

The group consisted of three men and three women, and the sessions lasted from half an hour to an hour. We felt successful after a session if members had not wandered off or fallen asleep. I sat in front of the group and touched the members to make sure they could see and hear me. Each week I told them who I was, where they were, why they were there, and who was present. I moved around a lot, making physical contact with each member; I called them by name. The other leader and I developed a routine of opening the session by providing chocolate candy or, in some cases, a cigar, and the members very much enjoyed this ritual. Once I brought in a bottle of perfume, let everyone smell it, and helped the women put it on, which brought many giggles. This allowed for touching, which these people very much needed. The members sat holding hands and sang favorite old tunes while one of them plucked away at a guitar. It was a touching experience to see these people enjoying singing an old and much-loved song; they still remembered the words but had to struggle with their physical handicap to sing them. I can still hear the group singing "You Are My Sunshine."

We generated another activity in the OBS group by bringing in a beach ball and encouraging the members to throw it to one another and to go through the struggle of retrieving it. This stimulated the members into activity. We brought in large, colorful pictures and had the members describe what they saw. The members had a tendency to talk very little, so we encouraged them to notice one another's presence and address one another. We brought a tape recorder to some sessions, recorded the songs, and then listened to everyone's voice. We brought in clay one day, but this proved to be a disaster because several members started eating it. This problem could have been prevented, though, had we paid closer attention to what was going on. Bringing my two daughters and introducing them to each member of both my groups delighted my children as well as the group members. This was a natural catalyst; afterward there was much talk among the members about the fun they had had with my children. Weather permitting, we took the members on walks, having them touch and smell flowers, trees, and shrubs. In all of these ways we encouraged members to employ all of their senses, so that they could be more alive.

Obviously, the goals of this group were much more limited in scope than those of the preplacement group. Few changes were observed outside of the group; members continued not to react to or recognize one another much of the time. However, I felt that it did them good to be aroused from their lethargy, if only for short periods of time. The following are notes I made after the second session:

> The OBS group was slow. In the beginning, two people insisted on going to sleep. One member kept wandering off. Later, some talked about a birthday party and shared the fun they had. Everyone sang some songs and held hands. I contacted everyone in group, touching and talking with each one. It is difficult not to get discouraged, and I have to continually keep my goal—to get any of them to converse or react about anything—in mind. As I did last time, I made a point of saying good-bye to each of them individually.

With this particular group, it was rewarding to see even the most minute changes. It was exciting for me to hear one 87-year-old man, who usually showed no responsiveness, giggle when I put some perfume behind my male co-leader's ear. During the initial sessions he had never uttered a word; now, slowly, he began to talk and sing with the rest. One lady who had not allowed anyone to touch her reached out one day and held another member's hand.

I visited this group three months after I had left it, not expecting to be remembered. I was touched when some members approached me in recognition and reminded me that I had not been to the group meetings!

Groups for Families of the Elderly

I see a pressing need for therapy groups for people who have aged relatives in an institution. Very often a family's feelings of guilt, anger, failure, and hopelessness will keep them away from their hospitalized member, depriving him or her of the joy of visits. Or the family members may visit but transmit their negative feelings to the old person. In either case, everyone suffers from the loss of true contact. By allowing families to share their concerns with other families, groups can relieve much of the tension that normally results from the responsibility of caring for a loved one who is old.

My co-leader and I experimented with this idea by holding several sessions with one member and his entire family. The family members talked about the shame they felt over having one of their relatives committed to a mental institution, and the patient expressed the anger he felt over being ignored by his family. After expressing their feelings, the family members made the decision to visit the institutionalized member more often.

Involvement with Other Ward Residents

Due to a lack of staff members qualified to lead groups, many patients were not assigned to a group. One way for me to make contact with these unassigned residents was by seeking them out, so each time I came to the hospital I spent some time walking around the ward. During my first day on the ward I noticed a woman who was crocheting and told her about my liking for this activity. On my next visit I brought wool and several crochet hooks. I put a table and several chairs in an area in which I could be seen by a lot of patients. I invited the woman who had been crocheting to sit with me. Very soon other women approached us and sat down. They took yarn and hooks and began to crochet, much to the amazement of the ward staff. One patient who seldom sat down and who instead usually ran around the ward cursing and uttering obscenities sat with me and crocheted. I crocheted in that spot again and again, and each time she stayed a little longer. It surprised everyone to hear her talk about her life. An informal group of five women and myself was thus spontaneously formed. It proved to be a great catalyst of interaction among ward members. Several men would often stand around and watch the women, who would show off what they had crocheted. I encouraged the women to get together and crochet during my absence, but they didn't do so. As with many other activities, this one only held them as long as a staff member was there to encourage them. I taught two staff members how to crochet, and it became a good means for them to make contact with patients.

I moved around on the ward, meeting as many members as possible. I talked with them, sat by their bedside, put my arms around one or held one's hand, laughed with them, and teased them. It was a good feeling to walk into the ward in the morning and hear many familiar hellos. I danced with many of them, and I encouraged them to dance with one another when the dance band came each week.

General Reactions and Observations

At times I felt depressed, hopeless, and angry, but these feelings were seldom directly connected with my activities with the patients; the smallest changes I observed in them were rewarding and gave me the incentive to go on. Rather, I experienced these feelings whenever I saw the system contributing to the physical and psychological deterioration of a person, such as when the staff appeared uncaring and lacking in enthusiasm. I've already mentioned that some patients were forced to stay in the institution because everyone claimed to be too busy to do the paperwork necessary to get them out. I felt angry when I saw student psychiatric technicians or other staff members show disrespect for the patients and when I heard these same individuals call an elderly person by his or her first name yet insist that they themselves be addressed by their surname. I felt discouraged and helpless when, as happened occasionally, an agitated patient would be restrained physically or with medication without ever being asked what had made him or her so upset in the first place. Another misuse of medication occurred, I felt, when patients were given strong doses to put them to sleep at night. In many cases a glass of wine would have had the same effect and might have stimulated satisfying socializing among the patients. Another upsetting sight was a patient in a wheelchair being pushed around and not being told where he or she was going.

At times the behavior of a patient was treated as crazy when in reality there was a good reason for it that could have been discovered if anybody had tried. One day a student brought a blind member of my OBS group to the meeting. The blind man proceeded to take off his shoes, and the student shouted at him to put them back on. I approached Mr. W. and kneeled in front of him. "Mr. W., you're taking your shoes off in our group session," I said. "How come?" He apologized, saying that he had thought he was being taken to the physical-therapy room.

In another case, a 75-year-old patient kept taking his shoes off all day long, always gathering up newspaper to put around his feet. Everyone considered this behavior bizarre. I remembered that during my childhood in Germany I was often told in the winter to put newspaper into my shoes to keep my feet warm. After spending some time with this man, I found that this "strange" behavior was based on the same experience. I learned to be careful not to judge a patient as bizarre or delusional too quickly but rather to take the time to find out whether there was a logical reason for a peculiar behavior.

I felt helpless when I had to struggle with the heavy diagnostic language used by the staff members to record the patients' behavior in their official records. I often found it difficult to understand the notes

in the records, and I was concerned that the simple language I was using to describe the members' behavior in the group might be considered
inappropriate. A number of staff members apparently had reservations
about the use of technical language, too, for one day, during an important hospital meeting, it was decided that from then on there would be
a minimum of labeling of patients and that, instead, their behavior would
be described in a way that anyone could understand. Instead of labeling a patient withdrawn, staff members would describe the behavior of
the patient that had led them to conclude that he or she was withdrawn.
This would, of course, be more time consuming, and several staff members resisted it.

It was sad to see that patients were sometimes discouraged or made
to feel shameful when they physically expressed affection for another
ward member. Sensuality was perceived by the staff as bad because of
"what it could lead to." There is one positive note, however. I had several
good discussions with staff members about our attitudes toward the sexuality of the aged. I felt encouraged by their willingness to explore their
attitudes and their openness to change. By dealing with our own attitudes, misperceptions, and fears, the staff members and I were able to
be more understanding and helpful to the patients. Several of us attended
seminars on the sexuality of the aging.

It was also sad to see an elderly person describe himself or herself
as ugly, having accepted the standard according to which only the young
are beautiful. In our groups my co-leader and I talked about attitudes
toward old people's physical appearance. We were able to work with the
members on accepting and liking themselves.

A Combined Group for the Elderly and Adolescents

At a convention of the American Association for Counseling and Development I met Michael Nakkula, who had designed an innovative group combining older people with adolescents. Nakkula's (1984) research design,
under the direction of Joseph Morris of the University of Minnesota at
Duluth, was aimed at assessing members' changes in attitude as a result
of their experiences in eight group sessions.

Basic Assumptions

Nakkula's study was based largely on a review of the literature and his
personal observations on the developmental tasks of the young and the
old. Some of his key assumptions were:

- Part of maintaining health in the elderly is staying in contact with
  all age groups.

- The old need to have an opportunity to pass on their wisdom to the younger generation.
- The young need exposure to the elderly to gain wisdom.
- The elderly can become a "living history book" to young people.
- There is a need to bring these two age groups together to exchange elderly wisdom and youthful vitality.
- Older people benefit from the knowledge that their investment in society can live on beyond their own life.
- Adolescents need role models for their developing value systems.
- The benefit of interaction between the young and the old is based not only on what they can learn from their differences but also on what they can learn from their similarities.
- Contact between the two age groups can lead to less fear and more realistic attitudes about the aging process among adolescents.
- The two age groups display a striking resemblance in their struggle to understand the purpose of their life.
- Both groups suffer from apparent alienation within our social structure.
- The elderly are stifled in their attempts to realize their full potential; adolescents are stifled by their limited power and control and lack experience in using the power they do have.

Based on the above assumptions, Nakkula hypothesized that combining the two age groups would result in positive changes in attitude toward members of the opposite age group due to increased knowledge and understanding. He also hypothesized that the group experience would lead to an increase of self-esteem in the elderly.

Structure of the Group

Participants were divided into two groups, each consisting of five junior-high-school students, aged 12 and 13, and five elderly people, all of whom lived in a nursing home. They met for eight sessions, with each session being structured as follows:

Session 1. The purpose of the group was explained. The members were asked to interview one another and later introduce one another to the rest of the group.

Session 2. The objective was to help members look at their similarities and differences. Classical music was played, and they were asked to think about the most critical task in their life. The differences and similarities of these task were then discussed in the group.

Session 3. The goal was to discuss what factors would lead to personal strength and, in turn, to personal happiness. The members were asked to think about their assets and how they thought their strengths contributed to their happiness. They were asked to choose a strength from the other age group they would like to possess.

Session 4. The purpose was to assist the elderly in putting their life experiences into perspective and to teach adolescents that life is an ongoing process that demands work. Members brought to the session photographs of themselves at different points in their life cycle. They talked about their favorite picture, explaining why it was associated with special meaning.

Session 5. The aim was to examine how the young and the old were represented in the media. Members shared and discussed news articles. They also identified adjectives used by the media in describing the young and the old.

Session 6. The purpose was to examine the messages found in music and to compare yesterday's with today's music, as well as to look for common themes. After listening to selected pieces of music, members discussed the feelings that were aroused and the people and situations they associated with each piece. They also talked about what was happening in the world at the time these songs were written. All the members sang a song known to everyone.

Session 7. The elderly were given an opportunity to share the significance of their heritage with the young, and the young had an opportunity to realize the importance of the elderly in connecting them with their roots. The members discussed their ethnic backgrounds. Adolescents discussed what they knew about their heritage. The elderly talked about how their families had come to the United States and what it had been like for them, their parents, and their grandparents from the beginning.

Session 8. The purpose was to say good-bye and to leave one another having earned mutual respect. The members divided into pairs and talked about what they had learned from and enjoyed about each other. They also identified at least one misconception they had had about the other age group and how it had been clarified. They exchanged names and addresses so that they might stay in touch.

Outcomes

This study included a pretest and posttest to assess adolescent attitudes toward the elderly and to assess the degree to which the elderly felt useful in society. It was found that young people who participated in the group were much less biased toward older people at the time of the posttesting. The elderly showed an increased sense of self-esteem. In addition, they appreciated the break from routine and the chance to socialize with curious and enthusiastic youngsters, who seemed to enjoy listening to their reminiscences.

Implications and Commentary

I am excited about a project like Nakkula's. Many people today grew up in single-parent families and can benefit from contact with other adults such as grandparents. In my talks to the elderly I encourage them to spend more time with young people, especially those who are significant to them. My message to them is not to underestimate the tremendous power and influence they can have in the lives of young people. In my adult therapy groups I often hear about a grandparent who had a strong impact on a person's life when a parent was too busy.

Groups combining old and young provide an economical response to the mental-health needs of the increasing elderly population while also creating a vehicle through which young people can contribute something valuable to the community. They target precisely what lies at the core of distress and despair for many old and young people alike: loneliness.

An example of having older people live with younger people is Advent Christian Village, a retirement, nursing, and child-care community in Dowling Park, Florida. A friend of mine who was orphaned grew up in the village. She fondly remembers her interaction with the older people who lived there. The elderly attended to the needs of the younger residents and in many cases became substitute parents. The younger residents were able to offer meaningful companionship to the elderly residents. It is remarkable that the village, which was founded in 1913 as a home for orphans and retired preachers, has managed to keep pace with the ever-changing concerns of contemporary society. It provides:

- professional care for neglected youths
- a serene and secure environment for active retirees
- competent care for impaired and frail elderly residents

At the time this chapter was first written in 1977, a place like the village was certainly the exception. By contrast, I now often hear of projects involving some creative combination of the young and the old. At St. Elizabeth Senior Day Care Center in Pompano Beach, Florida, for example, the elderly gather with preschoolers for activities like barbecues or finger painting with colored shaving cream. The director of this center commented: "It's an unwritten love agreement. The little ones— their parents have to work, so they're not here to give them warmth. The seniors are in the same situation, so we bring them together to fulfill the needs of both" ("A Home," 1990, p. 57). For more information on day-care centers in which the aged are involved, write to the National Council on the Aging, Department Y, 600 Maryland Avenue, SW, Washington, DC 20024.

There are many possibilities for designing programs that combine the elderly and the young. It is up to the creativity of the group practitioner to come up with variations. Should you like more detailed information regarding the structure and format of his group, write Michael Nakkula, 30 Lake Avenue, Newton Centre, MA 02159; telephone: (617) 244-6462.

Suggestions for Working with Healthy Aging People

It is crucial to realize that many elderly people who are not institutional-ized do have problems coping with the aging process. These people have to deal with the many losses associated with old age in addition to the pressures and conflicts that the younger generation experiences, and they can profit from personal-growth groups that serve people of all ages. The following are a few suggestions for helping healthy, well-functioning elderly people:

- I find it exciting to combine a group of people over 65 with a group of adolescents and have them explore their common struggles—their feelings of uselessness, difference, and isolation from the rest of society.
- Aging people can be employed or asked to volunteer as teacher aides in elementary and secondary schools.
- High school or college students who are learning to speak a foreign language can be given the assignment of visiting homes for the aged that include people who speak the language as their native tongue. This plan, in addition to helping the student, provides some badly needed stimulation for the elderly person.
- Groups of old people can be formed to explore such themes as love, sex, marriage, meaning in life, death, failing health, and body images. Many of the myths about the meaning of these issues for old people can be examined in depth.
- Teachers can invite elderly people to be guest speakers in their classes and ask them to discuss historical events they experienced that are being studied by the students.
- People in senior-citizen centers can be asked to teach young people arts and crafts and many other skills that are often not taught at home or at school.

Summary of Practical and Professional Considerations

Issues in the Group Process

All of the issues that were addressed in Part Two of this book pertain-ing to stages in the development of a group have some applicability to designing and conducting groups for the elderly. This section provides brief examples of practical issues for you to think about in forming specialized groups for older people.

The Group Proposal. It is especially important to develop a sound pro-posal, because you will often encounter resistance from agencies deal-ing with the elderly. I have already mentioned ways of enlisting the support of the agency. Refer to Chapter 3 for the elements that might be included in a proposal for groups for the elderly.

Screening and Selection Issues. As I have discussed, the needs of the elderly are diverse, so you need to consider the purposes of the group in determining who will or will not benefit from the experience. The decision to include or exclude members must be made appropriately and sensitively. For example, to mix regressed patients with relatively well-functioning older people is to invite fragmentation. There may be a rationale for excluding people who are highly agitated, are delusional, have severe physical problems that could inhibit their benefiting from the group, or display other behaviors that are likely to be counter-productive to the group as a whole.

Purpose of the Group. Elderly people generally need a clear, organized explanation of the specific purposes of a group and why they can benefit from it. Some of them are more closed to the potential values of group participation than are other populations. In short, it is important to be able to present a positive approach to the members. The anxiety level may be high among an elderly group, which calls for a clear structure and a repetition of the goals and procedures of the group.

Practical Issues. Practical considerations regarding the size, duration, setting, and techniques to be used depend on the level of functioning of a particular group. For example, more members could be included in a well-functioning group than in an OBS group. The attention span of a group of outpatients would be longer than that of patients who are out of contact with reality. It is essential for you to have a good understanding of the members' mental and physical capabilities.

Confidentiality. Institutional life is often not conducive to privacy. Elderly group members may be suspicious when they are asked to talk about themselves, for they may fear some sort of retaliation by the staff or fellow members. It will be important that you take great care in defining the boundaries of confidentiality to ensure that confidences will not be broken and to provide a safe and nonthreatening environment.

Labeling and Prejudging Group Members. Institutions are quick to diagnose and categorize people, and they are slow to remove such labels when they no longer fit. In working with the elderly, you must be careful not to be rigidly influenced by what you hear or read about a given member. Remain open to forming your own impressions, and be willing to challenge any limiting labels that are imposed on your elderly clients.

Visitors to Groups. As is often the case in institutions, visitors and other staff members may wish to attend a particular group session. A good practice with even severely regressed patients (who may not be aware of another's presence) is to announce visitors in advance of their attending a session and again at the beginning of the session. In addition, the purpose of their visit should be mentioned in order to lessen suspicion.

Value Differences. A good understanding of the social and cultural backgrounds of your members will enable you to work with their concerns in a sensitive way. As was true in my case, you may be younger than the members, and this age span can represent significant value differences. For example, a group leader in her early 20s might consider living together as an unmarried couple an acceptable norm, whereas a member in her mid-70s might suffer guilt and shame for doing so. This leader needs to take this member's anxiety seriously and not simply reassure her that she has no need to feel guilty. You are likely to assume that there is therapeutic value in discussing personal problems and conflicts openly. However, revealing personal matters may be extremely difficult for some elderly people because of their cultural conditioning, which has reinforced the notion that it is best to keep one's problems to oneself. It will be a challenge for you to teach these members about the benefits of self-exploration. Respect members' decisions to proceed at their own pace in revealing themselves.

The Issue of Touching. Aging people have a special need for being touched. They may be alone, and you and others in their group may be their only source of touching. Your own comfort level with touching will be a vital factor in determining how free members feel to exchange touches. It is also critical that you not misinterpret an older person's touching.

The need for touching among the elderly was vividly expressed during a visit to the respected home for the elderly in China. I observed an elderly woman lying on her bed, mumbling to herself and looking extremely withdrawn. As I stood near her bed, I struggled with myself over the appropriateness of touching her, not knowing if it would be accepted in a different cultural setting. I gave in to my urge to hold the woman's hand, and she reciprocated immediately by pressing my hand and turning toward me. She slowly began to talk and I asked our tour guide to translate. He introduced my daughters and me to her, and she showed great interest in where we were from and what we were doing. She kept repeating how lucky I was to have such daughters. She touched my daughters and me again and again. Within a short time this woman sat up on her bed and began laughing and talking. She had been an artist, and my daughters and I shared our interest in art with her. The young tour guide, who had never been in a home such as this, told me how surprised he was by her intellectual sharpness. When he initially saw her lying on her bed, he thought that she might be dying.

The attending nurse mentioned that this woman had indeed been very withdrawn and depressed, and the nurse was surprised over her excitement and interest in us. Within a span of 20 minutes she had become completely animated. This episode reminded me again how much we can communicate with a touch or a smile.

Difficult Group Members.   You may encounter many types of difficult members in this age group. Some may refuse to speak or make any contact, some may never stop talking or interrupting, and some may be highly agitated and hostile. Learn to set firm limits, and deal with these members nondefensively. Members who display problematic behaviors should not be labeled and categorized. The challenge is to understand the broader meaning of the behaviors that these members are manifesting in the group, rather than simply labeling them "resisters."

Some Cautions.   The following are a few cautions in your practice of group work with the elderly:

- Be careful not to treat people as frail when they are not.
- Don't keep your members busy with meaningless activities.
- Don't insult their dignity, intelligence, and pride.
- Make use of humor appropriately. Avoid laughing at your members for failing to accomplish tasks, but laugh with them when, for instance, they have created a funny poem.
- Be careful not to change your way of speaking with them. Avoid talking to them as if they were small children.
- Allow your members to nag and complain, even if there is nothing you can do about their complaints. You don't need to burden yourself with the feeling that you should do something about all of their grievances. Sometimes it is enough to simply let them get the problems off their chest.
- Avoid probing for the release of strong emotions that neither you nor they can handle effectively in the group sessions.
- Determine how much you can do without feeling depleted, and find avenues for staying vital and enthusiastic.
- Do not burden yourself with the belief that you *should* be capable of working with the demands often made by the elderly and that if you can't, you are a failure as a counselor. Decide where your interests and abilities are, and follow the lead they provide for you.

Attitudes and Skills of Leaders

It is especially critical to be aware of how your own feelings and attitudes will affect your work with the elderly. You will need to find ways to successfully deal with the emotions that are generated within you as a result of their work. If you want to work effectively with the concerns of the aged, it is necessary to acquire special skills and knowledge. Your range of life experiences, as well as your basic personality characteristics, can either help or hinder you in your work. (This would be a good time to review the personal characteristics of effective group leaders that we discussed in Chapter 1.) I consider the following as important assets for group work with the elderly:

- genuine respect for old people
- a history of positive experiences with old people
- a deep sense of caring for the elderly
- a respect for the elderly person's cultural values
- an understanding of the ways in which the individual's cultural background continues to influence present attitudes and behaviors
- an ability and desire to learn from old people
- an understanding of the biological aspects of aging
- the conviction that the last years of life can be challenging
- patience, especially with repetition of stories
- knowledge of the special biological, psychological, and social needs of the aged
- sensitivity to the burdens and anxieties of old people
- the ability to get old people to challenge many of the myths about old age
- a healthy attitude regarding one's own eventual old age
- an understanding of the developmental tasks of each period of life, from infancy to old age
- an appreciation for the effects that one period of life has on other stages of development
- a particular understanding of how one's ability to handle present life difficulties hinges on how well one dealt with problems in earlier stages
- a background in the pathology of aging
- the ability to deal with extreme feelings of depression, hopelessness, grief, hostility, and despair
- personal characteristics such as humor, enthusiasm, patience, courage, endurance, hopefulness, tolerance, nondefensiveness, freedom from limiting prejudices, and a willingness to learn
- an ability to be both gentle and challenging
- the sensitivity to know when it is therapeutic to provide support and when to challenge
- a working knowledge of the group process along with the special skills needed for group work with the elderly

A Personal Perspective

America is moving from its "greening" to its "graying" as the elderly increase more rapidly than the rest of the population. There are more than 30 million people age 65 and older in the United States today, which represents over 12% of the total population. This share is expected to increase to 21% by the year 2030 (Wright, Coley, & Corey, 1989).

It should be evident from this chapter that the elderly have special needs and problems that should not be ignored by any helping professional. Group workers of the future will increasingly be held account-able for developing programs to help the elderly in finding meaning in their lives and be productive after retirement. As mental-health profes-sionals become involved with the elderly, their challenge is to make a longer life also a better life (Wright et al., 1989). Counselors need to develop special programs for the elderly, and they must also find the means to reach this clientele.

I feel angry when old people are perceived as nearly dead, cute, or strange; I certainly will not care to be regarded as such when I'm older. As I once told a friend, if I am to get old in this country, I want to change a few things before I get there.

Bereavement Groups

The Therapeutic Value of Grief Work

Grief is a necessary and natural process after a significant loss. However, there are many forces in our society that make it difficult for people to completely experience grief. Social norms demand a "quick cure," and other people often cannot understand why it is taking "such a long time" for a grieving person to "get back to normal." As is the case with any emotion that is not expressed, unresolved grief lingers in the back-ground and prevents people from letting go of losses and forming new relationships.

Hospice centers help the terminally ill deal with their impending death and also help survivors who have lost a loved one feel their full range of emotions during bereavement. These hospices typically offer both closed groups and time-limited groups, as well as short-term groups with changing membership. Many survivors need the reassurance that they are not "going crazy."

Kübler-Ross (1969) made a significant contribution in describing the stages a dying person tends to go through, from denial to acceptance. But as she emphasized, all people who are dying do not conform to sequential stages in a neat and tidy way. Likewise, people who are work-ing through a loss also grieve in their own way, and they do not necessar-ily proceed from denial to acceptance of their losses. Some are never able to accept the death of a child or a spouse. They may get stuck by denying their feelings and by not facing and working through the pain over the loss. Those therapists who work with grieving clients know full well the therapeutic value of fully experiencing the pain. At some point in the grief process, people may feel numb, as if they were functioning on automatic pilot. Once this numbness wears off, the pain seems to in-tensify. People who are going through this pain need to learn that they may well get worse before they feel better. In order to put to rest un-resolved issues and unexpressed feelings, people need to express their anger, regrets, guilts, and frustrations. When they attempt to deny their pain, they inevitably wind up being stuck, for this unexpressed pain tends to eat away at them both physically and psychologically.

Unresolved grief accounts for many of the referrals for counseling and psychotherapy. This grief may be over many types of losses besides a death, such as the breakup of a relationship, the loss of one's career, and children's leaving home. In learning to resolve grief, regardless of its source, people need to be able to talk about what they are telling themselves internally and what they are feeling. They typically need to bewail the lack of fairness in their situation. They may eventually face up to the fact that there is no rational reason that will explain their loss.

The Advantage of Therapeutic Groups for Loss

Groups can be instrumental in helping people feel less isolated as they move at their own pace in their own way in working through their grief. The group process can be used to therapeutic advantage by individuals who are struggling to adjust to many of the changes that confront them because of their loss. Certainly this is not a task reserved for older people, since loss and grief can affect people regardless of their age. However, bereavement is a particularly critical developmental task that older people must often cope with, not only because of the loss of others who are close to them but also because of the loss of some of their capacities. Although death strikes at children as well as the elderly, facing one's own death and the death of significant others takes on special significance with aging.

If people who are experiencing bereavement are able to express the full range of their thoughts and feelings, they stand a better chance of adjusting to a new environment. Indeed, part of the grief process involves making basic life changes and experiencing new growth. If people have gone through the necessary cycle of bereavement, they are better equipped to take on a new purpose and a new reason for living. Group counseling can be especially helpful to people at this time.

The Structure and the Process of Bereavement Groups

The following discussion is based largely on an article by Yalom and Vinogradov (1988), who describe techniques and themes they found effective in co-leading several bereavement groups. The authors designed a group that met weekly for eight weeks. The members were individuals who had lost a spouse to cancer and who were undergoing normal grief and mourning. Most of the participants were between the ages of 50 and 70.

The co-leaders functioned as timekeepers of the group by reminding the participants of the time structure and the importance of working within this framework. At the first meeting they clarified their expectations for the group and expressed their hope that the members would direct their attention toward developing future coping strategies so that they could move forward in spite of the fact that they were still faced with loss, pain, and major life changes. They then invited the participants to describe their experiences with bereavement and to tell others in the group about their present life situation. The authors report that because of the supportive atmosphere, the members were self-revealing from the onset. The clients appeared to welcome a simple form in which they could talk openly about their concerns, and it was not necessary for the group leaders to impose an agenda or to tightly structure the meetings. Indeed, one of the key norms that the leaders attempted to shape during the early phase of the group was that the group would accept responsibility for its own direction.

Some group time was devoted to helping members explore their "shoulds." For example, some members had to deal with injunctions such as "I should grieve for a whole year, "I should give away my spouse's belongings," and "I should not be alone during the weekends." Members had an opportunity to explore their fears as they pertained to the here and now of the group process. Several people were afraid of losing control and sobbing in front of others, which is not too much different from the fears expressed by people in any group. The early sessions focused on examining unfinished business, and themes were identified and clarified for discussion in later group meetings.

About the middle of the group's life, it had developed a high level of cohesiveness, with many members feeling identification with others. Even though the circumstances of each individual's pain might be different, there was a common basis for connecting with others and not feeling alone in the world.

At the later meetings (during sessions 5 to 7), the bereavement groups had developed into cohesive and hard-working units. The co-leaders saw it as their task to monitor the remaining time of the group and to help members deal with their anticipated termination. Questions such as the following were useful: "What regrets might you anticipate having after this group is over?" "Are there any things that are left unsaid or unasked?" "What would you most like to accomplish during the remaining time in this group?"

The members had to face their feelings about dealing with the loss of this particular group, which included saying good-bye and facing their feelings evoked by the reality of termination. The authors (co-leaders) found that the discussion of the termination of the group rekindled members' feelings related to the loss of their spouse. The leaders reminded the group that the grieving process would take time and that intense feelings over painful loss would arise time and again. At the final meeting, the members exchanged phone numbers and made plans for a reunion or for continuing to meet as a leaderless group. The bonds that had formed during the preceding seven weeks apparently provided a strong supportive network from which they could continue to draw strength in working through and letting go of the pain of loss. All of the bereavement groups had a later social event such as a luncheon or meeting in which members could touch base.

Certain themes seemed to emerge time and again in each of the bereavement groups. These themes provided the material that would be explored during the sessions. They included facing the changes the survivor would have to make as a widow or widower. There was also the theme of time and ritual, which focused on the proper length of time for the grieving process. Members learned that prescribed limits to grief defied their individual experience in dealing with their feelings. New relationships presented a challenge. Members had to deal with their feelings of guilt over letting go of a loved one and establishing a new love relationship. Some felt that doing so would be a betrayal of their marriage.

Existential themes also grew out of these group sessions. For instance, members had to deal with their anger at life, at destiny, and at the unfairness of their fate. They had to struggle with the reality that at some time they would face their own death. Some members commented that their awareness of life's brevity served as a catalyst for them to decide on life's priorities and to take advantage of the moment by living as fully as possible and by not allowing themselves to be distracted by trivial concerns. For most of these group participants, the death of their wives or husbands served to teach them the lessons of existential responsibility: they learned that they alone were ultimately responsible for the direction of their life and for their choices.

The co-leaders hoped to create a climate in the group that would assist the survivors in sharing their experiences of bereavement with one another. Through this process, they expected that a temporary community would be created in which the members could feel deeply understood by others. Another goal was to aid these clients in creating action plans and exploring alternatives for their future. From the perspective of the co-leaders, these groups were highly successful as measured by the fact that members became deeply engaged, cohesion was high, attendance was excellent, and there were high levels of trust and self-disclosure. In follow-up assessments, all but two of the members gave testimonials about the value of the group. The co-leaders realized that specific structured exercises were occasionally helpful in eliciting new material for discussion or for facilitating self-disclosure. But they found that sometimes these exercises were counterproductive. They learned that they had to be aware of the timing of such exercises, lest they hamper the more spontaneous interactions that were naturally emerging within the group. The co-leaders learned that they were able to be most helpful to the groups by becoming aware of the issues and themes that preoccupy bereaved spouses and by facilitating the discussion of these themes in the group context. The co-leaders concluded that if people are able to live with the living, they can learn to live with the dead. The assumption that guided their practice as group facilitators was that it is best to concentrate on growth, self-knowledge, and existential responsibility. This focus proved to be more useful than dwelling on loss, pain, and emotional catharsis.

Where to Go from Here

If you are interested in working with the elderly, it would be a valuable experience to become involved with older people and their families. It is important that you explore your feelings about responsibilities toward older family members, which can help you understand the struggles of the members of the groups you lead. You can take a number of other steps to better prepare yourself to work with the elderly:

- Take courses and attend special workshops dealing with the problems of the aged.
- Get involved in fieldwork and internship experiences in working with the elderly.
- Visit agencies for the care of the elderly, both in your own country and on any trips you take abroad.
- Attend conventions on gerontology, a mushrooming field.
- Investigate institutes that provide training in leading groups for the elderly.
- Explore your feelings toward your own aging.

Hawkins (1983) maintains that counselors who lead groups for the elderly not only provide a valuable service for their clients but also grow themselves. Her recommendations for entry-level workers include doing extensive reading about the elderly, getting to know older people, demonstrating a genuine sense of caring, and imagining what their own life might be like as they age.

Irene Mortenson Burnside has had a valued impact on my views about working with the elderly. *Working with the Elderly: Group Processes and Techniques* (1984b) is a must for any person considering group work with the aged. Many people with experience in working with the elderly are contributors to the book. It contains a wealth of practical information on subjects such as training and supervision of group workers, suggestions for contracts in working with older people, group membership issues and procedures, responsibilities of group leaders, special groups, guidelines for group workers, and the future of group work with the aged.

Another good reference for group workers is the special issue "Counseling Psychology and Aging" in *The Counseling Psychologist* (1984). A resource listing articles and books of interest is *Group Work in the Helping Professions: A Bibliography* (Zimpfer, 1984). This reference guide has sections on types of group experience, groups for specific clienteles and in specific settings, and outcome studies. For references on group work pertaining to old age, suicide, death, survivor grief, and adaptation see section 9.4, pages 508–515.

For practical strategies in working with the elderly in groups, see *Inpatient Group Psychotherapy* (Yalom, 1983). It has especially good points on ways of helping group members work in the here and now and transfer group learning to everyday life. Yalom's book *Existential Psychotherapy* (1980) provides a superb philosophical foundation for the practice of group work.

Videotapes of Irvin Yalom conducting inpatient group therapy demonstrate his approach in breaking through the patients' isolation and resistance. Volume 2, *Inpatients*, consists of two 50-minute tapes, which are part of the *Understanding Group Psychotherapy* series. For more information on these tapes, contact Brooks/Cole Publishing Company, Pacific Grove, CA 93950-5098.

References and Suggested Readings*

*Altholz, J. A. S. (1984). Group psychotherapy with the elderly. In I. Burnside (Ed.), *Working with the elderly: Group process and techniques* (2nd ed.) (pp. 248–258). Boston: Jones & Bartlett.

*Booth, H. (1984). Dance/movement therapy. In I. Burnside (Ed.), *Working with the elderly: Group process and techniques* (2nd ed.) (pp. 211–224). Boston: Jones & Bartlett.

Brammer, L. M. (1984). Counseling theory and the older adult. *The Counseling Psychologist, 12*(2), 29–37.

Burnside, I. (1970). Loss: A constant theme in group work with the aged. *Hospital and Community Psychiatry, 21*(6), 173–177.

*Burnside, I. (1984a). Self-help groups. In I. Burnside (Ed.), *Working with the elderly: Group process and techniques* (2nd ed.) (pp. 234–247). Boston: Jones & Bartlett.

Burnside, I. (Ed.). (1984b). *Working with the elderly: Group process and techniques* (2nd ed.). Boston: Jones & Bartlett.

Capussi, D., & Fillion, N. G. (1979). Group counseling for the elderly. *Journal for Specialists in Group Work, 4*(3), 148–154.

Davidson, H. (1979). Development of a bereaved parents group. In M. A. Lieberman, L. D. Borman, & Associates (Eds.), *Self-help groups for coping with crisis*. San Francisco: Jossey-Bass.

*Dennis, H. (1984). Remotivation therapy. In I. Burnside (Ed.), *Working with the elderly: Group process and techniques* (2nd ed.) (pp. 187–197). Boston: Jones & Bartlett.

*Donahue, E. M. (1984). Reality orientation: A review of the literature. In I. Burnside (Ed.), *Working with the elderly: Group process and techniques* (2nd ed.) (pp. 165–176). Boston: Jones & Bartlett.

*Emery, G. (1981). Cognitive therapy with the elderly. In G. Emery, S. D. Hollon, & R. C. Bedrosian (Eds.), *New directions in cognitive therapy* (pp. 84–98). New York: Guilford Press.

*Books and articles marked with an asterisk are recommended for further reading.

*Erikson, E. H. (1982). *The life cycle completed.* New York: Norton.

Foster, J. R., & Foster, R. P. (1983). Group psychotherapy with the old and aged. In H. I. Kapland & B. J. Sadock (Eds.), *Comprehensive group psychotherapy* (2nd ed.) (pp. 269–278). Baltimore: Williams & Wilkins.

*Hammond, D. B., & Bonney, W. C. (1983). Counseling families of the elderly: A group experience. *Journal for Specialists in Group Work, 8*(4), 198–204.

*Hawkins, B. L. (1983). Group counseling as a treatment modality for the elderly: A group snapshot. *Journal for Specialists in Group Work, 8*(4), 186–193.

*Hennessey, M. J. (1984). Music therapy. In I. Burnside (Ed.), *Working with the elderly: Group process and techniques* (2nd ed.) (pp. 198–210). Boston: Jones & Bartlett.

A home away from home. (1990, July 2). *Newsweek,* pp. 56–58.

*Johnson, D. R. (1985). Expressive group psychotherapy with the elderly: A drama therapy approach. *International Journal of Group Psychotherapy, 25*(1), 109–127.

*Kalish, R. A. (1985). *Death, grief, and caring relationships* (2nd ed.). Pacific Grove, CA: Brooks/Cole.

Knight, B. (1986). *Psychotherapy with older adults.* Newbury Park, CA: Sage Publications.

*Kübler-Ross, E. (1969). *On death and dying.* New York: Macmillan.

*Kübler-Ross, E. (1975). *Death: The final stages of growth.* Englewood Cliffs, NJ: Prentice-Hall.

Leszcz, M., Feigenbaum, E., Sadavoy, J., & Robinson, A. (1985). A men's group: Psychotherapy of elderly men. *International Journal of Group Psychotherapy, 35*(2), 177–196.

*Lewis, M. I., & Butler, R. N. (1984). Life-review therapy: Putting memories to work. In I. Burnside (Ed.), *Working with the elderly: Group process and techniques* (pp. 50–59). Boston: Jones & Bartlett.

Lieberman, M. A., & Bliwise, N. G. (1985). Comparisons among peer and professionally directed groups for the elderly: Implications for the development of self-help groups. *International Journal of Group Psychotherapy, 35*(2), 155–175.

MacLennan, B. W. (1988). Discussion of "bereavement groups." *International Journal of Group Psychotherapy, 38*(4), 453–458.

*Martin, A. (1984). Family sculpting: A combination of modalities. In I. Burnside (Ed.), *Working with the elderly: Group process and techniques* (2nd ed.) (pp. 225–233). Boston: Jones & Bartlett.

Myers, J. E., & Blake, R. H. (1986). Preparing counselors for work with older people. *Counselor Education and Supervision, 26*(2), 137–145.

Nakkula, M. J. (1984). *Elderly and adolescence: A group approach to integrating the isolated.* Unpublished master's project, University of Minnesota, Duluth.

Nelson, R. C. (1989). Choice awareness: A group experience in a residential setting. *Journal for Specialists in Group Work, 14*(3), 158–169.

Parham, I. A., Priddy, J. M., McGovern, T. V., & Richman, C. M. (1982). Group psychotherapy with the elderly: Problems and prospects. *Psychotherapy: Theory, Research, and Practice, 19*(4), 437–443.

Sherman, B. (1979). Emergence of ideology in a bereaved parents group. In M. A. Lieberman, L. D. Borman, & Associates (Eds.), *Self-help groups for coping with crisis* (pp. 305–322). San Francisco: Jossey-Bass.

Shneidman, E. (1989). The Indian summer of life: A preliminary study of septuagenarians. *American Psychologist, 44*(4), 684–694.

Spiegel, D., & Glafkides, M. C. (1983). Effects of group confrontation with death and dying. *International Journal of Group Psychotherapy, 33*(4), 433–448.

*Spiegel, D., & Yalom, I. D. (1978). A support group for dying patients. *International Journal of Group Psychotherapy, 28*(2), 233–246.

Stone, W. N. (1988). Commentary on "bereavement groups." *International Journal of Group Psychotherapy, 38*(4), 447–452.

Waters, E. B. (1984). Building on what you know: Techniques for individual and group counseling with older people. *The Counseling Psychologist, 12*(2), 63–74.

Wellman, F. E., & McCormack, J. (1984). Counseling with older persons: A review of outcome research. *The Counseling Psychologist, 12*(2), 81–96.

Worthington, E. L. (1989). Religious faith across the life span: Implications for counseling and research. *The Counseling Psychologist, 17*(4), 555–613.

Wright, J., Coley, S., & Corey, G. (1989). Challenges facing human services education today. *Journal of Counseling and Human Service Professions, 3*(2), 3–11.

*Yalom, I. (1980). *Existential psychotherapy.* New York: Basic Books.

*Yalom, I. (1983). *Inpatient group psychotherapy.* New York: Basic Books.

*Yalom, I. D. (1989). *Love's executioner and other tales of psychotherapy.* New York: Basic Books.

*Yalom, I. D., & Vinogradov, S. (1988). Bereavement groups: Techniques and themes. *International Journal of Group Psychotherapy, 38*(4), 419–446.

Zimpfer, D. G. (1984). *Group work in the helping professions: A bibliography* (2nd ed.). Muncie, IN: Accelerated Development.

Name Index

SUBJECT INDEX

Exercise(s):
  aggressive, 53, 61–62
  brainstorming, 144, 340, 371
  to create trust, 144
  critical turning points, 415
  dealing with ethical issues, 68–70
  discounting, 245
  for the elderly, 407–408
  examining one's parents' point of view, 328–329
  feedback, 245
  at final stage, 245–246
  future projection, 246
  group planning, 103
  group-termination, 245
  incomplete-sentence, 407–408
  initial-session, 143
  at initial stages, 143–144
  inner and outer circles, 157
  interviewing, 103–104
  introducing yourself, 143
  in meeting with co-leader, 144
  opposite-sides, 329
  precautions in using, 52–53, 61–63, 355, 421
  at pregroup stage, 103–104
  remembering, 246
  for repeat dieters, 358–360
  reviewing the class experience, 246
  role-playing, 327–329, 379
  self-assessment, 33–34, 185–186
  sentence completion, 158
  for substance-abuse groups, 362–363
  termination-interview, 245
  at transition stage, 185–188
  use of "I" language, 372
  uses and abuses of, 61–63
  working on specific contracts, 122, 233
  at working stage, 222–223
Existential approach, 6, 426

Facilitating, 22–23
Fears, working with, 228–237
Feedback, 207–209, 218–219
Final stage of a group, 224–246
  characteristics of, 240
  exercises for, 245–246
  tasks of, 226–227
Follow-up procedures and suggestions, 242–244
Freedom of exit, 51–52
Freedom to experiment, 214

Gay Community Center, 370
Genuineness, of group leaders, 131–132
Gestalt therapy, 5, 23, 168, 327, 329
Goals, identifying and clarifying, 120–122
Goodwill, of group leaders, 16–17
Group cohesion, 201–202
  and conflict, 152

  defined, 123
  development and maintenance of, 126–127
  indicators of, 126
  research on, 216
  and universality, 209–210
  at working stage, 193
Group composition, 84–85
Group counseling, described, 10–12
Group leaders:
  basic skills of, 20–27
  challenges to, 152–153
  competence of, 40–42
  concerns of, 14–15
  ethical principles for, summary, 64–67
  evaluations of, 34–36
  legal safeguards for, 60–61
  licensing of, 41
  personal characteristics of, 15–20
  personal psychotherapy for, 44–45
  professional standards for training of, 42–46
  qualifications for working with children, 308–309
  reactions to resistance, 155
  self-assessment of, 33–34
  self-disclosure, 131–132, 204–206, 217–218
  self-exploration groups for, 45
  training and personal experience of, 45–49
  values of, 66
Group leadership:
  attitude questionnaire on, 31–33
  basic concepts and guidelines for, 257–260
  dealing with transference and counter-transference, 175–180
  effective, research on, 180–182
  facilitative attitudes, 421–422
  functions at final stage, summary, 241–242
  functions at initial stage, summary, 142–143
  functions at postgroup stage, summary, 244–245
  functions at pregroup stage, summary, 102–103
  functions at transition stage, summary, 185
  functions at working stage, summary, 222
  practicum in, 27, 45, 46–49
  problems and issues of, 14–15
  self-assessment, 33–34
  skills, 20–27
  tactics in groups for minors, 307–308
  therapeutic relationships, guidelines for creating, 182
  therapeutic structure, guidelines for providing, 136–137

To the owner of this book:

We hope that you have enjoyed this book and found it useful. We would like to know as much
as possible about your experiences with *Groups: Process and Practice* (Fourth Edition), so that
we can take your reactions into consideration in future editions. You can write your comments
on this form and send it to us care of Brooks/Cole Publishing Company. Many thanks for your
help.

School: _____

Your Instructor's Name: _____

1. In what class did you use this book? _____

2. What did you like *most* about *Groups: Process and Practice*? _____

_____

_____

3. What did you like *least* about the book? _____

_____

_____

4. How useful were the exercises at the end of the chapters in Parts One and Two? Did you use
any of them in class? _____

_____

_____

5. How useful and informative were the chapters on specific groups in Part Three? Were there
any chapters in this section that you did not read?

_____

_____

6. In the space below or in a separate letter, please make any other comments about the book you'd
like. For example, what were your general reactions to the book? Were any chapters *or* concepts
particularly difficult? Do you have any suggestions for future revisions? We'd be delighted to
hear from you!

Optional:

Your name: _____ Date: _____

May Brooks/Cole quote you, either in promotion for *Groups: Process and Practice* (Fourth Edition) or in future publishing ventures?

Yes: _____ No: _____

 Sincerely,

 Marianne Schneider Corey and Jerry Corey

FOLD HERE

FOLD HERE